The Family Guide to Classic Movies

by
J. S. Ringler

OSS Publishing
Company

White Plains, New York

The Family Guide to Classic Movies

Reprinted and Updated January 2005

Library of Congress Catalog Number: 97-92522

ISBN 10: 0-9660286-0-0
ISBN 13: 978-09660286-0-7

Printed in the United States of America

OSS Publishing Company
P.O. Box 610
White Plains, NY 10603
1-888-677-6521

Web Site: www.osspublishing.com

INTRODUCTION

This book was a number of years in the making. In an effort to find a more cheerful and uplifting alternative to the movies being offered in recent years, I began watching classic movies (from the 1930s through the 1960s). With the help of my uncle—an avid movie fan who had seen just about every major movie of his generation—I was able to make some very good choices. It soon became clear that these movies are still a valuable resource. They are entertaining, often present important lessons about life, and most can be enjoyed together by people of all ages.

Always a very involved family member, I am aware of the challenge that parents and grandparents face in finding wholesome entertainment to enjoy with their children and grandchildren. With toddlers, this is an easy proposition because there is no shortage of videos and TV programs for that age group. However, once children reach school age (about six or seven) and beyond, they have well outgrown these, and finding entertainment for them becomes much more difficult. When my eldest niece and nephew became old enough, I shared some classic films with them, and they took a liking to most of them. Family friends also tried these movies—they, their children and grandchildren enjoyed them too.

Knowing that not everyone my age had an older person to guide them through the vast collection of available classic movies, I decided to write this book. It serves as a starting point for people who want the wholesome kind of entertainment that classic movies can offer—providing guidance for younger people who are unfamiliar with that era and as a memory jogger for older people, who may have already seen some of these films in the past.

This guide is not a definitive listing of every movie ever made, but consists of a selection of 500-plus films that I have personally reviewed and found to have the greatest potential for appealing to modern viewers. It focuses on stories that are interesting, uplifting, or inspirational. These movies can be found on videotape or on television.

As my uncle familiarized me with the movie stars of this Hollywood era, I decided to do some research and create the second section of this book—**The Stars**. It consists of short biographical sketches of the actors and actresses who appeared most frequently in the films listed in the first section—**The Movies**. Knowing who these people are (or were) adds greatly to the value and enjoyment of these films.

CONTENTS

THE MOVIES

Movies are listed in alphabetical order. Each listing is presented in the following format:

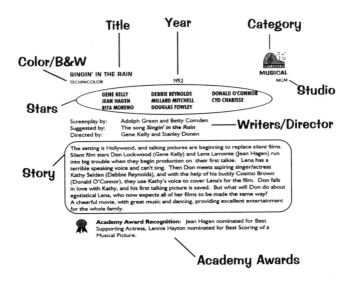

MOVIE CATEGORIES

These symbols are used either alone or in combination to best describe the theme of each movie:

ABBOTT AND COSTELLO
MEET FRANKENSTEIN

BLACK & WHITE 1948 UNIVERSAL INT'L

COMEDY/MYSTERY-SUSPENSE

BUD ABBOTT **LOU COSTELLO** **LON CHANEY**
BELA LUGOSI **GLENN STRANGE** **LENORE AUBERT**

Screenplay by: Robert Lees, Frederic I. Rinaldo, John Grant
Directed by: Charles T. Barton

This film pokes fun at the old Monster/Horror movies. Abbott and Costello are baggage handlers who get mixed up in some scary business when they must deliver two mysterious crates from Europe to a "House of Horrors" Museum. Lon Chaney plays the Wolfman, Bela Lugosi is Dracula, and Glenn Strange is Frankenstein's Monster. A great combination of laughs and scary stuff, suitable for children old enough to handle it. Especially fitting for Halloween time.

ABBOTT AND COSTELLO
MEET THE INVISIBLE MAN

BLACK & WHITE 1951 UNIVERSAL INT'L

COMEDY/MYSTERY-SUSPENSE

BUD ABBOTT **LOU COSTELLO** **NANCY GUILD**
ARTHUR FRANZ **ADELE JERGENS** **SHELDON LEONARD**
WILLIAM FRAWLEY **GAVIN MUIR**

Screenplay by: Robert Lees, Frederic I. Rinaldo and John Grant
Story by: Hugh Wedlock Jr. and Howard Snyder
Suggested by: H.G. Wells' *The Invisible Man*
Directed by: Charles Lamont

Bud Abbott and Lou Costello play detective school graduates who get their first case when a boxer named Tommy Nelson, who's wanted for the murder of his manager, comes into the agency's office. Nelson is innocent, but needs to prove it to the police, so he takes some special serum that his girlfriend's uncle—a doctor—is working on, making himself invisible so that he can buy some time. The two new detectives then set out to help "the invisible man" collect evidence against the real killer. They have lots of adventures and misadventures along the way, in an amusing comedy with a funny fight sequence where Lou goes into the ring against a big, strong bruiser. One word of caution, though—this movie does have a few special effects scenes that could be a little scary for fearful children. A good choice for Halloween.

ABOVE AND BEYOND
BLACK & WHITE   1953

DRAMA/MILITARY
MGM

ROBERT TAYLOR   ELEANOR PARKER   JAMES WHITMORE

Screenplay by: Melvin Frank, Norman Panama, and Beirne Lay, Jr.
Story by: Beirne Lay, Jr.
Directed by: Melvin Frank and Norman Panama

This is the story of Colonel Paul W. Tibbets, Jr., USAF. Robert Taylor stars in the leading role and Eleanor Parker portrays Tibbets' wife. During World War II, the U.S. developed B-29 long-range bombers capable of attacking Japan. Colonel Tibbets was an expert pilot who tested the B-29 and worked to bring it to full production. He was then put in charge of "Operation Silverplate"—the squad chosen to drop the atomic bomb on Japan. Besides the military aspects, the effect of this assignment on his personal life is explored as well. This is a strong drama which gives the viewer a real sense of what the men involved in the atomic attack must have experienced.

Academy Award Recognition: Beirne Lay, Jr. nominated for Best Motion Picture Story, Hugo Friedhofer nominated for Best Scoring of a Dramatic or Comedy Picture.

ABSENT-MINDED PROFESSOR, THE
BLACK & WHITE/COLORIZED   1961

COMEDY
WALT DISNEY

FRED MacMURRAY   NANCY OLSON   KEENAN WYNN
TOMMY KIRK   LEON AMES

Screenplay by: Bill Walsh
Based on: A story by Samuel W. Taylor
Directed by: Robert Stevenson

The setting: Medfield College of Technology, where Fred MacMurray stars as Professor Brainard—a chemistry teacher. Nancy Olson plays Betsy, his long-suffering fiancé, who keeps waiting for him, though he's already forgotten three wedding dates while getting lost in his work. On one such day, he makes a major discovery—"Flubber" (flying rubber). While trying to get the U.S. Government to recognize his invention, Brainard must keep a crooked businessman (Keenan Wynn) from stealing it. By this time, Betsy has reached the end of her rope and Brainard has his work cut out for him to try to win her back. Cute special effects and fun for the whole family.

ACROSS THE WIDE MISSOURI

DRAMA/WESTERN

TECHNICOLOR   1951   MGM

CLARK GABLE   **RICARDO MONTALBAN**   **JOHN HODIAK**
ADOLPHE MENJOU   **J. CARROL NAISH**

Screenplay by: Talbot Jennings
Story by: Talbot Jennings and Frank Cavett
Directed by: William A. Wellman

The story of a fur trapper as told by his son. Flint Mitchell (Clark Gable) is a beaver skin trapper who makes a trade to take a Blackfoot Indian woman named Kamiah (Maria Elena Marques) as his wife. He initially hopes to trade her away again for entry into good hunting territory, but they grow to love each other and he changes his mind, deciding to continue their marriage. The trials and tribulations of their pioneer life are played out in this well-done Western with a more personal story line than most and good performances by the whole cast.

ACTION IN THE
NORTH ATLANTIC

DRAMA/MILITARY/ACTION-ADVENTURE

BLACK & WHITE/COLORIZED   1943   WARNER BROTHERS

HUMPHREY BOGART   **RAYMOND MASSEY**   **ALAN HALE**
JULIE BISHOP   **RUTH GORDON**   **SAM LEVENE**

Screenplay by: John Howard Lawson; additional dialogue by
                  A.I. Bezzerides and W.R. Burnett
Based on: A story by Guy Gilpatric
Directed by: Lloyd Bacon

This is an adventure story about Merchant Marine sailors in World War II, who were responsible for shipping many goods to the front lines in Europe. Raymond Massey plays Steve Jarvis, the captain of a gasoline tanker, and Humphrey Bogart is Joe Rossi, his first mate. An interesting plot develops as they and their crew fight to survive dangerous missions while being attacked by German U-boats (submarines). A treat for fans of war movies, with lots of exciting action sequences of war at sea.

 Academy Award Recognition: Guy Gilpatric nominated for Best Original Story.

ADAM'S RIB
BLACK & WHITE/COLORIZED   1949

MGM

KATHARINE HEPBURN	SPENCER TRACY	JUDY HOLLIDAY
TOM EWELL	DAVID WAYNE	

Screenplay by: Ruth Gordon and Garson Kanin
Directed by: George Cukor

Katharine Hepburn and Spencer Tracy star as Amanda and Adam Bonner, a married couple, both of whom are New York City lawyers. When a woman (Judy Holliday) shoots and injures her husband in a domestic squabble, Amanda and Adam find themselves on opposite sides of the courtroom—Adam is the Assistant D.A., and Amanda is the Defense Attorney. Trouble begins when the courtroom action follows them home to their own marriage. A very clever comedy.

Academy Award Recognition, 1950: Ruth Gordon and Garson Kanin nominated for Best Story and Screenplay.

ADVENTURES OF ROBIN HOOD, THE
TECHNICOLOR   1938

DRAMA/ACTION-ADVENTURE
WARNER BROTHERS

ERROL FLYNN	OLIVIA de HAVILLAND	BASIL RATHBONE	CLAUDE RAINS
PATRIC KNOWLES	EUGENE PALLETTE	ALAN HALE	MELVILLE COOPER

Screenplay by: Norman Reilly Raine and Seton I. Miller
Based on: Ancient Robin Hood Legends
Directed by: Michael Curtiz and William Keighley

When a much-loved king, Richard the Lionhearted, goes off to fight in a crusade on foreign soil, his cruel and evil brother, Prince John (Claude Rains), takes over the throne.   Robin Hood (Errol Flynn), aided secretly by Maid Marian (played by Olivia de Havilland), leads a band of rebels in resistance to this new king. Along the way, Robin and Marian fall in love and, ultimately, he must rescue her from the king's heavily guarded castle. The stars and supporting players couldn't be more perfectly cast, and there's lots of swashbuckling action and loads of colorful costumes in this great adventure movie.

Academy Award Recognition: Erich Wolfgang Korngold won Best Original Score, nominated for Best Picture.

AFFAIR TO REMEMBER, AN

CINEMASCOPE & DELUXE COLOR   1957

DRAMA/ROMANCE
20TH CENTURY FOX

CARY GRANT   **DEBORAH KERR**

Screenplay by:	Delmer Daves and Leo McCarey
Based on:	A story by Leo McCarey and Mildred Cram
Directed by:	Leo McCarey

Cary Grant is Nick Ferrante and Deborah Kerr is Terry McKay, two single people who meet aboard an ocean liner. They fall in love in a whirlwind romance, but each is already involved in a romantic relationship at home. They are not sure that their new-found love will last, so they set a date to meet atop the Empire State Building in six months if they are still in love with each other. Six months later, they are both still in love with each other, but a mishap gets in the way of their appointment. The love story continues to unfold from there, with a chain of events leading up to a very dramatic and bittersweet ending.

Academy Award Recognition: Hugo Friedhofer nominated for Best Scoring of a Motion Picture, nominated for Best Song: *An Affair to Remember*, Music by Harry Warren and Lyrics by Harold Adamson and Leo McCarey.

AFFAIRS OF DOBIE GILLIS, THE

BLACK & WHITE   1953

COMEDY/MUSICAL
MGM

DEBBIE REYNOLDS	**BOBBY VAN**	**BARBARA RUICK**
BOB FOSSE	**HENLEY STAFFORD**	**LURENE TUTTLE**
HANS CONRIED		

Screenplay by:	Max Shulman
Directed by:	Don Weis

Dobie Gillis (Bobby Van) is a college freshman whose main concern is having a good time. Dobie meets Pansy Hammer (Debbie Reynolds), another freshman, who's been trained by her father to focus more on learning than having fun. She and Dobie fall in love and he teaches Pansy to make fun her priority. When Pansy's father becomes angry about Dobie's negative influence and separates the pair, they try to find a way to work things out. A cute and funny movie with some nice music and dancing.

AFRICAN QUEEN, THE
TECHNICOLOR   1951   **DRAMA/ACTION-ADVENTURE**
                                                           HORIZON, UNITED ARTISTS

HUMPHREY BOGART   **KATHARINE HEPBURN**   **ROBERT MORLEY**

Screenplay by: James Agee and John Huston
Based on: The novel **The African Queen** by C.S. Forester
Directed by: John Huston

Filmed on location in Africa

The story takes place in German East Africa in 1914. Katharine Hepburn plays Rose Sayer, a Methodist Missionary working in an African village. When the German army burns down the village and her brother (a minister) dies, she's left stranded. Rose is rescued by local steamboat driver Charlie Allnut (Humphrey Bogart), and together they must travel an almost impassable river to escape German troops. They don't get along at first, as she's a very proper lady and he's a gruff and crude sort of character, but through their struggle Rose and Charlie grow to care for each other. A top-notch film with a tale of adventure as well as a love story, and just a touch of humor added to the drama.

 Academy Award Recognition: Humphrey Bogart won Best Actor, Katharine Hepburn nominated for Best Actress, John Huston nominated for Best Director, James Agee and John Huston nominated for Best Screenplay.

AFTER THE THIN MAN
BLACK & WHITE   1936   **COMEDY/MYSTERY-SUSPENSE**
                                                               MGM

WILLIAM POWELL   **MYRNA LOY**   **JAMES STEWART**
ELISSA LANDI   **JOSEPH CALLEIA**   **JESSE RALPH**
SAM LEVENE   **ASTA**

Screenplay by: Frances Goodrich and Albert Hackett
From: The story by Dashiell Hammett
Directed by: W.S. Van Dyke

Powell and Loy star again as sleuths Nick and Nora Charles in another installment of the **Thin Man** movie series. In this one, they start out looking for a missing person— her cousin Selma's philandering husband. When he's found dead, Nick and Nora then have a difficult murder case to solve. A prime suspect is Selma's old boyfriend,

David (James Stewart), whom she had jilted when she married. A very intriguing mystery with some laughs as well.

 Academy Award Recognition: Frances Goodrich and Albert Hackett nominated for Best Screenplay.

ALEXANDER'S RAGTIME BAND
BLACK & WHITE   1938

MUSICAL/DRAMA
20TH CENTURY FOX

TYRONE POWER	**ALICE FAYE**	**DON AMECHE**
ETHEL MERMAN	**JACK HALEY**	**JEAN HERSHOLT**
HELEN WESTLEY	**JOHN CARRADINE**	

Screenplay by: Kathryn Scola and Lamar Trotti
Adaptation by: Richard Sherman
Directed by: Henry King

Lyrics and Music by Irving Berlin

The story begins in San Francisco, where aspiring concert violinist Roger Grant (Tyrone Power) works nights in a honky-tonk combo with piano player Charlie Dwyer (Don Ameche) and drummer Davey Lane (Jack Haley). When their paths cross with saloon singer Stella Kirby (Alice Faye), they become a hit as "Alexander's Ragtime Band" with Stella as their vocalist. What follows is a saga of the group's professional and personal ins and outs over the years, set to music with many of Irving Berlin's popular songs, which were mainstays of the musical culture of the early 1900s. Ethel Merman plays Jerry Allen, another singer who joins the group along the way. This is not only good entertainment, but also a historical showcase for Irving Berlin's famous music.

 Academy Award Recognition: Alfred Newman won Best Score, nominated for Best Picture, nominated for Best Song: *Now It Can Be Told*, Music and Lyrics by Irving Berlin, Lamar Trotti nominated for Best Original Story.

ALL THAT HEAVEN ALLOWS
TECHNICOLOR   1955

DRAMA/ROMANCE
UNIVERSAL INT'L

JANE WYMAN   **ROCK HUDSON**   **AGNES MOOREHEAD**
CONRAD NAGEL   **VIRGINIA GREY**   **GLORIA TALBOTT**
WILLIAM REYNOLDS

Screenplay by: Peg Fenwick
Based on: The story by Edna L. Lee and Harry Lee
Directed by: Douglas Sirk

Jane Wyman is Carrie Scott, a lonely well-to-do suburban widow. She finds true love with a younger man, gardener and outdoorsman Ron Kirby (Rock Hudson). There are plenty of problems though, as her children are against their relationship, and the two become victims of gossip from the snobbish townspeople. Despite their different backgrounds though, Carrie and Ron try their best to make things work. A good love story that most romance fans should find enjoyable.

ALLEGHENY UPRISING
BLACK & WHITE/COLORIZED   1939

DRAMA/ACTION-ADVENTURE
RKO

CLAIRE TREVOR   **JOHN WAYNE**   **GEORGE SANDERS**   **BRIAN DONLEVY**

Screenplay by: P.J. Wolfson
Based on: The factual story *The First Rebel* by Neil H. Swanson
Directed by: William A. Seiter

The setting: Pennsylvania, 16 years before the American Revolution. James Smith (John Wayne) and a band of men are fighting to protect their families from the Indians and those supplying the Indians with arms. When Smith and his men are falsely accused of destroying supplies intended for British troops, they rebel against the British forces. Claire Trevor plays Janie, the feisty young woman in love with Smith, who hopes he'll settle down with her. A good adventure movie with plenty of action.

ALONG THE GREAT DIVIDE

BLACK & WHITE   1951

DRAMA/WESTERN
WARNER BROTHERS

KIRK DOUGLAS   VIRGINIA MAYO   JOHN AGAR   WALTER BRENNAN

Screenplay by: Walter Doniger and Louis Meltzer
From: A story by Walter Doniger
Directed by: Raoul Walsh

Kirk Douglas stars as Len Merrick, a U.S. Marshal who interrupts the vigilante
hanging of cattle rustler "Pop" Keith (Walter Brennan) by a rancher who believes
that Keith has killed his favorite son. Merrick is devoted to upholding the law,
and vows to give Keith a fair trial. So, Merrick and his faithful assistant, Billy Shear
(John Agar), set out with "Pop" Keith and his daughter Ann (Virginia Mayo) on a
dangerous journey across the desert to the nearest court of law. Along the way,
Merrick has to deal with the crafty Keiths who keep trying to escape, as well as the
rancher and his posse, who want to stop him and hang the suspect themselves.
A very suspenseful Western drama with a riveting plot and great photography that's
suited more to older children and adults than very young ones.

AMERICAN IN PARIS, AN

TECHNICOLOR   1951

MUSICAL
MGM

GENE KELLY   LESLIE CARON   OSCAR LEVANT   NINA FOCH   GEORGES GUETARY

Screenplay by: Alan Jay Lerner
Directed by: Vincente Minnelli

Lyrics by Ira Gershwin, Music by George Gershwin, Choreography by Gene Kelly

The story takes place in Paris, where Jerry Mulligan (Gene Kelly), an American
painter, has stayed on after serving in World War II in order to make it in the art
world. While fighting off unwelcome romantic advances from a wealthy female art
fan, he falls in love with a young French woman named Lisa (Leslie Caron). However,
Lisa already has plans in place to marry her longtime boyfriend, and now she must
decide between him and her new love, Jerry. This film is more artistic than the
typical Hollywood musical, featuring ballet and modern dance, so it may be more
suitable for teenagers and adults than for younger children.

Academy Award Recognition: won Best Picture, Alan Jay Lerner
won Best Story and Screenplay, Johnny Green and Saul Chaplin won
Best Scoring of a Musical Picture, Vincente Minnelli nominated for
Best Director.

ANDY HARDY MEETS DEBUTANTE

COMEDY

BLACK & WHITE   1940   MGM

| LEWIS STONE | FAY HOLDEN | CECELIA PARKER | MICKEY ROONEY |
| JUDY GARLAND | ANN RUTHERFORD | DIANA LEWIS | |

Screenplay by: Annalee Whitmore and Thomas Seller
Based on: The characters created by Aurania Rouverol
Directed by: George B. Seitz

In this entry of the **Andy Hardy** series of films, Andy (Mickey Rooney) gets himself into hot water by bragging to his friends that he knows a beautiful New York
debutante. When Andy's family plans a trip to New York City, his pals challenge
him to return with a picture of the two of them together for the school paper.
Fortunately, his young admirer Betsy (Judy Garland) is there to lend a hand.
A cute and very appealing movie.

ANGEL IN MY POCKET

COMEDY

TECHNICOLOR   1969   UNIVERSAL

| ANDY GRIFFITH | LEE MERIWETHER | JERRY VAN DYKE | KAY MEDFORD |
| EDGAR BUCHANAN | GARY COLLINS | HENRY JONES | |

Screenplay by: Jim Fritzell and Everett Greenbaum
Directed by: Alan Rafkin

The Rev. Samuel Whitehead (Andy Griffith) is a minister and ex-Marine who's
assigned to a difficult parish in Wood Falls, Kansas. He arrives with his pregnant
wife Mary Elizabeth (Lee Meriwether), their three children, his annoying mother-in-
law and his delinquent, unemployed brother-in-law (Jerry Van Dyke) in tow. What
follows is an amusing tale of how he turns the community around while dealing with
a bickering, critical congregation and his own zany family. Family fun for all ages.

ANGELS IN THE OUTFIELD

BLACK & WHITE   1951

COMEDY

MGM

PAUL DOUGLAS	JANET LEIGH	KEENAN WYNN
LEWIS STONE	SPRING BYINGTON	BRUCE BENNETT
MARVIN KAPLAN	DONNA CORCORAN	

Screenplay by: Dorothy Kingsley and George Wells
Based on: A story by Richard Conlin
Directed by: Clarence Brown

This movie was filmed using the actual Pittsburgh Pirates baseball team and their ballpark, but is not a true story. Janet Leigh is Jennifer Paige, a newspaper reporter assigned to investigate why the Pirates are losing so many games, but she knows nothing about baseball. Despite that fact, she soon finds the reason—Guffy McGovern (Paul Douglas), the team's ill-tempered and offensive manager whom nobody likes. In response to the prayers of a little orphan girl named Bridget (Donna Corcoran), a group of angels are sent to help the players set Guffy straight. Lots of heavenly happenings ensue and Jennifer, Guffy and the little girl forge a special relationship. You'll notice that Guffy's foul language is made fun of in this movie by garbling his voice every time he is supposed to be swearing. This is an excellent and endearing comedy that can be enjoyed by the whole family.

ANNIE OAKLEY

BLACK & WHITE   1935

DRAMA

RKO

| BARBARA STANWYCK | PRESTON FOSTER | MELVYN DOUGLAS | MORONI OLSEN |

Screenplay by: Joel Sayre and John Twist
From: A story by Joseph A. Fields and Ewart Adamson
Directed by: George Stevens

Barbara Stanwyck plays the title role in this biographical drama of the famous female sharpshooting star. It depicts her rise from an unknown to the main draw of the Buffalo Bill Wild West Show that toured the country many years ago. Along the way, Annie competes with and falls in love with another star sharpshooter, Toby Walker (Preston Foster). Meanwhile, Jeff Hogarth (Melvyn Douglas), the show's manager, falls for her. An entertaining story of a good female role model that also presents morals of honor and respect for others. The plot may seem a little simplistic to adults by today's standards, but is easy for children to understand.

ANYTHING GOES

VISTAVISION & TECHNICOLOR · 1956

MUSICAL
PARAMOUNT

| BING CROSBY | DONALD O'CONNOR | JEANMAIRE |
| MITZI GAYNOR | PHIL HARRIS | |

Screenplay by: Sidney Sheldon
From: The play by Guy Bolton and P.G. Wodehouse
Directed by: Robert Lewis

Music and Lyrics by Cole Porter
New Songs by Sammy Cahn and James Van Heusen

A Broadway star (Bing Crosby) and a TV star (Donald O'Connor) are cast in a new Broadway show together and are scouting for a leading lady to join them. In Europe, they each offer the part to a different woman without the other's approval. They get a surprise when all four end up traveling on the same ship back to the United States. The two actors are forced to make a choice, and romance gets involved, making it a more complicated decision. A light and tuneful musical.

APPOINTMENT WITH DANGER

BLACK & WHITE · 1951

DRAMA/MYSTERY-SUSPENSE
PARAMOUNT

| ALAN LADD | PHYLLIS CALVERT | PAUL STEWART | JAN STERLING |
| JACK WEBB | STACY HARRIS | HENRY MORGAN | |

Screenplay by: Richard Breen and Warren Duff
Directed by: Lewis Allen

Alan Ladd stars as Al Goddard, a U.S. Postal Inspector. He is assigned to investigate the murder of a fellow Inspector, and the sole witness to the crime is a nun, Sister Augustine (Phyllis Calvert). She is able to identify the murderer, so Goddard must protect her life while he goes undercover to nab the entire band of criminals responsible. An extremely suspenseful film with a very intriguing story line. Some violence is involved, though tame by today's standards. This movie is more suitable for teenagers and adults than for younger children.

APRIL LOVE
CINEMASCOPE   1957

DRAMA/MUSICAL
20TH CENTURY FOX

PAT BOONE   SHIRLEY JONES

Screenplay by:	Winston Miller
Based on:	A novel by George Agnew Chamberlain
Directed by:	Henry Levin

A young man named Nick (Pat Boone), who has had a run-in with the law in Chicago, is sent to serve his probation with his aunt and uncle on their country farm. The uncle seems very mean at first, and when Nick befriends the neighbor's pretty daughter Liz (Shirley Jones), she tells him why. His uncle never recovered from the loss of his son in the Korean War, and has even given up on his specialty—raising trotting horses. With Liz's help, Nick learns to train and race horses, giving his uncle a new lease on life while turning his own life around, too. A nice story about personal growth and healing, with a handful of songs for good measure.

Academy Award Recognition: nominated for Best Song: *April Love*, Music by Sammy Fain, Lyrics by Paul Francis Webster.

ASK ANY GIRL
CINEMASCOPE & METROCOLOR   1959

COMEDY/ROMANCE
MGM

DAVID NIVEN   SHIRLEY MacLAINE   GIG YOUNG
ROD TAYLOR   JIM BACKUS   CLAIRE KELLY

Screenplay by:	George Wells
Based on:	The novel by Winifred Wolfe
Directed by:	Charles Walters

Shirley MacLaine is Meg Wheeler, a young woman from Pennsylvania who goes to New York City to seek her fortune. When Meg lands a job as a researcher with an ad agency, her bosses are the two Doughton brothers—the notorious playboy Evan (Gig Young), and Miles (David Niven), a very serious businessman who thinks she's weird. She wants to be noticed by Evan and gets Miles to assist in her plan, the results of which are surprising to all involved. An amusing romantic comedy with a great cast.

AT SWORD'S POINT

DRAMA/ACTION-ADVENTURE

COLOR   1951   RKO

CORNEL WILDE   **MAUREEN O'HARA**   **ALAN HALE, JR.**

Screenplay by: Walter Ferris and Joseph Hoffman
Story by: Aubrey Wisberg and Jack Pollexfen
Directed by: Lewis Allen

In this swashbuckler, the grown children of the original Three Musketeers step into
their father's shoes to save their Queen and her young Prince from being forced
into exile. One of the Musketeers' children is a daughter (Maureen O'Hara), but she
joins the men and fights side by side with them to save the day. It's a rare treat to
see such a strong female hero in an older action movie such as this one. A rousing
tale with lots of excitement.

AUNTIE MAME

COMEDY

TECHNIRAMA & TECHNICOLOR   1958   WARNER BROTHERS

ROSALIND RUSSELL   **FORREST TUCKER**   **CORAL BROWNE**   **FRED CLARK**
ROGER SMITH   **PATRIC KNOWLES**   **PEGGY CASS**   **JAN HANDZLIK**
JOANNA BARNES

Screenplay by: Betty Comden and Adolph Green
From: The novel **Auntie Mame** by Patrick Dennis, as adapted
                   for the stage by Jerome Lawrence and Robert E. Lee
Directed by: Morton DaCosta

Rosalind Russell stars as Mame Dennis, who becomes guardian of her nephew,
Patrick, when her brother passes away. She is an eccentric, off-the-wall character,
but loves the boy very much and tries to add excitement to his life—much to the
chagrin of Mr. Babcock (Fred Clark), the executor of Patrick's estate. Mr. Babcock
was directed by Patrick's father to keep an eye on Mame and protect the youngster
from her wild lifestyle. Roger Smith portrays Patrick as a grown-up young man.
A very amusing comedy with fine performances by the entire cast.

 Academy Award Recognition: nominated for Best Picture,
Rosalind Russell nominated for Best Actress, Peggy Cass nominated
for Best Supporting Actress.

BACHELOR AND THE BOBBY SOXER, THE

COMEDY

BLACK & WHITE/COLORIZED   1947   RKO

| CARY GRANT | MYRNA LOY | SHIRLEY TEMPLE | RUDY VALLEE |
| RAY COLLINS | HARRY DAVENPORT | JOHNNY SANDS | |

Screenplay by: Sidney Sheldon
Directed by: Irving Reis

Myrna Loy is Judge Margaret Turner. Her teenage sister, Susan (Shirley Temple), has a huge crush on handsome artist Richard Nugent (Cary Grant). He gets into big trouble with the law when Susan sneaks into his apartment one night. Margaret agrees to let Nugent off the hook if he helps in getting Susan over her infatuation with him. All of this sets the stage for the very amusing comedy that follows.

Academy Award Recognition: Sidney Sheldon won Best Original Screenplay.

BACHELOR MOTHER

COMEDY

BLACK & WHITE/COLORIZED   1939   RKO

| GINGER ROGERS | DAVID NIVEN | CHARLES COBURN |
| FRANK ALBERTSON | E.E. CLIVE | |

Screenplay by: Norman Krasna
Story by: Felix Jackson
Directed by: Garson Kanin

Ginger Rogers is Polly Parrish, a soon-to-be unemployed department store sales-woman who spots a baby being left on the front steps of an orphanage. When Polly knocks on the door to let the people inside know that the baby is there, she is mistaken for the child's unwed mother. David Merlin (played by David Niven), the son of her boss, is told of Polly's "plight," re-hires her, and she goes along with the charade in order to keep her job at the store. A very funny and genial comedy that has a happy ending.

Academy Award Recognition: Felix Jackson nominated for Best Original Story.

BAD DAY AT BLACK ROCK

CINEMASCOPE & EASTMAN COLOR   1955

DRAMA/MYSTERY-SUSPENSE

MGM

SPENCER TRACY	ROBERT RYAN	ANNE FRANCIS
DEAN JAGGER	WALTER BRENNAN	JOHN ERICSON
LEE MARVIN	ERNEST BORGNINE	

Screenplay by: Don McGuire and Millard Kaufman
Based on: A story by Howard Breslin
Directed by: John Sturges

Spencer Tracy stars as John J. MacReedy, a man with only one arm, who arrives in a tiny western town that's located in the middle of nowhere. It's a weird kind of place, and its few residents seem weirder still. The story is a very mysterious one, and for a good while, the audience is kept unsure of exactly what's going on. As events unfold, MacReedy stumbles upon a sinister town secret. He finds himself in very dangerous straits and will be lucky if he gets out of town alive. This is an excellent, at times spine-tingling, tale of suspense with great acting by Tracy.

 Academy Award Recognition: Spencer Tracy nominated for Best Actor, John Sturges nominated for Best Director, Millard Kaufman nominated for Best Screenplay.

BALL OF FIRE

BLACK & WHITE   1941

COMEDY

SAMUEL GOLDWYN

GARY COOPER	BARBARA STANWYCK	OSCAR HOMOLKA
DANA ANDREWS	DAN DURYEA	HENRY TRAVERS
S.Z. SAKALL	TULLEY MARSHALL	LEONID KINSKEY

Screenplay by: Charles Brackett and Billy Wilder
From: An original story by Billy Wilder and Thomas Monroe
Directed by: Howard Hawks

In this takeoff on the story of "Snow White and the Seven Dwarfs," a group of eight very intellectual men writing an encyclopedia share a house in New York City. Sugarpuss O'Shea, a nightclub singer (played by Barbara Stanwyck), accepts an offer to help them with an article on American slang, but she's really hiding out from the police—her fiancé is the prime suspect in a gangland murder. She brings fun and spirit to their humdrum lives, while growing especially fond of the youngest and most handsome of the group, Professor Bertram Potts (Gary Cooper). Things get very exciting when O'Shea's new friends must rescue her from her gangster boyfriend. The group of kind older gentlemen is really adorable in this delightful comedy.

 Academy Award Recognition: Barbara Stanwyck nominated for Best Actress, Thomas Monroe and Billy Wilder nominated for Best Original Story, Alfred Newman nominated for Best Scoring of a Dramatic Picture.

BALLAD OF JOSIE, THE
TECHNISCOPE & TECHNICOLOR   1968

COMEDY/WESTERN

UNIVERSAL

DORIS DAY	**PETER GRAVES**	**GEORGE KENNEDY**	**ANDY DEVINE**
WILLIAM TALMAN	**DAVID HARTMAN**	**GUY RAYMOND**	

Screenplay by: Harold Swanton
Directed by: Andrew V. McLaglen

Doris Day stars as Josie Minick, a woman in the west who's suddenly widowed by her no-good drunkard husband. She's left with almost nothing and faces losing her son to her well-to-do father-in-law. Josie decides to raise sheep in order to become self-sufficient, but there's a problem—her land is in cattle country, and sheep are unwelcome there. Peter Graves co-stars as Jason Meredith, a friend who grows closer to her as he defends her against angry cattle ranchers. An entertaining, pleasant story with a good mix of comedy, romance, and Western action—a little of something for everyone.

BAND WAGON, THE
TECHNICOLOR   1953

MUSICAL

MGM

FRED ASTAIRE	**CYD CHARISSE**	**OSCAR LEVANT**
NANETTE FABRAY	**JACK BUCHANAN**	

Screenplay by: Betty Comden and Adolph Green
Directed by: Vincente Minnelli

This movie is a series of very entertaining musical numbers held together by a slender plot. The story line follows the events surrounding the creation of a new Broadway show featuring musical star Tony Hunter (Fred Astaire). Cyd Charisse

plays Tony's co-star Gabrielle Girard. Good dancing, a talented cast and a happy
ending round out a nice showbiz story.

 Academy Award Recognition: Betty Comden and Adolph Green
nominated for Best Story and Screenplay, Adolph Deutsch nominated for
Best Scoring of a Musical Picture.

BAREFOOT EXECUTIVE, THE
TECHNICOLOR   1971

COMEDY/ANIMAL STORIES
WALT DISNEY

KURT RUSSELL	HARRY MORGAN	WALLY COX
HEATHER NORTH	ALAN HEWITT	HAYDEN RORKE
JOHN RITTER		

Screenplay by: Joseph L. McEveety
Story by: Lila Garrett, Bernie Kahn and Stewart C. Billett
Directed by: Robert Butler

Kurt Russell stars as Steven Post, a young man who works for a television network.
He makes it big when he discovers that his girlfriend's pet chimpanzee can pick hit
TV shows, but has his hands full keeping his source a secret. Both the cute story
and the chimp's humorous antics make this a fun movie.

BAREFOOT IN THE PARK
TECHNICOLOR   1967

COMEDY/ROMANCE
PARAMOUNT

ROBERT REDFORD   JANE FONDA   CHARLES BOYER   MILDRED NATWICK

Screenplay by: Neil Simon
From: The play by Neil Simon
Directed by: Gene Saks

Robert Redford and Jane Fonda play young newlyweds in this film version of the hit
Broadway show. This is the amusing tale of their adjustment to married life in a
low-rent New York City apartment. Not too interesting for young children—more
suitable for teenagers and adults.

 Academy Award Recognition: Mildred Natwick nominated for
Best Supporting Actress.

BARKLEYS OF BROADWAY, THE

MUSICAL

TECHNICOLOR   1949   MGM

FRED ASTAIRE   **GINGER ROGERS**   **OSCAR LEVANT**   **BILLIE BURKE**

Screenplay by: Betty Comden and Adolph Green
Directed by: Charles Walters

Fred and Ginger are The Barkleys, an often-bickering married team of musical stage stars. They reach a crossroads when she feels taken for granted and plans to build a career of her own in dramatic acting. Very enjoyable song and dance numbers are sprinkled between their marital spats as they work things out. This movie reunited Fred and Ginger after many years apart and is the last one that they made together.

BATTLE HYMN

DRAMA/MILITARY

CINEMASCOPE & TECHNICOLOR   1957   UNIVERSAL INT'L

ROCK HUDSON   **ANNA KASHFI**   **DAN DURYEA**
DON DeFORE   **MARTHA HYER**   **JOCK MAHONEY**

Screenplay by: Charles Grayson and Vincent B. Evans
Directed by: Douglas Sirk

Rock Hudson performs the starring role in the true story of Air Force Colonel Dean Hess. Colonel Hess served in Europe in World War II, and then became a minister after the war. But no matter what good he did, he was haunted by the war and his accidental killing of a group of children in an orphanage when a bombing mission went wrong. When the Korean War broke out, Hess went back into the service to train pilots, but also found a way to pay back his debt—saving Korean orphans. A well-done and very inspiring movie.

BATTLEGROUND
BLACK & WHITE/COLORIZED

DRAMA/MILITARY/ACTION-ADVENTURE

1949   MGM

VAN JOHNSON	JOHN HODIAK	RICARDO MONTALBAN
GEORGE MURPHY	MARSHALL THOMPSON	JEROME COURTLAND
DON TAYLOR	BRUCE COWLING	JAMES WHITMORE
LEON AMES	DENISE DARCEL	JIM ARNESS
SCOTTY BECKETT		

Screenplay by: Robert Pirosh
Directed by: William A. Wellman

A World War II drama that takes place at the Battle of the Bulge in Bastogne, France in 1944. This exciting story, portraying the experiences of a group of American GIs, features lots of action while exploring the personal side of war as well. A superior and realistic war drama, presented without graphic violence.

Academy Award Recognition: Robert Pirosh won Best Story and Screenplay, nominated for Best Picture, James Whitmore nominated for Best Supporting Actor, William A. Wellman nominated for Best Director.

BEAU JAMES
VISTAVISION & TECHNICOLOR

DRAMA/MUSICAL

1957   PARAMOUNT

| BOB HOPE | VERA MILES | PAUL DOUGLAS | ALEXIS SMITH |
| DARREN McGAVIN | GEORGE JESSEL | WALTER CATLETT | |

Screenplay by: Jack Rose and Melville Shavelson
Based on: The book by Gene Fowler
Directed by: Melville Shavelson

Cameo appearances by **JACK BENNY** and **JIMMY DURANTE**
Narration by **WALTER WINCHELL**

This biographical portrait of the famous New York City Mayor, Jimmy Walker, begins in 1925 and goes on to depict both his rise to power and eventual downfall. Bob Hope stars in the title role. Also appearing are Alexis Smith as Mrs. Walker, and Vera Miles as the mayor's mistress. A colorful and entertaining account that vividly recreates the atmosphere of the Roaring Twenties.

BEDKNOBS AND BROOMSTICKS

MUSICAL

TECHNICOLOR   1971   WALT DISNEY

ANGELA LANSBURY   **DAVID TOMLINSON**   **RODDY McDOWALL**

Screenplay by: Bill Walsh and Don DaGradi
Based on: The book by Mary Norton
Directed by: Robert Stevenson

Angela Lansbury stars as Eglantine Price, a woman living alone near the shores of England during World War II. She is sent three children to shelter in her home for safekeeping. The children are unhappy about their situation until they discover that Eglantine is taking a correspondence course in witchcraft. As she learns the ropes, she takes them on exciting adventures, using her bed as a vehicle to fly to fantasy worlds—these scenes creatively combine live action with cartoon animation. They also put together a plan to fight the Nazis if they should attack (which indeed they do near the end of the movie). An entertaining family film in the Disney tradition. One word of caution though—the somewhat spooky special effects during the group's clash with the Nazis could be a little scary for fearful younger children.

 Academy Award Recognition: Richard M. Sherman, Robert B. Sherman, and Irwin Kostal nominated for Best Scoring (Adaptation and Original Song Score), nominated for Best Song: *The Age of Not Believing*, by Richard M. Sherman and Robert B. Sherman.

BEDTIME FOR BONZO

COMEDY/ANIMAL STORIES

BLACK & WHITE   1951   UNIVERSAL INT'L

RONALD REAGAN   **DIANA LYNN**   **WALTER SLEZAK**
LUCILLE BARKLEY   **JESSE WHITE**   **BONZO**

Screenplay by: Val Burton and Lou Breslow
Story by: Raphael David Blau and Ted Berkman
Directed by: Frederick de Cordova

Peter Boyd (Ronald Reagan), a college professor and son of a convict, sets out to prove to his prospective father-in-law that criminal tendencies aren't genetic. He embarks on an experiment with a chimpanzee (Bonzo) to show that in a nurturing family, even a chimp can learn right from wrong. He acts as Bonzo's "father" and hires a young woman to be Bonzo's "mother", which further complicates Boyd's love life. A somewhat campy but funny film, thanks especially to the scene-stealing antics of the chimp.

BELL, BOOK AND CANDLE

COMEDY/MYSTERY-SUSPENSE

TECHNICOLOR   1958   COLUMBIA

| JAMES STEWART | KIM NOVAK | JACK LEMMON |
| ERNIE KOVACS | HERMIONE GINGOLD | ELSA LANCHESTER |

Screenplay by: Daniel Taradas
Based on: The play *Bell, Book and Candle* by John Van Druten
Directed by: Richard Quine

Shepard Henderson (James Stewart) is a publisher who finds himself immersed in the mysterious world of witchcraft. It all begins when a young witch named Gillian Holroyd (Kim Novak) decides to use her powers to win him over, even though he's already engaged. Also on the scene are two older and more experienced witches, Mrs. De Pass (Hermione Gingold) and Aunt Queenie (Elsa Lanchester), along with Gillian's warlock brother Nicky Holroyd (Jack Lemmon). The unusual story line, plus the great cast, combine to make this an entertaining and offbeat movie.

BELLE OF NEW YORK, THE

MUSICAL

TECHNICOLOR   1952   MGM

| FRED ASTAIRE | VERA-ELLEN | MARJORIE MAIN | KEENAN WYNN |

Screenplay by: Robert O'Brien and Irving Elinson
From: The play by Hugh Morton;
                  adapted for the screen by Chester Erskine
Directed by: Charles Walters

The setting is turn-of-the-century New York. Fred Astaire plays a high-living bachelor whose specialty is hanging around stage doors and romancing showbiz starlets. His aunt runs a moral guidance group called The Daughters of Right, but is unable to reform him, until he meets one of the members—a beautiful young woman (played by Vera-Ellen). He's in love at first sight, but has got to clean up his act in order to win the lady's heart. A pleasant musical, with a quaint story of days gone by.

BELLES ON THEIR TOES

TECHNICOLOR   1952   **COMEDY/DRAMA**

20TH CENTURY FOX

JEANNE CRAIN	MYRNA LOY	DEBRA PAGET
JEFFREY HUNTER	EDWARD ARNOLD	HOAGY CARMICHAEL
BARBARA BATES	ROBERT ARTHUR	VERNA FELTON

Screenplay by: Phoebe and Henry Ephron
Based on: The book by Frank B. Gilbreth, Jr. and Ernestine Gilbreth Carey
Directed by: Henry Levin

This sequel to *Cheaper By The Dozen* (1950) continues the story of the Gilbreth family. Myrna Loy carries forward her role as Lillian Gilbreth, a female engineer and recently widowed mother of 12 children. With her husband's passing, the whole family has to readjust and pull together to make ends meet while she fights for acceptance in a man's world. An appealing and inspiring story of family solidarity.

BELLS ARE RINGING

CINEMASCOPE & METROCOLOR   1960   **MUSICAL**

MGM

| JUDY HOLLIDAY | DEAN MARTIN | FRED CLARK | EDDIE FOY, JR. |
| JEAN STAPLETON | RUTH STOREY | FRANK GORSHIN | BERNIE WEST |

Screenplay by: Betty Comden and Adolph Green
Based on: The Broadway musical *Bells Are Ringing*;
                Music by Jule Styne, Lyrics by Betty Comden and Adolph Green
Directed by: Vincente Minnelli

Judy Holliday stars as a spirited telephone operator for an answering service, who takes a personal interest in her clients' lives and is determined to solve their problems. But she gets in too deep when she falls in love with one client in particular— a playwright (played by Dean Martin)—while helping him over the breakup of his writing partnership. She then attempts to keep her true identity a secret. A unique story and some fine music make this movie very enjoyable.

Academy Award Recognition: André Previn nominated for Best Scoring of a Musical Picture.

BELLS OF ST. MARY'S, THE
BLACK & WHITE/COLORIZED   1945

DRAMA/COMEDY/MUSICAL
RKO

BING CROSBY	INGRID BERGMAN	HENRY TRAVERS
WILLIAM GARGAN	RUTH DONNELLY	JOAN CARROLL
MARTHA SLEEPER	RHYS WILLIAMS	UNA O'CONNOR

Screenplay by: Dudley Nichols
Story by: Leo McCarey
Directed by: Leo McCarey

In this sequel to *Going My Way* (1944), Bing Crosby once again plays Father O'Malley, but this time Ingrid Bergman joins him as Sister Mary Benedict. They have very different ways of doing things, but as they work together to improve an aging Catholic parish school, they develop a strong and lasting friendship. A warm and touching story with some light moments and a few songs as well.

 Academy Award Recognition: nominated for Best Picture, Leo McCarey nominated for Best Director, Bing Crosby nominated for Best Actor, Ingrid Bergman nominated for Best Actress, Robert Emmett Dolan nominated for Best Musical Scoring of a Dramatic or Comedy Picture, nominated for Best Song: *Aren't You Glad You're You*, Music by James Van Heusen and Lyrics by Johnny Burke.

BEND OF THE RIVER
TECHNICOLOR   1952

DRAMA/WESTERN
UNIVERSAL INT'L

JAMES STEWART	ARTHUR KENNEDY	JULIA ADAMS	ROCK HUDSON

Screenplay by: Borden Chase
Based on: The novel *Bend of the Snake* by Bill Gulick
Directed by: Anthony Quinn

James Stewart is a man named McClintock who, in order to put a shady past behind him, signs on to guide a wagon train to Columbia River country. He finds a new friend, an accused horse thief whom he rescues from hanging, but the two become enemies when McClintock succeeds in turning his life around and his buddy does not. Along its journey, the wagon train encounters many dangers and challenges. A good Western drama and story of personal growth.

BEST FOOT FORWARD
TECHNICOLOR   1943

MUSICAL
MGM

LUCILLE BALL	**WILLIAM GAXTON**	**VIRGINIA WEIDLER**
TOMMY DIX	**NANCY WALKER**	**JUNE ALLYSON**
KENNY BOWERS	**GLORIA DeHAVEN**	**JACK JORDAN**

Screenplay by: Irving Brecher and Fred Finklehoffe
Based on: A stage play, with book written by John Cecil Holm
Directed by: Edward Buzzell

The story takes place at Winsocki Military Institute, where preparations are being made for the Senior Prom. One of the cadets writes a fan letter to Lucille Ball (who portrays herself) inviting her to be his date for the prom. She accepts the date as a publicity stunt, and pandemonium breaks out at the normally staid academy. Good music and a talented cast result in a perky musical.

BEST YEARS OF OUR LIVES, THE
BLACK & WHITE   1946

DRAMA
RKO

MYRNA LOY	**FREDRIC MARCH**	**DANA ANDREWS**
TERESA WRIGHT	**VIRGINIA MAYO**	**CATHY O'DONNELL**
HOAGY CARMICHAEL	**GLADYS GEORGE**	**HAROLD RUSSELL**

Screenplay by: Robert E. Sherwood
From: A novel by Mackinlay Kantor
Directed by: William Wyler

A moving story about three World War II veterans returning to the U.S. and how they readjust to the everyday civilian world. Two of them (Fredric March and Dana Andrews) face loved ones at home who have changed while they've been away, and the other one (real-life veteran Harold Russell) must rebuild a life as a disabled person. The women in their lives are portrayed by actresses Myrna Loy, Teresa Wright, and Virginia Mayo. A superb and very moving drama.

Academy Award Recognition: won Best Picture, Fredric March won Best Actor, Harold Russell won Best Supporting Actor, William Wyler won Best Director, Robert E. Sherwood won Best Screenplay, Hugo Friedhofer won Best Scoring of a Dramatic or Comedy Picture.

BIG COUNTRY, THE

COLOR   1958

DRAMA/WESTERN

UNITED ARTISTS

GREGORY PECK	**JEAN SIMMONS**	**CARROLL BAKER**
CHARLTON HESTON	**BURL IVES**	**CHARLES BICKFORD**
ALFONSO BEDOYA	**CHUCK CONNORS**	

Screenplay by: James R. Webb, Sy Bartlett, and Robert Wilder;
                        adaptation by Jessamyn West and Robert Wyler
From: The novel by Donald Hamilton
Directed by: William Wyler

Gregory Peck is James McKay, a sea captain who's engaged to Patricia Terrill (Carroll Baker), a western rancher's daughter. He faces a challenge from her former love Steve Leech (Charlton Heston), gets mixed up in a local water supply feud, and has trouble proving his manhood to Patricia and her father, who can't understand his dislike for violent tactics. He finds more in common with neighbor Julie Maragon (Jean Simmons), who becomes his confidante. The first half of the movie is mostly drama, and the second half has more action, building to a really big shootout at the end. A powerful and absorbing drama, more suitable for teenagers and adults than for younger children.

Academy Award Recognition: Burl Ives won Best Supporting Actor, Jerome Moross nominated for Best Musical Scoring of a Dramatic or Comedy Picture.

BIG HAND FOR THE LITTLE LADY, A

TECHNICOLOR   1966

DRAMA/COMEDY/WESTERN

WARNER BROTHERS

HENRY FONDA	**JOANNE WOODWARD**	**JASON ROBARDS**
CHARLES BICKFORD	**BURGESS MEREDITH**	

Screenplay by: Sidney Carroll
Directed by: Fielder Cook

An offbeat Western with an engrossing plot, no shootouts, and a touch of mystery. A stranger named Meredith (Henry Fonda), and his wife Mary (Joanne Woodward) pass through Laredo while the town is geared up for its annual high-stakes poker game. The suspense builds as the game begins, and Meredith is eventually drawn into the contest as a major player. A very well-acted, non-violent story with a great surprise ending.

BIG RED
TECHNICOLOR   1962

DRAMA/ANIMAL STORIES
WALT DISNEY

WALTER PIDGEON   GILLES PAYANT   EMILE GENEST   JANETTE BERTRAND

Screenplay by: Louis Pelletier
From: The novel by Jim Kjelgaard
Directed by: Norman Tokar

The story takes place in Quebec, Canada. Walter Pidgeon portrays a lonely man who has locked away his emotions in reaction to losing people he loved. He purchases a champion show dog—Big Red—and hires an orphaned French boy (Gille Payant) to train and care for the dog. Through their ups and downs with Big Red, the boy eventually teaches the man how to love again. A touching movie that the whole family can enjoy together.

BILLY ROSE'S DIAMOND HORSESHOE
TECHNICOLOR   1945

MUSICAL
20TH CENTURY FOX

BETTY GRABLE   DICK HAYMES   PHIL SILVERS
WILLIAM GAXTON   BEATRICE KAY   CARMEN CAVALLARO
WILLIE SOLAR   MARGARET DUMONT

Screenplay by: George Seaton
Suggested by: A play produced by Charles L. Wagner and
                   written by John Kenyon Nicholson
Directed by: George Seaton

Bonnie Collins (Betty Grable) is the star of the Diamond Horseshoe night club. Joe Davis, Jr. (Dick Haymes), the club owner's son, spends a lot of time there and has a big crush on Bonnie. He's thinking about quitting medical school and trying his hand at show business. To set things right, Bonnie attempts to convince Joe to continue his studies, but falls in love with him in the process. A trademark Betty Grable film—colorful, with lots of tunes and plenty of glamour.

BILLY ROSE'S JUMBO

PANAVISION & METROCOLOR   1962

MUSICAL

MGM

| DORIS DAY | STEPHEN BOYD | JIMMY DURANTE |
| MARTHA RAYE | DEAN JAGGER | |

Screenplay by: Sidney Sheldon
Based on: The musical play produced by Billy Rose
                   at the New York Hippodrome, with book by
                   Ben Hecht and Charles MacArthur
Directed by: Charles Walters

Music and Lyrics by Richard Rodgers and Lorenz Hart

Doris Day stars as the resourceful and talented daughter of a circus owner (Jimmy Durante). The show is practically bankrupt due to her father's carelessness, but she fights to save it. She also finds romance along the way with a handsome young man (Stephen Boyd) who tries to help her. A very colorful circus musical with good tunes and a happy ending.

Academy Award Recognition: George Stoll nominated for Best Scoring of Music (adaptation or treatment).

BISCUIT EATER, THE

TECHNICOLOR   1972

DRAMA/ANIMAL STORIES

WALT DISNEY

EARL HOLLIMAN	PATRICIA CROWLEY	LEW AYRES
GODFREY CAMBRIDGE	BEAH RICHARDS	CLIFTON JAMES
JOHNNY WHITAKER	GEORGE SPELL	

Screenplay by: Lawrence Edward Watkin
Based on: A story by James Street
Directed by: Vincent McEveety

The tale of two young boys, one white (Lonnie McNeil, played by Johnny Whitaker) and one black (Text Tomlin, played by George Spell), who work together to turn a rejected pup into a champion bird dog. A simple but charming story that is valuable in portraying positive interracial friendships to children.

BISHOP'S WIFE, THE   COMEDY/DRAMA/CHRISTMAS
BLACK & WHITE   1947   RKO

CARY GRANT	**LORETTA YOUNG**	**DAVID NIVEN**
MONTY WOOLLEY	**JAMES GLEASON**	**GLADYS COOPER**
ELSA LANCHESTER	**THE MITCHELL BOYCHOIR**	

Screenplay by: Robert E. Sherwood and Leonardo Bercovici
From: The novel by Robert Nathan
Directed by: Henry Koster

Cary Grant is Dudley, an angel who has come to the aid of Julia Brougham (Loretta Young), whose husband Henry (David Niven) is an overworked bishop. Between his regular duties and keeping demanding parishioners happy, Henry is so busy that he has begun to neglect his family life, but Dudley plans to fix that. A brilliant and amusing comedy with a Winter/Christmas theme—a special treat at holiday time.

 Academy Award Recognition: nominated for Best Picture, Henry Koster nominated for Best Director, Hugo Friedhofer nominated for Best Musical Scoring of a Dramatic or Comedy Picture.

BLACK BEAUTY   DRAMA/ANIMAL STORIES
BLACK & WHITE/COLORIZED   1946   20TH CENTURY FOX

MONA FREEMAN	**RICHARD DENNING**	**EVELYN ANKERS**

Screenplay by: Lillie Hayward and Agnes Christine Johnston
Loosely based on: The book by Anna Sewall
Directed by: Max Nosseck

Set in rural England in the late 1880s, this is the story of Anne Wendon (played by Mona Freeman), a teenage girl on the verge of womanhood. She loves horses—especially her own, Black Beauty. She also begins to discover another kind of love with a young man who sees her only as a child, so she tries to convince him she's not. Girls should find this sweet story especially appealing.

BLACKBOARD JUNGLE, THE
BLACK & WHITE   1955

DRAMA

MGM

GLENN FORD	**ANNE FRANCIS**	**LOUIS CALHERN**
MARGARET HAYES	**JOHN HOYT**	**RICHARD KILEY**
SIDNEY POITIER	**VIC MORROW**	**JAMEEL FARAH**

Screenplay by: Richard Brooks
Based on: The novel by Evan Hunter
Directed by: Richard Brooks

A serious look at juvenile delinquency in the 1950s and the beginning of violence in America's schools. Glenn Ford is Richard Dadier, a teacher who arrives at an inner city school with good intentions, but he and fellow teachers are terrorized by their defiant students. Eventually, Dadier is the only teacher to stand up and meet the challenge of reinstating authority. Featured as some of the high school students are: Vic Morrow, Sidney Poitier, and Jamie Farr (billed as Jameel Farah). A strong drama that teaches a lesson about taking a stand, even against tough odds.

Academy Award Recognition: Richard Brooks nominated for Best Screenplay.

BLOSSOMS IN THE DUST
TECHNICOLOR   1941

DRAMA

MGM

GREER GARSON	**WALTER PIDGEON**	**FELIX BRESSART**
MARSHA HUNT	**FAY HOLDEN**	**SAMUEL S. HINDS**

Screenplay by: Anita Loos
Story by: Ralph Wheelwright
Directed by: Mervyn LeRoy

In this true story, Greer Garson portrays Edna Gladney, a Texas woman of the early 1900s who, through a chain of events in her life, became a champion for orphaned and illegitimate children. She set up an orphanage despite great obstacles, and cared for the children until she could find homes for them. Walter Pidgeon plays Edna's husband, Sam. A drama with a somewhat somber theme, but a view of how such children were neglected by society at that time.

Academy Award Recognition: nominated for Best Picture, Greer Garson nominated for Best Actress.

BLUE DAHLIA, THE
BLACK & WHITE

1946

DRAMA/MYSTERY-SUSPENSE
PARAMOUNT

ALAN LADD	**VERONICA LAKE**	**DORIS DOWLING**
WILLIAM BENDIX	**HUGH BEAUMONT**	**HOWARD DaSILVA**

Screenplay by: Raymond Chandler
Directed by: George Marshall

Alan Ladd is John Morrison, a man who returns from World War II with his pals (William Bendix and Hugh Beaumont). Morrison finds out that while he's been away, his wife Helen (Doris Dowling) has been dating a nightclub owner. When Helen is found dead next to Morrison's own gun, he must search for the real murderer in order to prove his innocence. Veronica Lake co-stars as Joyce Harwood, the nightclub owner's wife. A whodunit of exceptional quality.

Academy Award Recognition: Raymond Chandler nominated for Best Original Screenplay.

BLUE SKIES
TECHNICOLOR

1946

MUSICAL
PARAMOUNT

BING CROSBY	**FRED ASTAIRE**	**JOAN CAULFIELD**

Screenplay by: Arthur Sheckman
Adapted by: Allan Scott from an idea by Irving Berlin
Directed by: Stuart Heisler

Music and Lyrics by Irving Berlin

The setting: the 1920s. Fred Astaire is Jed Potter, a dancer and a sure, steady fellow. Bing Crosby is Johnny Adams, a nightclub owner and singer, who's a romantic wanderer. Both are in love with the same woman, Mary O'Hara (played by Joan Caulfield), and the story continues from there, following the romantic triangle over time, with enjoyable songs by Irving Berlin sprinkled here and there, making for a pleasant musical.

Academy Award Recognition: Robert Emmett Dolan nominated for Best Scoring of a Drama or Comedy Picture, nominated for Best Song: *You Keep Coming Back Like a Song*, Music and Lyrics by Irving Berlin.

BOATNIKS, THE

TECHNICOLOR

1970

COMEDY

WALT DISNEY

ROBERT MORSE	**STEFANIE POWERS**	**PHIL SILVERS**
NORMAN FELL	**MICKEY SHAUGHNESSY**	**WALLY COX**
DON AMECHE		

Screenplay by: Arthur Julian
Based on: A story by Marty Roth
Directed by: Norman Tokar

Ensign Garland (Robert Morse) is an accident-prone Coast Guard officer beginning a new assignment. At the marina, he befriends Kate (Stefanie Powers), a woman who operates the boat rental concession and a sailing school. When Garland crosses paths with three bungling jewel thieves fleeing to Mexico, he and Kate work together to expose and capture them. If successful, Garland will get a chance to prove himself to his boss, Commander Taylor (played by Don Ameche). A genial comedy with lots of slapstick and sight gags.

BON VOYAGE!

TECHNICOLOR

1962

COMEDY

WALT DISNEY

FRED MacMURRAY	**JANE WYMAN**	**DEBORAH WALLEY**	**MICHAEL CALLAN**

Screenplay by: Bill Walsh
Based on: The book by Marrijane and Joseph Hayes
Directed by: James Neilson

The adventures and misadventures of Harry and Catherine Willard (played by Fred MacMurray and Jane Wyman) as they fulfill their lifelong dream of touring Europe—but with their three children in tow. The harried parents try to keep the younger kids occupied while keeping tabs on their teenage daughter's first serious romance. A funny family story with nice scenery of Europe.

BONZO GOES TO COLLEGE

BLACK & WHITE   1952

COMEDY/ANIMAL STORIES

UNIVERSAL INT'L

MAUREEN O'SULLIVAN   **EDMUND GWENN**   **CHARLES DRAKE**
GIGI PERREAU   **GENE LOCKHART**   **IRENE RYAN**
BONZO

Screenplay by: Leo Lieberman and Jack Henley
Story by: Leo Lieberman, based on the character **Bonzo**
                 created by Raphael David Blau and Ted Berkman
Directed by: Frederick de Cordova

In this sequel to **Bedtime for Bonzo** (1951), Bonzo the chimpanzee runs away from a traveling carnival and is found by the granddaughter of a college football coach (Edmund Gwenn). The chimp becomes the lonely little girl's companion, and when she and her grandfather discover that Bonzo can really throw a football, he's recruited as quarterback for the college team. A cute story with plenty of humorous stunts by Bonzo.

BOOM TOWN

BLACK & WHITE/COLORIZED   1940

DRAMA

MGM

CLARK GABLE   **SPENCER TRACY**   **CLAUDETTE COLBERT**   **HEDY LAMARR**
LIONEL ATWILL   **CHILL WILLS**   **FRANK MORGAN**

Screenplay by: John Lee Mahin
Based on: A story by James Edward Grant
Directed by: Jack Conway

In 1918 in the oil fields of Burkburnett, Texas, John Sand (Spencer Tracy) and John McMasters (Clark Gable) are two wildcatters who become business partners. This is the story of their long and stormy friendship, in which one of their biggest sources of trouble is McMasters' marriage to Sand's old flame, Betsy (Claudette Colbert). An exciting drama with a quick pace and many unexpected turns.

BORN FREE

PANAVISION & TECHNICOLOR   1966

COLUMBIA

VIRGINIA McKENNA   **BILL TRAVERS**   **GEOFFREY KEEN**

Screenplay by: Gerald L.C. Copley
Based on: The book by Joy Adamson
Directed by: James Hill

Chief Technical Adviser: George Adamson

The true story of George and Joy Adamson, an Africa game warden and his wife. When a lioness is killed, George and Joy take in her three cubs and raise them to adulthood. When they become too big and troublesome, the Adamsons send two of them to a zoo, but cannot bear the thought of the most spirited one, Elsa, living in captivity. They decide to try something never done before—teaching a tame lion how to live in the wild. A story that's fascinating and touching at the same time.

Academy Award Recognition: won Best Song: *Born Free*, Music by John Barry and Lyrics by Don Black; John Barry won Best Original Music Score.

BORN YESTERDAY

BLACK & WHITE   1950

COMEDY/DRAMA

COLUMBIA PICTURES

JUDY HOLLIDAY   **BRODERICK CRAWFORD**   **WILLIAM HOLDEN**

Screenplay by: Albert Mannheimer
From: The play by Garson Kanin
Directed by: George Cukor

Judy Holliday stars as Billie Dawn, a good-hearted but uneducated blonde bomb-shell. She's the girlfriend of crooked businessman Harry Brock (played by Broderick Crawford) and they're in Washington to lobby Congress for legislation that will benefit his business. He hires Paul Verrall (William Holden), a writer/reporter, to tutor her so that she can hobnob with the upper class. But Brock's plan backfires as Billie discovers a whole new world and falls in love with her teacher. A great comedy combined with a dramatic theme about the important role that knowledge plays in maintaining freedom.

Academy Award Recognition: Judy Holliday won Best Actress, nominated for Best Picture, George Cukor nominated for Best Director, Albert Mannheimer nominated for Best Screenplay.

BOYS' TOWN
BLACK & WHITE/COLORIZED   1938

DRAMA
MGM

SPENCER TRACY   **MICKEY ROONEY**   **HENRY HULL**

Screenplay by:	John Meehan and Dore Schary
From:	An original story by Dore Schary and Eleanore Griffin
Directed by:	Norman Taurog

A story about the beginnings of the renowned Boys' Town, the home that grew to become a city for homeless and abandoned boys in Nebraska. Spencer Tracy plays Father Flanagan, the priest who actually founded Boys' Town, but all of the other characters are fictional. Mickey Rooney portrays one of the boys at the home, orphaned and troubled by the criminal life of his older brother. A simple but inspiring story, showing how the horrible fate that many orphans faced years ago was changed for the better by the founding of this kind of institution.

 Academy Award Recognition: Eleanore Griffin and Dore Schary won Best Original Story and were nominated for Best Screenplay, Spencer Tracy won Best Actor, nominated for Best Picture, Norman Taurog nominated for Best Director.

BRIDGES AT TOKO-RI, THE
TECHNICOLOR   1954

DRAMA/MILITARY
PARAMOUNT

WILLIAM HOLDEN	**GRACE KELLY**	**FREDRIC MARCH**
MICKEY ROONEY	**ROBERT STRAUSS**	**CHARLES McGRAW**
KEIKO AWAJI	**EARL HOLLIMAN**	

Screenplay by:	Valentine Davies
Based on:	The novel by James A. Michener
Directed by:	Mark Robson

William Holden is Lt. Harry Brubaker, a Navy pilot and World War II veteran who's been called back from civilian life to serve in the Korean War. Grace Kelly co-stars as his wife Nancy and Mickey Rooney is his buddy, helicopter pilot Mike Farney. Brubaker and his shipmates are assigned to a dangerous mission over the bridges at Toko-Ri, a well-protected target in Korea. There's tense drama as all prepare for the possible outcomes of the attack, and lots of action as the plan unfolds.

BRIGADOON

MUSICAL

CINEMASCOPE & ANSCO COLOR   1954   MGM

GENE KELLY   VAN JOHNSON   CYD CHARISSE   ELAINE STEWART

Screenplay by: Alan Jay Lerner
Based on: The musical play with book and lyrics written
                    by Alan Jay Lerner, and music by Frederick Loewe
Directed by: Vincente Minnelli

Choreography by Gene Kelly

Two Americans, Tommy Albright and Jeff Douglas (played by Gene Kelly and Van Johnson), stumble upon a quaint village named Brigadoon while on a hunting trip in Scotland. Tommy falls in love with a beautiful villager, Fiona Campbell (played by Cyd Charisse). But there is a catch—the magical town only exists for one day every 100 years, and Tommy would have to become a permanent part of Brigadoon in order to be with Fiona forever. A lovely fantasy with fine music and dancing.

BRIGHT EYES

DRAMA/MUSICAL

BLACK & WHITE   1934   20TH CENTURY FOX

SHIRLEY TEMPLE   JAMES DUNN   JANE DARWELL
JUDITH ALLEN   LOIS WILSON   CHARLES SELLON
WALTER JOHNSON   JANE WITHERS

Screenplay by: William Conselman
Story by: David Butler and Edwin Burke
Directed by: David Butler

Shirley Temple portrays Shirley Blake, a little girl whose widowed mother works as a live-in maid for the well-to-do Smythe family. Fortunately for Shirley, she also has her godfather, Loop Merritt (James Dunn), an airplane pilot and all-around nice guy. She is suddenly orphaned when her mother dies in an accident, and then a battle for custody begins between Loop and the Smythe's family patriarch, Uncle Ned. As in all of her films, Shirley charms just about everyone, and gets a very happy ending. Jane Withers (whom many will remember as "Josephine the Plumber" in TV commercials) is priceless as Joy, the Smythe's spoiled-rotten daughter.

BRINGING UP BABY
BLACK & WHITE/COLORIZED   1938

COMEDY
RKO

KATHARINE HEPBURN	**CARY GRANT**	**CHARLIE RUGGLES**
WALTER CATLETT	**BARRY FITZGERALD**	**MAY ROBSON**
FRITZ FELD	**LEONA ROBERTS**	**GEORGE IRVING**

Screenplay by: Dudley Nichols and Hagar Wilde
From: The story by Hagar Wilde
Directed by: Howard Hawks

Cary Grant plays a bookish dinosaur expert with a fiancé who is planning a predictable and boring future for him. Enter a wacky heiress (Katherine Hepburn), whose antics turn his life upside down. While chasing around after her pet leopard named "Baby" and a missing dinosaur bone, they fall in love. A zany 30s comedy, complete with plenty of slapstick humor and a happy ending.

BUCCANEER, THE
VISTAVISION & TECHNICOLOR   1958

DRAMA/ACTION-ADVENTURE
PARAMOUNT

YUL BRYNNER	**CLAIRE BLOOM**	**CHARLES BOYER**
INGER STEVENS	**HENRY HULL**	**E.G. MARSHALL**
LORNE GREENE	**CHARLTON HESTON**	

Screenplay by: Jesse L. Lasky, Jr. and Berenice Mosk
From: A screenplay by Harold Lamb, Edwin Justus Mayer and
                      C. Gardner Sullivan, based on Jeanie MacPherson's
                      adaptation of *LaFitte, The Pirate* by Lyle Saxon
Directed by: Anthony Quinn
Supervised by: Cecil B. DeMille

Yul Brynner stars as the pirate Jean Lafitte. The story is set in New Orleans during the War of 1812, with the United States counting on Lafitte to help them win the war and survive as a nation, though he had been previously condemned as a criminal. The able cast also includes Charlton Heston as General Andrew Jackson and Inger Stevens as Lafitte's love interest, the daughter of the Louisiana governor. A lively adventure with very colorful costumes.

BY THE LIGHT OF THE SILVERY MOON

TECHNICOLOR   1953

MUSICAL

WARNER BROTHERS

DORIS DAY	**GORDON MacRAE**	**LEON AMES**
ROSEMARY DeCAMP	**BILLY GRAY**	**MARY WICKES**

Screenplay by: Robert O'Brien and Irving Elinson
Suggested by: Booth Tarkington's Penrod Stories
Directed by: David Butler

This charming tale of family life in small town America in the early 1900s is the sequel to **On Moonlight Bay** (1951). Doris Day is Marjorie Winfield, an 18 year old girl engaged to the boy across the street, William Sherman (Gordon MacRae), who has just returned from World War I. Their romance becomes bumpy when he decides to delay their marriage and build a little nest egg first. In addition, Marjorie's entire family has a crisis when her brother Wesley (Billy Gray) and the housekeeper Stella (Mary Wickes) misinterpret a note they find in her father's pocket. Mr. and Mrs. Winfield are portrayed by Leon Ames and Rosemary DeCamp. A cheerful musical with some nice tunes, for the whole family.

BYE, BYE BIRDIE

PANAVISION & COLOR   1963

MUSICAL

COLUMBIA PICTURES

JANET LEIGH	**DICK VAN DYKE**	**ANN-MARGRET**
MAUREEN STAPLETON	**BOBBY RYDELL**	**JESSE PEARSON**
PAUL LYNDE	**MARY LAROCHE**	**ED SULLIVAN (as himself)**

Screenplay by: Irving Brecher
Based on: The play **Bye, Bye Birdie**, with book by Michael Stewart
Directed by: George Sidney

Teenage American girls are in a panic because their heartthrob Conrad Birdie (an Elvis Presley-like character) is being drafted into military service. Birdie's final public appearance is to be on the **Ed Sullivan Show**, giving a goodbye kiss to a lucky teenage girl (Ann-Margret). Dick Van Dyke plays a struggling songwriter trying to hit it big so that he can marry his fiancé (Janet Leigh). He gets his chance when Birdie uses one of his songs for the farewell show. This movie version of the Broadway musical provides entertainment by poking fun at the teen idols of the 1950s .

Academy Award Recognition: John Green nominated for Best Scoring of Music (adaptation or treatment).

CADDY, THE

BLACK & WHITE   1953   **COMEDY**

PARAMOUNT

DEAN MARTIN   **JERRY LEWIS**   **DONNA REED**   **BARBARA BATES**

Screenplay by:	Edmund Hartmann and Danny Arnold; additional dialogue by Ken Englund
Story by:	Danny Arnold
Directed by:	Norman Taurog

Harvey Miller (Jerry Lewis) is the son of a golf pro, but is a failure in tournament play due to his fear of crowds. He meets his future brother-in-law, Joe Anthony (Dean Martin), who has a natural talent for golf but doesn't know much about the game. The two decide to form an unusual partnership, with Joe as the golfer and Harvey as his caddy and coach. The fun begins when things don't go according to plan. Donna Reed is featured as Joe's love interest in this funny and entertaining comedy.

Academy Award Recognition: nominated for Best Song: *That's Amore*, Music by Harry Warren, Lyrics by Jack Brooks.

CAINE MUTINY, THE

TECHNICOLOR   1954   **DRAMA/MILITARY**

COLUMBIA

HUMPHREY BOGART	**JOSE FERRER**	**VAN JOHNSON**
FRED MacMURRAY	**ROBERT FRANCIS**	**TOM TULLY**
E.G. MARSHALL	**LEE MARVIN**	**CLAUDE AKINS**

Screenplay by:	Stanley Roberts; additional dialogue by Michael Blankfort
Based on:	The Pulitzer Prize winning novel by Herman Wouk
Directed by:	Edward Dmytryk

The story takes place during World War II on a U.S. Navy ship called the Caine—an old beat-up mine sweeper. A new commanding officer, Captain Queeg (Humphrey Bogart), comes aboard, sent by his superiors to crack down on sloppy habits and slack discipline. But before long, it becomes apparent that Queeg is mentally unstable and the rest of the officers on board ship must decide what to do about it. An intelligent and suspenseful Navy drama.

 Academy Award Recognition: nominated for Best Picture, Humphrey Bogart nominated for Best Actor, Tom Tully nominated for Best Supporting Actor, Stanley Roberts nominated for Best Screenplay, Max Steiner nominated for Best Scoring of a Dramatic or Comedy Picture.

CALAMITY JANE
TECHNICOLOR   1953   MUSICAL
                                                        WARNER BROTHERS

DORIS DAY	**HOWARD KEEL**	**ALLYN McLERIE**
PHILIP CAREY	**DICK WESSON**	

Screenplay by: James O'Hanlon
Directed by: David Butler

Doris Day stars as Calamity Jane, a rough and tough western gal whose bravery and skill are admired by the men in her town. However, her good friend Wild Bill Hickok (co-star Howard Keel) wishes she would dress and act in a more ladylike way. When Jane imports a very feminine aspiring actress to entertain at the town's saloon, she suddenly finds herself competing for the attention of men. First-rate tunes and good performances make this a very enjoyable musical.

 Academy Award Recognition: won Best Song: *Secret Love*, Music by Sammy Fain, Lyrics by Paul Francis Webster; Ray Heindorf nominated for Best Scoring of a Musical Picture.

CALL ME MADAM

TECHNICOLOR   1953

MUSICAL

20TH CENTURY FOX

ETHEL MERMAN	DONALD O'CONNOR	VERA-ELLEN
GEORGE SANDERS	BILLY DeWOLFE	HELMUT DANTINE
WALTER SLEZAK	LILIA SKALA	CHARLES DINGLE

Screenplay by: Arthur Sheekman
Based on: The musical comedy *Call Me Madam*,
                   with book by Howard Lindsay and Russell Crouse
Directed by: Walter Lang

Music and Lyrics by Irving Berlin

The main character in this story is based on the real-life U.S. Ambassador to Luxembourg, Perle Mesta. It takes place in 1951 in the fictional country of Lichtenburg, to which Sally Adams (Ethel Merman) becomes the new American Ambassador. Donald O'Connor plays Kenneth Gibson, a reporter and expert in European politics, who becomes her press attaché. Sally is a noted Washington party hostess (which is why she was chosen for the job) but knows nothing about her new country or her duties as Ambassador. Gibson teaches her the ropes, and Sally brings excitement to the staid society of Lichtenburg, while she and Gibson each find a new romance. Entertaining and funny with good songs and dances.

 Academy Award Recognition: Alfred Newman won Best Scoring of a Musical Picture.

CALL ME MISTER

TECHNICOLOR   1951

MUSICAL

20TH CENTURY FOX

| BETTY GRABLE | DAN DAILEY | DANNY THOMAS |
| DALE ROBERTSON | BENAY VENUTA | |

Screenplay by: Albert E. Lewin and Burt Styler
Suggested by: The musical revue by Harold J. Rome and Arnold M. Aurbach
Directed by: Lloyd Bacon

The setting is post-World War II Japan, where entertainer Kay Hudson (Betty Grable) runs into her GI ex-husband Shep Dooley (played by Dan Dailey). She's not quite over him yet, but is still suspicious of his irresponsible and womanizing ways. As Kay tours Japan entertaining the troops Shep follows her, trying to win her back. A pleasant and enjoyable musical.

CALLAWAY WENT THATAWAY

COMEDY

BLACK & WHITE   1951   MGM

FRED MacMURRAY	**DOROTHY McGUIRE**	**HOWARD KEEL**
JESSE WHITE	**FAY ROOPE**	**NATALIE SHAFER**

Screenplay by: Norman Panama and Melvin Frank
Directed by: Norman Panama and Melvin Frank

Mike Frye (Fred MacMurray) and Deborah Patterson (Dorothy McGuire) are a public relations team who find a man, "Stretch" Barnes (Howard Keel), who looks exactly like a former cowboy movie star. They decide to use this lookalike to stage the star's "comeback," but find that things don't happen according to their original, simple plan. A funny story that also conveys an important message about honesty.

CANTERVILLE GHOST, THE

DRAMA/COMEDY

BLACK & WHITE   1944   MGM

CHARLES LAUGHTON	**ROBERT YOUNG**	**MARGARET O'BRIEN**

Screenplay by: Edwin Harvey Blum
Based on: *The Canterville Ghost* by Oscar Wilde
Directed by: Jules Dassin

The tale begins in medieval times, and cowardly Sir Simon de Canterville (Charles Laughton) is ordered to be sealed into an alcove of the family castle as punishment for running away from a fight. After he dies, he becomes a ghost and, according to his father's wishes, is forced to haunt the halls of the castle until a descendant does a brave deed and frees his soul. The action then moves ahead in time to World War II, when American GI Cuffy Williams (Robert Young) discovers he is a Canterville descendant and joins forces with a little girl, Lady Jessica de Canterville (Margaret O'Brien) in an attempt to release Sir Simon from his unhappy existence. An unusual and entertaining ghost story, but it does have a few scenes that could be a little too scary for some fearful younger children.

CANYON PASSAGE

TECHNICOLOR   1946

DRAMA/WESTERN

UNIVERSAL

DANA ANDREWS	**BRIAN DONLEVY**	**SUSAN HAYWARD**
PATRICIA ROC	**WARD BOND**	**HOAGY CARMICHAEL**
FAY HOLDEN	**STANLEY RIDGES**	**LLOYD BRIDGES**
ANDY DEVINE		

Screenplay by: Ernest Pascal
Adapted from: ***The Saturday Evening Post*** novel *"Canyon Passage"*
                          by Ernest Haycox
Directed by: Jacques Tourneur

This story is set in an Oregon mining town in the Old West. It tells the tale of a man who tries to uphold what is right in the face of the gambling, corruption and greed that arose with the Gold Rush. This movie has a multi-faceted plot that weaves together drama, action and romance. The cast does an excellent job in providing good Western entertainment.

Academy Award Recognition: nominated for Best Song: ***Ole Buttermilk Sky***, Music by Hoagy Carmichael and Lyrics by Jack Brooks.

CAPTAIN JANUARY

BLACK & WHITE/COLORIZED   1936

DRAMA/MUSICAL

20TH CENTURY FOX

SHIRLEY TEMPLE	**GUY KIBBEE**	**SLIM SUMMERVILLE**
BUDDY EBSEN	**SARA HADEN**	**JANE DARWELL**
JUNE LANG		

Screenplay by: Sam Hellman, Gladys Lehman and Harry Tugend
Based on: A story by Laura E. Richards
Directed by: David Butler

Shirley Temple is Star, a young orphan girl rescued from a shipwreck by Captain January (Guy Kibbee), an elderly lighthouse keeper who now is raising her as his own daughter. She adores Captain January, as he is very kind and loving to her, and their world is a perfect one until a sourpuss truant officer sets her mind on taking Star away from him. The rest of the story involves how January and his seafaring friends try to keep Star out of an orphanage. In her usual style, Shirley Temple's character in this movie charms everyone and gets a happy ending while enjoying some songs and dances.

CAPTAINS COURAGEOUS

BLACK & WHITE/COLORIZED   1937

DRAMA
MGM

FREDDIE BARTHOLOMEW	**SPENCER TRACY**	**LIONEL BARRYMORE**
MELVYN DOUGLAS	**JOHN CARRADINE**	**MICKEY ROONEY**

Screenplay by: John Lee Mahin, Marc Connelly, and Dale Van Every
Based on: Rudyard Kipling's Story
Directed by: Victor Fleming

Freddie Bartholomew is Harvey, a wealthy, spoiled and manipulative boy whose father doesn't pay enough attention to him. While traveling on an ocean liner, Harvey falls overboard and is rescued by a Portuguese fisherman named Manuel (Spencer Tracy). The entire crew of the fishing boat is disgusted by Harvey's bad behavior and puts Manuel in charge of him for the duration of their three-month voyage. The two develop a special relationship as Manuel teaches Harvey to be an honorable young man. A movie with an important message and a dramatic, unexpected ending.

 Academy Award Recognition: Spencer Tracy won Best Actor; nominated for Best Picture; Marc Connolly, John Lee Mahin and Dale Van Every nominated for Best Screenplay.

CAPTAINS OF THE CLOUDS

TECHNICOLOR   1942

DRAMA/ACTION-ADVENTURE
WARNER BROTHERS

JAMES CAGNEY	**DENNIS MORGAN**	**BRENDA MARSHALL**
ALAN HALE	**GEORGE TOBIAS**	**REGINALD GARDINER**

Screenplay by: Arthur T. Horman, Richard Macaulay and Norman Reilly Raine
From: A story by Arthur T. Horman and Roland Gillett
Directed by: Michael Curtiz

This tribute to the Royal Canadian Air Force chronicles the adventures of a group of "Bush Pilots" in Canada, as civilians and then as members of the Royal Canadian Air Force in World War II. Cagney plays a stubborn renegade who competes relentlessly with other pilots in business and in romance. This movie has lots of aviation action and good acting by the talented cast.

CARBINE WILLIAMS

BLACK & WHITE/COLORIZED   1952

DRAMA

MGM

| JAMES STEWART | JEAN HAGEN | WENDELL COREY | JAMES ARNESS |

Screenplay by: Art Cohn
Based on: The true life story of David Marshall Williams
Directed by: Richard Thorpe

David Marshall Williams (played by James Stewart) got involved in moonshining, which led to a shootout with federal agents. While serving a 30-year term in a North Carolina prison for his crime, Williams worked in the blacksmith's shop. His life turned around when he invented a new gun and got a contract offer from the Winchester Rifle Company. This is all shown in retrospect, as Williams' son is told his father's life story by a friend. A good biographical portrait.

CAROUSEL

CINEMASCOPE & DELUXE COLOR   1956

MUSICAL

20TH CENTURY FOX

| GORDON MacRAE | SHIRLEY JONES | CAMERON MITCHELL |
| BARBARA RUICK | CLARAMAE TURNER | ROBERT ROUNSVILLE |

Screenplay by: Phoebe and Henry Ephron
From: The musical play *Carousel*, with music by Richard Rodgers, book and lyrics by Oscar Hammerstein II
Directed by: Henry King

Billy Bigelow (Gordon MacRae) is a soul in heaven, and needs to go back to earth because he hears that someone in his family is in trouble. As he bargains for a chance to return for one day and help out, his life is played out in flashbacks. On earth, he was a deceitful, smooth-talking carnival barker who fell for a lovely and innocent young mill worker named Julie (Shirley Jones). He married her, but took her life astray before meeting his untimely demise. The Rodgers and Hammerstein songs, plus the fine voices of MacRae and Jones, bring this story of an in-love but mismatched couple to life in an unusual kind of musical.

CASABLANCA

BLACK & WHITE/COLORIZED   1942

DRAMA

WARNER BROTHERS

HUMPHREY BOGART	**INGRID BERGMAN**	**PAUL HENREID**
CLAUDE RAINS	**CONRAD VEIDT**	**SYDNEY GREENSTREET**
PETER LORRE	**S.Z. SAKALL**	

Screenplay by: Julius J. and Philip G. Epstein and Howard Koch
From: A play by Murray Burnett and Joan Alison
Directed by: Michael Curtiz

This famous World War II drama takes place in Casablanca, French Morocco, where Europeans fleeing the war wait for exit visas so they can pass through Lisbon to the United States. Humphrey Bogart stars as a saloon owner who tries to stay out of the conflicts generated by the war. However, he's drawn into them when a former love (co-star Ingrid Bergman) asks him to help her and her husband, who is a member of the French Resistance. First-class performances and an intriguing plot, along with the well-known tune *As Time Goes By*.

 Academy Award Recognition: won Best Picture; Michael Curtiz won Best Director; Julius J. Epstein, Philip G. Epstein and Howard Koch won Best Screenplay; Humphrey Bogart nominated for Best Actor; Claude Rains nominated for Best Supporting Actor; Max Steiner nominated for Best Scoring of a Dramatic or Comedy Picture.

CAT AND THE CANARY, THE

BLACK & WHITE   1939

COMEDY/MYSTERY-SUSPENSE

PARAMOUNT

BOB HOPE	**PAULETTE GODDARD**	**JOHN BEAL**
DOUGLASS MONTGOMERY	**GALE SONDERGAARD**	**ELIZABETH PATTERSON**

Screenplay by: Walter de Leon and Lynn Starling
Based on: The stage play by John Willard
Directed by: Elliott Nugent

The tale of strange happenings in a creepy old mansion when a group of relatives gather for the reading of an uncle's will. Among them are Wally Campbell (Bob Hope), a radio personality, and Joyce Norman (Paulette Goddard), an artist. Joyce is named the first heir, but there is a mystery second heir who will inherit the fortune if Joyce should become insane or be killed. Lots of spooky things start happening as the second heir attempts to get rid of Joyce. A hilarious spoof of horror movies that's an especially good choice for Halloween viewing.

CHARADE
DRAMA/MYSTERY-SUSPENSE
TECHNICOLOR   1963   UNIVERSAL

CARY GRANT   AUDREY HEPBURN   WALTER MATTHAU
JAMES COBURN   GEORGE KENNEDY

Screenplay by: Peter Stone, story by Peter Stone and Marc Behm
Directed by: Stanley Donen
Music by: Henry Mancini

Audrey Hepburn is Regina Lampert, who returns home to Paris from a ski vacation to find that her husband has been killed and was wanted by the CIA. Regina is in extreme danger, as several thugs are chasing her for $250,000 that her husband had stolen, but she has no idea where it is. The handsome Peter Joshua (Cary Grant), who's trying to solve his brother's murder, comes to her aid. A riveting mystery with lots of twists and turns, plenty of action, and a touch of romance. One word of caution, though—a couple of scenes could be a little scary for younger children.

 Academy Award Recognition: nominated for Best Song: *Charade*, Music by Henry Mancini, Lyrics by Johnny Mercer.

CHEAPER BY THE DOZEN
COMEDY/DRAMA
COLOR   1950   20TH CENTURY FOX

CLIFTON WEBB   MYRNA LOY   JEANNE CRAIN   BETTY LYNN
EDGAR BUCHANAN   BARBARA BATES   MILDRED NATWICK   SARA ALLGOOD

Screenplay by: Lamar Trotti
Based on: The novel by Frank Gilbreth, Jr.
Directed by: Walter Lang

Clifton Webb plays Frank Gilbreth, and Myrna Loy his wife, Lillian. Both were industrial engineers of the 1920s and they had a family of 12 children. This is the story of how their household was run, the children being taught to be efficient at both work and play. It ends with Mr. Gilbreth's passing, but this doesn't take away from enjoyment of the story as whole. A charming family story, with both funny and serious moments, based on a book written by one of their sons.

CHINA CLIPPER

BLACK & WHITE   1936   **DRAMA**

WARNER BROTHERS

PAT O'BRIEN   **BEVERLY ROBERTS**   **HUMPHREY BOGART**

Screenplay by: Frank Wead
Directed by: Raymond Enright

A fictional story about the first trans-Pacific flight, showing how commercial aviation began after World War I, despite the disbelief of many skeptics. Pioneering flights were made over water to establish trade routes. The main character of this tale is Dave Logan (Pat O'Brien), a former World War I pilot trying to start his own airline. His buddy, Hap Stuart (a very young Humphrey Bogart), becomes a pilot for the infant airline, and Logan has difficulties with his wife caused by his obsession with his work. An interesting drama that sheds some light on an important part of aviation history.

CHRISTMAS IN CONNECTICUT

BLACK & WHITE/COLORIZED   1945   **COMEDY/CHRISTMAS**

WARNER BROTHERS

BARBARA STANWYCK   **DENNIS MORGAN**   **SYDNEY GREENSTREET**
REGINALD GARDINER   **S.Z. SAKALL**

Screenplay by: Lionel Houser and Adele Commandini
From: An original story by Aileen Hamilton
Directed by: Peter Godfrey

Barbara Stanwyck stars as Elisabeth Lane, a writer for a women's housekeeping magazine who provides recipes and stories about her life as a married homemaker in a beautiful Connecticut country home. But the truth is that she's actually single, can't cook, and lives in a city apartment. Elisabeth gets her delicious recipes from her friend Felix (S.Z. Sakall), who runs a restaurant. When her publisher (Sydney Greenstreet) offers a home-style Christmas to a recently hospitalized GI (Dennis Morgan), Elisabeth is forced to turn her fabricated lifestyle into reality. Lots of confusion follows, along with a little romance, in this funny holiday classic.

CLOCK, THE

BLACK & WHITE 1945 DRAMA/ROMANCE MGM

JUDY GARLAND   **ROBERT WALKER**   **JAMES GLEASON**
KEENAN WYNN   **MARSHALL THOMPSON**

Screenplay by: Robert Nathan and Joseph Schrank
Based on: A story by Paul Gallico and Pauline Gallico
Directed by: Vincente Minnelli

Judy Garland stars as Alice Maybery, a working girl in New York City who accidental-ly crosses paths with Joe Allen (co-star Robert Walker), a serviceman on a very short leave before shipping out to World War II. They hit it off, and she shows him the sights around town. They very quickly fall in love, and race against time to push the proper paperwork through in order to get married before his leave is over. This poignant and suspenseful love story is a first-class wartime romance.

COME SEPTEMBER

CINEMASCOPE & TECHNICOLOR 1961 COMEDY/ROMANCE UNIVERSAL INT'L

ROCK HUDSON   **GINA LOLLOBRIGIDA**   **SANDRA DEE**
BOBBY DARIN   **RONALD HOWARD**   **JOEL GREY**

Screenplay by: Stan Shapiro and Maurice Richlin
Directed by: Robert Mulligan

Rock Hudson is Robert Talbot, an affluent businessman with a villa in Italy, where he goes to vacation every September. Gina Lollobrigida is Lisa Fellini, a beautiful Italian lady who is his vacation girlfriend every year. She tries to get him to settle down with her permanently, but to no avail. Their story takes a new turn when he comes for an early visit in July and finds that in his absence the caretaker has rented the villa to a group of college girls (one of them played by Sandra Dee). While the couple chaperones the girls, they re-evaluate their own relationship. A light and engaging romantic comedy.

COME TO THE STABLE
BLACK & WHITE   1949

COMEDY/DRAMA/CHRISTMAS
20TH CENTURY FOX

LORETTA YOUNG	**CELESTE HOLM**	**HUGH MARLOWE**
ELSA LANCHESTER	**THOMAS GOMEZ**	

Screenplay by: Oscar Millard and Sally Benson
From: A story by Clare Boothe Luce
Directed by: Henry Koster

Two nuns (Loretta Young and Celeste Holm) arrive in a small New England town, named Bethlehem, with a mission—to build a children's hospital and fulfill a promise made to God by one of the nuns during World War II in France. They start with nothing, but use ingenuity and persuasion to work toward their goal, despite many obstacles. Elsa Lanchester is featured as a painter of religious pictures, whose studio the nuns use as their home base. A winsome and amusing tale that's very entertaining, and especially fitting for holiday viewing.

Academy Award Recognition: Loretta Young nominated for Best Actress, Celeste Holm and Elsa Lanchester nominated for Best Supporting Actress, Claire Boothe Luce nominated for Best Motion Picture Story, nominated for Best Song: ***Through a Long and Sleepless Night***, Music by Alfred Newman, Lyrics by Mack Gordon.

COMMAND DECISION
BLACK & WHITE/COLORIZED   1948

DRAMA/MILITARY
MGM

CLARK GABLE	**WALTER PIDGEON**	**VAN JOHNSON**	**BRIAN DONLEVY**
CHARLES BICKFORD	**JOHN HODIAK**	**EDWARD ARNOLD**	

Screenplay by: William R. Laidlaw and George Froeschel
Based on: The play by William Wister Haines
Directed by: Sam Wood

In this World War II drama, Clark Gable is U.S. Brigadier General K.C. Dennis, an officer known for arranging risky attacks that often claim large losses of personnel. He is in charge of an American plan to use air strikes to destroy German factories that are starting to produce jet planes. As the mission unfolds, it takes its toll on the men in the control center. Also featured are Walter Pidgeon as Major General

Roland Goodlow and Van Johnson as Sergeant Kane, Dennis' loyal assistant. Realistic shots of the air war, and all of its dangers, are expertly combined with the backstage view of the battle strategy, resulting in a top-notch war movie.

COMPUTER WORE TENNIS SHOES, THE
TECHNICOLOR   1970

COMEDY
WALT DISNEY

KURT RUSSELL	**CESAR ROMERO**	**JOE FLYNN**
WILLIAM SCHALLERT	**ALAN HEWITT**	**RICHARD BAKALYAN**
DEBBIE PAINE	**MICHAEL McGREEVEY**	**JON PROVOST**

Screenplay by: Joseph L. McEveety
Directed by: Robert Butler

Kurt Russell stars as Dexter, a bored college student. He and a group of friends convince a businessman to donate a computer to their school, which suddenly excites and inspires them. During a freak electrical accident in the computer room, Dexter acquires the computer's "brain." His new-found superintelligence propels him to fame and he experiences plenty of new adventures. Jon Provost of TV's *Lassie* series appears as one of Dexter's friends. A well-done comedy with a unique story that the whole family can enjoy together.

COURT JESTER, THE
TECHNICOLOR & VISTAVISION   1956

MUSICAL/COMEDY
PARAMOUNT

DANNY KAYE	**GLYNIS JOHNS**	**BASIL RATHBONE**	**ANGELA LANSBURY**
CECIL PARKER	**MILDRED NATWICK**	**JOHN CARRADINE**	

Screenplay by: Norman Panama and Melvin Frank
Directed by: Norman Panama and Melvin Frank

Danny Kaye stars in this Medieval tale with very colorful costumes. As a character named Hawkins, he joins a band of rebels planning to overthrow a tyrant king and install the rightful heir, an infant whom they hold in their protection. Hawkins' mission is to pose as the king's court jester and infiltrate the castle. He gets help (and some romance) from the beautiful but rugged rebel leader Maid Jean (Glynis Johns). Of course, things don't go too smoothly—Hawkins experiences many close calls and is also courted by the king's daughter, Princess Gwendolyn (Angela Lansbury), who's hoping to escape an arranged marriage. An excellent plot with good songs and swashbuckling action makes this a treat for the whole family.

COURTSHIP OF ANDY HARDY, THE
BLACK & WHITE   1942

COMEDY
MGM

LEWIS STONE	**MICKEY ROONEY**	**CECELIA PARKER**	**FAY HOLDEN**
ANN RUTHERFORD	**SARA HADEN**	**DONNA REED**	

Screenplay by: Agnes Christine Johnston
Based on: The characters created by Aurania Rouverol
Directed by: George B. Seitz

Another entry in the *Andy Hardy* series. This time, Judge Hardy (Lewis Stone) is mediating a dispute between a divorced couple and notices that their fighting has taken its toll on their daughter Melodie (Donna Reed). The judge asks his son Andy (Mickey Rooney) to take Melodie to a dance and help her to gain social confidence. Some unexpected things happen, and both Andy and his sister Marian (Cecelia Parker), who also has some growing to do, learn some valuable lessons. A cute story about the social lives of young people.

COURTSHIP OF EDDIE'S FATHER, THE
COLOR   1963

COMEDY/DRAMA/ROMANCE
MGM

GLENN FORD	**SHIRLEY JONES**	**STELLA STEVENS**
DINA MERRILL	**ROBERTA SHERWOOD**	**RONNY HOWARD**
JERRY VAN DYKE		

Screenplay by: John Gay
Based on: The novel by Mark Toby
Directed by: Vincente Minnelli

Glenn Ford is Tom Corbett, a recently widowed executive. He and his young son, Eddie (Ronny Howard), try to adjust to life on their own without a wife and mother. Shirley Jones is Elizabeth, a neighbor and friend of Tom's deceased wife. She steps in to help Eddie cope with his loss and soon grows closer to Tom. Complications emerge as Tom dates another woman (played by Dina Merrill) who has no room in her heart for Eddie. A very sweet family drama with a happy ending.

CRASH DIVE
COLOR

DRAMA/MILITARY/ACTION-ADVENTURE
1943
20TH CENTURY FOX

TYRONE POWER   **DANA ANDREWS**   **ANNE BAXTER**

Screenplay by: Jo Swerling
Directed by: Archie Mayo
Based on: A story by W.R. Burnett

Two men (Tyrone Power, Dana Andrews) are shipmates on a submarine and both are in love with the same woman (Anne Baxter). Despite this, they fight their way through a dangerous mission together, trying not to let their personal problems get in the way. This movie does a good job of combining personal drama and exciting wartime action.

DADDY LONG LEGS
CINEMASCOPE & COLOR BY DELUXE   1955

MUSICAL/ROMANCE
20TH CENTURY FOX

FRED ASTAIRE   **LESLIE CARON**   **TERRY MOORE**
THELMA RITTER   **FRED CLARK**

Screenplay by: Phoebe and Henry Ephron
From: The novel by Jean Webster
Directed by: Jean Negulesco

Fred Astaire appears in the title role as a wealthy man who happens upon an orphanage while visiting France. He admires a charming teenage girl (Leslie Caron) and decides to anonymously sponsor her for a college education in the United States. She writes him many letters and, as she grows up and he observes her from afar, they fall in love without his true identity being known to her. Fred Clark and

Thelma Ritter also appear as Astaire's business manager and secretary. This musical romance is done in a whimsical style with fine dance numbers by Astaire and Caron.

 Academy Award Recognition: Alfred Newman nominated for Best Scoring of a Musical Picture, nominated for Best Song: *Something's Gotta Give*, Music and Lyrics by Johnny Mercer.

DANGEROUS WHEN WET
TECHNICOLOR   1953   **MUSICAL**
                                                        MGM

ESTHER WILLIAMS	FERNANDO LAMAS	JACK CARSON
CHARLOTTE GREENWOOD	DENISE DARCEL	WILLIAM DEMAREST
DONNA CORCORAN	BARBARA WHITING	

Screenplay by: Dorothy Kingsley
Directed by: Charles Walters

Esther Williams stars as Katie Higgins, a very athletic farmer's daughter who is sponsored by a vitamin elixir company to swim the English Channel. While in Europe, she meets and falls for Andre Lanet (Fernando Lamas), an attractive and wealthy bachelor. William Demarest and Charlotte Greenwood play Katie's health-and-fitness conscious parents. There's lots of fun for the whole family in this light and cheery musical which also features a special sequence where Esther swims with cartoon characters Tom & Jerry.

DARK COMMAND
BLACK & WHITE/COLORIZED   1940   **DRAMA/WESTERN/ACTION-ADVENTURE**
                                            REPUBLIC PICTURES

| CLAIRE TREVOR | JOHN WAYNE | WALTER PIDGEON | ROY ROGERS |
| GEORGE HAYES | PORTER HALL | MARJORIE MAIN | |

Screenplay by: Grover Jones, Lionel Houser, and Hugh Herbert
Based on: A novel by W.R. Burnett
Directed by: Raoul Walsh

This is a fictionalized story, based partly on fact. It takes place in Kansas, which was on the verge of statehood just before the Civil War. Settlers flowed into the territory from both the North and the South, attempting to claim the state for their side. John Wayne is a Texas cowboy traveling the countryside with a dentist (George "Gabby" Hayes). When they arrive in Lawrence, Kansas, the cowboy is smitten with a banker's daughter (Claire Trevor) and decides to stay for a while. However, she is dating the town schoolteacher (Walter Pidgeon), who leads a dull life but aspires to greatness. Each of these characters takes part in the historic events and conflicts of the time in his/her own way. The plot is stirring, with lots of action, and the cast is excellent, resulting in a first-rate Western.

 Academy Award Recognition: Victor Young nominated for Best Original Score.

DARK PASSAGE
BLACK & WHITE/COLORIZED

DRAMA/MYSTERY-SUSPENSE
1947   WARNER BROTHERS

HUMPHREY BOGART	LAUREN BACALL	BRUCE BENNETT	AGNES MOOREHEAD

Screenplay by: Delmer Daves
Based on: The novel by David Goodis
Directed by: Delmer Daves

Vincent Parry (Humphrey Bogart) is a man wrongly convicted of murdering his wife, and he escapes from San Quentin Prison. On the run, he is aided by a lovely young woman, Irene Jansen (Lauren Bacall), who believes in his innocence. She conceals him in her apartment as he works to find the real murderer while staying under-cover from authorities. Parry even has secret plastic surgery done to change his appearance and help protect his true identity. An unusual, intriguing mystery with great performances by the entire cast.

DATE WITH JUDY, A
TECHNICOLOR

MUSICAL
1948   MGM

WALLACE BEERY	JANE POWELL	ELIZABETH TAYLOR	CARMEN MIRANDA
ROBERT STACK	SCOTTY BECKETT	SELENA ROYLE	LEON AMES

Screenplay by: Leon Ames, Dorothy Cooper and Dorothy Kingsley
Based on: The characters created by Aleen Leslie
Directed by: Richard Thorpe

In Santa Barbara, California, Judy Foster (Jane Powell) is a high school girl who sings with a band for school dances. Carol (Elizabeth Taylor) is Judy's friend. Carol's brother Oogie is the leader of the band Judy sings with (and also her boyfriend). There are some story lines about the kids' romances, as well as happenings within their families—Carol and Oogie's problems with their absentee businessman father and Judy's parents' impending anniversary. Robert Stack plays a slightly older soda fountain attendant who is attracted to Carol. Also featured in this movie is Xavier Cugat and his orchestra, a popular band at that time. A charming and pleasant family film providing light entertainment.

DEAD RECKONING

BLACK & WHITE

1947

DRAMA/MYSTERY-SUSPENSE

COLUMBIA

HUMPHREY BOGART   LIZABETH SCOTT

Screenplay by:	Oliver H.P. Garrett and Steve Fisher; adaptation by Allen Rivkin
Story by:	Gerald Adams and Sidney Biddell
Directed by:	John Cromwell

Humphrey Bogart plays Rip Murdoch, a paratrooper returning from World War II. He and his army buddy, Sgt. Drake, are whisked off to Washington, D.C. to receive military honors, but Drake becomes camera shy and disappears. Sensing that something is very wrong, Murdoch investigates and finds that Drake has a secret identity and is on the run from the law. From there, Murdoch embarks on an odyssey to clear his pal's name, uncovering clues with the help of Drake's girlfriend, Coral Chandler (Lizabeth Scott).

DESIGNING WOMAN

CINEMASCOPE & METROCOLOR

1957

COMEDY/ROMANCE

MGM

GREGORY PECK   LAUREN BACALL   DOLORES GRAY   SAM LEVENE

Screenplay by:	George Wells
From:	A suggestion by Helen Rose
Directed by:	Vincente Minnelli

Gregory Peck portrays a newspaper sports columnist and Lauren Bacall is a prominent clothing designer—both from New York City. They meet while on vacation, fall in love and marry in a whirlwind romance. But the real fun begins when they return home and discover how little they know about each other's lifestyle and friends. A very enjoyable love story, done in a lush and beautiful style.

 Academy Award Recognition: George Wells won Best Story and Screenplay (written directly for the screen).

DESPERATE JOURNEY
BLACK & WHITE

DRAMA/MILITARY/ACTION-ADVENTURE
1942 WARNER BROTHERS

ERROL FLYNN	**RONALD REAGAN**	**NANCY COLEMAN**
RAYMOND MASSEY	**ALAN HALE**	**ARTHUR KENNEDY**

Screenplay by: Arthur T. Horman
Directed by: Raoul Walsh

Flynn, Reagan, Kennedy, Hale and Sinclair portray the crew of a bomber plane shot down over Germany in World War II. They are picked up by the German army, but with ingenuity, manage to escape and take with them military secrets found in a commander's office. The rest of the story follows their dangerous escape route through Germany to freedom, with many close calls along the way. Raymond Massey plays the German commander who is desperate to track them down. Lots of riveting action and the fantastic acts of heroism typical of morale-boosting movies of the wartime era.

DESTINATION TOKYO
BLACK & WHITE/COLORIZED

DRAMA/ACTION-ADVENTURE/MILITARY
1943 WARNER BROTHERS

CARY GRANT	**JOHN GARFIELD**	**ALAN HALE**	**JOHN RIDGELY**
DANE CLARK	**WARNER ANDERSON**	**WILLIAM PRINCE**	**ROBERT HUTTON**
TOM TULLY	**JOHN FORSYTHE**		

Screenplay by: Delmer Daves and Albert Maltz
Original story by: Steve Fisher
Directed by: Delmer Daves

A World War II submarine adventure with Cary Grant as the sub's captain, who is carrying out secret orders to attack Tokyo. The suspense builds as the complicated and perilous mission evolves. A state-of-the-art war movie with lots of exciting combat action.

 Academy Award Recognition: Steve Fisher nominated for Best Original Story.

DIVE BOMBER
TECHNICOLOR   1941

DRAMA/MILITARY
WARNER BROTHERS

ERROL FLYNN	**FRED MacMURRAY**	**RALPH BELLAMY**
ALEXIS SMITH	**ROBERT ARMSTRONG**	**REGIS TOOMEY**

Screenplay by: Frank Wead and Robert Buckner
From a story by: Frank Wead
Directed by: Michael Curtiz

This movie was dedicated to the military flight surgeons, who set out to solve the medical problems that emerged as airplane flight developed and became an essential part of the armed forces. A fictional story is used to show how some actual problems were solved. Errol Flynn plays Lt. Douglas Lee, a young Navy doctor who becomes devoted to helping pilots prepare for battle, assisting Dr. Lance Rogers (Ralph Bellamy), an experienced flight surgeon. Fred MacMurray portrays Commander Joe Blake, an expert flier, who along with his buddy Tim Griffin (Regis Toomey), distrusts the doctors and doubts their ability to improve the pilots' working conditions. The result is a superior aviation drama with excellent photography of flight scenes.

DON'T GO NEAR THE WATER
CINEMASCOPE & METROCOLOR   1957

COMEDY/MILITARY
MGM

GLENN FORD	**GIA SCALA**	**EARL HOLLIMAN**	**ANNE FRANCIS**	**KEENAN WYNN**
FRED CLARK	**EVA GABOR**	**RUSS TAMBLYN**	**JEFF RICHARDS**	

Screenplay by: Dorothy Kingsley and George Wells
Based on: The novel *Don't Go Near The Water* by William Brinkley
Directed by: Charles Walters

Glenn Ford stars in this light and amusing service comedy about a Naval public relations installation on a remote Pacific Island in World War II. The men there don't see much action—they're busy catering to journalists, congressmen and the like. Even though they have cushy jobs, they have misfortunes and hilarious adventures all their own.

DONOVAN'S REEF

TECHNICOLOR   1963

COMEDY

PARAMOUNT

JOHN WAYNE	LEE MARVIN	ELIZABETH ALLEN
JACK WARDEN	CESAR ROMERO	DICK FORAN
DOROTHY LAMOUR		

Screenplay by: Frank Nugent and James Edward Grant
Story by: Edmund Beloin
Directed by: John Ford

A wealthy, conservative Boston heiress (Elizabeth Allen) travels to a Pacific island to contact her father (Jack Warden), whom she has never seen. He's a doctor who settled there after World War II, and tries to hide the details of his life (and his other children) from his newly-arrived daughter. She becomes enchanted by the island's people, some of whom are oddball characters (played by Lee Marvin and Dorothy Lamour), and embarks on a stormy romance with her father's crusty but lovable ex-GI friend (John Wayne). The tropical locale provides beautiful scenery for this charming and funny comedy that the whole family can enjoy.

DOUBLE INDEMNITY

BLACK & WHITE   1944

DRAMA/MYSTERY-SUSPENSE

PARAMOUNT

| FRED MacMURRAY | BARBARA STANWYCK | EDWARD G. ROBINSON |

Screenplay by: Billy Wilder and Raymond Chandler
Based on: The novel by James M. Cain
Directed by: Billy Wilder

In a departure from his usual roles, Fred MacMurray plays a mysterious tough-guy, insurance salesman Walter Neff. Barbara Stanwyck is Phyllis Didrikson, a wife who wants to get a secret insurance policy on her husband's life. Neff refuses her request at first, because he suspects that Phyllis is up to no good. But he falls for her, and ends up involved in her sinister plan to murder her husband. This is a gripping and suspenseful film with a dark atmosphere and a roller coaster plot that's ideal for mystery lovers, and more suitable for teenagers and adults rather than young children.

 Academy Award Recognition: nominated for Best Picture, Barbara Stanwyck nominated for Best Actress, Billy Wilder nominated for Best Director, Raymond Chandler and Billy Wilder nominated for Best Screenplay, Miklos Rozsa nominated for Best Scoring of a Dramatic or Comedy Picture.

DOUBLE WEDDING
BLACK & WHITE   1937

COMEDY/ROMANCE
MGM

| WILLIAM POWELL | MYRNA LOY | FLORENCE RICE |
| JOHN BEAL | JESSIE RALPH | EDGAR KENNEDY |

Screenplay by: Jo Swerling
From: A play by Ferenc Molnar
Directed by: Richard Thorpe

Myrna Loy is Margit Agnew, a successful and single businesswoman who's very proud of being level-headed and organized. She runs the life of her younger sister, who is soon to be married to a faithful but dull young man. Enter Charlie Lodge (William Powell), a vagabond actor/painter who lives in a trailer. Margit finds his lifestyle deplorable at first but is soon attracted to him, though she denies it. Confusion and hysteria abound as Margit's altar-bound sister also falls for the wacky artist. A zany comedy with the Powell-Loy team in good form.

DOWN ARGENTINE WAY
TECHNICOLOR   1940

MUSICAL
20TH CENTURY FOX

| DON AMECHE | BETTY GRABLE | CARMEN MIRANDA | CHARLOTTE GREENWOOD |

Screenplay by: Darrell Ware and Karl Tunberg
Directed by: Irving Cummings

Glenda Crawford (Betty Grable), the daughter of a wealthy American businessman, goes to a horse show and meets Ricardo Quintana (Don Ameche), the handsome son of an Argentinean horse breeder. They like each other very much, but a feud between their fathers gets in the way of their friendship, so Glenda travels to

Buenos Aires with her Aunt Binnie (Charlotte Greenwood) to try and work things out. While there, Glenda and Ricardo train a race horse together and fall deeply in love. Some nice music and a festive South American atmosphere make this a pleasant musical.

 Academy Award Recognition: nominated for Best Song: ***Down Argentine Way***, Music by Harry Warren, Lyrics by Mack Gordon.

DREAM WIFE
COMEDY/ROMANCE

BLACK & WHITE/COLORIZED   1953   MGM

CARY GRANT	DEBORAH KERR	WALTER PIDGEON	BETTA ST. JOHN

Screenplay by: Sidney Sheldon, Herbert Baker, and Alfred Lewis Levitt
Directed by: Sidney Sheldon

Cary Grant is American businessman Clemson Reade, who, on an overseas trip, meets and admires Tarji (Betta St. John), the lovely daughter of a Middle Eastern dignitary. However, Reade has already has a fiancé, Priscilla "Effie" Effington (Deborah Kerr), an executive with the U.S. State Department. Feeling neglected by Effie, who's dedicated to her work, he becomes engaged to the more subservient and attentive Tarji. The engagement becomes an international event, and the fun begins when Effie is assigned to oversee the situation for the State Department. A pleasant and diverting romantic comedy.

DUCHESS OF IDAHO
MUSICAL

TECHNICOLOR   1950   MGM

ESTHER WILLIAMS	VAN JOHNSON	JOHN LUND	PAULA RAYMOND
CLINTON SUNDBERG	CONNIE HAINES	MEL TORME	AMANDA BLAKE

Screenplay by: Dorothy Cooper and Jerry Davis
Directed by: Robert Z. Leonard

Esther Williams is Christine Riverton Duncan, the star of a Chicago water ballet show. Her roommate Ellen (Paula Raymond) works as a secretary for bachelor businessman Douglas J. Morrissen, Jr. (John Lund) and is in love with him, but he takes no notice of her. When Morrissen plans a business trip to Sun Valley, Idaho, Chris devises a plan to help Ellen win him over, and along the way finds love herself, with dashing bandleader Dick Layn (Van Johnson). This enjoyable movie has music, dancing and of course, some of Esther's swimming.

EAGLE AND THE HAWK, THE
TECHNICOLOR   1950

DRAMA/WESTERN
PARAMOUNT

JOHN PAYNE	RHONDA FLEMING	DENNIS O'KEEFE

Screenplay by: Geoffrey Homes and Lewis R. Foster
Based on: A story by Jess Arnold
Directed by: Lewis R. Foster

A fictional story based on history, in 1863, when Napoleon III attempted to install Maximilian as Emperor of Mexico by taking advantage of U.S. Civil War discord. Texas Ranger Todd Croyden (John Payne) and American spy Whitney Randolph (Dennis O'Keefe) are dispatched to find the people who are plotting to overthrow the Mexican government. Along the way, they meet an attractive lady, Madeleine Danzeeger (Rhonda Fleming), whom Croyden falls for, and they unhappily discover that her father is part of the rebel movement. A good Western drama, with a complex historical element that makes it better suited for an older audience, teenagers and adults.

EASTER PARADE
TECHNICOLOR   1948

MUSICAL
MGM

JUDY GARLAND	FRED ASTAIRE	PETER LAWFORD
ANN MILLER	JULES MUNSHIN	CLINTON SUNDBERG

Screenplay by: Sidney Sheldon, Frances Goodrich and Albert Hackett
Original story by: Frances Goodrich and Albert Hackett
Directed by: Charles Walters

Lyrics and Music by Irving Berlin

The setting is New York in the early 1900s, where the Easter Parade tradition began. Fred Astaire portrays Don Hewes, a dancer whose partner Nadine Gale (Ann Miller) breaks up the team to begin her own solo career. Don recruits chorus girl Hannah Brown (Judy Garland) as his new partner, and works to groom her for stardom. Nadine is jealous of Don's new and attractive partner. His best friend, Jonathan Harrow III (Peter Lawford), begins to care for Hannah also, adding to the romantic confusion. Light, cheerful entertainment with nice Irving Berlin tunes and great dance numbers.

 Academy Award Recognition: Johnny Green and Roger Edens won Best Scoring of a Musical Picture .

EASY TO LOVE

TECHNICOLOR   1953

MUSICAL
MGM

ESTHER WILLIAMS	VAN JOHNSON	TONY MARTIN
JOHN BROMFIELD	EDNA SKINNER	KING DONOVAN
PAUL BRYAR	CARROLL BAKER	

Screenplay by: Lazlo Vadnay and William Roberts
Based on: A story by Lazlo Vadnay
Directed by: Charles Walters

Esther Williams is Julie Hallerton, a Cypress Gardens swimming and waterskiing star and Van Johnson is Ray Lloyd, the manager of the Gardens. On the surface, Ray values Julie as an important part of his business, but deep down has truly grown to love her. As a confirmed bachelor, though, he is reluctant to give in to his feelings. Ray invites Julie to New York on a business trip, but his real motive is to get her away from her current admirer, Hank (John Bromfield). Once in New York, Julie meets singer Barry Gordon (Tony Martin), a womanizer who tries to sweep her off her feet. When Julie and Ray return to Florida , Barry follows, and she now has three men competing for her affections. Beautiful swimming and waterskiing scenes are featured in this enjoyable and fun musical.

EASY TO WED

TECHNICOLOR   1946

COMEDY/MUSICAL

MGM

| VAN JOHNSON | ESTHER WILLIAMS | LUCILLE BALL |
| KEENAN WYNN | CECIL KELLAWAY | |

Screenplay: Adapted by Dorothy Kingsley from the screenplay
                Libeled Lady by Maurine Watkins,
                Howard Emmett Rogers and George Oppenheimer
Directed by: Edward Buzzell

In this remake of *Libeled Lady* (1936), Esther Williams plays Connie Allenbury, a wealthy heiress who intends to sue a newspaper that wrote an unfavorable article about her. Newspaperman Warren Haggerty (Keenan Wynn) must stop the lawsuit and enlists the help of his fiancé Gladys Benton (Lucille Ball), and a former colleague, Bill Chandler (Van Johnson). While trying to convince her to drop the litigation, Bill falls for Connie. A fast-paced story with good stars, providing light entertainment.

EDGE OF DARKNESS

BLACK & WHITE   1943

DRAMA/ACTION-ADVENTURE

WARNER BROTHERS

ERROL FLYNN	ANN SHERIDAN	WALTER HUSTON
NANCY COLEMAN	HELMUT DANTINE	JUDITH ANDERSON
RUTH GORDON	JOHN BEAL	MORRIS CARNOVSKY

Screenplay by: Robert Rossen
Based on: The novel by William Woods
Directed by: Lewis Milestone

Errol Flynn and Ann Sheridan star as leaders of the resistance in a small Norwegian fishing village during the German occupation of World War II. This is a classic morale-boosting movie of the war era which depicts the bravery of those who uphold freedom, and the defeat of the Germans with many daring acts of heroism. A good choice for those who relish war stories.

EDISON, THE MAN

BLACK & WHITE

DRAMA

1940

MGM

| SPENCER TRACY | RITA JOHNSON | LYNNE OVERMAN | CHARLES COBURN |
| GENE LOCKHART | HENRY TRAVERS | FELIX BRESSART | |

Screenplay by: Talbot Jennings and Bradbury Foote
Original story by: Dore Schary and Hugo Butler
Directed by: Clarence Brown

Technical Advisors: William A. Simonds, of The Edison Institute, Dearborn,
                     Michigan, and Norman R. Speiden, Director of Historical
                     Research, Thomas A. Edison, Inc., West Orange, NJ

Spencer Tracy plays out the highlights of Thomas Edison's adult life—from his first invention through his struggle to fulfill his vision of bringing electric light to the world. A good supporting cast portrays Edison's faithful and hard-working assistants. An excellent biographical drama with great educational value.

Academy Award Recognition: Hugo Butler and Dore Schary nominated for Best Original Story.

EGG AND I, THE

BLACK & WHITE

COMEDY

1947

UNIVERSAL INT'L

| CLAUDETTE COLBERT | FRED MacMURRAY | MARJORIE MAIN |
| PERCY KILBRIDE | LOUISE ALLBRITTON | |

Screenplay by: Chester Erskine and Fred F. Finklehoffe
From: The best selling book by Betty MacDonald
Directed by: Chester Erskine

Claudette Colbert plays Betty MacDonald, a woman accustomed to city life, whose husband Bob MacDonald (Fred MacMurray) has purchased an old broken-down farm, where he plans for them to raise chickens. Betty doesn't adjust too well at first, and many funny things happen to the couple as they work to whip the farm into shape. A very endearing movie that provides family-style entertainment.

Academy Award Recognition: Marjorie Main nominated for Best Supporting Actress.

ESCAPADE IN JAPAN
TECHNIRAMA & TECHNICOLOR   1957

DRAMA/ACTION-ADVENTURE

RKO

TERESA WRIGHT   **CAMERON MITCHELL**   **JON PROVOST**
ROGER NAKAGAWA   **PHILIP OBER**

Screenplay by: Winston Miller
Directed by: Arthur Lubin

John Provost (from the Lassie TV series) plays an American boy named Tony who is flying to Tokyo to join his parents, who anxiously await his arrival. Tony's plane goes down at sea and he is picked up by a Japanese family on their fishing boat. When the Japanese parents talk of notifying the police, their young son, Hiko, misunderstands and tells Tony that if he's caught, the police will put him in jail. The two little boys then run off together, and while the police search for them, the pair become good friends and see plenty of Japan. A good family film with cute acting by the two boys and a look at the beauty of Japanese culture.

ESCAPE FROM FORT BRAVO
ANSCO COLOR   1953

DRAMA/WESTERN/ACTION-ADVENTURE

MGM

WILLIAM HOLDEN   **ELEANOR PARKER**   **WILLIAM DEMAREST**
JOHN ANDERSON   **POLLY BERGEN**   **JOHN LUPTON**
CARL BENSON REID   **WILLIAM CAMPBELL**   **JOHN FORSYTHE**

Screenplay by: Frank Fenton
Story by: Phillip Rock and Michael Pate
Directed by: John Sturges

At Fort Bravo during the Civil War, a group of Southern soldiers are held prisoner. Their colonel (John Forsythe) has plans to escape, aided by the undercover work of his fiancé, Carla Forester (Eleanor Parker). William Holden is Captain Roper, the Union man in charge of the fort, who leads the pursuit of the four prisoners who do manage to get out. Then everything is complicated further by an unexpected Indian attack. A top-notch Western with plenty of action.

EVERY GIRL SHOULD BE MARRIED

BLACK & WHITE/COLORIZED   1948

COMEDY/ROMANCE

RKO

CARY GRANT	FRANCHOT TONE	DIANA LYNN	BETSY DRAKE
ALAN MOWBRAY	ELISABETH RISDON	EDDIE ALBERT	

Screenplay by: Stephen Morehouse Avery and Don Hartman
Story by: Eleanor Harris
Directed by: Don Hartman

Betsy Drake is Anabel Sims, a department store clerk who is determined to snag a husband. She sets her sights on Dr. Madison Brown (Cary Grant), and pursues this confirmed bachelor with a vengeance, exhausting all of her feminine wiles while he keeps trying to avoid the inevitable. This was Betsy Drake's first film appearance, and she later became the real-life wife of Cary Grant. Since marriage is no longer the only opportunity for women, the premise of this movie is rather dated, but those who like romance stories should still find it enjoyable.

EXCUSE MY DUST

TECHNICOLOR   1951

MUSICAL/COMEDY

MGM

RED SKELTON	SALLY FORREST	MacDONALD CAREY
WILLIAM DEMAREST	MONICA LEWIS	RAYMOND WALBURN

Screenplay by: George Wells
Directed by: Roy Rowland

The story is set in 1895. Red Skelton is Joe Beldon, a wacky inventor who's working on building an automobile in the early days of the "horseless carriage." He enters a road race, hoping to win enough prize money to open an automobile factory. Joe has a girlfriend named Liz Bullitt (played by Sally Forrest), but his interest in autos puts him at odds with her father, Harvey (William Demarest). Harvey not only thinks that Joe is a nut, but is also worried that, if successful, the automobile could put his livery stable out of business. A funny movie about the old days, providing cheery family entertainment.

FACE OF A FUGITIVE

EASTMAN COLOR BY PATHÉ   1959

DRAMA/WESTERN

COLUMBIA

| FRED MacMURRAY | LIN McCARTHY | DOROTHY GREEN |
| ALAN BAXTER | MYRNA FAHEY | JAMES COBURN |

Screenplay by: David T. Chantler and Daniel B. Ullman
From: A story by Peter Dawson
Directed by: Paul Wendkos

Fred MacMurray portrays a bank robber on the run from the law. In a small town, he meets a sweet little girl and her widowed mother, but they do not know his true identity. He develops a romantic interest in the widow, whose brother just happens to be the town's acting sheriff, and ends up helping the sheriff in dealing with some very dangerous trouble-makers. It becomes apparent that this bank robber is truly a good man who has simply been going down the wrong path. A rather interesting Western drama with some action and a personal story line as well.

FAITHFUL IN MY FASHION

BLACK & WHITE   1946

COMEDY/ROMANCE

MGM

DONNA REED	TOM DRAKE	EDWARD EVERETT HORTON
SPRING BYINGTON	SIG RUMAN	HARRY DAVENPORT
WM. "BILL" PHILLIPS	MARGARET HAMILTON	

Screenplay by: Lionel Houser
Directed by: Sidney Salkow

Jean Kendrick (Donna Reed) works in the shoe department of a New York store. She had become engaged to her co-worker boyfriend, Jeff Compton (Tom Drake), before he was shipped out to World War II. He returns on a two-week leave believing that Jean waited for him and that everything is the same as he left it. In the meantime, she has been promoted from stock clerk to buyer and has met another man. She doesn't want to hurt Jeff and doesn't know how to tell him the truth. Encouraged by her friends at the store, Jean decides to keep up the pretense of their engagement for the two weeks, with unexpected results. A light romantic comedy with a sweet story.

FAMILY HONEYMOON
BLACK & WHITE   1948

COMEDY
UNIVERSAL INT'L

CLAUDETTE COLBERT   **FRED MacMURRAY**   **RITA JOHNSON**
WILLIAM DANIELS   **GIGI PERREAU**

Screenplay by: Dane Lussier
Based on: Novel by Homer Croy
Directed by: Claude Binyon

Claudette Colbert is Katie Armstrong Jordan, the widowed mother of three who just remarried Grant Jordan (co-star Fred MacMurray). When their babysitter breaks her leg, they end up taking the kids along on their honeymoon. Their plans for a relaxing and romantic trip are sabotaged not only by Katie's badly behaved children, but also by an old girlfriend who is still pursuing Grant with a vengeance even though he is now married. A pleasant family comedy with a happy ending.

FANCY PANTS
TECHNICOLOR   1950

COMEDY/MUSICAL
PARAMOUNT

BOB HOPE   **LUCILLE BALL**

Screenplay by: Edmund Hartmann and Robert O'Brien
Based on: A story by Harry Leon Wilson
Directed by: George Marshall

In this remake of **Ruggles of Red Gap** (1935), Lucille Ball is Agatha "Aggie" Floud, the daughter of a newly-rich American family. Taken by her mother to Europe in an attempt to impart some culture to her, Aggie meets an English Earl who wants to impress her and hires actors to masquerade as his upper crust family and servants. Bob Hope plays the actor who impersonates the butler, "Humphrey." Aggie's mother then hires Humphrey as their butler, and they take him back to America. Once they reach home, the townspeople mistake Humphrey for the Earl who was courting Aggie. To help the family impress their neighbors, Humphrey follows along by impersonating the English Earl, but falls in love with Aggie himself. An enjoyable movie with a couple of musical numbers and classic slapstick comedy.

FARMER'S DAUGHTER, THE
BLACK & WHITE   1947

COMEDY/ROMANCE
RKO

| LORETTA YOUNG | JOSEPH COTTEN | ETHEL BARRYMORE |
| CHARLES BICKFORD | ROSE HOBART | RHYS WILLIAMS |

Screenplay by: Allen Rivkin and Laura Kerr
Suggested from: A play by Juhni Tervataa
Directed by: H.C. Potter

Katrin Holstrom (Loretta Young) leaves her family's farm for nursing school in the
big city. When she's swindled out of just about every penny she's got, Katrin takes
a job as a maid in the home of a Senator's widow, Mrs. Morley (Ethel Barrymore),
to re-earn her nursing tuition. But all of Katrin's plans change when she meets and falls
in love with Mrs. Morley's son Glenn (Joseph Cotten), a newly-elected Congressman.
Katrin turns out to be more spirited and informed about politics than the Morleys
had expected, runs for Congress herself (for the opposing party) and gets into a lot
more trouble than she bargained for! A heartwarming and endearing tale.

Academy Award Recognition: Loretta Young won Best Actress,
Charles Bickford nominated for Best Supporting Actor.

FAR COUNTRY, THE
TECHNICOLOR   1955

DRAMA/WESTERN
UNIVERSAL INT'L

JAMES STEWART	RUTH ROMAN	CORINNE CALVET
WALTER BRENNAN	JOHN McINTIRE	JAY C. FLIPPEN
HENRY MORGAN	CONNIE GILCHRIST	JACK ELAM

Screenplay by: Borden Chase
Directed by: Anthony Mann

The setting is Seattle in 1896. James Stewart is Jeff, a cynical cowboy driving his
cattle to Alaska. A sequence of events brings him to lead an expedition to Canada,
which is delivering supplies to a saloon owner named Ronda (Ruth Roman). She is
opening a new establishment in the Klondike gold-mining country. Jeff's old-timer
buddy, Ben, is played by Walter Brennan and Corinne Calvet is Reneé, a young
woman who competes with Ronda for Jeff's affections. At the beginning of his
journey, Jeff distrusts everyone, but eventually comes to realize that people have
the capacity to help each other for their common good. A very well-done Western
with an important story about human relationships.

FAR HORIZONS, THE

VISTAVISION & TECHNICOLOR   1955

DRAMA/WESTERN

PARAMOUNT

FRED MacMURRAY   **CHARLTON HESTON**   **DONNA REED**
BARBARA HALE   **WILLIAM DEMAREST**

Screenplay by: Winston Miller and Edmund H. North
From: The novel *Sacajawea of the Shoshones*
                 by Della Gould Emmons
Directed by: Rudolph Mate

This is a fictional story based on the true account of the expedition of Lewis (Fred MacMurray) and Clark (Charlton Heston). When the Louisiana Purchase was made by the United States, President Jefferson commissioned Lewis and Clark to explore and map its vast wilderness. An Indian woman named Sacajawea (played by Donna Reed) helped guide them through the territory that she knew so well. In this movie version, she and Clark grow very close and fall in love along the way—much to the dismay of a jealous Lewis. The adventures of their expedition are combined with the romance story line and beautiful panoramic photography to make a very entertaining movie experience.

FASTEST GUN ALIVE, THE

BLACK & WHITE/COLORIZED   1956

DRAMA/WESTERN

MGM

GLENN FORD   **JEANNE CRAIN**   **BRODERICK CRAWFORD**
RUSS TAMBLYN   **ALLYN JOSLYN**   **LEIF ERICKSON**
JOHN DEHNER   **NOAH BEERY**

Screenplay by: Frank D. Gilroy and Russell Rouse
Based on: The story *The Last Notch* by Frank D. Gilroy
Directed by: Russell Rouse

Glenn Ford stars as George Temple, a store owner who's a very fast gun, but has a deep, dark secret that drives him to keep his abilities hidden. Broderick Crawford is Vinnie Harold, a mean character who claims he is the fastest gun alive and proves it by shooting and killing anyone who claims to be faster. Eventually, Temple is forced to reveal his shooting skills, and becomes the one responsible for defending the entire town against Harold. A very suspenseful and absorbing Western with lots of shootout action.

FATHER GOOSE

TECHNICOLOR   1964

COMEDY/ROMANCE

UNIVERSAL

CARY GRANT   LESLIE CARON   TREVOR HOWARD

Screenplay by:	Peter Stone and Frank Tarloff
Based on:	A story by S.H. Barnett
Directed by:	Ralph Nelson

Walter Ekland (Cary Grant) is an American wanderer in Australia during World War II. Because he owns a boat, Ekland is coerced into helping the Australian Navy keep watch for Japanese attack forces from an uninhabited island. When checking out another nearby island, he discovers a woman named Catherine (Leslie Caron) and a group of school girls marooned there. For their protection, Ekland takes them back to his island. His carefree (and rather crude) bachelor lifestyle rubs the very proper Catherine the wrong way and the responsibility of looking after the girls cramps his style. The story continues from there, as they all try to get along while staying safe from the Japanese. A rather amusing movie in which Cary Grant departs from his usual role of the suave gentleman.

 Academy Award Recognition: S.H. Barnett, Peter Stone and Frank Tarloff won Best Story and Screenplay (written directly for the screen).

FATHER OF THE BRIDE

BLACK & WHITE/COLORIZED   1950

COMEDY

MGM

SPENCER TRACY   JOAN BENNETT   ELIZABETH TAYLOR   DON TAYLOR
BILLIE BURKE   LEO G. CARROLL   MORONI OLSEN

Screenplay by:	Frances Goodrich and Albert Hackett
Based on:	The novel by Edward Streeter
Directed by:	Vincente Minnelli

Spencer Tracy stars as Stanley Banks, the harried father of a young bride, Kay (Elizabeth Taylor). Poor Stanley suddenly has to deal with huge bills, his excitable wife Ellie (Joan Bennett), and new in-laws, all at once. A rather funny look at the changes and ordeals that a family goes through for a formal wedding—from the initial planning stage right through the big day itself. Excellent family entertainment.

 Academy Award Recognition: nominated for Best Picture, Spencer Tracy nominated for Best Actor, Frances Goodrich and Albert Hackett nominated for Best Screenplay.

FATHER WAS A FULLBACK

BLACK & WHITE   1949   **COMEDY**

20TH CENTURY FOX

FRED MacMURRAY   **MAUREEN O'HARA**   **BETTY LYNN**
RUDY VALLEE   **THELMA RITTER**   **NATALIE WOOD**
JAMES G. BACKUS

Screenplay by: Aleen Leslie, Casey Robinson, Mary Loos and Richard Sale
Suggested by: A play by Clifford Goldsmith
Directed by: John M. Stahl

Fred MacMurray is George Cooper, the head football coach at a state university whose team is on a very bad losing streak. Maureen O'Hara co-stars as his wife, Elizabeth. George is hounded by everyone in town about how poorly the team is doing and, at the same time, is barraged by the antics of his two daughters who are going through wacky teenage phases. Natalie Wood is Ellen, the younger daughter, and Betty Lynn is Connie, the older one who is boy crazy and constantly lovesick. Thelma Ritter plays Geraldine, the clan's cynical and wise-cracking housekeeper. An appealing comedy that the whole family can enjoy together.

FATHER'S LITTLE DIVIDEND

BLACK & WHITE   1951   **COMEDY**

MGM

SPENCER TRACY   **JOAN BENNETT**   **ELIZABETH TAYLOR**
DON TAYLOR   **BILLIE BURKE**   **MORONI OLSEN**

Screenplay by: Albert Hackett and Frances Goodrich
Based on: Characters created by Edward Streeter
Directed by: Vincente Minnelli

This is the sequel to *Father of the Bride* (1950), again featuring Spencer Tracy as Stanley Banks, but this time focusing on his adjustment to becoming a grandfather. Joan Bennett co-stars once more as Ellie, his wife, and Elizabeth Taylor continues her role as Kay, their daughter and new mother-to-be. Just when Stanley thinks that things will quiet down after Kay's big wedding, along comes the next major event. First there are the trials and tribulations of helping the young couple through the pregnancy and delivery, then Stanley's adjustment to having a little baby around again. In his famous style, Tracy plays a character who's gruff on the outside but soft and warm on the inside. A very entertaining movie about family life.

FIGHTING FATHER DUNNE

DRAMA

BLACK & WHITE   1948   RKO

| PAT O'BRIEN | DARRYL HICKMAN | CHARLES KEMPER |
| UNA O'CONNOR | ARTHUR SHIELDS | BILLY GRAY |

Screenplay by: Martin Rackin and Frank Davis
Based on: Story by William Rankin
Directed by: Ted Tetzlaff

The setting: St. Louis in 1905. Being a newspaper boy was a tough business in those days, when papers were delivered mostly by street kids (homeless boys) who could be hired for very low wages. Pat O'Brien stars as Father Dunne, a priest who sets out to help such children and establish a home to care for them properly. With a lot of ingenuity and the powers of persuasion, Father Dunne works hard, against great odds, to try and save the boys from their predicament. An inspiring story that teaches how a little determination can go a long way.

FIGHTING KENTUCKIAN, THE

DRAMA/ACTION-ADVENTURE

BLACK & WHITE/COLORIZED   1949   REPUBLIC

| JOHN WAYNE | VERA RALSTON | PHILIP DORN | OLIVER HARDY |

Screenplay by: George Waggner
Directed by: George Waggner

John Wayne stars as John Breen, a Kentucky militiaman on the march in Alabama. At a French settlement he meets a southern belle named Fleurette (Vera Ralston), and they are immediately attracted to each other—but she is engaged to another. While Breen sticks around to try and win Fleurette's heart, he unwittingly stumbles upon a plan by some evildoers to swindle the French settlers out of their land. An enjoyable tale about a rugged adventurer.

FIGHTING SULLIVANS, THE

BLACK & WHITE   1944

DRAMA

20TH CENTURY FOX

ANNE BAXTER   THOMAS MITCHELL   SELENA ROYLE   EDWARD RYAN

Screenplay by: Mary C. McCall, Jr.
Story by: Edward Doherty and Jules Schermer
Directed by: Lloyd Bacon

The true story of the five Sullivan brothers who served in World War II. Raised in a close-knit Irish clan, they grew up defending each other in neighborhood scraps, so it was natural for them to want to fight side-by-side in the war. Their story became famous because all five young men were killed in the same battle, prompting the military to change its rules, prohibiting family members from serving in the same unit. An interesting tale of family life and patriotic sacrifice, with the expected dramatic ending.

 Academy Award Recognition: Edward Doherty and Jules Schermer nominated for Best Original Story.

FIRST LOVE

BLACK & WHITE   1939

DRAMA/MUSICAL/ROMANCE

UNIVERSAL

DEANNA DURBIN   ROBERT STACK   EUGENE PALLETTE   HELEN PARRISH
FRANK JENKS   MARY TREEN   KATHLEEN HOWARD

Screenplay by: Bruce Manning and Lionel Houser
Directed by: Henry Koster

Deanna Durbin stars as Constance Harding, an orphaned young lady who goes to live with her wealthy uncle, James Clinton (Eugene Pallette), and his family after she graduates from school. The family is quite a collection of oddballs—her aunt is into astrology, one cousin is a lazy do-nothing, and the other cousin is a spoiled brat. Then Constance meets her cousin's boyfriend, Ted Drake (Robert Stack), and falls in love with him, which creates complications. This film received a lot of publicity when it was released because it included Deanna Durbin's first on-screen kiss. A pleasant, entertaining movie that shows off Deanna's classical singing style with a song here and there.

 Academy Award Recognition: Charles Previn nominated for Best Musical Score.

FIVE PENNIES, THE

VISTAVISION & TECHNICOLOR   1959

MUSICAL/DRAMA

PARAMOUNT

DANNY KAYE	**BARBARA BEL GEDDES**	**LOUIS ARMSTRONG**
HARRY GUARDINO	**BOB CROSBY**	**SUSAN GORDON**
TUESDAY WELD	**RAY ANTHONY**	

Screenplay by: Jack Rose and Melville Shavelson
Story by: Robert Smith, suggested by the life of Loring "Red" Nichols
Directed by: Melville Shavelson

Trumpet solos for Danny Kaye by Red Nichols

This is the true story of famous trumpet player Red Nichols. It begins in New York City in 1924 when Red arrives in town from Ogden, Utah to launch his musical career. There, he meets, falls for and marries a showgirl named Bobbie (Barbara Bel Geddes) who wholeheartedly supports his career. The Nichols' later have a baby girl and take her on the road with them. But, as she gets older, they become torn between the traveling and providing a settled home for her. When the little girl is stricken with polio, their decision is made for them. The rest of the story tells how they fight back against her polio and build new a life for themselves outside of the music world. A good biographical movie that shows a family coping with and triumphing over adversity, with some nice songs along the way.

Academy Award Recognition: Leith Stevens nominated for Best Scoring of a Musical Picture, nominated for Best Song: *The Five Pennies*, Music and Lyrics by Sylvia Fine.

FLAME OF THE BARBARY COAST

BLACK & WHITE/COLORIZED   1945

DRAMA

REPUBLIC

JOHN WAYNE	**ANN DVORAK**	**JOSEPH SCHILDKRAUT**
WILLIAM FRAWLEY	**VIRGINIA GREY**	**RUSSELL HICKS**
PAUL FIX	**BUTTERFLY McQUEEN**	**JACK NORTON**

Screenplay by: Borden Chase
Directed by: Joseph Kane

John Wayne is Duke Fergus, a cowboy who has come to San Francisco from Montana to collect money owed him by Barbary Coast gambler Tito Morell (Joseph Schildkraut). Morell also owns a nightclub where a woman named Floxen Tarry (Ann Dvorak) sings—and Duke falls in love with her. Helped by Floxen, Duke gets into gambling, wins a lot of money but loses it just as fast. So he goes back home to

Montana, sells his cattle ranch, returns to the Barbary Coast with enough money to build a nightclub that's bigger and better than Morell's, and hires Floxen to sing there. More trouble is in store, though, when the 1906 San Francisco Earthquake hits. An entertaining tale with a good story line and a happy ending.

 Academy Award Recognition: Dale Butts and Morton Scott nominated for Best Scoring of a Dramatic or Comedy Picture.

FLIPPER
COLOR   1963

DRAMA/ANIMAL STORIES
MGM

CHUCK CONNORS   LUKE HALPIN

Screenplay by: Arthur Weiss
Story by: Ricou Browning and Jack Cowden
Directed by: James B. Clark

Luke Halpin plays Sandy, the young son of a Florida fisherman (Chuck Connors). He befriends a dolphin by saving its life when it is accidentally speared, and names the loving creature Flipper. Sandy has a hard time convincing his father to love Flipper as much as he does, though, since a plague has killed many fish in the area and dolphins are now competing with fishermen in catching the remaining fish. This amiable story of a growing relationship between human and animal is a good choice for the whole family.

FLIPPER'S
NEW ADVENTURE
METROCOLOR   1964

DRAMA/ANIMAL STORIES
MGM

LUKE HALPIN   PAMELA FRANKLIN   HELEN CHERRY
TOM HELMORE   FRANCESCA ANNIS   BRIAN KELLY

Screenplay by: Art Arthur
Story by: Ivan Tors, based on characters created by
                   Ricou Browning and Jack Cowden
Directed by: Leon Benson

Luke Halpin again stars as Sandy in this sequel to *Flipper* (1963), the predecessor of the *Flipper* TV series. In this tale, Sandy's mother has passed away, and his father is away at Park Ranger School. When Sandy and Flipper are evicted from their home by a state road project, the neighbor looking after them decides that the only solution is to separate the two by sending the boy to his aunt's house and the dolphin to the seaquarium. But Sandy can't bear being apart from his faithful friend, and runs away to hide out with Flipper until his father's return. Their true adventure begins when he and Flipper try to help a family whose boat is hijacked by three escaped convicts. A good family-style movie for those who love animals .

FLOWER DRUM SONG
PANAVISION & TECHNICOLOR   1961

MUSICAL/ROMANCE
UNIVERSAL INT'L

| **NANCY KWAN** | **JAMES SHIGETA** | **BENSON FONG** |
| **JACK SOO** | **JUANITA HALL** | **MIYOSHI UMEKI** |

Screenplay by: Joseph Fields
Based on: The novel *The Flower Drum Song* by C.Y. Lee
Directed by: Henry Koster

Music by Richard Rodgers, Lyrics by Oscar Hammerstein II

A beautiful young Asian woman named Mei Li (Miyoshi Umeki) arrives in San Francisco with her father because she has been summoned to America for an arranged marriage. Her intended turns out to be nightclub owner Sammy Fong (Jack Soo), who already has a girlfriend, singer Linda Low (Nancy Kwan). His mother, however, wants to choose his wife for him. Sammy tries to pass Mei Li off to another family who is also looking for a traditional Asian wife for their young man, Wang Ta (James Shigeta). Mei Li falls in love with Wang almost immediately, but Wang has eyes for Linda Low, who considers him a much better catch than Sammy. Romantic chaos follows, but all involved get a surprise happy ending. A humorous look at the clash between old Asian tradition and the newer Asian-American customs, done with some enjoyable songs.

Academy Award Recognition: Alfred Newman and Ken Darby nominated for Best Scoring of a Musical Picture.

FOLLOW ME, BOYS!

COLOR

1966

COMEDY/DRAMA

WALT DISNEY

FRED MacMURRAY	VERA MILES	LILLIAN GISH
CHARLIE RUGGLES	KURT RUSSELL	

Screenplay by: Louis Pelletier
Based on: The book *God and My Country* by MacKinlay Kantor
Directed by: Norman Tokar

Fred MacMurray is Lemuel Siddons, a saxophone player with a 1930s traveling band. The band arrives in a small town called Hickory, and Siddons decides that it's high time he put down some roots. Hickory has a growing problem with young boys running the streets and getting into trouble, so he offers to start a Boy Scout troop, partly to impress a lovely lady, Vida Downey (Vera Miles). What follows is the tale of Siddons' adventures while becoming the cornerstone of the town's scouting tradition and a local hero. He also helps a particular boy (played by Kurt Russell) through some tough personal difficulties. A well-done Disney family movie that shows the importance of helping others.

FOR ME AND MY GAL

BLACK & WHITE

1942

MUSICAL

MGM

JUDY GARLAND	GEORGE MURPHY	GENE KELLY

Screenplay by: Richard Sherman, Fred Finkelhoffe, and Sid Silvers
Original story by: Howard Emmett Rogers
Directed by: Busby Berkeley

Harry Palmer (Gene Kelly) and Jo Hayden (Judy Garland) are vaudeville entertainers in 1916. They meet while working in separate acts, and then team up with each other. What follows is the story of their showbiz career and romance, which are both interrupted by World War I. This is a more dramatic musical than most, as it was released early in World War II, when people's minds were turning once again to the difficulties facing them. Today, though, it still holds up as a touching wartime love story, featuring popular songs of the World War I era and solid performances by the talented cast.

 Academy Award Recognition: Roger Edens and Georgie Stoll nominated for Best Scoring of a Musical Picture.

FOREST RANGERS, THE
COLOR   1942   DRAMA/ACTION-ADVENTURE
                                                  PARAMOUNT

FRED MacMURRAY	PAULETTE GODDARD	SUSAN HAYWARD
LYNNE OVERMAN	ALBERT DEKKER	EUGENE PALLETTE
REGIS TOOMEY	ROD CAMERON	CLEM BEVANS

Screenplay by: Harold Shumate
Story by: Thelma Strabel
Directed by: George Marshall

Fred MacMurray is Don Stuart, a forest ranger whose large territory experiences a suspicious fire. He speculates that the fire was intentionally set, and goes into town to investigate. While there, Stuart meets pretty socialite Celia Huston (played by Paulette Goddard), and he courts and marries her, much to the chagrin of Tana Mason (Susan Hayward). Tana loves Stuart herself, but is a logger whom he sees as "just one of the guys," so he has no romantic interest in her. The rest of the story involves both the love triangle and the resolution of the mystery surrounding the forest fire. A movie with something for everyone, including plenty of action and an exciting ending.

FRANCIS
BLACK & WHITE   1949   COMEDY/ANIMAL STORIES
                                                  UNIVERSAL INT'L

DONALD O'CONNOR	PATRICIA MEDINA	ZASU PITTS
RAY COLLINS	JOHN McINTIRE	CHILL WILLS

Screenplay by: David Stern
Based on: The novel by David Stern
Directed by: Arthur Lubin

In Burma, during World War II, Peter Stirling (Donald O'Connor), a former bank teller, is wounded. He is saved by a mule—a talking mule—named Francis. After recovering from his wound, Stirling lands an Intelligence position. Francis relays tips to him regarding enemy positions and plans, making him a hero, but everyone thinks Stirling's crazy when he reveals that his source is a talking mule. Actor Chill Wills performs the voice of Francis. This movie launched a popular series of *Francis* movies, and inspired the television series "Mister Ed." Light entertainment that should be enjoyable for children.

FRANCIS IN THE NAVY
BLACK & WHITE   1955   COMEDY/ANIMAL STORIES

UNIVERSAL INT'L

DONALD O'CONNOR	**MARTHA HYER**	**RICHARD ERDMAN**
JIM BACKUS	**CLINT EASTWOOD**	**DAVID JANSSEN**
LEIGH SNOWDEN	**MARTIN MILNER**	**CHILL WILLS**

Screenplay by: Devery Freeman
Based on: The character *Francis* created by David Stern
Directed by: Arthur Lubin

In this movie, one in a series of *Francis* films, Francis the talking mule becomes merchandise on the way to a Navy surplus sale. Peter Stirling (Donald O'Connor), an Army soldier who is his human confidante, arrives to rescue him from his predicament. When Stirling's identity is switched with a Navy sailor who is his exact look-alike, confusion abounds as Francis and Stirling try to help each other escape from the Navy. A pleasant and amusing comedy that kids should enjoy.

FRANCIS JOINS THE WACS
BLACK & WHITE   1954   COMEDY/ANIMAL STORIES

UNIVERSAL INT'L

DONALD O'CONNOR	**JULIA ADAMS**	**CHILL WILLS**
MAMIE VAN DOREN	**LYNN BARI**	**ZASU PITTS**

Screenplay by: Devery Freeman and James B. Allardice
Story by: Herbert Baker
Based on: The character *Francis* created by David Stern
Directed by: Arthur Lubin

In this entry of the *Francis* movie series, Peter Stirling (Donald O'Connor) is re-called into military service and, through a clerical error, is assigned to the WACS (Women's Army Corps). He is now at the mercy of female officers Major Simpson (Lynn Bari) and Captain Parker (Julia Adams), who don't take kindly to his condescending attitude toward women in the armed forces. Simpson and Parker make Stirling stay in the WACS, and put him in charge of their ailing camouflage unit. He prepares them for test maneuvers, where they will have to prove themselves to the male-chauvinist General Kaye. Stirling is once again assisted by his pal, Francis the talking mule, who relays military secrets to him. A very amusing service comedy with a cute story, and possibly the best movie in the *Francis* series. Chill Wills plays two roles: the voice of Francis, and General Kaye.

FRIENDLY PERSUASION
COLOR   1956

DRAMA
ALLIED ARTISTS

GARY COOPER   DOROTHY McGUIRE   TONY PERKINS
MARJORIE MAIN   ROBERT MIDDLETON   RICHARD EYER

From: The book by Jessamyn West
Directed by: William Wyler

In this story of a Quaker family in Indiana during the Civil War, Gary Cooper and
Dorothy McGuire play Jess and Eliza Birdwell, parents who are trying to hang on to
their pacifist values and simple way of life as the front lines of battle approach their
farm. Anthony Perkins is Josh, their eldest son, who is approaching manhood. He
questions his family's values (Quakers are strictly devoted to a peaceful existence)
while deciding whether or not to go off and fight in the war. A charming portrait
of family life, which examines both sides of some important questions, with a touch
of humor too. An excellent drama, well-acted by the distinguished cast.

Academy Award Recognition: nominated for Best Picture, Anthony
Perkins nominated for Best Supporting Actor, William Wyler nominated
for Best Director, nominated for Best Song: ***Friendly Persuasion (Thee
I Love)***, Music by Dimitri Tiomkin, Lyrics by Paul Francis Webster.

FUNNY FACE
VISTAVISION & TECHNICOLOR   1957

MUSICAL
PARAMOUNT

AUDREY HEPBURN   FRED ASTAIRE   KAY THOMPSON

Screenplay by: Leonard Gershe
Directed by: Stanley Donen

Music and Lyrics by George and Ira Gershwin
Additional Music and Lyrics by Roger Edens and Leonard Gershe

Kay Thompson is Maggie Prescott, the chief of a fashion magazine who feels the
publication is stale and needs a fresh approach. During a photo shoot in a book-
store, she and Dick Avery (Fred Astaire), her star photographer, cross paths with a
beautiful young store clerk named Jo Stockton (Audrey Hepburn). Avery is quite
impressed by her, and sees the opportunity to create a new image—the gorgeous
model who also has depth of personality and a fine mind. Jo is then reluctantly

transformed into the magazine's new star and falls in love with Avery as well. Very smooth and entertaining, with some unusual touches that make it a little different than the standard movie musical.

 Academy Award Recognition: Leonard Gershe nominated for Best Story and Screenplay (written directly for the screen).

FUNNY GIRL
TECHNICOLOR   1968

MUSICAL
COLUMBIA

BARBRA STREISAND	OMAR SHARIF	KAY MEDFORD
ANN FRANCIS	WALTER PIDGEON	FRANK FAYLEN
GERALD MOHR		

Screenplay by: Isobel Lennart
Based on: The stage musical *Funny Girl*
Directed by: William Wyler

In this movie about the life of famous entertainer Fanny Brice, Barbara Streisand plays the starring role, which she had originated earlier on the Broadway stage. The story tells of Fanny's rise to stardom in the famous Ziegfeld Follies, and her rocky marriage to gambler Nick Arnstein (Omar Sharif), who eventually went to prison for embezzlement. The film's producer was Ray Stark, Fanny's son-in-law. A superior musical with great songs and fine performances by the cast.

 Academy Award Recognition: Barbra Streisand won Best Actress, nominated for Best Picture, Kay Medford nominated for Best Supporting Actress, Walter Scharf nominated for Best Score of a Musical Picture (adaptation), nominated for Best Song: *Funny Girl*, Music by Jule Styne and Lyrics by Bob Merrill.

GANG'S ALL HERE, THE

TECHNICOLOR   1943

MUSICAL

20TH CENTURY FOX

ALICE FAYE	CARMEN MIRANDA	PHIL BAKER	CHARLOTTE GREENWOOD

Screenplay by: Walter Bullock
From: A story by Nancy Winter, George Root Jr. and Tom Bridges
Directed by: Busby Berkeley

Alice Faye and Carmen Miranda star as Edie & Dorita, showgirls at the Club New Yorker, during World War II. Benny Goodman and his orchestra play at the Broadway Canteen, where Edie meets a serviceman and falls in love. Conflict arises when she finds he is already engaged to marry another woman. The finale is a huge show to help sell war bonds, where all is resolved. Pleasant and light musical entertainment.

GAZEBO, THE

CINEMASCOPE,   1959
BLACK & WHITE/COLORIZED

COMEDY/MYSTERY-SUSPENSE

MGM

GLENN FORD	DEBBIE REYNOLDS	CARL REINER
JOHN McGIVER	MABEL ALBERTSON	DORO MERANDE

Screenplay by: George Wells
Based on: The play written by Alec Coppel,
                   from a story by Myra and Alec Coppel
Directed by: George Marshall

Elliot Nash (Glenn Ford) is a hard working writer-director. He's a nervous wreck because he is being blackmailed for a large amount of money by someone who says they have possession of compromising photos of his wife, Nell Nash (Debbie Reynolds), a star of the New York stage. Even though he is a very meek and mild character, Elliot is so upset that he devises a plan to do away with the blackmailer when he shows up to collect the cash. Elliot follows through with it, but is shocked to find out later that he may have eliminated the wrong person. A hilarious and unique murder mystery with lots of unexpected developments.

GEISHA BOY, THE

VISTAVISION/TECHNICOLOR   1958

COMEDY

PARAMOUNT

JERRY LEWIS	**MARIE McDONALD**	**SESSUE HAYAKAWA**
BARTON MacLANE	**SUZANNE PLESHETTE**	**THE LOS ANGELES DODGERS**

Screenplay by: Frank Tashlin
Based on: A story by Rudy Makoul
Directed by: Frank Tashlin

Jerry Lewis is The Great Wooley, a bumbling magician who travels to Japan with the USO because he can't find work in America. Along the way, he is befriended by an airline stewardess (Suzanne Pleshette), a young Japanese boy, and the boy's aunt. The child is an orphan who has withdrawn from the world around him—until Wooley's antics make him happy again. A sweet story mixed with zany comedy that the entire family can enjoy together.

GENTLEMAN JIM

BLACK & WHITE   1942

DRAMA/COMEDY

WARNER BROTHERS

ERROL FLYNN	**ALEXIS SMITH**	**JACK CARSON**
ALAN HALE	**JOHN LODER**	**WILLIAM FRAWLEY**
MINOR WATSON	**WARD BOND**	**RHYS WILLIAMS**

Screenplay by: Vincent Lawrence and Horace McCoy
Based on: The life of James J. Corbett
Directed by: Raoul Walsh

The setting: San Francisco in 1889, when boxing was illegal. This is the life story of James J. Corbett (Gentleman Jim), starring Errol Flynn. Corbett gets involved in boxing when some wealthy men try to raise boxing above its illegal status by show-casing more classy fighters, rather than the usual back-alley brutes. He and his best buddy, Walter Lowrie (Jack Carson), leave their jobs as bank tellers to launch his boxing career. Corbett also experiences a very rocky romance with Victoria Ware (Alexis Smith), the daughter of one of his well-to-do sponsors. Good, clean classic movie fun.

GENTLE GIANT

COLOR 1967

DRAMA/ANIMAL STORIES

PARAMOUNT

DENNIS WEAVER	VERA MILES	RALPH MEEKER
CLINT HOWARD	GENTLE BEN	

Screenplay by: Edward J. Lakso and Andy White
From: A novel by Walt Morey
Directed by: James Neilson

Clint Howard is Mark Wedloe, a young boy who loves animals. He befriends a Black Bear cub, whom he names Ben, when the cub's mother is shot and killed by poachers (illegal hunters). Mark's parents Tom and Ellen (played by Dennis Weaver and Vera Miles), along with their neighbors, are very worried, because they have always known Black Bears to be very powerful and dangerous wild animals. But Mark's caring way with Ben has made the bear very gentle, and he's determined to prove everyone wrong. This adorable story of a child's love for an animal became the basis for the television series *Gentle Ben*.

GHOST AND MRS. MUIR, THE

BLACK & WHITE 1947

DRAMA

20TH CENTURY FOX

GENE TIERNEY	REX HARRISON	GEORGE SANDERS
EDNA BEST	VANESSA BROWN	NATALIE WOOD

Screenplay by: Philip Dunne
From: The novel by R.A. Dick
Directed by: Joseph L. Mankiewicz

In London at the turn of the century, recently widowed Mrs. Lucy Muir (played by Gene Tierney) has a daughter Anna (Natalie Wood) and a housekeeper, Martha (Edna Best). She has been living with her mother and sister, but decides to rent the oceanside home that was formerly owned by Captain Gregg (Rex Harrison), a seafaring man. Lucy is fascinated by the house, and despite the fact that it is haunted by Gregg's ghost, moves in. Captain Gregg appears to Lucy, and attempts to scare her away from his home, but she stays anyway. The ornery ghost develops a soft spot for her and over the years they develop a very close and uncommon relationship. A unique drama with a supernatural theme and a bittersweet ending.

GIANT
WARNER COLOR   1956

DRAMA
WARNER BROTHERS

ELIZABETH TAYLOR	**ROCK HUDSON**	**JAMES DEAN**	**CARROLL BAKER**
DENNIS HOPPER	**MERCEDES McCAMBRIDGE**	**CHILL WILLS**	**JANE WITHERS**
ROD TAYLOR	**EARL HOLLIMAN**	**SAL MINEO**	

Screenplay by:	Fred Guiol and Ivan Moffat
From:	The novel by Edna Ferber
Directed by:	George Stevens

Rock Hudson is Bick Benedict, a Texas rancher who travels to an estate in the East to purchase a horse. While there, he and Leslie (Elizabeth Taylor), the beautiful daughter of the estate's owner, fall in love and marry. Bick returns to his huge Texas ranch with his new wife, who needs to adjust to a different way of life and establish herself as the lady of the house. The rest of this saga traces the Benedicts' marital ups and downs, the raising of their children, and then their growing older while watching Texas' main industry change from ranching to oil drilling. James Dean portrays Jett Rink, the Benedicts' ranch hand. A very impressive drama done in a big way, with big stars. It is a rather long film, though, and some may prefer to watch it in more than one sitting.

 Academy Award Recognition: George Stevens won Best Director, nominated for Best Picture, Rock Hudson and James Dean nominated for Best Actor, Mercedes McCambridge nominated for Best Supporting Actress, Fred Guiol and Ivan Moffat nominated for Best Screenplay (adapted), Dimitri Tiomkin nominated for Best Scoring of a Dramatic or Comedy Picture.

GIGI
CINEMASCOPE & METROCOLOR   1958

MUSICAL
MGM

LESLIE CARON	**MAURICE CHEVALIER**	**LOUIS JOURDAN**	**HERMIONE GINGOLD**
EVA GABOR	**JACQUES BERGERAC**	**ISABEL JEANS**	**JOHN ABBOTT**

Screenplay by:	Alan Jay Lerner
Based on:	The novel by Colette
Directed by:	Vincente Minnelli

Lyrics by Alan Jay Lerner and Music by Frederick Loewe

The story takes place in Paris, France, at the turn of the century. Gigi (Leslie Caron) is an exuberant schoolgirl approaching womanhood. Hermione Gingold plays the grandmother who is raising and grooming Gigi to become a proper young lady. Things start to change when Gigi is befriended by playboy Gaston (Louis Jordan), a very eligible bachelor. Gaston is captivated by her, as she is so different than his usual girlfriends, who have now become boring. However, Gigi's grandmother is concerned that the young lady's good reputation will be compromised by dating such a man. Maurice Chevalier plays Gaston's confidante, his Uncle Honore, a charming older French gentleman. A very entertaining musical with beautiful scenery and charming songs.

 Academy Award Recognition: won Best Picture, Vincente Minnelli won Best Director, Alan Jay Lerner won Best Screenplay (based on material from another medium), Andre Previn won Best Scoring of a Musical Picture, won Best Song: *Gigi,* Music by Frederick Loewe, Lyrics by Alan Jay Lerner.

GIRL CRAZY

BLACK & WHITE   1943   MGM

MUSICAL

| MICKEY ROONEY | JUDY GARLAND | JUNE ALLYSON |
| NANCY WALKER | GUY KIBBEE | TOMMY DORSEY and his orchestra |

Screenplay by: Fred F. Finklehoffe
Based on: The musical play by Guy Bolton and Jack McGowan
Directed by: Norman Taurog

Music by George Gershwin and Lyrics by Ira Gershwin

Danny Churchill (Mickey Rooney) is the son of a wealthy publisher. A college student at Yale, he's also a slacker who parties constantly and doesn't apply himself to his schoolwork. In an effort to straighten him out, his father sends him to an all-male agricultural college out west (in the middle of nowhere). On the way, he meets Ginger Gray (Judy Garland), a mail carrier whose grandfather is the college dean (played by Guy Kibbee). Though Danny is attracted to her, Ginger has no interest because she thinks he's just a spoiled brat and a clumsy city slicker. But when the state plans to close the college due to low enrollment, Danny and Ginger pull together to try and save it. Excellent songs and dances along with a cute story make this a very cheerful outing.

GIVE A GIRL A BREAK

TECHNICOLOR 1953

MUSICAL
MGM

MARGE CHAMPION	GOWER CHAMPION	DEBBIE REYNOLDS
HELEN WOOD	BOB FOSSE	KURT KASZNAR
RICHARD ANDERSON		

Screenplay by: Albert Hackett and Frances Goodrich
Based on: A story by Vera Caspary
Directed by: Stanley Donen

Music by Burton Lane; Lyrics by Ira Gershwin

Gower Champion is Ted Sturgis, the producer and star of a stage musical. Only a few weeks before opening night, his leading lady quits and he's stuck with no co-star. At first, Ted won't consider hiring his former dancing partner Madelyn Corlane (Marge Champion) because they parted on bad terms, so he holds open auditions to replace the departing star with a newcomer. Debbie Reynolds plays Suzy Doolittle, one of the unknowns chosen as a finalist. Then hot competition for the lead role begins when Madelyn decides to audition for it as well. A pleasant and enjoyable musical with very good dance numbers, some featuring Bob Fosse, who later went on to become a major Broadway star and choreographer.

GIVE MY REGARDS TO BROADWAY

TECHNICOLOR 1948

MUSICAL
20TH CENTURY FOX

| DAN DAILEY | CHARLES WINNINGER | NANCY GUILD |
| CHARLIE RUGGLES | FAY BAINTER | BARBARA LAWRENCE |

Screenplay by: Samuel Hoffenstein, Elizabeth Reinhardt
Based on: A story by John Klempner
Directed by: Lloyd Bacon

Dan Dailey is Bert Norwick, the son of ex-vaudevillians Albert and Fay Norwick (Charles Winninger and Fay Bainter) who had to leave showbiz in order to properly raise their family. Albert has trained son Bert and daughters May (Jane Nigh) and June (Barbara Lawrence) for show business, planning for the day that vaudeville would return. However, as many years have gone by, the kids have other plans for their lives and have trouble getting through to their father, who continues to hang on to the dream of his children becoming stars. A pleasant family story punctuated by some good music.

GLENN MILLER STORY, THE

TECHNICOLOR   1954

DRAMA

UNIVERSAL INT'L

| JAMES STEWART | JUNE ALLYSON | HENRY MORGAN |
| CHARLES DRAKE | GEORGE TOBIAS | BARTON MacLANE |

Screenplay by: Valentine Davies and Oscar Brodney
Directed by: Anthony Mann

Technical Consultant: Chummy MacGregor

This is the true story of renowned orchestra leader Glenn Miller (James Stewart).
It traces his rise from road musician to superstar leader of his very own big band,
including his courtship and marriage to his devoted wife, Helen (June Allyson), who
believed in him and helped him work his way to the top. Henry Morgan portrays
Chummy MacGregor, Miller's good friend, who served as technical advisor of this
film. An exceptional biographical profile with lots of music—many of Glenn Miller's
biggest hits are featured.

Academy Award Recognition: Valentine Davies and Oscar Brodney
nominated for Best Story and Screenplay, Joseph Gershenson and
Henry Mancini nominated for Best Scoring of a Musical Picture.

GO FOR BROKE!

BLACK & WHITE   1951

DRAMA/ACTION-ADVENTURE/MILITARY

MGM

VAN JOHNSON	LANE NAKANO	GEORGE MIKI
AKIRA FUKUNAGA	KEN K. OKAMOTO	HENRY OYASATO
HARRY HAMADA	HENRY NAKAMURA	

Screenplay by: Robert Pirosh
Directed by: Robert Pirosh

A World War II story about the 442nd Infantry Regiment—a whole unit made
up of Japanese-Americans—who volunteered to fight for the U.S., despite the
prejudices held against them. Van Johnson stars as Lt. Michael Grayson, who's
(reluctantly) assigned to command the unit. Initially, he has a low opinion of
Japanese-Americans and is not at all pleased to be there. But as time goes on,
Grayson bridges the culture gap that exists between the group and himself.
When the regiment displays their bravery and devotion to the American cause

in battle, he becomes very proud of and even more attached to his men. Light moments are mixed in with the drama, and there are good action scenes of the troops in battle. A quality movie well worth seeing.

 Academy Award Recognition: Robert Pirosh nominated for Best Story and Screenplay.

GOING MY WAY
BLACK & WHITE   1944

DRAMA/COMEDY/MUSICAL
PARAMOUNT

BING CROSBY	BARRY FITZGERALD	FRANK McHUGH	JAMES BROWN
GENE LOCKHART	JEAN HEATHER	PORTER HALL	RISE STEVENS

Screenplay by: Frank Butler and Frank Cavett
Story by: Leo McCarey
Directed by: Leo McCarey

Bing Crosby is Father Charles O'Malley, a young priest assigned to the Church of St. Dominic, whose aging pastor, Father Fitzgibbon (Barry Fitzgerald), is experiencing financial troubles—he can't make the mortgage payments on the church. At first, O'Malley's new-fangled ways don't sit too well with the older priest, but as his efforts become successful, Fitzgibbon accepts him and a special friendship grows between the two. This heartwarming drama also has a little subtle comedy, some pleasant songs, and a happy ending.

 Academy Award Recognition: won Best Picture, Leo McCarey won Best Director, Bing Crosby won Best Actor, Barry Fitzgerald won Best Supporting Actor, Leo McCarey won Best Original Story, Frank Butler and Frank Cavett won Best Screenplay, won Best Song: *Swinging on a Star*, Music by James Van Heusen and Lyrics by Johnny Burke; Barry Fitzgerald nominated for Best Actor.

GONE WITH THE WIND

DRAMA/ROMANCE

TECHNICOLOR   1939   MGM

CLARK GABLE	**VIVIEN LEIGH**	**LESLIE HOWARD**	**OLIVIA de HAVILLAND**
HATTIE McDANIEL	**BUTTERFLY McQUEEN**	**THOMAS MITCHELL**	**ONA MUNSON**
ANN RUTHERFORD	**EVELYN KEYES**		

Screenplay by: Sidney Howard, Jo Swerling, Charles MacArthur, Ben Hecht, John Lee Mahin, John Van Druten, Oliver H.P. Garrett, Winston Miller, John Balderston, Michael Foster, Edwin Justus Mayer, F. Scott Fitzgerald, David O. Selznick

Based on: The novel by Margaret Mitchell

Directed by: Victor Fleming, George Cukor, Sam Wood

Vivien Leigh portrays the headstrong and impetuous Scarlett O'Hara, and Clark Gable is the very masculine Rhett Butler in this epic that ranks among the best-known movies ever. It tells the tale of Scarlett and Rhett's stormy romance with the Old South/Civil War era as its backdrop. Supporting actress Hattie McDaniel made history with her role, becoming the first African-American ever to win an Academy Award. A magnificent entertainment experience, but it is rather long, so the viewer may prefer to watch it in more than one sitting.

 Academy Award Recognition: won Best Picture, Vivien Leigh won Best Actress, Hattie McDaniel won Best Supporting Actress, Victor Fleming won Best Director, Sidney Howard won Best Screenplay, Clark Gable nominated for Best Actor, Olivia de Havilland nominated for Best Supporting Actress, Max Steiner nominated for Best Original Score.

GOOD NEWS

MUSICAL/COMEDY

TECHNICOLOR   1947   MGM

JUNE ALLYSON	**PETER LAWFORD**	**PATRICIA MARSHALL**
JOAN McCRACKEN	**RAY McDONALD**	**MEL TORME**

Screenplay by: Betty Comden and Adolph Green

Based on: The musical comedy by Lawrence Schwab, Lew Brown, Frank Mandel, B.G. Desylva and Ray Henderson

Directed by: Charles Walters

The story takes place in 1927 at Tait College. Tommy Marlowe (Peter Lawford) is the big man on campus—a handsome football star. He pursues Pat McClellan

(Patricia Marshall), a snobby and egotistical girl, but is rejected by her. In an attempt to learn French and impress Pat, he enlists the help of Connie Lane (June Allyson), an intelligent and hard-working student. In the process, Connie falls for Tommy, and must find a way to make him realize that she loves him more than Pat ever could. A fun movie with lots of songs and dances from that era, depicting college life in the old days.

 Academy Award Recognition: nominated for Best Song: *Pass That Peace Pipe*, Music and Lyrics by Ralph Blane, Hugh Martin and Roger Edens.

GOODBYE, MR. CHIPS
BLACK & WHITE   1939

DRAMA
MGM

ROBERT DONAT   GREER GARSON

Screenplay by: R.C. Sheriff, Claudine West and Eric Maschwitz
From: The book **Goodbye, Mr. Chips!** By James Hilton
Directed by: Sam Wood

Robert Donat is Charles Chipping, "Mr. Chips," as his students at Brookfield Boys' School in England call him. The story begins with his difficulties as a young teacher, and traces his career with various students over many years until he retires as the most cherished teacher at the academy . Along his journey, he also finds love with Katherine Ellis (Greer Garson) who becomes his wife and helpmate. A touching and sentimental movie with fine performances by both Donat and Garson.

 Academy Award Recognition: Robert Donat won Best Actor, nominated for Best Picture, Greer Garson nominated for Best Actress, Sam Wood nominated for Best Director; Eric Maschwitz, R.C. Sheriff and Claudine West nominated for Best Screenplay.

GREAT ESCAPE, THE
PANAVISION & DELUXE COLOR

DRAMA/ACTION-ADVENTURE/MILITARY

1963

UNITED ARTISTS

STEVE McQUEEN	JAMES GARNER	RICHARD ATTENBOROUGH
JAMES DONALD	CHARLES BRONSON	DONALD PLEASENCE
JAMES COBURN	HANNES MESSEMER	DAVID McCALLUM

Screenplay by: James Clavell and W.R. Burnett
Based on: The book by Paul Brickhill
Directed by: John Sturges

This is an amazing true story. A group of Allied World War II soldiers are prisoners
in a strict German P.O.W. camp, but they are the tough sort who are not about to
take their captivity lying down. With ingenuity and courage they undertake a risky
escape plan: digging underground tunnels to try and get 250 men out. The all-star
cast, action and suspense make this an excellent choice for fans of war movies.

GREAT ZIEGFELD, THE
BLACK & WHITE

1936

DRAMA

MGM

WILLIAM POWELL	MYRNA LOY	LUISE RAINER
FRANK MORGAN	FANNY BRICE	VIRGINIA BRUCE
REGINALD OWENS	RAY BOLGER	

Screenplay by: William Anthony McGuire
Directed by: Robert Z. Leonard

This is the true life story of entertainment mogul Flo Ziegfeld (William Powell).
He rises from carnival barker to the grandest showman on Broadway, where he
glorifies many American beauties in his stage shows, which are called "Follies."
He marries Anna Sten (Luise Rainer), a European star whom he has turned into an
American star, but they divorce. Ziegfeld then marries the famous Broadway star
Billie Burke (played by Myrna Loy). Even with tremendous success, Ziegfeld is
always in debt, and has even more trouble when the Stock Market crashes in 1929.
A good biographical account with a superb cast, punctuated by lavish and glamorous
musical numbers.

 Academy Award Recognition: won Best Picture, Luise Rainer won
Best Actress, William Anthony McGuire nominated for Best Original
Story, Robert Z. Leonard nominated for Best Director.

GREATEST SHOW ON EARTH, THE

DRAMA

TECHNICOLOR   1952   PARAMOUNT

| BETTY HUTTON | CORNEL WILDE | CHARLTON HESTON | DOROTHY LAMOUR |
| GLORIA GRAHAME | EMMETT KELLY | JAMES STEWART | |

Screenplay by: Fredric M. Frank, Barre Lyndon, and Theodore St. John
Story by: Fredric M. Frank, Theodore St. John, and Frank Cavett
Directed by: Cecil B. DeMille

Technical Advisor: John Ringling North
Produced with the cooperation of Ringling Brothers–Barnum & Bailey Circus

An all-star cast presents this behind-the-scenes view of a circus production. All but Charlton Heston portray circus performers; he is the show's road manager, who keeps it all going. The story line follows the performers' lives on the road, their ups and downs, and their love lives. There's also a little bit of intrigue thrown in, as James Stewart portrays a clown with a mysterious past. Betty Hutton, who plays a trapeze artist, did all of her own stunts for this film. This movie expertly combines human drama with a realistic and dazzling circus atmosphere, providing very colorful entertainment.

Academy Award Recognition: won Best Picture; Frederic M. Frank, Theodore St. John and Frank Cavett won Best Motion Picture Story; Cecil B. DeMille nominated for Best Director.

GUESS WHO'S COMING TO DINNER?

DRAMA

COLOR   1967   COLUMBIA

SPENCER TRACY	KATHARINE HEPBURN	SIDNEY POITIER
KATHARINE HOUGHTON	CECIL KELLAWAY	ROY E. GLENN, SR.
BEAH RICHARDS	ISABEL SANFORD	VIRGINIA CHRISTINE

Screenplay by: William Rose
Directed by: Stanley Kramer

Spencer Tracy and Katharine Hepburn are Matt and Christina Drayton, a middle-aged white couple whose daughter Joey (Katharine Houghton) returns from a vacation to announce that she is engaged to a doctor, John Prentice (Sidney Poitier), who happens to be black. John is against going ahead with their marriage without the support of the Draytons, so it is up to them—whether they will approve or disapprove of the union. The drama unfolds as the Draytons work their way toward a decision, with input from John's parents (played by Roy E. Glenn, Sr. and Beah Richards) as well. An interesting and thought-provoking movie with a talented cast, that explores interracial issues in a dignified way.

 Academy Award Recognition: Katharine Hepburn won Best Actress, William Rose won Best Story and Screenplay (written directly for the screen), nominated for Best Picture, Spencer Tracy nominated for Best Actor, Cecil Kellaway nominated for Best Supporting Actor, Beah Richards nominated for Best Supporting Actress, Stanley Kramer nominated for Best Director, Frank DeVol nominated for Best Scoring of Music (adaptation or treatment).

GUY NAMED JOE, A
BLACK & WHITE   1944

DRAMA/ROMANCE
MGM

SPENCER TRACY	IRENE DUNNE	VAN JOHNSON	WARD BOND
JAMES GLEASON	LIONEL BARRYMORE	BARRY NELSON	ESTHER WILLIAMS
HENRY O'NEILL	DON DeFORE		

Screenplay by: Dalton Trumbo
Adaptation by: Frederick Hazlitt Brennan
From: An original story by Chandler Sprague and David Boehm
Directed by: Victor Fleming

Spencer Tracy is Pete Sandidge, a reckless World War II flying ace. Irene Dunne is lady flyer Dorinda Durston, Pete's sweetheart. Dorinda is very much in love with Pete, and worries about his safety, as she has a growing feeling that each dangerous mission he flies brings him closer to catastrophe. Her intuition proves correct, when one day he takes off but does not return. However, Pete goes on to heaven, where he becomes an angel and is sent back to earth to help train young pilots. His first subject is handsome Ted Randall (Van Johnson), who meets and falls in love with Dorinda. She cares for Ted, but is still devastated by the loss of Pete, and isn't sure she could bear to risk losing Ted the same way. Of course, Pete is insanely jealous and doesn't want anyone else to have Dorinda. An unusual tale that combines romance with a story of personal growth and sacrifice. It has a happy ending, but may produce a few tears along the way.

 Academy Award Recognition: David Boehm and Chandler Sprague nominated for Best Original Story.

GUYS AND DOLLS

CINEMASCOPE & COLOR   1955

MUSICAL
SAMUEL GOLDWYN

MARLON BRANDO	**JEAN SIMMONS**	**FRANK SINATRA**
VIVIAN BLAINE	**ROBERT KEITH**	**STUBBY KAYE**
REGIS TOOMEY	**SHELDON LEONARD**	**THE GOLDWYN GIRLS**

Screenplay by: Joseph L. Mankiewicz
Based on: The play *Guys and Dolls*, with book by Jo Swerling and
                   Abe Burrows, from a Damon Runyon Story
Directed by: Joseph L. Mankiewicz

Music and Lyrics by Frank Loesser

Skye Masterson (Marlon Brando) and Nathan Detroit (Frank Sinatra) are two small-time crooks who run illegal dice games. They are always in search of a secret location in which to operate. Meanwhile, Sarah Brown (Jean Simmons), a prim and proper Salvation Army missionary, attempts to reform the people of their neighborhood. Masterson and Sarah are complete opposites, but they somehow end up in love. Nathan Detroit's long-suffering fiancé, Miss Adelaide (Vivian Blaine), keeps trying to corral him into marriage while their never-ending engagement continues year after year. An enjoyable musical with a funny story and good songs.

 Academy Award Recognition: Jay Blackton and Cyril J. Mockridge nominated for Best Scoring of a Musical Picture.

GYPSY

TECHNIRAMA & TECHNICOLOR   1962

MUSICAL/COMEDY
WARNER BROTHERS

ROSALIND RUSSELL	**NATALIE WOOD**	**KARL MALDEN**	**ANN JILLIAN**

Screenplay by: Leonard Spigelgass
Based on: The stage play directed and choreographed by Jerome Robbins,
                   book by Arthur Laurents, from the memoirs of Gypsy Rose Lee
Directed by: Mervyn Leroy

The story of Rose Hovick (Rosalind Russell), the mother of both the famous stripper, Gypsy Rose Lee (Natalie Wood plays Gypsy as an adult) and actress June Havoc (Ann Jillian plays June as a child). Rose was quite a character and a notorious stage mother, promoting her daughters in showbiz from the time they were youngsters. She had always dreamed of hitting the big time herself but didn't, so the next best thing was for her children to be famous. This film version of the Broadway musical has both funny and serious moments, as well as good songs. A note for parents: Natalie Wood does imitate some of Gypsy Rose Lee's dance routines, but they are tastefully done and there is no nudity.

 Academy Award Recognition: Frank Perkins nominated for Best Scoring of Music (adaptation or treatment).

GYPSY COLT
ANSCO COLOR & TECHNICOLOR   1954

DRAMA/ANIMAL STORIES
MGM

DONNA CORCORAN   **WARD BOND**   **FRANCES DEE**

Screenplay by: Martin Berkeley
Based on: A story by Eric Knight
Directed by: Andrew Marton

This movie is a remake of *Lassie Come Home* (1943), but featuring a horse rather than a collie. An American farming community is suffering from a drought, and farmer Frank MacWade (Ward Bond) finds it financially necessary to sell Gypsy, the family's most prized horse. Gypsy and McWade's daughter, Meg (Donna Corcoran), have a special relationship, so the horse keeps running away from his new owner to return home to her—traveling as many as 500 miles. A sweet, classic animal story that kids should enjoy.

HANS CHRISTIAN ANDERSON
TECHNICOLOR   1952

MUSICAL/DRAMA
SAMUEL GOLDWYN, RKO

DANNY KAYE   **FARLEY GRANGER**   **JEANMAIRE**
JOEY WALSH   **PHILIP TONGE**   **ROLAND PETIT**

Screenplay by: Moss Hart
Based on: A story by Myles Connolly
Directed by: Charles Vidor

This is a fairy tale about the great story teller, Hans Christian Anderson, with Danny Kaye in the starring role. Hans works as a shoemaker to earn a living, and is a sweet man who enjoys entertaining children with his stories. When he falls in love with a beautiful ballerina who is married to a very cruel man, good-hearted Hans tries to rescue her from her predicament. An enchanting musical that is geared toward children, with songs that they can understand and enjoy.

 Academy Award Recognition: Walter Scharf nominated for Best Scoring of a Musical Picture, nominated for Best Song: *Thumbelina*, Music and Lyrics by Frank Loesser.

HAPPY YEARS, THE
TECHNICOLOR   1950

DRAMA/COMEDY
MGM

| DEAN STOCKWELL | DARRYL HICKMAN | SCOTTY BECKETT |
| LEON AMES | MARGALO GILLMORE | LEO G. CARROLL |

Screenplay by: Harry Ruskin
Based on: *The Lawrenceville School Stories* by Owen Johnson
Directed by: William A. Wellman

The story takes place in 1896, in New Jersey at a boys' boarding school called Lawrenceville. It involves a boy named John Humperdinck Stover (Dean Stockwell), who is a die-hard troublemaker and has been expelled from many other schools. His parents have sent him to Lawrenceville with the hope that he can be straightened out there. For the first time, John is up against other schoolboys who are as tough as he is. These boys and John's Latin teacher somehow manage to turn him around and set his feet on the road to becoming an honorable young man. A very well-done and charming movie with lessons for people of all ages.

HARVEY
BLACK & WHITE   1950

COMEDY
UNIVERSAL INT'L

| JAMES STEWART | JOSEPHINE HULL | VICTORIA HORNE | JESSE WHITE |

Screenplay by: Mary Chase and Oscar Brodney
Based on: The Pulitzer Prize play by Mary Chase
Directed by: Henry Koster

Elwood P. Dowd (James Stewart) lives with his sister Veta (Josephine Hull) and niece Myrtle Mae (Victoria Horne). Both his family and the townspeople think Elwood (who drinks quite a bit) is crazy because he acquaints himself with an imaginary friend—a six-foot-tall white rabbit named Harvey. So that she won't be the laughing stock of her high society friends, Veta decides that she has to get Elwood out of her house. She commits him to a rest home, but when she tells Elwood's odd story to the psychiatrist, he erroneously concludes that Veta is the lunatic. After letting Elwood go, the staff of the rest home eventually realizes that they've made a mistake. Then all are involved in a frantic chase to track Elwood down so they can straighten him out. A very amusing, madcap comedy with an unusual plot and a great cast.

 Academy Award Recognition: Josephine Hull won Best Supporting Actress, James Stewart nominated for Best Actor.

HARVEY GIRLS, THE   MUSICAL
TECHNICOLOR   1946   MGM

JUDY GARLAND	JOHN HODIAK	RAY BOLGER
ANGELA LANSBURY	PRESTON FOSTER	VIRGINIA O'BRIEN
KENNY BAKER	MARJORIE MAIN	CHILL WILLS

Screenplay by: Edmond Beloin, Nathaniel Curtis, Harry Crane,
                 James O'Hanlon and Samuel Raphaelson;
                 additional dialogue by Kay Van Riper
Based on: The book by Samuel Hopkins Adams and
                 the original story by Griffin and Rankin
Directed by: George Sidney

As the railroad expands west, the Harvey restaurant chain follows. Young women are recruited from far and wide to waitress in these top-drawer restaurants. One such restaurant has a major effect on a small western town, as the girls—particularly the spunky Susan Bradley (Judy Garland)—bring with them their classy and wholesome demeanor. The owner of the town's only saloon, Ned Trent (John Hodiak), now has competition working against his establishment, and his girlfriend Em (Angela Lansbury) is none too happy about his growing interest in Susan. A fun and delightful musical with very nice tunes.

 Academy Award Recognition: won Best Song: *On the Atchison, Topeka and Santa Fe*, Music by Harry Warren, Lyrics by Johnny Mercer; Lennie Hayton nominated for Best Scoring of a Musical Picture.

HAS ANYBODY SEEN MY GAL

TECHNICOLOR   1952

COMEDY
UNIVERSAL INT'L

PIPER LAURIE   **ROCK HUDSON**   **CHARLES COBURN**
GIGI PERREAU   **LYNN BARI**

Screenplay by:	Joseph Hoffman
Based on:	A story by Eleanor H. Porter
Directed by:	Douglas Sirk

It's the late 1920s, and a wealthy elderly man, Samuel J. Fulton (Charles Coburn) is making out his will. He has no living relatives and wishes to leave his fortune to the Blaisdells—the family of a woman he was in love with 40 years earlier. He travels to Vermont to check the people out first and see if they are worthy of the inheritance. To keep his identity secret he poses as a boarder in their home. As a test, he has $100,000 sent to them anonymously and watches how they react. Their newfound wealth changes their lives—and not all for the better. A quaint family comedy which recreates the Roaring Twenties and teaches the lesson that money doesn't necessarily buy happiness.

HEAVEN KNOWS, MR. ALLISON

CINEMASCOPE & DELUXE COLOR   1957

DRAMA/ACTION-ADVENTURE
20TH CENTURY FOX

DEBORAH KERR   **ROBERT MITCHUM**

Screenplay by:	John Lee Mahin and John Huston
Based on:	The novel by Charles Shaw
Directed by:	John Huston

Deborah Kerr is Sister Angela, a Catholic nun stranded alone on a South Pacific island in 1944, during World War II. An American Marine, Corporal Allison (played by Robert Mitchum), finds her when he washes ashore in a raft. Together, they work to survive until some kind of help can arrive—hopefully before the Japanese do. Though they come from very different worlds, they forge a very special friendship during their time together. An excellent movie with stellar performances by Kerr and Mitchum.

Academy Award Recognition: Deborah Kerr nominated for Best Actress, John Lee Mahin and John Huston nominated for Best Screenplay.

HEIDI

BLACK & WHITE   1937

DRAMA

20TH CENTURY FOX

SHIRLEY TEMPLE   **JEAN HERSHOLT**   **ARTHUR TREACHER**
MARY NASH   **SIDNEY BLACKMER**

Screenplay by: Walter Ferris and Julien Josephson
Based on: The book by Johanna Spyri
Directed by: Allan Dwan

Heidi (Shirley Temple) is brought to her grandfather's house in the mountains when her aunt (Mary Nash) no longer wishes to care for her. Her grandfather (played by Jean Hersholt) is a reclusive, bitter man, but Heidi touches his heart and makes him happy again. But her selfish aunt later returns and, for a fee, whisks Heidi away to live in Frankfurt as a companion for an invalid girl. Heidi's indomitable cheerfulness confounds her new and ornery governess. She also befriends the family's kind butler, Andrews (Arthur Treacher). Meanwhile, Heidi's grief-stricken grandfather sets out on foot, trudging many miles through the snow to try and find her and bring her home again. A very sweet children's drama with some funny moments mixed in, and a happy ending as well.

HEIRESS, THE

BLACK & WHITE   1949

DRAMA

PARAMOUNT

OLIVIA de HAVILLAND   **RALPH RICHARDSON**   **MONTGOMERY CLIFT**
MIRIAM HOPKINS   **VANESSA BROWN**   **MONA FREEMAN**
RAY COLLINS   **SELENA ROYLE**

Screenplay by: Ruth Goetz and Augustus Goetz
Based on: Their play and the Henry James novel *Washington Square*
Directed by: William Wyler

Olivia de Havilland is Catherine Sloper, a shy, plain, and socially inept spinster of the 1840s who is dominated by her father, the well-to-do Dr. Austin Sloper (Ralph Richardson). Along comes the ne'er-do-well Morris Townsend (Montgomery Clift), who begins to court Catherine. Her father suspects that Morris is after the family's money and wants to get rid of him. What follows is an excellent, well-acted drama with a great ending.

 Academy Award Recognition: Olivia de Havilland won Best Actress, Aaron Copland won Best Scoring of a Dramatic or Comedy Picture, nominated for Best Picture, Ralph Richardson nominated for Best Supporting Actor, William Wyler nominated for Best Director.

HELLO, DOLLY!

COLOR BY DELUXE   1969

MUSICAL/COMEDY

20TH CENTURY FOX

BARBRA STREISAND	WALTER MATTHAU	MICHAEL CRAWFORD
MARIANNE McANDREW	TOMMY TUNE	LOUIS ARMSTRONG

Screenplay by: Ernest Lehman
Based on: The stage play **Hello, Dolly!**, with book by Michael Stewart,
                   based on **The Matchmaker** by Thornton Wilder
Directed by: Gene Kelly

New York City, 1890. Barbara Streisand stars as Dolly Levi, an expert matchmaker. Now, she also wishes to make a match for herself. Dolly wants to land Horace Vandergelder (Walter Matthau), a wealthy shopowner. Standing in her way are his plans to marry another woman, so Dolly tries to fix the other woman up with someone else so that she can have Vandergelder for herself. This movie version of the hit Broadway show features beautiful photography and the songs are well done by Streisand—her many fans should especially enjoy this musical.

  Academy Award Recognition: Lennie Hayton and Lionel Newman won Best Score of a Musical Picture (adaptation), nominated for Best Picture.

HELLO, FRISCO, HELLO

TECHNICOLOR   1943

MUSICAL

20TH CENTURY FOX

ALICE FAYE	JOHN PAYNE	JACK OAKIE	JUNE HAVOC

Screenplay by: Robert Ellis, Helen Hogan, and Richard Macauley
Directed by: Bruce Humberstone

Trudy Evans (Alice Faye) and Johnny Cornell (John Payne) start out as part of an entertainment troupe—with buddies Dan Daley (Jack Oakie) and Beulah Clancy (June Havoc)—that performs in saloons on San Francisco's Barbary Coast. Cornell is an ambitious young man who pushes his way to the top to become an important businessman, running his own saloon. Trudy becomes the star attraction at his establishment, and though she loves him very much, Cornell is more dazzled by the Nob Hill society girl whom he eventually marries. Their lives continue in separate directions for a while until their paths cross again at the story's climax. A colorful movie with lots of old-time atmosphere and great costumes.

  Academy Award Recognition: won Best Song: **You'll Never Know**, Music by Harry Warren, Lyrics by Mack Gordon.

HER TWELVE MEN

ANSCO COLOR, TECHNICOLOR   1954

COMEDY/DRAMA

MGM

| GREER GARSON | ROBERT RYAN | BARRY SULLIVAN | RICHARD HAYDN |
| BARBARA LAWRENCE | JAMES ARNESS | TIM CONSIDINE | |

Screenplay by: William Roberts and Laura Z. Hobson
From: A story by Louise Baker
Directed by: Robert Z. Leonard

Greer Garson is Jan Stewart, who's recently been widowed, and with no prior teaching experience takes a job as a teacher at a boys' boarding school. Over time, Jan learns how to manage the boys, helping them with their personal problems and adding a special touch of feminine warmth to the school. There are both amusing and touching moments in this good, wholesome family film.

HERE COMES MR. JORDAN

BLACK & WHITE   1941

DRAMA

COLUMBIA

| ROBERT MONTGOMERY | CLAUDE RAINS | EVELYN KEYES |
| RITA JOHNSON | JAMES GLEASON | EDWARD EVERETT HORTON |

Screenplay by: Sidney Buchman and Seton I. Miller
Based on: The play *Halfway to Heaven* by Harry Segall
Directed by: Alexander Hall

Robert Montgomery stars as Joe Pendleton, a professional boxer who is involved in a plane crash. An angel (played by Edward Everett Horton) takes him to heaven by mistake—Pendleton was supposed to survive. Now, another angel, Mr. Jordan (Claude Rains), must fix the error and find Pendleton a new body in which to finish his destiny. The first body he tries out is that of a murdered wealthy businessman, Bruce Farnsworth. James Gleason plays Sam Corkle, Joe Pendleton's manager, who is completely puzzled by the whole thing, but believes Joe's story. Of course, all does not go so smoothly, and the result is an interesting and unusual story with a surprise ending.

Academy Award Recognition: Harry Segall won Best Original Story, Sidney Buchman and Seton I. Miller won Best Screenplay, nominated for Best Picture, Robert Montgomery nominated for Best Actor, James Gleason nominated for Best Supporting Actor, Alexander Hall nominated for Best Director.

HERE COMES THE GROOM
BLACK & WHITE   1951

COMEDY/ROMANCE/MUSICAL
PARAMOUNT

BING CROSBY	**JANE WYMAN**	**ALEXIS SMITH**
FRANCHOT TONE	**JAMES BARTON**	**IAN WOLFE**
CONNIE GILCHRIST	**ELLEN CORBY**	**ANNA MARIA ALBERGHETTI**

Screenplay by: Virginia Van Upp, Liam O'Brien and Myles Connolly
Story by: Robert Riskin and Liam O'Brien
Directed by: Frank Capra

Pete Garvey (Bing Crosby) is a newspaper reporter in post-war Europe. He is a wanderer who leaves his long-time love, Emmadel Jones (Jane Wyman) waiting at home for years. Then he returns to the U.S. with two French orphans, planning to marry Emmadel and start a family. However, he finds that he has left her waiting too long and that she is now engaged to marry her wealthy boss. He tries every angle he can think of to win Emmadel back, but she fights him every step of the way. She does still love him, but wants the more stable kind of life her new fiancé can give her. An amiable and enjoyable romantic comedy with a few good songs.

 Academy Award Recognition: won Best Song: *In the Cool, Cool, Cool of the Evening*, Music by Hoagy Carmichael, Lyrics by Johnny Mercer; Robert Riskin and Liam O'Brien nominated for Best Motion Picture Story.

HIGH NOON
BLACK & WHITE/COLORIZED   1952

DRAMA/WESTERN
UNITED ARTISTS

GARY COOPER	**THOMAS MITCHELL**	**LLOYD BRIDGES**
KATY JURADO	**GRACE KELLY**	**OTTO KRUGER**
LON CHANEY	**HENRY MORGAN**	

Screenplay by: Carl Foreman
Based on: The magazine story *The Tin Star* by John W. Cunningham
Directed by: Fred Zinnemann

Gary Cooper is Will Kane, the Marshall of a western town, and Grace Kelly is his fiancé, Amy Fowler. Kane is retiring from his post because of his marriage to Amy. But on the day that they are to be married, a criminal whom Kane sent to prison for murder plans to return and get revenge. Instead of running away, Kane opts to stay and confront the evildoer. The townspeople are reluctant to back him, and Amy doesn't understand his need to take this stand, as all events lead up to a dramatic one-on-one showdown. This movie does have a dark and intense atmosphere, but is very well done and should appeal to die-hard Western fans.

 Academy Award Recognition: Gary Cooper won Best Actor, Dimitri Tiomkin won Best Musical Scoring of a Dramatic or Comedy Picture, won Best Song: *High Noon (Do Not Forsake Me, Oh My Darlin')*, Music by Dimitri Tiomkin, Lyrics by Ned Washington; nominated for Best Picture, Fred Zinnemann nominated for Best Director, Carl Foreman nominated for Best Screenplay.

HIGH SOCIETY
VISTAVISION & TECHNICOLOR   1956

MUSICAL
MGM

BING CROSBY	GRACE KELLY	FRANK SINATRA
CELESTE HOLM	JOHN LUND	LOUIS CALHERN
SIDNEY BLACKMER	LOUIS ARMSTRONG	

Screenplay by: John Patrick
Based on: A play by Philip Barry
Directed by: Charles Walters

Music and Lyrics by Cole Porter

In this musical remake of **The Philadelphia Story** (1940), the setting is Newport, Rhode Island among the wealthy society set. C.K. Dexter-Haven (Bing Crosby) and Tracy Lord (Grace Kelly) are a divorced couple with neighboring mansions. Tracy is now getting remarried to a bland, boring man (Lund), but the reforming playboy Dexter-Haven still loves her and keeps trying to win her back. Two society columnists (Celeste Holm and Frank Sinatra) arrive to cover the wedding as the Lord family scurries to hide a family secret, and there are lots of romantic entanglements leading up to the wedding. The classic story plus pleasant tunes and a colorful atmosphere combine to make this movie a pleasant diversion.

 Academy Award Recognition: Johnny Green and Saul Chaplin nominated for Best Scoring of a Musical Picture, nominated for Best Song: *True Love*, Music and Lyrics by Cole Porter.

HIRED WIFE
BLACK & WHITE   1940   **COMEDY/ROMANCE**
                                                               UNIVERSAL

ROSALIND RUSSELL	BRIAN AHERNE	VIRGINIA BRUCE
JOHN CARROLL	ROBERT BENCHLEY	HOBART CAVANAGH
RICHARD LANE		

Screenplay by: Richard Connell and Gladys Lehman
Story by: George Beck
Directed by: William Seiter

Rosalind Russell is Kendal Browning, secretary and valuable right hand to her boss Stephen Dexter (Brian Aherne). She is very much in love with him, but he has a roving eye, so she is relegated to rescuing him from frequent romantic predicaments. When he spots Phyllis Walden (Virginia Bruce) on a billboard, he wants to use the beauty in his own company's ads, and of course, Kendal does everything she can to prevent this—but to no avail. When a competitor threatens to bankrupt his business, Dexter is advised by his lawyer (Robert Benchley) to marry and put the company in his wife's name. Kendal manages to get Dexter to marry her instead of billboard queen Phyllis, and then the fun begins. An amusing romantic comedy with an unusual story line.

HIS GIRL FRIDAY
BLACK & WHITE   1940   **COMEDY**
                                                                  COLUMBIA

CARY GRANT	ROSALIND RUSSELL	RALPH BELLAMY
GENE LOCKHART	HELEN MACK	PORTER HALL

Screenplay by: Charles Lederer
Based on: The play ***The Front Page*** by Ben Hecht and
                      Charles MacArthur
Directed by: Howard Hawks

The story of Walter Burns (Cary Grant) and Hildy Johnson (Rosalind Russell), a divorced couple who are reporters for the same newspaper. Hildy is leaving the paper to marry another man, Bruce Baldwin (Ralph Bellamy), but Walter wants her back. He has only one day to stop them before they leave town and tie the knot, and goes through all kinds of antics to halt the wedding. In a last-ditch effort to stall her departure, Walter talks Hildy into covering one last story—about a man awaiting execution for murder, a story that Walter is sure will drag on for a while until he can win Hildy back. An enjoyable and very fast-moving comedy with crisp dialogue.

HOLIDAY

BLACK & WHITE   1938   **COMEDY**

COLUMBIA PICTURES

KATHARINE HEPBURN	**CARY GRANT**	**DORIS NOLAN**
LEW AYRES	**EDWARD EVERETT HORTON**	

Screenplay by: Donald Ogden Stewart and Sidney Buchman
Based on: The play by Philip Barry
Directed by: George Cukor

Johnny Case (Cary Grant) is a somewhat wacky and free-spirited fellow who becomes engaged to be married during a whirlwind romance while on vacation. He finds out later that his new fiancé, Julia Seton (played by Doris Nolan) comes from an extremely wealthy and very stodgy family. Johnny provides a breath of fresh air for Julia's sister Linda (Katharine Hepburn) and brother Ned (Lew Ayres), who are free spirits themselves, trapped in the rigidity and coldness of their family's way of life. As the engagement progresses, it becomes obvious that Johnny's plans for his life are very different from Julia's and much more like Linda's. This movie seems a little dated at first, but this fades away quickly, because both the story and dialogue are very sharp, and the cast gives fine performances.

HOLIDAY AFFAIR

BLACK & WHITE   1949   **DRAMA/CHRISTMAS**

RKO

ROBERT MITCHUM	**JANET LEIGH**	**WENDELL COREY**
GRIFF BARNETT	**ESTHER DALE**	**HENRY O'NEILL**
HENRY MORGAN	**GORDON GEBERT**	

Screenplay by: Isobel Lennart
Based on: The story *Christmas Gift* by John D. Weaver
Directed by: Don Hartman

Connie (Janet Leigh) is a young war widow left to raise her son alone, and since her husband's death, she has retreated to an over-organized and dull life. She's been dating "the right kind of man," Carl (Wendell Corey), but is reluctant to marry him. Then one day while Christmas shopping (she works as a comparison shopper for a department store), Connie meets Steve (Robert Mitchum). He comes into her life, bringing spontaneity and fun, and wins the approval of her son as well. She falls for him and then must decide which man to marry, Carl or Steve. A heartwarming tale that should appeal to all ages. A good choice for viewing at Christmas time.

HOLIDAY INN
BLACK & WHITE   1942

MUSICAL/CHRISTMAS
PARAMOUNT

BING CROSBY   **FRED ASTAIRE**   **MARJORIE REYNOLDS**
VIRGINIA DALE   **WALTER ABEL**   **LOUISE BEAVERS**

Screenplay by: Claude Binyon, adaptation by Elmer Rice
Based on: An idea by Irving Berlin
Directed by: Mark Sandrich

Lyrics and Music by Irving Berlin

This story begins with an entertainment trio, Jim Hardy (Bing Crosby), Ted Hanover (Fred Astaire) and Lila Dixon (Virginia Dale).   Jim and Lila are engaged, and he buys a farm so they can settle down. But Lila isn't interested in farm life and stays on the road in show business as Ted's dance partner. Now alone and stuck with a farm, Jim gets an interesting idea—he'll open a country inn, but one that operates only on holidays, offering great entertainment. Then along comes Linda Mason (Marjorie Reynolds), an out-of-work singer/dancer whom Jim hires, and she falls in love with him. In the meantime, Ted loses partner Lila to a millionaire, spots lovely Linda at the Holiday Inn, and plans to steal her away from Jim. Placed around the entertaining showbiz/romance story line are many good songs by Irving Berlin, including his most famous holiday tune *White Christmas*.

Academy Award Recognition: won Best Song: *White Christmas*, Music and Lyrics by Irving Berlin, Irving Berlin nominated for Best Original Story, Robert Emmett Dolan nominated for Best Scoring of a Musical Picture.

HONKY TONK
BLACK & WHITE   1941

DRAMA
MGM

CLARK GABLE   **LANA TURNER**   **CLAIRE TREVOR**   **FRANK MORGAN**
MARJORIE MAIN   **CHILL WILLS**   **ALBERT DEKKER**

Screenplay by: Marguerite Roberts
Directed by: Jack Conway

Clark Gable is con man Candy Johnson, who along with his sidekick The Sniper (played by Chill Wills) is run out of town everywhere he goes. On a train, Candy spots Elizabeth Cotton (Lana Turner), who he thinks is just another floozie. But when they both get off at the next town, Yellow Creek, he finds out that Elizabeth's father (played by Frank Morgan) is the Justice of the Peace, who Candy secretly knows is a con man just like himself. Candy decides to work in collusion with this Judge, and the rest of the plot unfolds from there. An interesting story, well-acted by a talented cast.

HORSE IN THE GRAY FLANNEL SUIT, THE

COMEDY/ANIMAL STORIES

TECHNICOLOR   1968   WALT DISNEY

| DEAN JONES | DIANE BAKER | LLOYD BOCHNER | FRED CLARK |
| ELLEN JANOV | MOREY AMSTERDAM | KURT RUSSELL | LURENE TUTTLE |

Screenplay by: Louis Pelletier
Based on: The book **The Year of the Horse** by Eric Hatch
Directed by: Norman Tokar

Dean Jones is Fredrick Bolton, an advertising executive and single parent to his daughter Helen, who takes riding lessons and longs to have her very own horse, which he cannot afford. Opportunity arises when Tom Dugan (Fred Clark), a client whose company manufactures Aspercel, a stomach remedy, demands a new ad campaign to reach more upper-crust customers. Fredrick comes up with a novel idea to help both his client and his daughter—a race horse named Aspercel, with Helen as the rider. But what starts out as an easy plan takes a lot of unexpected turns, including Fredrick's surprise romance with Helen's attractive riding teacher Suzie Clemens (Diane Baker), and Helen's new friendship with nice young man Ronnie Gardner (Kurt Russell). An amiable and enjoyable family-oriented comedy.

HOUDINI

DRAMA

TECHNICOLOR   1953   PARAMOUNT

TONY CURTIS   JANET LEIGH

Screenplay by: Philip Yordan
Based on: A book by Harold Kellock
Directed by: George Marshall

This true story about Harry Houdini (Tony Curtis), the famous escape artist, traces Houdini's career from his early sideshow appearances to his own popular magic shows, and then on to his great escape events as a superstar attraction. His court-ship and marriage to his wife, Bess (Janet Leigh) is also shown. It is a fascinating biographical drama that ends when Houdini dies trying to escape from a tank full of water. That last scene may be too scary for very young children, though, making this film more suitable for older children and adults.

HOUSEBOAT
TECHNICOLOR   1958

COMEDY/ROMANCE
PARAMOUNT

CARY GRANT   SOPHIA LOREN   MARTHA HYER

Screenplay by: Melville Shavelson and Jack Rose
Directed by: Melville Shavelson

Cary Grant is Tom Winston, a government man and widower with three children, two boys and a girl. Tom had never spent much time with his children, but now decides that he should be the one to raise them and takes the children with him to Washington, D.C. Enter the attractive Cinzia Zaccardi (Sophia Loren), an Italian symphony conductor's daughter, who takes an interest in the motherless children because their father seems to have an inept and gruff manner with them. The children like Cinzia so much that they convince Tom to hire her as their governess. Pretty soon, it becomes obvious that his apartment is too small in which to raise a family, so Tom purchases a houseboat and moves them all to the country so they can have more space. Cinzia teaches Tom how to care for his children, and the two end up caring for each other in the process. A very funny and charming movie that the whole family can enjoy together.

 Academy Award Recognition: Melville Shavelson and Jack Rose nominated for Best Story and Screenplay (written directly for the screen), nominated for Best Song: ***Almost in Your Arms (Love Song from Houseboat)***, Music and Lyrics by Jay Livingston and Ray Evans.

HOW THE WEST WAS WON
CINERAMA & METROCOLOR　　　　1963

DRAMA/WESTERN
MGM

DEBBIE REYNOLDS	**CARROLL BAKER**	**LEE J. COBB**	**HENRY FONDA**
CAROLYN JONES	**KARL MALDEN**	**GREGORY PECK**	**GEORGE PEPPARD**
ROBERT PRESTON	**JAMES STEWART**	**ELI WALLACH**	**JOHN WAYNE**
RICHARD WIDMARK	**WALTER BRENNAN**	**ANDY DEVINE**	**AGNES MOOREHEAD**
ANDY DEVINE	**RAYMOND MASSEY**	**THELMA RITTER**	**HARRY MORGAN**

Screenplay by:　　James R. Webb
Suggested by:　　The series *How The West Was Won*, from *LIFE* Magazine
Directed by:　　John Ford, George Marshall, and Henry Hathaway

Narrated by Spencer Tracy

A huge, all-star saga about the settlement and development of the Old West, and the people who struggled to achieve it. This movie is divided into segments with different characters and stories. It is long, and it's possible that one may want to watch it in more than one sitting. The photography of this film is excellent, with breathtaking on-location scenery, and fine performances from the entire cast.

Academy Award Recognition: James R. Webb won Best Story and Screenplay (written directly for the screen), Alfred Newman and Ken Darby nominated for Best Music Score (substantially original), nominated for Best Picture.

HOW TO MARRY A MILLIONAIRE
CINEMASCOPE & TECHNICOLOR　　　　1953

COMEDY
20TH CENTURY FOX

BETTY GRABLE	**MARILYN MONROE**	**LAUREN BACALL**	**DAVID WAYNE**
RORY CALHOUN	**CAMERON MITCHELL**	**FRED CLARK**	**WILLIAM POWELL**

Screenplay by:　　Nunnally Johnson
Based on:　　Plays by Zoe Akins, Dale Eaason, and Katherine Albert
Directed by:　　Jean Negulesco

In New York City, three beautiful women (Betty Grable, Marilyn Monroe and Lauren Bacall) rent an apartment in a luxury building for one year to be in the proper hunting ground for meeting and marrying rich men. The story is a simple one, but plenty of funny things happen to them as they work to fulfill their dreams. A perky and glamorous comedy.

HOW TO SUCCEED IN BUSINESS
WITHOUT REALLY TRYING

MUSICAL

PANAVISION & COLOR BY DELUXE   1967

UNITED ARTISTS

ROBERT MORSE   **MICHELE LEE**   **RUDY VALLEE**

Screenplay by: David Swift
Based on: The novel by Shepherd Mead and the original Broadway musical
Directed by: David Swift

Music and Lyrics by Frank Loesser

Robert Morse is Pierpont Finch, a young man who purchases a book about how to
succeed in the business world. He gets a small job in the mailroom at the Worldwide
Wicket Company, follows the steps outlined in the book, and within days, finds himself rapidly climbing the corporate ladder.   Along the way, Finch also finds romance
with a pretty company secretary, Rosemary Pilkington (Michele Lee). Rudy Vallee
portrays the corporation's president. This satire of corporate culture in America is
funny, tuneful and enjoyable.

HUCKSTERS, THE

DRAMA

BLACK & WHITE   1947

MGM

CLARK GABLE   **DEBORAH KERR**   **SYDNEY GREENSTREET**   **ADOLPHE MENJOU**
AVA GARDNER   **KEENAN WYNN**   **EDWARD ARNOLD**

Screenplay by: Luther Davis; adaptation by Edward Chodorov
                  and George Wells
Based on: The novel by Frederic Wakeman
Directed by: Jack Conway

Clark Gable is Victor Albee Norman, an advertising executive returning to business
after serving in World War II. He meets and falls in love with Kay Dorrance (played
by Deborah Kerr), a widow with two young children. Victor's plans for a new life
with Kay make him start to think about the moral ramifications of certain aspects
of his job. He's also not sure about continuing to jump through hoops to please
demanding clients, like the bombastic and ruthless soap company president, Evan
Llewellyn Evans (Sydney Greenstreet). An excellent, well-acted drama about the
kinds of moral dilemmas that people often face in the business world.

I LOVE MELVIN

TECHNICOLOR   1953

MUSICAL

MGM

| DONALD O'CONNOR | DEBBIE REYNOLDS | UNA MERKEL | RICHARD ANDERSON |
| ALLYN JOSLYN | LES TREMAYNE | JIM BACKUS | |

Screenplay by: George Wells;
                  additional dialogue by Ruth Brooks Flippen
Based on: A story by Laslo Vadnay
Directed by: Don Weis

Debbie Reynolds is Judy LeRoy, a chorus girl, and Donald O'Connor is magazine
writer Melvin Hoover. They bump into each other accidentally and then meet again
backstage at her show. While Melvin shoots photos of Judy for his magazine, the
two fall in love. However, her family prefers the boyfriend that she had dated before Melvin, a fellow with a lot more money. Judy and Melvin try to find a way to
be together in this cheery and breezy musical with nice song and dance numbers.

I LOVE YOU AGAIN

BLACK & WHITE   1940

COMEDY/ROMANCE

MGM

WILLIAM POWELL   MYRNA LOY

Screenplay by: Charles Lederer, George Oppenheimer and Harry Kurnitz
Original story by: Leon Gordon and Maurine Watkins,
                    based on the novel by Octavus Roy Cohen
Directed by: W.S. Van Dyke II

William Powell is Larry Wilson, a meek and mild, clean-cut businessman from a
small town who's traveling on an ocean liner. An accidental bump on the head gives
him amnesia, but he reverts to his real personality as a former con man, George
Carey—who had become Larry Wilson as the result of *another* bump on the head
he had sustained several years earlier. As his real self, George plans to make off
with all of Larry Wilson's money. Then he meets Larry's wife Kay (Myrna Loy),
who is about to divorce Larry for being cheap and boring. George finds her
attractive, and sets out to win her back with Larry's "new" personality. A quite
amusing and zany comedy with an ingenious story line.

I REMEMBER MAMA

BLACK & WHITE   1948

DRAMA

RKO

IRENE DUNNE	**BARBARA BEL GEDDES**	**OSCAR HOMOLKA**	**PHILIP DORN**
SIR CEDRIC HARDWICKE	**EDGAR BERGEN**	**RUDY VALLEE**	**ELLEN CORBY**

Screenplay by: Dewitt Bodeen
Based on: The play *I Remember Mama*,
                  adapted and directed by John Van Druten,
                  from the novel *Mama's Bank Account* by Kathryn Forbes
Directed by: George Stevens

The tale of a Norwegian clan in San Francisco and how their mother (Irene Dunne) holds them together through awkward family politics and tough times. She's the family's hero, and the story is told from the perspective of one of her daughters (played by Barbara Bel Geddes). Ellen Corby (Grandma of TV's *The Waltons*) appears as an aunt. A touching drama about the depth of a mother's love for her children, done by a very gifted crew of actors.

Academy Award Recognition: Irene Dunne nominated for Best Actress, Barbara Bel Geddes and Ellen Corby nominated for Best Supporting Actress, Oscar Homolka nominated for Best Supporting Actor.

I WAKE UP SCREAMING

BLACK & WHITE   1941

DRAMA/MYSTERY-SUSPENSE

20TH CENTURY FOX

BETTY GRABLE	**VICTOR MATURE**	**CAROLE LANDIS**

Screenplay by: Dwight Taylor
Based on: The novel *I Wake Up Screaming* by Steve Fisher
Directed by: Bruce Humberstone

The story begins with the murder of beautiful model Vicki Lynn (Carole Landis). She had previously worked as a waitress, and got her modeling career started with the help of one of her customers, sports promoter Frankie Christopher (Victor Mature). Frankie is the prime suspect in her murder, because he was angry that Vicki had recently signed a movie contract with another talent scout. Vicki's sister, Jill Lynn (Betty Grable), who lived with her, is also a possible suspect. The rest of the movie is a chronicle of the events leading up to Vicki's murder as told by Frankie and Jill, and the unfolding of the investigation. A very suspenseful and intriguing mystery, and one of the few times Betty Grable was able to show her dramatic talents in a serious role.

I WAS A MALE WAR BRIDE

BLACK & WHITE · 1949

COMEDY/ROMANCE · 20TH CENTURY FOX

CARY GRANT   ANN SHERIDAN

Screenplay by:	Charles Lederer, Leonard Spigelgass, and Hagar Wilde
From:	A story by Henri Rochard
Directed by:	Howard Hawks

After World War II, many "war brides" were brought to America—they were European women who had married American soldiers while they were overseas. This movie puts a comic twist on that concept. Cary Grant is Captain Henri Rochard, a French soldier, and Ann Sheridan is Lt. Cathy Gates, the American WAC (Women's Army Corps) who wants to bring her husband home with her. Since Henri is a man, he does not qualify as a war bride, so he disguises himself as another WAC in order to travel home to America with Cathy. The crazy challenges that they face in order to remain together generate a rather amusing romantic comedy.

ICELAND

BLACK & WHITE · 1942

COMEDY/MUSICAL/ROMANCE · 20TH CENTURY FOX

SONJA HENIE   JOHN PAYNE   JACK OAKIE   FELIX BRESSART

Screenplay by:	Robert Ellis and Helen Logan
Directed by:	H. Bruce Humberstone

During World War II, the Marines arrive in Iceland. Sonja Henie stars as Katina, a young and pretty Icelander whose younger sister is all set to marry into a well-to-do family. But according to tradition, an older sister must marry before her younger sister can. This presents a big problem for Katina, whose current boyfriend is a boring nebbish she dreads being stuck with. Enter the handsome, smooth-talking, American Marine Corporal James Murfin (John Payne), who sweeps Katina off her feet, and she decides that he is the one she will marry. The fun begins when Katina tells her parents about her new fiancé, the unsuspecting Marine, who's a confirmed bachelor. Jack Oakie is Corporal Murfin's faithful sidekick, Slip Riggs. An amusing romantic comedy with a few nice tunes and some of Sonja's famous skating.

I'LL SEE YOU IN MY DREAMS
BLACK & WHITE   1951

DRAMA/MUSICAL
WARNER BROTHERS

DORIS DAY   **DANNY THOMAS**   **FRANK LOVEJOY**
PATRICE WYMORE   **JAMES GLEASON**   **MARY WICKES**

Screenplay by: Melville Shavelson and Jack Rose
Directed by: Michael Curtiz

This is the biography of famous composer Gus Kahn, portrayed by Danny Thomas. The story begins in Chicago, where Kahn delivers crockery while writing song lyrics. He finally gets a break when he meets a young lady, Gracie LeBoy (Doris Day), who works as a demonstrator for a music publishing company. Gracie sees something special in Gus. She gives him some advice, puts his lyrics to music, helps him to launch his career, and falls in love with him. Though Gracie remains his inspiration, Gus goes on to team up with other composers and becomes very successful. Gracie and Gus marry, and the rest of the movie recounts the journey of their life together. A very charming portrayal of Mr. and Mrs. Kahn and the times in which they lived. People who think they are unfamiliar with Kahn's music will realize how many of his hits they already know when they hear the songs featured in this movie.

IMITATION GENERAL
CINEMASCOPE & BLACK AND WHITE   1958

COMEDY/MILITARY
MGM

GLENN FORD   **RED BUTTONS**   **TAINA ELG**   **DEAN JONES**

Screenplay by: William Bowers
Based on: The story by William Chamberlain
Directed by: George Marshall

The setting: France, 1944. Master Sgt. Murphy (Glenn Ford) and a corporal (Red Buttons) are escorting a General through a World War II battle zone. The General is killed and the troops in their sector find themselves surrounded by Germans. In order to prevent disaster, Murphy decides to impersonate the now-deceased General. He comes up with some interesting and unusual ideas to save the day, but because impersonating an officer is a major offense, he must avoid being recognized by the other men. An engaging service comedy, suitable for the entire family.

IN OLD CALIFORNIA

BLACK & WHITE

1942

DRAMA/COMEDY/WESTERN
REPUBLIC

JOHN WAYNE   **BINNIE BARNES**   **ALBERT DEKKER**
HELEN PARRISH   **PATSY KELLY**

Screenplay by: Gertrude Purcell and Frances Hyland
Original story by: J. Robert Bren and Gladys Atwater
Directed by: William McGann

John Wayne plays a pharmacist from Boston who goes to California to set up shop and establish a new life for himself. In the process, he makes new friends, finds romance, and goes head-to-head against the town's outlaws. This enjoyable Western is an old-fashioned good guys vs. bad guys story, with some laughs and light-hearted moments sprinkled in as well.

INDISCREET

TECHNICOLOR

1958

COMEDY/ROMANCE
WARNER BROTHERS

CARY GRANT   **INGRID BERGMAN**   **CECIL PARKER**   **PHYLLIS CALVERT**

Screenplay by: Norman Krasna
Based on: His play, **Kind Sir**
Directed by: Stanley Donen

Ingrid Bergman is Anna Kalman, an attractive well-known European actress who cannot find a man who suits her tastes. Cary Grant is Philip Adams, an American businessman who's being offered a position with NATO. Anna is immediately interested in him, but Philip tells her that he is a married man, although separated, and chances for a divorce are slim. Throwing caution to the wind, she dates him anyway, and falls in love. Eventually, Anna finds out that Philip is not really married, but made up the whole story in order to avoid commitment, and then the real fireworks begin. A glamorous and very witty romantic comedy.

IT HAPPENED ONE NIGHT

BLACK & WHITE   1934

COMEDY

COLUMBIA

CLARK GABLE   CLAUDETTE COLBERT

Screenplay by: Robert Riskin
Based on: The story **Night Bus** by Samuel Hopkins Adams
Directed by: Frank Capra

Claudette Colbert is Ellie Andrews, an heiress who is running away from her father
to assert her independence. While attempting to travel from Florida to New York,
she meets a brusque and enterprising reporter, Peter Warne (Clark Gable). He
offers to help her escape if she will let him write her story later. At the start, Ellie
and Peter have nothing in common, but get to know each other very well along
the way. Before they know it, they become an unlikely couple in love. They have
plenty of comic adventures on the road in this timeless and charming classic.

 Academy Award Recognition: won Best Picture, Clark Gable won
Best Actor, Claudette Colbert won Best Actress, Frank Capra won Best
Director, Robert Riskin won Best Screenplay (adaptation).

IT HAPPENED TO JANE

EASTMAN COLOR   1959

COMEDY

COLUMBIA PICTURES

DORIS DAY   JACK LEMMON   ERNIE KOVACS
STEVE FORREST   MARY WICKES

Screenplay by: Norman Katkov
From: A story by Max Wilk and Norman Katkov
Directed by: Richard Quine

Doris Day is Jane Osgood, a widow struggling to support two children by running a
Maine lobster farm. A railroad error causes a large shipment of her live lobsters to
be ruined, along with her business reputation. Jack Lemmon is George Denham,
her best friend and lawyer, who agrees to handle the lawsuit she files against the rail
company. Surprisingly, the legal case becomes bigger than either one thought—
drawing national attention—and they embark on quite an odd adventure. Romantic
confusion erupts when a reporter falls for Jane and wants to marry her while
George keeps his love for her a secret. A cheerful comedy with a good message
about what can be accomplished when people pitch in together against great odds.

IT HAPPENS EVERY THURSDAY

BLACK & WHITE   1953

COMEDY/DRAMA

UNIVERSAL INT'L

LORETTA YOUNG	JOHN FORSYTHE	FRANK McHUGH
EDGAR BUCHANAN	PALMER LEE	HARVEY GRANT
JANE DARWELL	WILLARD WATERMAN	

Screenplay by: Dane Lussier
Adaptation by: Leonard Praskins and Barney Slater
Based on: The novel by Jane S. McIlvaine
Directed by: Joseph Pevney

Loretta Young and John Forsythe star as Jane and Bob MacAvoy, a young New York couple living in a crowded apartment with their young son and another baby on the way. Bob is a newspaper reporter who works nights, and he and Jane hardly see each other. One day, Jane reads a newspaper ad about a small-town newspaper in California that's for sale, and convinces Bob to pursue his dream of having his own paper—so they pack up and take off. Unfortunately, when they arrive at their destination they find that the newspaper is practically defunct, but there's no turning back now, and the people there seem nice enough. Together they work very hard and come up with some unusual and funny schemes to promote subscriptions, but can they make a go of it? A very amusing tale with a few serious moments and an important message about the value of a strong marriage partnership.

IT STARTED WITH EVE

BLACK & WHITE   1941

COMEDY/MUSICAL

UNIVERSAL

DEANNA DURBIN	CHARLES LAUGHTON	ROBERT CUMMINGS
GUY KIBBEE	MARGARET TALLICHET	CATHERINE DOUCET
WALTER CATLETT	CHARLES COLEMAN	

Screenplay by: Norman Krasna and Leo Townsend
Based on: A story by Hans Kraly
Directed by: Henry Koster

Jonathan Reynolds (Charles Laughton), a wealthy tycoon, is on his deathbed and his son Jonathan Jr. (Robert Cummings) is called home from Mexico. Jonathan Jr. brings along his fiancé and her mother, putting them up at a local hotel. The elder Reynolds, who could pass away at any moment, asks to meet his son's fiancé. Jonathan Jr. goes to the hotel to retrieve her, but she is not there. In desperation, he asks the hatcheck girl, Anne Terry (Deanna Durbin) to pose as his fiancé. She does him the favor, but his father makes an unexpected and miraculous recovery, and now mistakenly believes that Anne is really Jonathan's future wife. Light entertainment, with very funny acting by the whole cast and Deanna's pleasant singing.

 Academy Award Recognition: Charles Previn and Hans Salter nominated for Best Scoring of a Musical Picture.

IT'S A MAD, MAD, MAD, MAD WORLD
ULTRA PANAVISION & TECHNICOLOR   1963

COMEDY

UNITED ARTISTS

SPENCER TRACY	**MILTON BERLE**	**SID CAESAR**
BUDDY HACKETT	**ETHEL MERMAN**	**MICKEY ROONEY**
DICK SHAWN	**PHIL SILVERS**	**JONATHAN WINTERS**

Screenplay by: William and Tania Rose
Directed by: Stanley Kramer

Some passersby come to the aid of a crook (Jimmy Durante) who is fatally injured in a car accident. Before he dies, he tells the group about a huge sum of money he has hidden, and then they all set out on a wild goose chase in search of the cash. Spencer Tracy plays the police detective who's out to recover the criminal's loot. He plans to find it by following the crowd of treasure-seekers. There's an abundance of old-fashioned slapstick in this wacky comedy with an all-star cast.

 Academy Award Recognition: Ernest Gold nominated for Best Music Score (substantially original), nominated for Best Song: *It's a Mad, Mad, Mad, Mad World*, Music by Ernest Gold, Lyrics by Mack David.

IT'S A WONDERFUL LIFE

DRAMA/CHRISTMAS

BLACK & WHITE/COLORIZED   1946   RKO

JAMES STEWART	DONNA REED	LIONEL BARRYMORE	THOMAS MITCHELL
HENRY TRAVERS	BEULAH BONDI	FRANK FAYLEN	WARD BOND
GLORIA GRAHAME			

Screenplay by: Frances Goodrich, Albert Hackett, and Frank Capra;
                   additional scenes by Jo Swerling
Based on: A story by Philip Van Doren Stern
Directed by: Frank Capra

In the small town of Bedford Falls, George Bailey (James Stewart) works at a bank that fails and loses everything just before Christmas. He's depressed and he can't go home to face his wife and children, so he goes to a bar and has a few drinks—after which he decides to jump off a bridge to his death in an icy river. At the last moment, an angel named Clarence (Henry Travers) appears to save him. Clarence tries to convince George that his life is still valuable by looking back at his past and forward to what the world would be like without him for his wife Mary (Donna Reed), his children, and his good friends. This endearing and touching drama was not a box-office hit when it was originally released, but has now become a Christmas favorite.

Academy Award Recognition: nominated for Best Picture, Frank Capra nominated for Best Director, James Stewart nominated for Best Actor.

IT'S A WONDERFUL WORLD

COMEDY/MYSTERY-SUSPENSE

BLACK & WHITE   1939   MGM

CLAUDETTE COLBERT	JAMES STEWART	GUY KIBBEE
NAT PENDLETON	FRANCES DRAKE	EDGAR KENNEDY
ERNEST TRUEX		

Screenplay by: Ben Hecht
Based on: An original story by Ben Hecht and Herman J. Mankiewicz
Directed by: W.S. Van Dyke II

Guy Johnson (James Stewart) is a private investigator who's wrongly convicted of conspiracy when his client is framed for murder. Johnson escapes while being transported to prison, and when Edwina Corday (Claudette Colbert) witnesses his escape, he's forced to take her along. Edwina eventually comes to believe his story and decides to help him prove his innocence—so they're off on an exciting adventure. Her quick wit and enthusiasm turn out to be real assets. Good performances by the stars and a story that moves at a brisk pace make this a very enjoyable movie.

JET PILOT

TECHNICOLOR

DRAMA/ACTION-ADVENTURE/MILITARY

1957

RKO

JOHN WAYNE	**JANET LEIGH**	**JAY C. FLIPPEN**	**PAUL FIX**
RICHARD ROBER	**ROLAND WINTERS**	**HANS CONRIED**	**IVAN TRIESAULT**

Screenplay by: Jules Furthman
Directed by: Josef von Sternberg

John Wayne is Colonel Shannon, an American jet pilot, and Janet Leigh is Anna, a Russian jet pilot whose plane is forced down at Shannon's American air base in Alaska. The two fall in love, but the Cold War constantly threatens to come between them. International intrigue and romance mix together here to make a rather interesting story. This action movie is different than most of its time because Anna becomes the hero in the story, rather than the typical damsel in distress.

JOHNNY COME LATELY

BLACK & WHITE

1943

DRAMA

WARNER BROTHERS

JAMES CAGNEY	**GRACE GEORGE**	**MARJORIE MAIN**
MARJORIE LORD	**HATTIE McDANIEL**	**EDWARD McNAMARA**

Screenplay by: John Van Druten
Based on: The novel *McLeod's Folly* by Louis Bromfield
Directed by: William K. Howard

Vinnie McLeod (Grace George), an elderly lady, is the editor of an almost defunct small-town newspaper, "The Shield & Banner," having lost out to another newspaper company controlled by the corrupt W.W. Dougherty (played by Edward McNamara). James Cagney is Tom Richards, a former newspaper man passing through town who's arrested for vagrancy. Vinnie McLeod offers Richards a job with her newspaper to save him from going to jail. Vinnie has tried for a long time to bring Dougherty down by exposing his wrongdoing and is hopeful that Richards can help her—but he is reluctant to get involved at first. However, he takes a liking to her and decides to join forces with her to eliminate corruption from the town. What follows is a good old-fashioned story of good vs. evil and Cagney plays the hero with his usual flair.

 Academy Award Recognition: Leigh Harline nominated for Best Scoring of a Dramatic or Comedy Picture

JUNE BRIDE
BLACK & WHITE

1948

COMEDY/ROMANCE
WARNER BROTHERS

BETTE DAVIS	**ROBERT MONTGOMERY**	**FAY BAINTER**
BETTY LYNN	**TOM TULLY**	**BARBARA BATES**
JEROME COWAN	**MARY WICKES**	

Screenplay by:	Ranald MacDougall
Based on:	A play by Eileen Tighe and Graeme Lorimer
Directed by:	Bretaigne Windust

Robert Montgomery is Cary Jackson, a foreign correspondent who is let go and transferred to *Home Life* magazine for women, which is run by a tough editor, Linda Gilman (Bette Davis). Since the two had a romance three years earlier and he dumped her because he didn't want to be tied down, Linda isn't happy at all about the situation. They travel to Indiana to cover a small-town wedding for the June issue of the magazine, and become involved in some romantic complications leading up to the ceremony—in addition to re-thinking their own relationship. Incidentally, the "June" wedding actually takes place in winter, to be ready for the spring printing of the magazine. A humorous tale about the ins and outs of male-female relationships.

JUST FOR YOU

TECHNICOLOR   1952   **COMEDY/DRAMA/MUSICAL**

PARAMOUNT

BING CROSBY   JANE WYMAN   ETHEL BARRYMORE   NATALIE WOOD

Screenplay by: Robert Carson
Based on: *Famous* by Stephen Vincent Benet
Directed by: Elliot Nugent

The story is set in New York City. Bing Crosby is Jordan Blake, a famous Broadway producer, and Jane Wyman is Carolina Hill, the leading lady of his current show. He's a widower who's kept himself totally involved in his work and distant from his son and daughter. While romancing Carolina, he tries to repair his relationship with his children by focusing on becoming a better father. A good story and some nice tunes make this an entertaining movie.

 Academy Award Recognition: nominated for Best Song: *Zing a Little Zong*, Music by Harry Warren, Lyrics by Leo Robin.

KEY TO THE CITY

BLACK & WHITE   1950   **COMEDY/ROMANCE**

MGM

**CLARK GABLE   LORETTA YOUNG   FRANK MORGAN
MARILYN MAXWELL   RAYMOND BURR   JAMES GLEASON**

Screenplay by: Robert Riley Crutcher
Based on: A story by Albert Beich
Directed by: George Sidney

Clark Gable is Steve Fisk, and Loretta Young is Clarissa Standish, two mayors attending the Annual Mayors' convention in San Francisco. He's a tough-as-nails former longshoreman and she's a prim and proper Harvard graduate. At first, each is annoyed by the other, but then nature takes its course and they embark on a bumpy romance. A very endearing and funny love story.

KING SOLOMON'S MINES

TECHNICOLOR   1950

DRAMA/ACTION-ADVENTURE

MGM

DEBORAH KERR   **STEWART GRANGER**   **RICHARD CARLSON**
HUGO HAAS   **LOWELL GILMORE**

Screenplay by: Helen Deutsch
Based on: The novel by H. Rider Haggard
Directed by: Compton Bennett and Andrew Marton

The setting is Africa in 1897. Allan Quartermain (Stewart Granger), an English safari guide, is hired by Elizabeth Curtis (Deborah Kerr) to help her search for her missing husband, who was on a treasure hunt for a diamond mine in uncharted African wilderness. It's an almost impossible mission, but Quartermain agrees to take the job. The pair experience many perils and close calls on their dangerous quest, while a special relationship begins to develop between them as well. A superior adventure story with plenty of action and suspense.

 Academy Award Recognition: nominated for Best Picture.

KISS IN THE DARK, A

BLACK & WHITE   1949

COMEDY/ROMANCE

WARNER BROTHERS

DAVID NIVEN   **JANE WYMAN**   **VICTOR MOORE**
WAYNE MORRIS   **BRODERICK CRAWFORD**

Screenplay by: Harry Kurnitz
From: A story by Everett and Devery Freeman
Directed by: Delmer Daves

David Niven is Eric Phillips, a concert pianist who for years has been sheltered from the real world and controlled by his managers. Jane Wyman is Polly Haines, a pretty model who lives in the apartment building that has been purchased for him as an investment. Eric considers selling the building, but in the process grows attached to his tenants. He also falls in love with Polly, who teaches him how to have some fun and become a part of the outside world. A quiet and simple story made interesting by the talented stars.

KISS ME KATE

ANSCO COLOR & TECHNICOLOR   1953

MUSICAL
MGM

KATHRYN GRAYSON	HOWARD KEEL	ANN MILLER
KEENAN WYNN	BOBBY VAN	TOMMY RALL
JAMES WHITMORE	KURT KASZNAR	BOB FOSSE

Screenplay by: Dorothy Kingsley
Based on: The play by Samuel and Bella Spewack
Directed by: George Sidney

Music and Lyrics by Cole Porter

This is a show within a show—the story of the production (a musical version) of Shakespeare's *The Taming of the Shrew*. The action takes place both on-stage and behind-the-scenes. Actor/Director Fred Graham (Howard Keel) maneuvers to get his talented ex-wife Lilli Vanessi (Kathryn Grayson) to perform a role in the show, while his co-star, Lois Lane (Ann Miller) attempts to capture his attention. At the same time, Lois is working to straighten out her wayward boyfriend. Good music and dancing, and things get amusing when the real-life quarreling of the cast showed through in their on-stage performances.

 Academy Award Recognition: Andre Previn and Saul Chaplin nominated for Best Scoring of a Musical Picture.

KITTY FOYLE

BLACK & WHITE   1940

DRAMA/ROMANCE
RKO

GINGER ROGERS	DENNIS MORGAN	JAMES CRAIG

Screenplay by: Dalton Trumbo;
                   additional dialogue by Donald Ogden Stewart
Based on: A novel by Christopher Morley
Directed by: Sam Wood

Ginger Rogers stars as Kitty Foyle, a young working woman in New York who must decide between two life choices on a fateful night. One option is a marriage proposal from her current boyfriend Mark (James Craig), a doctor, and the other is an offer to run away with her longtime love, Wyn Strafford (Dennis Morgan), a wealthy but already married Philadelphian. Mark is the steady man who could provide a pleasant but simple life, and Wyn offers the more passionate love, but at a price that Kitty may not be willing to pay. The plot unfolds as a retrospective on Kitty's life leading up to the present moment. This is an excellent drama that displays Ginger Rogers' talent as a dramatic actress, and there is a great deal of suspense leading up to the ending—Kitty's decision isn't revealed until the last line of the film.

 Academy Award Recognition: Ginger Rogers won Best Actress, nominated for Best Picture, Dalton Trumbo nominated for Best Screenplay, Sam Wood nominated for Best Director.

KNUTE ROCKNE - ALL AMERICAN
BLACK & WHITE/COLORIZED   1940

DRAMA

WARNER BROTHERS

| PAT O'BRIEN | RONALD REAGAN | GALE PAGE | DONALD CRISP |

Screenplay by: Robert Buckner
Directed by: Lloyd Bacon

This is the true life story of Notre Dame football coach Knute Rockne. His family emigrated from Norway to Chicago, and Rockne played football as a child. He grew up and worked for the post office before attending college at Notre Dame. Though he played football there, he was also a very bright student of chemistry. He made history by being the first man to receive a forward pass in a football game, and stayed on at Notre Dame after graduation to teach chemistry. He later focused on coaching football, which made both Rockne and his star player, George Gipp (Ronald Reagan) famous. Gipp was the one who uttered the now-legendary phrase "Win one for the Gipper." Knute Rockne revolutionized the game of football by instituting new kinds of plays and setting a standard for great coaching. An excellent portrayal of a man who inspired many.

LADY FROM CHEYENNE, THE

BLACK & WHITE   1941

DRAMA/WESTERN

UNIVERSAL

| LORETTA YOUNG | ROBERT PRESTON | EDWARD ARNOLD | FRANK CRAVEN |
| GLADYS GEORGE | JESSIE RALPH | STANLEY FIELDS | WILLIE BEST |

Screenplay by: Warren Duff and Kathryn Scola
Based on: An original story by Jonathan Finn and Theresa Oaks
Directed by: Frank Lloyd

The story begins at a land auction in Wyoming in the 1860s where a young woman, Annie Morgan (Loretta Young), buys a valuable piece of riverfront land, spoiling plans for a land grab and control of the local water supply by the crooked Jim Cork (Edward Arnold) and his accomplice, Steve Lewis (Robert Preston). At first, Cork has Steve befriend Annie and offer her a large sum of money for the land, but when she flatly refuses, Cork decides to get rough with her. One thing leads to another, and finally the only way to destroy Jim Cork's power is for the town's women to obtain the right to vote. Annie heads for the state legislature in Cheyenne and finds herself faced with an impossible task—until she gets help from the legislature's attending servant, George (Willie Best), who knows the political ropes. An unusual and quaint Western tale of good vs. evil, with a happy ending.

LASSIE COME HOME

TECHNICOLOR   1943

DRAMA/ANIMAL STORIES

MGM

RODDY McDOWALL	DONALD CRISP	DAME MAY WITTY
EDMUND GWENN	NIGEL BRUCE	ELSA LANCHESTER
ELIZABETH TAYLOR	LASSIE	

Screenplay by: Hugo Butler
Based on: The novel by Eric Knight
Directed by: Fred M. Wilcox

The story takes place in Yorkshire, England during desperate economic times. Sam Carraclough (Donald Crisp) owns a prized collie named Lassie, and she is the only valuable possession he has left. The dog is especially attached to his son Joe (Roddy McDowall), but Sam is forced to sell her to a wealthy Duke in order to keep the family going. Missing Joe terribly, Lassie keeps escaping from her new kennel and returning home. When the Duke takes Lassie to Scotland, his granddaughter, Priscilla (Elizabeth Taylor), allows her to escape and the rest of the movie follows Lassie's trek from Scotland all the way home to England. A very sentimental and touching tale of the love between a child and a dog.

LAST HURRAH, THE
BLACK & WHITE   1958

DRAMA
COLUMBIA

SPENCER TRACY	**JEFFREY HUNTER**	**DIANNE FOSTER**
PAT O'BRIEN	**BASIL RATHBONE**	**DONALD CRISP**
JAMES GLEASON	**EDWARD BROPHY**	**JOHN CARRADINE**

Screenplay by: Frank Nugent
Based on: The novel by Edwin O'Connor
Directed by: John Ford

In this film, Spencer Tracy is superb in his portrayal of Frank Skeffington, an aging politician running his last re-election campaign for office in a New England city. His son is a playboy and of no help to him, but his nephew Adam Caulfield (played by Jeffrey Hunter) lends him personal support even though he works for a newspaper run by Skeffington's political rivals. Although he has been in office for a long time and has many old political allies, the tide is turning against him and the campaign is a tough one. This look into the sometimes darker side of politics is well acted, with a good supporting cast, although it does have a somber ending.

LAURA
BLACK & WHITE   1944

DRAMA/MYSTERY-SUSPENSE
20TH CENTURY FOX

GENE TIERNEY	**DANA ANDREWS**	**CLIFTON WEBB**
VINCENT PRICE	**JUDITH ANDERSON**	

Screenplay by: Jay Dratler, Samuel Hoffenstein, and Betty Reinhardt
Based on: The novel by Vera Caspary
Directed by: Otto Preminger

The murder of Laura Hunt (Gene Tierney), a young career woman, is being investigated. Thanks to the striking portrait hanging on the wall of her apartment,

Mark McPherson (Dana Andrews), a young hard-boiled homicide detective, finds himself falling in love with her during the course of his work. There are three prime suspects for McPherson to consider—a newspaper writer named Waldo Lydecker (Clifton Webb), Laura's fiancé, Shelby Carpenter (Vincent Price), and Laura's aunt, Anne Treadwell (Judith Anderson). An excellent, sophisticated murder mystery with great acting by everyone in the cast.

 Academy Award Recognition: Clifton Webb nominated for Best Supporting Actor, Otto Preminger nominated for Best Director; Jay Dratler, Samuel Hoffenstein and Betty Reinhardt nominated for Best Screenplay.

LET'S MAKE IT LEGAL
BLACK & WHITE   1951

COMEDY
20TH CENTURY FOX

CLAUDETTE COLBERT	**MacDONALD CAREY**	**ZACHARY SCOTT**	**BARBARA BATES**
ROBERT WAGNER	**MARILYN MONROE**	**FRANK CADY**	

Screenplay by: F. Hugh Herbert and I.A.L. Diamond
Based on: A story by Mortimer Braus
Directed by: Richard Sale

Claudette Colbert and MacDonald Carey are Miriam and Hugh Hallsworth, a middle-aged suburban couple who are getting divorced after 20 years of marriage. Their household also includes their daughter Barbara (Barbara Bates), son-in-law Jerry (Robert Wagner), and baby granddaughter. Jerry feels that Barbara is too spoiled by Miriam, and wants them to get their own place, but Barbara does not want to leave her mother in crisis. On the last day before their divorce becomes final, Miriam's old boyfriend Victor MacFarland (Zachary Scott) returns—he just happens to be a millionaire and the most eligible bachelor in the country. As Victor resumes courting Miriam, the family members root for different outcomes. Hugh and Barbara hope that Miriam will dump Victor, and Jerry looks forward to Victor marrying Miriam so that he and Barbara can get their own home. A winning and genial family comedy with a happy ending.

LETTER TO THREE WIVES, A

BLACK & WHITE   1949

DRAMA/ROMANCE
20TH CENTURY FOX

| JEANNE CRAIN | LINDA DARNELL | ANN SOTHERN | KIRK DOUGLAS |
| PAUL DOUGLAS | BARBARA LAWRENCE | JEFFREY LYNN | |

Screenplay by:	Joseph L. Mankiewicz
Adapted by:	Vera Caspary
From:	A *Cosmopolitan Magazine* novel by John Klempner
Directed by:	Joseph L. Mankiewicz

Just before departing for a day-long boat trip, three married suburban women, Debby Bishop (Jeanne Crain), Lora Mae Hollingsway (Linda Darnell) and Rita Phipps (Ann Sothern) receive a letter. The letter is from another woman in town, informing them that she has run off with one of their husbands, but without identifying which one. Leading up to a surprise ending are retrospectives on each couple's relationship, as each of the three wives ponders what could have gone wrong and if her husband is the one who left. The male co-stars who play the three husbands are: Kirk Douglas as George Phipps, Paul Douglas as Porter Hollingsway, and Jeffrey Lynn as Brad Bishop. An excellent cast does a great job in presenting a very interesting and rather suspenseful story.

 Academy Award Recognition: Joseph L. Mankiewicz won for Best Director and Best Screenplay, nominated for Best Picture.

LIBELED LADY

BLACK & WHITE   1936

COMEDY/ROMANCE
MGM

| JEAN HARLOW | WILLIAM POWELL | MYRNA LOY |
| SPENCER TRACY | WALTER CONNOLLY | |

Screenplay by:	Maurine Watkins, Howard Emmett Rogers, and George Oppenheimer
From:	The story by Wallace Sullivan
Directed by:	Jack Conway

Spencer Tracy is Warren Haggerty, a newspaper executive whose paper runs a false story about Connie Allenbury (Myrna Loy), an heiress who subsequently sues the paper for libel to the tune of five million dollars. This fiasco interrupts Haggerty's wedding plans with fiancé Gladys Benton (Jean Harlow), and he hires Bill Chandler (William Powell), a former newspaper employee and a smooth operator, to get Connie Allenbury to drop her lawsuit. The plan is to recreate the circumstances of the article and turn it into the truth, thus negating the lawsuit. Then Bill and Connie fall in love, complicating the whole plot. First-class entertainment—a great story with an all-star cast.

 Academy Award Recognition: nominated for Best Picture.

LIFE BEGINS FOR ANDY HARDY

BLACK & WHITE   1941

COMEDY/DRAMA

MGM

| LEWIS STONE | MICKEY ROONEY | FAY HOLDEN | ANN RUTHERFORD |
| SARA HADEN | PATRICIA DANE | RAY McDONALD | JUDY GARLAND |

Screenplay by: Agnes Christine Johnston
Based on: The characters created by Aurania Rouverol
Directed by: George B. Seitz

Of the **Andy Hardy** series of movies, this may be the one with the most serious, but educational, story lines. Rather than going straight to college, Andy Hardy (Mickey Rooney) first heads to New York to experience life on his own, outside of his small town—much to the objection of his parents. Once there, Andy has many trials and tribulations, finding that the world is a much tougher and more complex place than he thought. Luckily, his friend Betsy Booth (played by Judy Garland) lives in New York, and she tries to look out for him. A very interesting, well-acted story that teaches some valuable lessons.

LIFE WITH FATHER

TECHNICOLOR   1947

COMEDY/DRAMA

WARNER BROTHERS

| WILLIAM POWELL | IRENE DUNNE | ELIZABETH TAYLOR | MARTIN MILNER |
| EDMUND GWENN | ZASU PITTS | JIMMY LYDON | MORONI OLSEN |

Screenplay by: Donald Ogden Stewart
Based on: The play by Howard Lindsay and Russell Crouse,
      and a book by Clarence Day, Jr.
Directed by: Michael Curtiz

Set in New York City during the 1880s, this is the account of a particular family, based on a book by one of the sons. William Powell portrays Clarence Day, a brusque Victorian man who presides over an entire household of redheaded children, and whose wife Vinnie (Irene Dunne) is a sweet woman who knows how to work around him. The story is a fairly simple one, chronicling various events in the family's everyday life, but the charm of the characters is what makes this movie come alive. Excellent, family-style entertainment.

 Academy Award Recognition: William Powell nominated for Best Actor, Max Steiner nominated for Best Musical Scoring of a Dramatic or Comedy Picture.

LILIES OF THE FIELD
BLACK & WHITE   1963

DRAMA/COMEDY
UNITED ARTISTS

SIDNEY POITIER   LILIA SKALA

Screenplay by: James Poe
Based on: A novel by William E. Barrett
Directed by: Ralph Nelson

Sidney Poitier stars as Homer Smith, a traveling handyman who stops at a convent of German nuns when he requires water for his car's radiator. He takes care of some minor repairs for the nuns, unaware that their leader, Mother Maria (played by Lilia Skala) has bigger plans for him. She has prayed for God to send her a strong man to build the chapel that the community needs and would be so dear to them, since they had to flee their own country. An exceptionally heartwarming and inspiring story.

 Academy Award Recognition: Sidney Poitier won Best Actor, nominated for Best Picture, Lilia Skala nominated for Best Supporting Actress, James Poe nominated for Best Screenplay (based on material from another medium).

LISTEN, DARLING

BLACK & WHITE   1938   **COMEDY/MUSICAL**

                                                               MGM

JUDY GARLAND	FREDDIE BARTHOLOMEW	MARY ASTOR
WALTER PIDGEON	ALAN HALE	SCOTTY BECKETT

Screenplay by: Elaine Ryan and Anne Morrison Chapin
From: The story by Katherine Brush
Directed by: Edwin L. Marin

Judy Garland is Pinkie, the daughter of Dottie Wingate (Mary Astor), a young widow in financial trouble who feels her only choice is to marry the town banker, a well-fixed older man who is fond of her. Pinkie is upset and unhappy that her mother should marry someone she doesn't really love, just for the sake of her little brother Billy (Scotty Beckett) and herself. With the help of friend Buzz Mitchell (Freddie Bartholomew), Pinkie finds Richard Thurlow (Walter Pidgeon), a bachelor who has a lot in common with Dottie. The kids then go to work to get Dottie and Richard together as a couple. A sweet and enjoyable movie with some nice songs.

LITTLE NELLIE KELLY

BLACK & WHITE   1940   **COMEDY/DRAMA/MUSICAL**

                                                                        MGM

JUDY GARLAND	GEORGE MURPHY	CHARLES WINNINGER

Screenplay by: Jack McGowan
Based on: The musical comedy written, composed and
                         produced by George M. Cohan
Directed by: Norman Taurog

In this movie, Judy Garland plays two roles—a mother and her daughter. Jerry and Nellie Kelly (George Murphy and Judy Garland) are an Irish couple who come to New York with Nellie's father, Michael Noonan (Charles Winninger), to fashion a new life for themselves. Sadly, Nellie dies while giving birth to their daughter, who is then named after her. Raised by her father and grandfather (a traditional, crusty old Irishman), Little Nellie grows up well. But when they disapprove of the young man she loves, it's up to Little Nellie to work things out so that she can be with him. A good story that combines both humor and drama, with a few nice tunes.

LITTLE MISS BROADWAY

BLACK & WHITE   1938

MUSICAL/COMEDY

20TH CENTURY FOX

SHIRLEY TEMPLE	**GEORGE MURPHY**	**JIMMY DURANTE**
PHYLLIS BROOKS	**EDNA MAE OLIVER**	**DONALD MEEK**

Screenplay by: Harry Tugend and Jack Yellen
Directed by: Irving Cummings

Shirley Temple is Betsy, a cute little orphan girl who is adopted by the operators of a residential hotel in New York City. She grows to love her new family and the motley crew of show biz people who live there. When the hotel's existence is threatened by a cranky old landlord, Betsy helps fight to save it. Naturally, Betsy brings cheer to all along the way, with music, dancing and some laughs.

LITTLE PRINCESS, THE

TECHNICOLOR   1939

DRAMA

20TH CENTURY FOX

SHIRLEY TEMPLE	**RICHARD GREENE**	**ANITA LOUISE**
CESAR ROMERO	**ARTHUR TREACHER**	**IAN HUNTER**
MARY NASH		

Screenplay by: Ethel Hill and Walter Ferris
Based on: The novel by Frances Hodgson Burnett
Directed by: Walter Lang

The setting is England in 1899, during the Boer War. Shirley Temple stars as young Sara Crewe, whose widowed father, Captain Crewe (Ian Hunter), goes off to war, leaving her in a girls' boarding school. Miss Minchin, a mean-spirited grouch, runs the school, but since Sara's father is a very wealthy owner of diamond mines, Sara is given special attention. Despite this, Sara is a very unspoiled, kind girl and is liked by all of the teachers. When her father is reported to have died in battle, Sara's life is changed in an instant, as Miss Minchin begins to treat her terribly, like a pauper. But through it all, the indomitable Sara keeps believing that her father is still alive and is determined to find him somehow. A well-done film version of a classic children's story that has a happy ending.

LITTLE WOMEN

TECHNICOLOR   1949

DRAMA

MGM

JUNE ALLYSON	**PETER LAWFORD**	**MARGARET O'BRIEN**
ELIZABETH TAYLOR	**JANET LEIGH**	**ROSSANO BRAZZI**
MARY ASTOR	**LUCILE WATSON**	**SIR C. AUBREY SMITH**
ELIZABETH PATTERSON	**LEON AMES**	**HARRY DAVENPORT**
RICHARD STAPLEY	**CONNIE GILCHRIST**	**ELLEN CORBY**

Screenplay by: Andrew Solt, Sarah Y. Mason and Victor Herman
From: The novel by Louisa May Alcott
Directed by: Mervyn LeRoy

This is the classic tale of the March family (consisting of four daughters) of Concord, Massachusetts during the Civil War Era. It tells of how the young women's lives change as they grow to adulthood. The story centers around Jo (June Allyson), the tomboy of the family. Peter Lawford plays Laurie, the young man who lives across the street and is in love with Jo. She loves him also, but can't marry him because they're too different. So Jo goes to New York as a governess and takes a chance on finding love and understanding with the older Professor Bhaer (Rossano Brazzi). In addition, plenty of things happen to the rest of the family: Beth (Margaret O'Brien), Amy (Elizabeth Taylor) , Meg (Janet Leigh), and their mother (played by Mary Astor). A good film version of the classic novel, providing family-style entertainment.

LONE STAR

BLACK & WHITE   1952

DRAMA/WESTERN

MGM

CLARK GABLE	**AVA GARDNER**	**BRODERICK CRAWFORD**
LIONEL BARRYMORE	**BEULAH BONDI**	**ED BEGLEY**

Screenplay by: Borden Chase
From: The magazine story by Borden Chase
Based on: The screen story by Howard Estabrook
Directed by: Vincent Sherman

In 1845, Texas was an independent nation awaiting annexation to the United States. People in both the U.S. and Texas were divided in opinion—some for annexation, and some against. This story begins in Nashville, Tennessee, the home of U.S. President Andrew Jackson (Lionel Barrymore), who is in favor of annexation for patriotic reasons. Devereaux Burke (Clark Gable) is in favor of annexation for business reasons, but on behalf of President Jackson, sets out for Austin, Texas to enlist Sam Houston's help. To get there, Burke has to cross many miles of dangerous country. While in Austin, Burke meets Martha Ronda (Ava Gardner), who's opposed to Texas joining the U.S., because of the civil unrest and violence that could possibly follow. The rest of the story unfolds from there, as all try to achieve their objectives. The result is an interesting drama, with a good mix of political conflict and Western action.

LONG GRAY LINE, THE

CINEMASCOPE & TECHNICOLOR   1955

DRAMA/MILITARY
COLUMBIA PICTURES

TYRONE POWER	**MAUREEN O'HARA**	**ROBERT FRANCIS**	**DONALD CRISP**
WARD BOND	**BETSY PALMER**	**PHIL CAREY**	**HARRY CAREY, JR.**
PATRICK WAYNE	**PETER GRAVES**		

Screenplay by: Edward Hope
Based on: ***Bringing Up the Brass*** by Marty Maher
                   and Nardi Reeder Campion
Directed by: John Ford

This is the true story of Marty Maher (Tyrone Power) who served at the West Point Military Academy for 50 years. He came to the U.S. as an Irish immigrant, and began at West Point as a waiter in the dining room. Maher later enlisted in the Army and eventually became an instructor, helping to train the Cadets. Along the way, he wed Mary O'Donnell (Maureen O'Hara), the housekeeper of his command-ing officer. This excellent and educational drama depicts both Maher's personal life and his career, including his close friendships with the many Cadets he taught over the years and the hardships of two World Wars.

LONG, LONG TRAILER, THE

COMEDY

ANSCO COLOR & TECHNICOLOR   1954   MGM

LUCILLE BALL	**DESI ARNAZ**	**MARJORIE MAIN**	**KEENAN WYNN**
GLADYS HURLBUT	**MORONI OLSEN**	**BERT FREED**	

Screenplay by: Albert Hackett and Frances Goodrich
Based on: The novel by Clinton Twiss
Directed by: Vincente Minnelli

Lucy and Desi play newlyweds, Tracy and Nicky Collini. Because Nicky's job requires that he travel a great deal, Tracy comes up with the idea that they should buy a trailer so that she can go along and make a real home for Nicky, no matter where he works. When they first embark on their adventure, the inexperienced pair know nothing about trailer life, but they spend plenty of time learning the hard way. A very funny movie with some hilarious scenes done only as Lucy and Desi could do them.

LONGEST DAY, THE

DRAMA/MILITARY

BLACK & WHITE   1962   20TH CENTURY FOX

JOHN WAYNE	**HENRY FONDA**	**ROBERT RYAN**
RED BUTTONS	**RICHARD BURTON**	**RICHARD TODD**
MEL FERRER	**ROBERT MITCHUM**	

Screenplay by: Andrew Marton, Bernhard Wicki, and Ken Annakin
Based on: The book by Cornelius Ryan
Directed by: Andrew Marton, Bernhard Wicki and Ken Annakin

This movie employs a large, all-star cast to depict the story of D-Day, the Allied invasion of Normandy, France on June 6, 1944. It is done on a grand scale, and chronicles the events of the entire day, on the various battle fronts and behind the enemy lines, where paratroopers were dropped. Great pains were taken by the production staff to make the portrayal as authentic as possible. Cornelius Ryan interviewed D-Day survivors for his book, on which this movie is based. A very impressive and educational war movie with great, realistic photography that makes for a fine viewing experience.

 Academy Award Recognition: nominated for Best Picture.

LOUISA

BLACK & WHITE   1950

COMEDY

UNIVERSAL INT'L

RONALD REAGAN	CHARLES COBURN	RUTH HUSSEY
EDMUND GWENN	SPRING BYINGTON	PIPER LAURIE
SCOTTY BECKETT	JIMMY HUNT	CONNIE GILCHREST

Story and Screenplay: Stanley Roberts
Directed by: Alexander Hall

Hal Norton (Ronald Reagan) is a hard-working engineer who's raising a family and has a nice, quiet suburban life. One day his wife Meg (Ruth Hussey) informs him that his widowed mother Louisa (Spring Byington), who recently moved in with them, is interfering too much in the running of their household. Hal suggests to his mother that she find some social activities of her own to occupy her time. Little does he know what he has suggested—Louisa begins dating again. When the town grocer (Edmund Gwenn) and Hal's boss (Charles Coburn) do battle for Louisa's hand in marriage, the entire family is thrown into chaos. An amusing and sweet family story with a happy ending.

LOVE BUG, THE

TECHNICOLOR   1969

COMEDY

WALT DISNEY

| DEAN JONES | MICHELE LEE | BUDDY HACKETT | DAVID TOMLINSON |

Screenplay by: Don DaGradi and Bill Walsh
Based on: A story by Gordon Buford
Directed by: Robert Stevenson

Jim Douglas (played by Dean Jones) is a race car driver who's experiencing a losing streak. One day, he visits an auto showroom to check out a new car, and a pretty saleswoman named Carole (Michele Lee). Jim defends an aging Volkswagen beetle that's being treated like a reject by Mr. Thorndyke (David Tomlinson), the dealership's unscrupulous owner. The spunky little car, which has a mind of its own, takes a liking to Jim and follows him home. Jim discovers that the car is lightning fast, and decides to race it. His buddy Tennessee Steinmetz (Buddy Hackett) names the car Herbie. However, when Jim starts to win races with the tiny Volkswagen, greedy Thorndyke decides that he wants Herbie back. Eventually, Jim ends up competing against Thorndyke in the El Dorado Road Race, and the winner will get ownership of Herbie. Luckily, Carole and Tennessee are there to help Jim and Herbie every step of the way. An appealing and delightful family-style comedy.

LOVE CRAZY
BLACK & WHITE   1941   COMEDY/ROMANCE
                                                         MGM

WILLIAM POWELL	**MYRNA LOY**	**GAIL PATRICK**
JACK CARSON	**FLORENCE BATES**	**SIDNEY BLACKMER**

Screenplay by: William Ludwig, Charles Lederer, and David Hertz
Original story by: David Hertz and William Ludwig
Directed by: Jack Conway

William Powell and Myrna Loy are Steven and Susan Ireland, a very happily married couple who are so in love that they always go all out to celebrate their anniversaries. But then Isobel (Gail Patrick), an aggressive old flame of Steven's, moves into their apartment building and causes enough trouble to prompt Susan to ask for a divorce. The only way Steven can stop the divorce is to be declared insane—so he stops at nothing to convince the world that he's nuts, in order to buy enough time to win Susan back. A fast-paced and zany comedy, with the Powell–Loy team in fine form.

LOVE FINDS ANDY HARDY
BLACK & WHITE   1938   COMEDY
                                                         MGM

MICKEY ROONEY	**LEWIS STONE**	**FAY HOLDEN**	**CECILIA PARKER**
JUDY GARLAND	**LANA TURNER**	**ANN RUTHERFORD**	

Screenplay by: William Ludwig
From: The stories by Vivien R. Bretherton; based upon
                 the characters created by Aurania Rouverol
Directed by: George B. Seitz

In this entry of the **Andy Hardy** series, Andy (Mickey Rooney) has problems with his love life. His girlfriend, Polly, cancels their date for the Christmas Eve country club dance because her family is leaving town for the holidays. But there's a possible substitution, the lovely Cynthia, whom Andy is supposed to keep occupied while her boyfriend (and Andy's best buddy) is away. Meanwhile, the neighbor's visiting granddaughter, Betsy (played by Judy Garland), has a tremendous crush on Andy, but can't seem to capture his attention. In addition, Andy's trying to save enough money for a car to drive on the big night. A quaint and funny story of teenage romance in the old days.

LT. ROBINSON CRUSOE U.S.N.
TECHNICOLOR   1966

COMEDY
WALT DISNEY

DICK VAN DYKE   NANCY KWAN   AKIM TAMIROFF

Screenplay by: Bill Walsh and Dan DaGradi
Based on: A story by Retlaw Yensid
Directed by: Byron Paul

Dick Van Dyke stars as Lt. Robinson Crusoe, a navy pilot whose plane catches fire
and goes down in the Pacific during a routine mission. He drifts ashore on an island,
and discovers a chimp lost by the U.S. space program. Crusoe lives off the land,
doing the best he can to set up housekeeping while enjoying the companionship of
the chimp. His peaceful existence is shattered when a native girl (Nancy Kwan) is
exiled to his island by her father (Akim Tamiroff), the tribal chief, for not going
through with an arranged marriage. Crusoe must then come up with a plan, not
only to help the native girl, but also to save himself from the angry chief who will
someday return to the island. A pleasant comedy with an unusual story line.

LUCY GALLANT
VISTAVISION & TECHNICOLOR   1955

DRAMA
PARAMOUNT

JANE WYMAN   CHARLTON HESTON   CLAIRE TREVOR
THELMA RITTER   WILLIAM DEMAREST   EDITH HEAD

Screenplay by: John Lee Mahin and Winston Miller
From: The novel *The Life of Lucy Gallant* by Margaret Cousins
Directed by: Robert Parrish

Jane Wyman is Lucy Gallant, a woman whose life changes when the train she's riding
becomes stranded in an oil boom town in 1941 Texas. She decides to stay there
and opens a clothing store that caters to the wealthy women who are benefiting
from the oil boom. Lucy's store becomes a big success, selling fine quality merchandise that the townspeople once could only buy in far away places like New York.
Charlton Heston plays Casey Cole, a rancher who looked after Lucy when she first
arrived in town, and is now in love with her. Casey wants to marry Lucy, but insists
that she give up her business career first. She is then forced to decide whether to
maintain her financial independence and stay single, or to get married and become a
homemaker. A very colorful and interesting drama, even though these days very
few women face this kind of decision.

MADAME CURIE

BLACK & WHITE   1943

DRAMA

MGM

GREER GARSON	WALTER PIDGEON	HENRY TRAVERS
ROBERT WALKER	C. AUBREY SMITH	DAME MAY WHITTY
REGINALD OWEN	VAN JOHNSON	MARGARET O'BRIEN

Screenplay by: Paul Osborn and Paul H. Rameau
Based on: The book *Madame Curie* by Eve Curie
Directed by: Mervyn LeRoy

This is a biography of renowned scientist Madame Marie Curie with Greer Garson in the title role. At the Sorbonne University in France, Marie Sklodowska, a native of Poland, studied Physics and Mathematics. There, she met Pierre Curie (Walter Pidgeon), a man dedicated to science with little interest in women—but Marie fascinated him. The story focuses on their work together and their discovery of radium, as well as their marriage and devotion to each other. A superb drama that helps us appreciate the tremendous effort involved in the Curies' discovery.

Academy Award Recognition: nominated for Best Picture, Walter Pidgeon nominated for Best Actor, Greer Garson nominated for Best Actress, Herbert Stothart nominated for Best Musical Scoring of a Dramatic or Comedy Picture.

MAGIC TOWN

BLACK & WHITE/COLORIZED   1947

COMEDY/DRAMA

RKO

| JAMES STEWART | JANE WYMAN | KENT SMITH | NED SPARKS |
| WALLACE FORD | REGIS TOOMEY | ANN DORAN | DONALD MEEK |

Screenplay by: Robert Riskin
Based on: A story by Robert Riskin and Joseph Krumgold
Directed by: William A. Wellman

Lawrence "Rip" Smith (James Stewart) is a pollster searching for a mathematical miracle—a shortcut method of gauging public opinion without having to interview thousands of people. He finds a small town, Grandview, whose population's make-up and opinions exactly mirror that of the U.S. as a whole. Smith works there tallying opinions while posing as an insurance salesman and falls in love with Mary Peterman (Jane Wyman). She is the editor of the town paper and a proponent of a plan to modernize the town. Their separate agendas complicate their courtship. A rather enjoyable movie with an unusual story to tell.

MAGNIFICENT OBSESSION

TECHNICOLOR   1954   **DRAMA/ROMANCE**

UNIVERSAL INT'L

JANE WYMAN	ROCK HUDSON	AGNES MOOREHEAD	BARBARA RUSH

Screenplay by: Robert Blees
Based on: The novel by Lloyd C. Douglas,
       and a screenplay by Sarah Y. Mason and Victor Heerman,
       as adapted by Wells Root
Directed by: Douglas Sirk

Rock Hudson is Bob Merrick, a reckless millionaire playboy and medical school dropout who's injured in a boating accident. Jane Wyman is Helen Phillips, the wife of a prominent doctor who dies of a heart attack while emergency equipment is being used to save Merrick. Helen and Bob meet later on and are attracted to each other, but her husband's death still stands between them. When she's blinded in an accident, he's inspired to return to medicine in order to cure her. A colorful and classy soap opera with a great cast.

 Academy Award Recognition: Jane Wyman nominated for Best Actress.

MAIL ORDER BRIDE

PANAVISION & METROCOLOR   1964   **COMEDY/DRAMA/WESTERN**

MGM

BUDDY EBSEN	KEIR DULLEA	LOIS NETTLETON	WARREN OATES

Screenplay by: Burt Kennedy
Based on: A short story by Van Cort
Directed by: Burt Kennedy

According to a friend's last will and testament, drifter Will Lane (Buddy Ebsen) is put in charge of a ranch until the deceased man's wild and carousing son, Lee Carey (Keir Dullea) is fit to run it. Lane is eager to move on, and decides that taking a wife would be just the thing to settle Lee down. So Lane orders one through a mail order catalog—Annie Boley (played by Lois Nettleton). The story continues from there, as Lane oversees the relationship that evolves between the newly married strangers, and Lee finally grows up. An enjoyable and unusual Western.

MALTESE FALCON, THE

BLACK & WHITE   1941

DRAMA/MYSTERY-SUSPENSE

WARNER BROTHERS

HUMPHREY BOGART	**MARY ASTOR**	**GLADYS GEORGE**	**PETER LORRE**
BARTON MacLANE	**LEE PATRICK**	**SYDNEY GREENSTREET**	**WARD BOND**

Screenplay by: Jerome Cowan
Based on: The novel by Dashiell Hammett
Directed by: John Huston

Humphrey Bogart stars as San Francisco private eye, Sam Spade. A young woman, Brigid O'Shaughnessy (Mary Astor) enlists his help in locating her missing sister. When Sam's partner and the missing woman's supposed boyfriend are both murdered, Sam finds himself plunged into a riddle involving a coveted artifact—the Maltese Falcon. A superior mystery movie with lots of intrigue and suspense.

Academy Award Recognition: nominated for Best Picture, Sydney Greenstreet nominated for Best Supporting Actor, John Huston nominated for Best Screenplay.

MAN FROM LARAMIE, THE

COLOR   1955

DRAMA/WESTERN

COLUMBIA

JAMES STEWART	**ARTHUR KENNEDY**	**DONALD CRISP**	**CATHY O'DONNELL**
ALINE McMAHON	**WALLACE FORD**	**ALEX NICOL**	

Screenplay by: Philip Yordan and Frank Burt
Based on: A *Saturday Evening Post* story by Thomas T. Flynn
Directed by: Arthur Mann

James Stewart stars as Will Lockhart, who has traveled from his hometown of Laramie, Wyoming to Coronado, New Mexico. He is undercover, posing as a freight transporter in order to track down the party who sold rifles to the Apache Indians, who in turn used the guns to ambush his brother's cavalry unit. While carrying out his mission, Lockhart gets into plenty of trouble with Alec Waggoman (Donald Crisp), the tyrannical rancher who controls the territory—and suddenly finds himself involved in a fierce battle for turf. A well-acted, very edgy Western that's more suitable for teenagers and adults than younger children.

MAN WHO CAME TO DINNER, THE

COMEDY

BLACK & WHITE   1941   WARNER BROTHERS

BETTE DAVIS   **ANN SHERIDAN**   **MONTY WOOLEY**
RICHARD TRAVIS   **JIMMY DURANTE**   **BILLIE BURKE**
REGINALD GARDINER   **ELISABETH FRASER**   **GRANT MITCHELL**
GEORGE BARBIER   **RUSSELL ARMS**   **MARY WICKES**

Screenplay by: Julius J. and Philip G. Epstein
From: The stage play by George S. Kaufman and Moss Hart
Directed by: William Keighley

The Stanleys (Grant Mitchell, Billie Burke), a well-to-do Midwestern couple, invite
famous author and radio host Sheridan Whiteside (Monty Wooley) to dinner at their
home. Whiteside is accompanied by his faithful and efficient assistant Maggie Cutler
(Bette Davis). But when Whiteside slips and falls on the Stanleys' icy front steps, his
short visit becomes a long stay. While he recuperates, the obnoxious tyrant takes
over their home, entertaining a string of unusual guests and turning the family's life
upside down. Meanwhile, Maggie finds the love of her life, but Whiteside brings in
an actress friend (Ann Sheridan) to try and break them up. This movie version of
the popular stage play maintains somewhat of a stage-like atmosphere. The nimble
dialogue moves at a quick pace, with great performances by the entire cast.

MAN WHO KNEW TOO MUCH, THE

DRAMA/MYSTERY-SUSPENSE

TECHNICOLOR   1956   UNIVERSAL

JAMES STEWART   **DORIS DAY**

Screenplay by: John Michael Hayes
Based on: A story by Charles Bennett and D.B. Wyndham Lewis
Directed by: Alfred Hitchcock

Dr. Ben McKenna (James Stewart) and his actress/singer wife Jo (Doris Day) are
visiting Morocco, with their young son in tow. They meet a mysterious Frenchman
who is soon murdered, having spoken his last words to Dr. McKenna, passing along
information about the planned assassination of a London statesman. The McKennas
then become the target of anonymous threats, and their son is kidnaped. In order
to save their son's life, the couple must search for the boy on their own without

spilling the beans to authorities. In the height of Hitchcock style, this movie is loaded with suspense and has an edge-of-your-seat ending.

 Academy Award Recognition: won Best Song: *Whatever Will Be, Will Be (Que Sera, Sera)*, Music and Lyrics by Jay Livingston and Ray Evans.

MAN WHO SHOT LIBERTY VALANCE, THE
BLACK & WHITE   1962

DRAMA/WESTERN
PARAMOUNT

JAMES STEWART	JOHN WAYNE	VERA MILES	LEE MARVIN
EDMOND O'BRIEN	ANDY DEVINE	JOHN CARRADINE	

Screenplay by: James Warner Bellah and Willis Goldbeck
Based on: The story by Dorothy M. Johnson
Directed by: John Ford

James Stewart is Ransom Stoddard, a young lawyer who arrives in the town of Shinbone with plans to bring law and order to the wild west. However, he and his plans are threatened at every turn by a ruthless outlaw, Liberty Valance (played by Lee Marvin). Stoddard is befriended by Tom Doniphon (John Wayne), a tough but good-hearted cowboy, and Hallie (Vera Miles), a restaurant waitress. Both admire Stoddard's idealism, but Doniphon tries to teach him that sometimes in the lawless west a man must use force to obtain his own justice. A riveting drama that builds to a phenomenal ending.

MAN WITHOUT A STAR
TECHNICOLOR   1955

DRAMA/WESTERN
UNIVERSAL INT'L

KIRK DOUGLAS	JEANNE CRAIN	CLAIRE TREVOR
WILLIAM CAMPBELL	RICHARD BOONE	JAY C. FLIPPEN

Screenplay by: Borden Chase and D.D. Beauchamp
Based on: A novel by Dee Linford
Directed by: King Vidor

Kirk Douglas is Dempsey Rae, a veteran cowboy who's just starting a new job at Reed Bowman's (played by Jeanne Crain) ranch, and she's embroiled in a feud with a neighbor over herds' grazing rights. Dempsey's experienced enough to know that the conflict could become vicious, and tries to avoid involvement, but eventually he is drawn into it. An extra dimension is added to the story as he meets Jeff Jimson (William Campbell) a young man who has just left home, and takes him under his wing to teach him the trade. Claire Trevor has a supporting role as Dempsey's friend Idonee, a woman who owns a saloon in town. A tense Western drama with some good action scenes.

MANY RIVERS TO CROSS
CINEMASCOPE & EASTMAN COLOR 1955

COMEDY
MGM

ROBERT TAYLOR	ELEANOR PARKER	JAMES ARNESS
ALAN HALE, JR.	ROSEMARY DeCAMP	

Screenplay by: Harry Brown and Guy Trosper
Based on: A story by Steve Frazee
Directed by: Roy Rowland

Bushrod Gentry (Robert Taylor) is a fur trapper who roams the wilderness and never intends to settle down. That's before Mary Stuart Chernee (Eleanor Parker), a tough pioneer woman, sets her sights on marrying him. She tries every trick in the book to win him over, but Bushrod swears to restless bachelorhood until she traps him into a shotgun wedding. He runs off in a last-ditch effort to regain his freedom, but Mary heads out to track him down. A very amusing story with plenty of action.

MARGIE
TECHNICOLOR 1946

COMEDY/DRAMA
20TH CENTURY FOX

JEANNE CRAIN	GLENN LANGAN	LYNN BARI
ALAN YOUNG	BARBARA LAWRENCE	CONRAD JANIS
ESTHER DALE	HOBART CAVANAUGH	HATTIE McDANIEL

Screenplay by: F. Hugh Herbert
Based on: Stories by Ruth McKenney and Richard Bransten
Directed by: Henry King

A sensitive portrait of an awkward teenage girl coming of age in the 1920s. This story is a fine blend of comedy and drama, with a little music. Jeanne Crain stars in the title role as Margie McDuff, and Alan Young (of **Mr. Ed** TV fame) is

Roy Hornsdale, her shy young boyfriend. The story revolves around a crush that Margie develops on a teacher at school, the dashing Professor Ralph Fontayne (played by Glenn Langan). It depicts very well both the joy and heartache that goes along with such teenage crushes. A top-notch family film with excellent perform-ances by the entire cast.

MARY POPPINS
TECHNICOLOR   1964

MUSICAL
WALT DISNEY

JULIE ANDREWS	DICK VAN DYKE	DAVID TOMLINSON
GLYNIS JOHNS	HERMIONE BADDELEY	KAREN DOTRICE
MATTHEW GARBER	ELSA LANCHESTER	ARTHUR TREACHER
REGINALD OWEN	ED WYNN	RETA SHAW

Screenplay by: Bill Walsh and Don Da Gradi
Based on: The *Mary Poppins* books by P.L. Travers
Directed by: Robert Stevenson

Julie Andrews stars as Mary Poppins, the perfect and magical nanny. She takes on the case of two incorrigible children who have already caused a long line of nannies to flee. Mary finds that the children are neglected by their father, a banker who puts business first and expects the youngsters to behave like miniature adults. Of course, she manages to solve all of the family's problems with cheerfulness and songs. An excellent, must-see movie for the entire family with great music and animation special effects.

Academy Award Recognition: Julie Andrews won Best Actress, Richard M. Sherman and Robert B. Sherman won Best Music Score (substantially original), won Best Song: *Chim Chim Cher-ee*, Music and Lyrics by Richard M. Sherman and Robert B. Sherman; nominated for Best Picture, Robert Stevenson nominated for Best Director, Bill Walsh and Don Dagradi nominated for Best Screenplay (based on material from another medium), Irwin Kostal nominated for Best Scoring of Music (adaptation or treatment).

MATING GAME, THE

CINEMASCOPE & METROCOLOR   1959

COMEDY

MGM

DEBBIE REYNOLDS   TONY RANDALL

Screenplay by: William Roberts
Based on: The novel ***The Darling Buds of May*** by H.E. Bates
Directed by: George Marshall

Debbie Reynolds stars as Mariette Larkin, a carefree farmer's daughter, and Tony Randall co-stars as Lorenzo Charlton, a picky IRS auditor. He is assigned to perform an audit of her parents' farm, as demanded by an irate neighbor during a fierce feud. However, Lorenzo's objective changes when he falls in love with Mariette, and he tries to help her family out of their predicament, which won't be easy. A breezy comedy that's good family fare.

McCONNELL STORY, THE

CINEMASCOPE   1955

DRAMA/MILITARY

WARNER BROTHERS

ALAN LADD   JUNE ALLYSON   JAMES WHITMORE

Screenplay by: Ted Sherdeman and Sam Rolfe
Story by: Ted Sherdeman
Directed by: Gordon Douglas

The true story of Joseph McConnell, Jr. (Alan Ladd), who began his military career as a mischievous young soldier in the medical corps during World War II, and yearned to become a pilot. After a long struggle and plenty of support from his loving wife, Pearl (June Allyson), he eventually became one of the United States' top fighter pilots in the Korean War. After his service in Korea, McConnell became a test pilot, despite Pearl's urging that he retire from flying. She was worried about losing him, which eventually did happen—he was killed one day while testing a jet. A very interesting biographical drama with a lot of action.

McLINTOCK!
TECHNICOLOR & PANAVISION   1963

COMEDY/WESTERN
UNITED ARTISTS

JOHN WAYNE	**MAUREEN O'HARA**	**PATRICK WAYNE**
STEFANIE POWERS	**JACK KRUSCHEN**	**CHILL WILLS**
YVONNE DeCARLO	**JERRY VAN DYKE**	**EDGAR BUCHANAN**

Original Screenplay by: James Edward Grant
Directed by: Andrew V. McLaglen

John Wayne stars as George Washington McLintock, a wealthy, rough-and-ready cattle ranch owner. When his estranged wife Katie (Maureen O'Hara) arrives in town, fireworks begin. She has come to take their daughter, Rebecca (Stefanie Powers), back east with her to live a more refined life. Meanwhile, McLintock has hired a new ranch hand named Devlin (played by Patrick Wayne, John's son), a young man with potential whom he takes under his wing. In addition to the explosive quarreling between Mr. and Mrs. McLintock, a rocky romance develops between Devlin and Rebecca. Yvonne DeCarlo (TV's Lily Munster) portrays Devlin's mother, who is hired as the ranch cook. A fun Western comedy that all can enjoy together.

MEET ME IN LAS VEGAS
CINEMASCOPE & COLOR   1956

MUSICAL
MGM

DAN DAILEY	**CYD CHARISSE**	**AGNES MOOREHEAD**	**JIM BACKUS**

Screenplay by: Isobel Lennart
Directed by: Roy Rowland

Chuck Rodwell (Dan Dailey), a rancher, and Maria Corvier (Cyd Charisse), a ballet dancer, meet in a Las Vegas casino. Maria becomes Rodwell's lucky charm because when she's with him, he wins at every game table or slot machine he tries. They decide to cash in on their gambling success as much as possible, but of course, not without some romance, music, and dancing. A light and entertaining outing.

Academy Award Recognition: George Stoll and Johnny Green nominated for Best Scoring of a Musical Picture.

MEET ME IN ST. LOUIS
TECHNICOLOR 1944

MUSICAL
MGM

JUDY GARLAND	MARGARET O'BRIEN	MARY ASTOR
LEON AMES	MARJORIE MAIN	LUCILLE BREMER
TOM DRAKE	HARRY DAVENPORT	JUNE LOCKHART

Screenplay by: Irving Brecher and Fred F. Finklehoffe
Based on: The book by Sally Benson
Directed by: Vincente Minnelli

This story is about the Smith family, living in St. Louis, Missouri at the turn of the century, as all are awaiting the opening of the World's Fair. Esther (Judy Garland), the family's second oldest daughter, meets and falls in love with John Truett (Tom Drake), the boy next door. When the Smith's father (Leon Ames) is offered a job in New York City and they may have to move, the whole family becomes concerned about losing their gracious way of life. An excellent portrayal of a bygone era, with some great tunes.

Academy Award Recognition: Irving Brecher and Fred F. Finkelhoffe nominated for Best Screenplay, Georgie Stoll nominated for Best Scoring of a Musical Picture, nominated for Best Song: *The Trolley Song*, Music and Lyrics by Ralph Blane and Hugh Martin.

MILLION DOLLAR DUCK, THE
TECHNICOLOR 1971

COMEDY/ANIMAL STORIES
WALT DISNEY

| DEAN JONES | SANDY DUNCAN | JOE FLYNN |
| TONY ROBERTS | JAMES GREGORY | LEE HARCOURT MONTGOMERY |

Screenplay by: Roswell Rogers
Based on: A story by Ted Key
Directed by: Vincent McEveety

Dean Jones plays Professor Albert Dooley, a young scientist struggling to pay the bills for his family. When Dooley brings home an unwanted duck from the lab, he's shocked to discover that, as a result of an accidental exposure to radiation, it lays eggs with solid gold yolks. From then on, it seems the family's life will never be the same. Sandy Duncan co-stars as Katie Dooley, Albert's sweet but slightly wacky wife. A pleasant and enjoyable family-style comedy.

MILLION DOLLAR MERMAID

TECHNICOLOR   1952

MUSICAL
MGM

ESTHER WILLIAMS   VICTOR MATURE   WALTER PIDGEON

Screenplay by: Everett Freeman
Directed by: Mervyn LeRoy

Esther Williams stars in the life story of swimming star Annette Kellerman. In the early 1900s Australia, Annette was a little girl with braces on her legs, longing to be a ballet dancer, which was impossible. But, she found that she could move in the water without being hindered by her handicap and became a great swimmer, healing her legs in the process. She started as a competitive swimmer in Australia and rose to become a water ballet star at the New York Hippodrome Theater. Victor Mature co-stars as James Sullivan, Annette's manager, with whom she also had a romance. Walter Pidgeon portrays Annette's father, music teacher Frederick Kellerman. Pleasant, light entertainment in Williams' usual style—and a positive message about overcoming life's obstacles.

MIRACLE ON 34TH STREET

BLACK & WHITE/COLORIZED   1947

DRAMA/CHRISTMAS
20TH CENTURY FOX

MAUREEN O'HARA   JOHN PAYNE   EDMUND GWENN   GENE LOCKHART
NATALIE WOOD   WILLIAM FRAWLEY

Screenplay by: George Seaton
Story by: Valentine Davies
Directed by: George Seaton

This is a charming Christmas story involving a little New York City girl named Susan Walker (played by Natalie Wood). Maureen O'Hara is Doris Walker, Susan's mother, a divorcée working for Macy's department store and a very practical realist with little tolerance for fantasy. Doris gets a big surprise when she unknowingly hires the real Santa Claus (Edmund Gwenn) as the department store's Santa, and he sets out to make all of Susan's dreams come true. Also on the scene is good friend FredGailey (John Payne), who hopes to once again interest Doris in love. A heartwarming and charming holiday classic that's a treat for the whole family.

Academy Award Recognition: Edmund Gwenn won Best Supporting Actor, Valentine Davies won Best Original Story, George Seaton won Best Screenplay, nominated for Best Picture.

MISTER ROBERTS
CINEMASCOPE & WARNER COLOR   1955

COMEDY/MILITARY
WARNER BROTHERS

HENRY FONDA	**JAMES CAGNEY**	**WILLIAM POWELL**	**JACK LEMMON**
BETSY PALMER	**WARD BOND**	**PHIL CAREY**	

Screenplay by: Frank Nugent and Joshua Logan
Based on: The play by Thomas Heggen and Joshua Logan;
            from the novel by Thomas Heggen
Directed by: John Ford and Mervyn LeRoy

Henry Fonda and Jack Lemmon star as Lt. Roberts and Ensign Pulver in this Navy comedy set aboard a cargo ship in the waning days of World War II. Roberts wishes he were seeing real action rather than just marking time, but his hard-nosed and mean Captain (played by James Cagney) will not allow him a transfer. The Captain has also not given the ship's crew liberty in quite a long time—so there's a lot of tension among the men on board.   While Roberts is busy standing up for his ship-mates' rights, the wacky Ensign Pulver impersonates the Captain to impress and romance pretty Navy nurses. William Powell also appears as the ship's doctor. The whole cast gives good performances in this fine movie version of the popular Broadway play.

 Academy Award Recognition: Jack Lemmon won Best Supporting Actor, nominated for Best Picture.

MOGAMBO
TECHNICOLOR   1953

DRAMA/ROMANCE
MGM

CLARK GABLE	**AVA GARDNER**	**GRACE KELLY**
DONALD SINDEN	**PHILIP STAINTON**	

Screenplay by: John Lee Mahin
Based on: A play by Wilson Collison
Directed by: John Ford

In this remake of **Red Dust** (1932), Clark Gable stars as Victor Marswell, a macho safari hunter in the wilds of Africa. Along comes New Yorker Eloise Kelly (played by Ava Gardner), who is in Africa to visit a friend and gets stranded at Marswell's camp, waiting for the next transport out. Anthropologist Donald Nordley (Donald Sinden) and his wife Linda (Grace Kelly) also spend time at the camp while studying gorillas. When Victor courts both women, a romantic triangle emerges. This movie was considered rather steamy when it was released, but is pretty tame by today's standards. The complex story line makes this movie more suitable for teenagers and adults, rather than young children.

 Academy Award Recognition: Ava Gardner nominated for Best Actress, Grace Kelly nominated for Best Supporting Actress.

MONKEY BUSINESS
BLACK & WHITE   1952

COMEDY
20TH CENTURY FOX

CARY GRANT	GINGER ROGERS	CHARLES COBURN
MARILYN MONROE	HUGH MARLOW	ESTHER DALE

Screenplay by: Ben Hecht, Charles Lederer, I.A.L. Diamond
Story by: Harry Segall
Directed by: Howard Hawks

Nearsighted scientist Barnaby Fulton (Cary Grant) is working—so far, without success—to discover a youth serum. He tests his various potions on chimpanzees in his lab. One day, a chimp gets loose, makes a concoction of his own from Barnaby's collection of chemicals, and dumps it into the water cooler. The fun begins when Barnaby and his wife Edwina (Ginger Rogers) begin drinking from the water cooler and the chimp's formula works, turning them back to progressively younger ages with each dose! Then it's one wacky mishap after another, some involving Barnaby's stodgy boss Oliver Oxley (Charles Coburn) and Oxley's voluptuous secretary, Lois Laurel (Marilyn Monroe). An amusing romp that should appeal to people of all ages.

MOON OVER MIAMI

TECHNICOLOR   1941

MUSICAL

20TH CENTURY FOX

DON AMECHE   **BETTY GRABLE**   **ROBERT CUMMINGS**   **CAROLE LANDIS**
JACK HALEY   **CHARLOTTE GREENWOOD**   **COBINA WRIGHT, JR.**

Screenplay by: Vincent Lawrence and Brown Holmes;
                 adaptation by George Seaton and Lynn Starling
From: The play *Three Blind Mice* by Stephen Powys
Directed by: Walter Lang

The story begins in Texas, where two sisters, Kay and Barbara Latimer (played by Betty Grable and Carole Landis), and their Aunt Susan (Charlotte Greenwood) inherit a small sum of money. They decide to spend the cash and head for Miami. They check into a luxury hotel, where Kay plans to hunt down and marry a millionaire. As part of their charade Aunt Susan poses as Kay's maid, and sister Barbara acts as her secretary. Though things don't go exactly as they had planned, all three do find romance. A very colorful and breezy musical.

MORE THE MERRIER, THE

BLACK & WHITE   1943

COMEDY/ROMANCE

COLUMBIA

JEAN ARTHUR   **JOEL McCREA**   **CHARLES COBURN**

Screenplay by: Robert Russell and Frank Ross,
                 Richard Flournoy and Lewis R. Foster
Story by: Robert Russell and Frank Ross
Directed by: George Stevens

Jean Arthur is Connie Milligan, a young working woman living in Washington, DC during its World War II housing shortage. She has always led a well-organized and predictable life, but all that changes when she rents half of her apartment to a funny older man, Mr. Dingle (Charles Coburn). Mr. Dingle feels that Connie needs to shake things up a bit and find a nice young man to enjoy life with. So Mr. Dingle sublets half of his half of the apartment to handsome Joe Carter (Joel McCrea), and sets out to achieve his objective. A well-done and charming romantic comedy.

Academy Award Recognition: Charles Coburn won Best Supporting Actor, Jean Arthur nominated for Best Actress, nominated for Best Picture, George Stevens nominated for Best Director, Robert Russell and Frank Ross nominated for Best Original Story; Robert Russell, Frank Ross, Richard Flournoy and Lewis R. Foster nominated for Best Screenplay.

MOTHER WORE TIGHTS
TECHNICOLOR   1947

MUSICAL
20TH CENTURY FOX

BETTY GRABLE	**DAN DAILEY**	**MONA FREEMAN**
CONNIE MARSHALL	**WILLIAM FRAWLEY**	**SENOR WENCES**

Screenplay by: Lamar Trotti
Based on: The book by Mariam Young
Directed by: Walter Lang

A retrospective on an aging couple's show business career. The story begins at the turn of the century. Betty Grable is Myrtle McKinley, a talented young woman who goes to San Francisco to attend business college, but unexpectedly gets a job as a chorus girl. Then Myrtle meets entertainer Frank Burt (Dan Dailey), and they work together while having a stormy romance. Later, as a married couple, they become major vaudeville stars. The rest of the story goes on to show how they manage to continue their show biz careers while raising a family as well. A pleasant story about the old days, featuring vaudeville-style tunes.

Academy Award Recognition: Alfred Newman won Best Scoring of a Musical Picture, nominated for Best Song: *You Do*, Music by Josef Myrow, Lyrics by Mack Gordon.

MOVE OVER, DARLING
CINEMASCOPE & COLOR   1963

COMEDY/ROMANCE
20TH CENTURY FOX

DORIS DAY	**JAMES GARNER**	**POLLY BERGEN**
THELMA RITTER	**FRED CLARK**	**DON KNOTTS**
EDGAR BUCHANAN	**CHUCK CONNORS**	

Screenplay by: Hal Kanter and Jack Sher
Directed by: Michael Gordon

In this remake of *My Favorite Wife* (1940), Doris Day is Ellen Arden, a wife and mother who was lost in a plane crash and is presumed dead. Her husband, Nicholas (James Garner), goes on to marry a second wife, Bianca (Polly Bergen). Then Ellen turns up shortly after the ceremony, having returned from a deserted island. Their two children don't remember her—but she wants them to be a family again. Ellen's mother-in-law tries to help her halt Nicholas' honeymoon and annul his new marriage. Meanwhile, Nicholas goes to great lengths to buy time and avoid dropping the bomb-shell on Bianca. A light and enjoyable comedy.

MR. BLANDINGS BUILDS HIS DREAM HOUSE
BLACK & WHITE   1948

COMEDY
RKO

| CARY GRANT | MYRNA LOY | MELVYN DOUGLAS |
| JASON ROBARDS | LURENE TUTTLE | LEX BARKER |

Screenplay by: Norman Panama and Melvin Frank
Based on: The novel by Eric Hodgins
Directed by: H.C. Potter

Cary Grant and Myrna Loy are Jim and Muriel Blandings, a couple who lives in a crowded New York City apartment with their two young daughters. Muriel tries to talk Jim into remodeling the apartment, but he decides it would be better to put their money into a house in the country. A slick real estate agent tricks them into buying a dilapidated house that they later find must be torn down and completely rebuilt. Jim and Muriel know nothing about building a home, but soon learn much more than they ever expected. A cute and very funny family-style comedy.

MR. DEEDS GOES TO TOWN
BLACK & WHITE   1936

COMEDY
COLUMBIA

| GARY COOPER | JEAN ARTHUR | LIONEL STANDER | GEORGE BANCROFT |

Screenplay by: Robert Riskin
Based on: A story by Clarence Budington Kelland
Directed by: Frank Capra

Gary Cooper is Longfellow Deeds, a greeting card poet from a small Vermont town. When a distant uncle leaves him a $20 million estate, he heads for New York City. A smart man who always lived a simple life, Deeds is not sure what to do with his brand new fortune, but there is no shortage of wily characters trying to swindle him out of it. Babe Bennett (Jean Arthur), a female reporter, pretends to meet Deeds by chance in order to write articles about him for her newspaper. They wind up falling in love, and then she feels guilty about the whole situation. A fine film by great director Frank Capra, that ends with a big courtroom scene.

Academy Award Recognition: Frank Capra won Best Director, nominated for Best Picture, Gary Cooper nominated for Best Actor, Robert Riskin nominated for Best Screenplay.

MR. HOBBS TAKES A VACATION

COMEDY

CINEMASCOPE & COLOR   1962   20TH CENTURY FOX

JAMES STEWART   **MAUREEN O'HARA**   **FABIAN**

Screenplay by: Nunnally Johnson
Based on: A novel by Edward Streeter
Directed by: Henry Koster
Music by: Henry Mancini

Roger Hobbs (James Stewart) is a St. Louis banker and Peggy Hobbs (Maureen O'Hara) is his wife. He plans a vacation for just the two of them to be alone together, but she plans a vacation for the entire family (including their children and grandchildren) at a beach house in California. The hilarity begins when the beach house turns out to be a broken-down wreck. Then the kids drive Mr. Hobbs crazy with all of their problems, which he must help solve. A very amusing family comedy with something for everyone.

MR. PEABODY AND THE MERMAID

COMEDY

BLACK & WHITE   1948   UNIVERSAL INT'L

WILLIAM POWELL   **ANN BLYTH**   **IRENE HERVEY**

Screenplay by: Nunnally Johnson
Based on: The novel *Peabody's Mermaid* by Guy and Constance Jones
Directed by: Irving Pichel

William Powell is Mr. Peabody, a man who is approaching his 50th birthday and is rather down about it. While vacationing with his wife Polly (Irene Hervey) in the British West Indies, he goes boating and discovers a magical mermaid (played by Ann Blyth). He takes her back to his hotel and puts her in the fish pond for safe keeping. The mermaid cannot speak, but she makes Mr. Peabody feel young again, and he falls in love with her. A sweet and enjoyable fantasy.

MR. SMITH GOES TO WASHINGTON

BLACK & WHITE   1939

COMEDY/DRAMA

COLUMBIA

JAMES STEWART	**JEAN ARTHUR**	**CLAUDE RAINS**	**GUY KIBBEE**
EUGENE PALETTE	**BEULAH BONDI**	**HARRY CAREY**	**H.B. WARNER**

Screenplay by: Sidney Buchman
Story by: Lewis R. Foster
Directed by: Frank Capra

A senator dies and the state governor must appoint a replacement. Jefferson Smith (James Stewart), a Boy Ranger troop leader, is chosen to fill the seat. It is expected that he will cast votes for influential constituents without asking any questions of the powers that be. But once in Washington, Smith plans to do things his own way and fight against corruption, with the help of his new office assistant, Saunders (played by Jean Arthur), who teaches him how the government process works. A classic story of the average citizen standing up for what's right—well done by a great cast and masterful director Capra.

Academy Award Recognition: Lewis R. Foster won Best Original Story, nominated for Best Picture, James Stewart nominated for Best Actor, Claude Rains and Harry Carey nominated for Best Supporting Actor, Frank Capra nominated for Best Director, Sidney Buchman nominated for Best Screenplay, Dimitri Tiomkin nominated for Best Score.

MRS. MINIVER

BLACK & WHITE   1942

DRAMA

MGM

GREER GARSON	**WALTER PIDGEON**	**TERESA WRIGHT**
DAME MAY WITTY	**REGINALD OWEN**	**HENRY TRAVERS**
RICHARD NEY	**HENRY WILCOXON**	

Screenplay by: Arthur Wimperis, George Froeschel,
                   James Hilton, and Claudine West
Based on: The book by Jan Struther
Directed by: William Wyler

The critically acclaimed saga of a middle-class English family enduring World War II. The story begins just before war breaks out in England, and then goes on to show the changes and hardships the family experiences in wartime. Greer Garson stars in the title role, and Walter Pidgeon portrays her husband. A powerful and realistic portrayal of what people of that time and place must have experienced. Too strong a drama for very young children though; more suitable for older children and adults. Excellent performances by the entire cast.

 Academy Award Recognition: won Best Picture, Greer Garson won Best Actress, Teresa Wright won Best Supporting Actress, William Wyler won Best Director; George Froeschel, James Hilton, Claudine West and Arthur Wimperis won Best Screenplay, Walter Pidgeon nominated for Best Actor, Dame May Whitty nominated for Best Supporting Actress, Henry Travers nominated for Best Supporting Actor.

MRS. PARKINGTON
BLACK & WHITE   1944   DRAMA
                                                   MGM

GREER GARSON	**WALTER PIDGEON**	**EDWARD ARNOLD**
AGNES MOOREHEAD	**CECIL KELLAWAY**	**GLADYS COOPER**
TOM DRAKE	**PETER LAWFORD**	**DAN DURYEA**

Screenplay by: Robert Thogred and Polly James
Based on: A novel by Louis Bromfield
Directed by: Tay Garnett

Mrs. Susie Parkington (Greer Garson) is an 84-year-old family matriarch—her husband, Major Augustus Parkington (Walter Pidgeon), died years earlier. The story looks back on their romance out west, where the Major owned a silver mine, their personal ups and downs over years, and their amassing of great wealth. In the present time, there is still some trouble for Mrs. Parkington to deal with, caused by her grandson's embezzlement. A very well-done family saga with a great cast.

 Academy Award Recognition: Greer Garson nominated for Best Actress, Agnes Moorehead nominated for Best Supporting Actress.

MUNSTER, GO HOME
COLOR   1966

COMEDY/MYSTERY-SUSPENSE
UNIVERSAL

FRED GWYNNE   **YVONNE DeCARLO**   **AL LEWIS**   **BUTCH PATRICK**
HERMIONE GINGOLD   **JOHN CARRADINE**   **RICHARD DAWSON**

Screenplay by: George Tibbles, Joe Connelly and Bob Mosher
Based on: The TV series *The Munsters*
Directed by: Earl Bellamy

Herman Munster (Fred Gwynne) inherits an English Title and the whole Munster family travels to Europe to claim it. However, the English branch of the clan is determined to grab the fortune for themselves. The Munsters have many funny adventures on board ship during their trans-Atlantic voyage. Then in England, their relatives have transformed the Munster Hall mansion into a haunted house to scare the newcomers off, but no such luck—the Munsters love it! There are lots of mysterious doings that follow, as Herman and Grandpa (Al Lewis) set out to discover the secret of Munster Hall. Fans of the TV series will probably get a kick out of this amusing movie.

MURDER AT THE GALLOP
BLACK & WHITE   1963

DRAMA/MYSTERY-SUSPENSE
MGM

MARGARET RUTHERFORD   **ROBERT MORLEY**   **FLORA ROBSON**

Screenplay by: James P. Cavanagh
Based on: The novel *After The Funeral* by Agatha Christie
Directed by: George Pollack

This is one of a series of films in which Margaret Rutherford portrays Miss Marple, the elderly amateur detective from Agatha Christie's mystery novels. An old man dies of a heart attack, but she believes that he was purposely frightened to death. When the man's sister is also murdered, Miss Marple now has a double murder to solve. An intriguing and suspenseful mystery.

MURDER, HE SAYS
BLACK & WHITE   1945

COMEDY/MYSTERY-SUSPENSE
PARAMOUNT

FRED MacMURRAY   **HELEN WALKER**   **MARJORIE MAIN**

Screenplay by: Lou Breslow
Story by: Jack Moffitt
Directed by: George Marshall

Fred MacMurray is Pete Marshall, a pollster taking a survey about the modern way
of life in rural areas. He thinks his job is a piece of cake until he meets the Fleagles,
a family that strikes fear in hearts of people for miles around. He finds himself in a
weird household of hillbillies, and their dying grandmother gives Marshall the secret
clue to the whereabouts of a pile of cash that was stolen in a bank robbery. Then
Marshall is in for big trouble, and will be lucky to escape with his life. This is an offbeat movie—a skillful combination of zany comedy and eerie mystery.

MURDER, SHE SAID
BLACK & WHITE   1961

DRAMA/MYSTERY-SUSPENSE
MGM

MARGARET RUTHERFORD   **ARTHUR KENNEDY**

Screenplay by: David Pursall and Jack Seddon
Based on: The novel *4-50 From Paddington* by Agatha Christie,
                   adapted by David Osborn
Directed by: George Pollack

This is the first in a series of films where Margaret Rutherford plays Miss Marple,
the elderly amateur detective from Agatha Christie's mystery novels. While on a
train ride, she witnesses a murder on another passing train, and reports it to the
police. They do not believe her story, so Miss Marple sets out to solve the mystery
on her own. As her cover, she takes a job as a maid in a household of wealthy but
strange people. An excellent and entertaining whodunit.

MUSIC MAN, THE
TECHNIRAMA & TECHNICOLOR   1962   **MUSICAL**
                                                 WARNER BROTHERS

ROBERT PRESTON	**SHIRLEY JONES**	**BUDDY HACKETT**
HERMIONE GINGOLD	**PAUL FORD**	**PERT KELTON**
RONNY HOWARD	**THE BUFFALO BILLS**	**MARY WICKES**

Screenplay by: Marion Hargrove
Based on: Meredith Willson's Broadway musical ***The Music Man***,
                             Book written in collaboration with Franklin Lacey
Directed by: Morton Da Costa

Music and Lyrics by Meredith Willson

Robert Preston is Harold Hill, a con man and traveling salesman who arrives in the small town of River City, Iowa. His angle: he poses as a bandleader, promising to turn the local boys into a fabulous marching band while selling musical instruments and uniforms to their parents. Hill plans on making a quick buck and skipping town, but the unexpected happens—he falls for the town librarian, Marian Paroo (played by Shirley Jones). Young Ronny Howard turns in a fine performance as Marian's adorable little brother Winthrop. This is a sparkling musical with an excellent cast and great songs that people of all ages can enjoy together.

 Academy Award Recognition: Ray Heindorf won Best Scoring of Music (adaptation or treatment), nominated for Best Picture.

MY DARLING CLEMENTINE
BLACK & WHITE   1946   **DRAMA/WESTERN**
                                                 20TH CENTURY FOX

HENRY FONDA	**LINDA DARNELL**	**VICTOR MATURE**
CATHY DOWNS	**WALTER BRENNAN**	**TIM HOLT**
WARD BOND	**ALAN MOWBRAY**	**JOHN IRELAND**

Screenplay by: Samuel G. Engel and Winston Miller
From: A story by Sam Hellman
Based on: A book by Stuart N. Lake
Directed by: John Ford

Henry Fonda is Wyatt Earp, a former marshal who has given up the law to herd cattle with his three brothers. When they arrive at the outskirts of the town of Tombstone, the three older men go to town, leaving the youngest behind to watch over the herd. They return to find their brother robbed and murdered, and that's enough to make Earp stay in Tombstone a while to find the killer. The ensuing hunt involves the Clanton clan (the father played by Walter Brennan) and Doc Holliday (Victor Mature), a former doctor gone wrong. A touch of romance is added with the arrival of Clementine (Linda Darnell), Doc Holliday's former love to whom Wyatt Earp takes a liking. An interesting and intense Western.

MY FAVORITE BLONDE

COMEDY/MYSTERY-SUSPENSE

BLACK & WHITE   1942   PARAMOUNT

BOB HOPE   **MADELEINE CARROLL**   **GALE SONDERGAARD**

Screenplay by: Don Hartman and Frank Butler
Story by: Melvin Frank and Norman Panama
Directed by: Sidney Lanfield

Madeleine Carroll is Karen Bentley, who is assigned to deliver a mysterious gold scorpion, which contains wartime flight plans, to a safe destination. Unfortunately, she is being followed and threatened by evildoers who want to gain possession of the scorpion. Bob Hope is Larry Haines, a vaudeville entertainer whose partner is a small (and very cute) penguin named Percy. Haines finds Karen very attractive, and decides to help her out. Haines, Karen and Percy share many adventures and close calls while ensuring the scorpion's proper delivery. An exciting and fun mystery tale.

MY FAVORITE BRUNETTE

COMEDY/MYSTERY-SUSPENSE

BLACK & WHITE   1947   PARAMOUNT

BOB HOPE   **DOROTHY LAMOUR**   **PETER LORRE**   **LON CHANEY**

Screenplay by: Edmund Beloin and Jack Rose
Directed by: Elliott Nugent

Bob Hope is Ronnie Jackson, a baby photographer who dreams of being a private investigator, like the man whose office is across the hall from his studio. Enter Carlotta Montay (Dorothy Lamour), a woman who mistakenly hires Jackson as a private investigator to help her search for a missing person. Suddenly, he and Carlotta are plunged into a very complex and dangerous mystery. Jackson's inexperience shows as he stumbles along the way to solving the case. A neat and fun combination of comedy and suspense.

MY FAVORITE WIFE
BLACK & WHITE/COLORIZED   1940

COMEDY
RKO

IRENE DUNNE   **CARY GRANT**   **RANDOLPH SCOTT**   **GAIL PATRICK**

Screenplay by:	Bella and Samuel Spewack
Original story by:	Bella and Samuel Spewack and Leo McCarey
Directed by:	Garson Kanin

Nick Arden (Cary Grant) is a lawyer whose wife Ellen (Irene Dunne) was lost at sea for 7 years and presumed dead. Just when she is declared legally dead and he remarries, Ellen returns. Not only does this interfere with his new marriage, but what will he tell their two children, who believe their mother is dead? This amusing comedy was remade in 1963 as **Move Over, Darling**.

Academy Award Recognition: Leo McCarey, Bella Spewack and Samuel Spewack nominated for Best Original Story; Roy Webb nominated for Best Original Musical Score.

MY FRIEND FLICKA
TECHNICOLOR   1943

DRAMA/ANIMAL STORIES
20TH CENTURY FOX

RODDY McDOWALL	**PRESTON FOSTER**	**RITA JOHNSON**
JAMES BELL	**DIANA HALE**	**JEFF COREY**

Screenplay by:	Lillie Hayward, adaptation by Francis Edwards Faragoh
From:	The novel by Mary O'Hara
Directed by:	Harold Schuster

Roddy McDowall is Ken, the son of horse rancher Rob McLaughlin (Preston Foster). Ken longs for a colt of his own to train and care for, so his father lets him select one. But Ken chooses a colt that is descended from a long line of renegade horses. Then, despite his father's warnings, Ken accepts the challenge, fighting many obstacles to raise and train the horse he loves. A very good family movie for fans of animal stories, with important lessons about responsibility and perseverance.

MY PAL GUS
BLACK & WHITE   1952

COMEDY/DRAMA
20TH CENTURY FOX

RICHARD WIDMARK   **JOANNE DRU**   **AUDREY TOTTER**   **GEORGE WINSLOW**

Screenplay by: Fay and Michael Kanin
Directed by: Robert Parrish

Richard Widmark is Dave Jennings, the divorced father of a little boy named Gus (George Winslow). Mr. Jennings is a very gruff and busy businessman who spends very little time with Gus, causing him to be an unhappy child who gets into trouble often. Gus ends up in a nursery school which requires parent participation, and his teacher (played by Joanne Dru) attempts to show Mr. Jennings how to become a good father and make the boy his first priority. Excellent family fare with a good mixture of both comedy and drama.

MY SIX LOVES
TECHNICOLOR   1963

COMEDY/DRAMA
PARAMOUNT

DEBBIE REYNOLDS   **CLIFF ROBERTSON**   **DAVID JANSSEN**
EILEEN HECKART   **HANS CONRIED**   **MARY McCARTY**
JOHN McGIVER   **ALICE GHOSTLEY** ·   **JIM BACKUS**

Screenplay by: John Fante, Joseph Calvelli, and William Wood
Based on: The story by Peter V.K. Funk
Directed by: Gower Champion

Debbie Reynolds stars as Janice Courtney, a famous actress who experiences exhaustion and is ordered by her doctor to spend six weeks at her country home in Connecticut. When she arrives there, Janice finds that six abandoned children have been living on her property in her absence. Janice's lifestyle then changes in a big way, as she grows to care for the children and falls in love with the local minister, Rev. Jim Larkin (Cliff Robertson). A charming comedy that the whole family can enjoy together.

NAKED SPUR, THE
TECHNICOLOR   1953   DRAMA/WESTERN
                                                                MGM

JAMES STEWART   JANET LEIGH   ROBERT RYAN   RALPH MEEKER   MILLARD MITCHELL

Screenplay by: Sam Rolfe and Harold Jack Bloom
Directed by: Anthony Mann

James Stewart is Howard Kemp, a bounty hunter searching for Ben Vandergroat (Robert Ryan), a man wanted for murdering a Marshal in Kansas. After combing the Colorado countryside for a while alone, Kemp finally succeeds in capturing Vandergroat with the aid of two acquaintances (played by Ralph Meeker and Millard Mitchell). Janet Leigh is Lina Patch, Vandergroat's female traveling companion. The whole group stays together for the long ride back to justice in Kansas. The rest of the story chronicles the experiences of the group along its journey, while each member angles for his or her own desired outcome. An unusual and interesting Western with good scenic photography.

Academy Award Recognition: Sam Rolfe and Harold Jack Bloom nominated for Best Story and Screenplay.

NATIONAL VELVET
TECHNICOLOR   1944   DRAMA/ANIMAL STORIES
                                                                MGM

MICKEY ROONEY   DONALD CRISP   ELIZABETH TAYLOR   ANNE REVERE
ANGELA LANSBURY   JACKIE JENKINS   ARTHUR TREACHER

Screenplay by: Theodore Reeves and Helen Deutsch
Based on: The novel *National Velvet* by Enid Bagnold
Directed by: Clarence Brown

This story takes place in England during the late 1920s. Elizabeth Taylor stars as Velvet Brown, a young girl who loves horses. With the help of a trainer/stable hand named Mi Taylor (Mickey Rooney), Velvet trains to race Pie, her favorite horse, at the Grand National competition. But since girls are not permitted to be jockeys, their plan must remain a secret. Donald Crisp and Anne Revere portray Velvet's parents, Mr. and Mrs. Brown, while Angela Lansbury appears as her sister Edwina. A classic children's novel transferred expertly to the screen, creating a family-style movie that all generations can enjoy together.

Academy Award Recognition: Anne Revere won Best Supporting Actress, Clarence Brown nominated for Best Director.

NAVY BLUE AND GOLD
BLACK & WHITE   1937

DRAMA/MILITARY
MGM

ROBERT YOUNG	**JAMES STEWART**	**FLORENCE RICE**	**BILLIE BURKE**
LIONEL BARRYMORE	**TOM BROWN**	**SAMUEL S. HINDS**	

Screenplay by:	George Bruce
From:	The book by George Bruce
Directed by:	Sam Wood

Three young men enter the Naval Academy at Annapolis—Roger Ash (Robert Young), Truck Cross (James Stewart), and Richard Gates (Tom Brown)—each for his own personal reasons. They become roommates and football teammates, sticking with each other through thick and thin. A rousing story of old-time college buddies, played out by a very talented cast.

NEPTUNE'S DAUGHTER
TECHNICOLOR   1949

MUSICAL
MGM

ESTHER WILLIAMS	**RED SKELTON**	**RICARDO MONTALBAN**
BETTY GARRETT	**KEENAN WYNN**	**XAVIER CUGAT and his orchestra**

Screenplay by:	Dorothy Kingsley
Additional dialogue by:	Ray Singer and Dick Chevillat
Directed by:	Edward Buzzell
Songs by:	Frank Loesser

Esther Williams stars as Eve Barrett, a swimming star turned swimsuit company executive. Betty Garrett plays Eve's sister Betty. When a South American polo team comes to town, romance is in the air for both young ladies. Then lots of unexpected things happen when Eve falls for the handsome and wealthy Jose O'Rourke (Ricardo Montalban), and in a case of mistaken identity, Betty falls for wacky masseuse Jack Spratt (Red Skelton). Light entertainment at a relaxed pace, with some good songs.

 Academy Award Recognition: won Best Song: *Baby It's Cold Outside*, Music and Lyrics by Frank Loesser.

NEVER A DULL MOMENT

BLACK & WHITE   1950   COMEDY

                                                              RKO

IRENE DUNNE	FRED MacMURRAY	WILLIAM DEMAREST
ANDY DEVINE	GIGI PERREAU	NATALIE WOOD
PHILIP OBER	JACK KIRKWOOD	ANN DORAN

Screenplay by: Lou Breslow and Doris Anderson
Based on: A novel by Kay Swift
Directed by: George Marshall

Fred MacMurray is Chris Hayward, a widower rancher, and Irene Dunne is Kay
Kingsley, a New York City songwriter. The two meet at a rodeo, quickly fall in love
and marry. Then they go back to his ranch to start a new life with his two young
daughters (played by Gigi Perreau and Natalie Wood). Kay has some big adjust-
ments to make while learning about life in the country and motherhood. Plenty of
humorous mishaps occur on their way to becoming a family. A pleasant comedy
that all ages can enjoy together.

NEVER LET ME GO

BLACK & WHITE   1953   DRAMA

                                                              MGM

| CLARK GABLE | GENE TIERNEY | BERNARD MILES | RICHARD HAYDN |
| BELITA | KENNETH MORE | KAREL STEPANEK | |

Screenplay by: Ronald Millar and George Froeschel
Adapted from: The novel *Came The Dawn* by Roger Bax
Directed by: Delmer Daves

Clark Gable is Philip Sutherland, a reporter stationed in Moscow during and after
World War II. At a U.S. Embassy, he marries Marya Lamarkina (Gene Tierney), a
Russian ballerina. When Sutherland is transferred out of Russia by authorities, the
couple finds out that Marya will not be permitted to leave the country, so Philip puts
together a plan to escape with her. A very dramatic story that builds to a highly
suspenseful climax as their secret and dangerous mission unfolds.

NO TIME FOR LOVE

BLACK & WHITE   1943

COMEDY/ROMANCE

PARAMOUNT

CLAUDETTE COLBERT   **FRED MacMURRAY**   **ILKA CHASE**
RICHARD HAYDN   **JUNE HAVOC**

Screenplay by: Claude Binyon; adaptation by Warren Duff
Based on: A story by Robert Lees and Fred Rinaldo
Directed by: Mitchell Leisen

Katherine Grant (Claudette Colbert) is a magazine photographer who is assigned to report on work at the construction site of an underwater tunnel. Once there, she meets big and burly James Ryan (MacMurray), one of the men building the project. At first, the only thing they have in common is a mutual dislike for each other, but as time goes on, they fall in love. A fun romantic comedy with an exciting ending that features some good action scenes.

NO TIME FOR SERGEANTS

BLACK & WHITE   1958

COMEDY

WARNER BROTHERS

ANDY GRIFFITH   **MYRON McCORMICK**   **NICK ADAMS**
MURRAY HAMILTON   **DON KNOTTS**

Screenplay by: John Lee Mahin
Based on: The play by Ira Levin as presented by Maurice Evans,
                 based on the novel by Mac Hyman
Directed by: Mervyn Leroy

Andy Griffith stars as Will Stockdale, a country boy from Georgia who's drafted into the Air Force. It's a whole new world for Will, and every step of the way he has many new experiences. However, the Air Force will never be the same again. Will is a constant headache for his drill sergeant (played by Myron McCormick) and his barracks buddies, but he doesn't give up trying to fit in. A very amusing service comedy.

NORTH BY NORTHWEST
VISTAVISION & TECHNICOLOR   1959

DRAMA/MYSTERY-SUSPENSE
MGM

CARY GRANT   **EVA MARIE SAINT**   **JAMES MASON**

Screenplay by: Ernest Lehman
Directed by: Alfred Hitchcock

Cary Grant stars as Roger Thornhill, a New York advertising executive. In a case
of mistaken identity, he is thrust into the center of a dangerous mystery—suddenly
strangers are trying to hunt him down and kill him. With no help from the police,
Thornhill's only way out is to solve the riddle on his own. Then he meets Eve
Kendall (Eva Marie Saint), a beautiful young woman who says she will help him—
but does she mean it? While he works to unravel the mystery, Thornhill has some
awesome and frightening adventures. A superb and absorbing movie with director
Hitchcock's trademark edge-of-your-seat suspense.

Academy Award Recognition: Ernest Lehman nominated for Best
Story and Screenplay (written directly for the screen).

NORTH TO ALASKA
TECHNICOLOR   1960

COMEDY/ACTION-ADVENTURE
20TH CENTURY FOX

JOHN WAYNE   **STEWART GRANGER**   **ERNIE KOVACS**
FABIAN   **CAPUCINE**

Screenplay by: John Lee Mahin, Martin Rackin and Claude Binyon
Based on: The play *Birthday Gift* by Laslo Fodor
Directed by: Henry Hathaway

The setting: the Gold Rush days in Nome, Alaska circa 1900. Three partners in a
goldmine hit it big—Sam McCord (John Wayne), George Pratt (Stewart Granger),
and George's brother Billy (played by Fabian). Staying behind to ready things for
her arrival, George sends Sam to Seattle to retrieve his fiancé. Once there, Sam
finds the girl already married to another, but refuses to return to Alaska empty-
handed. He finds another pretty young woman named Michelle (Capucine) to
bring back to George instead. But Michelle prefers Sam, causing complications.
Meanwhile, the three men have their hands full protecting their mine from claim
jumpers, especially sneaky con artist Frankie Canon (Ernie Kovacs). A rousing
adventure with lots of action, spirit and fun.

NORTHWEST MOUNTED POLICE

TECHNICOLOR · 1940

DRAMA/ACTION-ADVENTURE

PARAMOUNT

GARY COOPER   **MADELEINE CARROLL**   **PAULETTE GODDARD**
ROBERT PRESTON   **PRESTON FOSTER**

Screenplay by: Alan Le May, Jesse Lasky, Jr., and C. Gardner Sullivan
Based on: The book ***Royal Canadian Mounted Police***
       by R.C. Fetherston-Haugh
Directed by: Cecil B. DeMille

The story takes place in 1880s Canada, where the Native Americans who live in the wilderness are being forced from their land as European settlers expand into their territory. When these people rebel against the settlers, the Mounties, otherwise known as the Royal Canadian Mounted Police, are called into action. Preston Foster and Robert Preston play two such Mounties, Sgt. Jim Brett and Constable Ronnie Logan. Gary Cooper is a Texas Ranger who has entered the territory in pursuit of an American fugitive. A colorful, multifaceted and action-packed adventure story unfolds from there. The main female roles are played by Madeleine Carroll (April Logan, a nurse) and Paulette Goddard (Louvette Corbeau, the fugitive's daughter).

Academy Award Recognition: Victor Young nominated for Best Original Musical Score.

NOTORIOUS

BLACK & WHITE · 1946

DRAMA/MYSTERY-SUSPENSE

RKO

CARY GRANT   **INGRID BERGMAN**   **CLAUDE RAINS**

Screenplay by: Ben Hecht
Directed by: Alfred Hitchcock

Ingrid Bergman is Alicia Huberman, the daughter of a man convicted as a Nazi spy and traitor to the United States. Cary Grant is Devlin, a U.S. secret agent who requests her assistance with his current investigation, that she might provide him with some of her father's old contacts. Alicia is then set up to romance and marry one of her father's friends, Alexander Sebastian (Claude Rains), in order to get secret information. An exceptionally suspenseful and gripping tale develops as she and Devlin work together undercover to solve the case.

Academy Award Recognition: Claude Rains nominated for Best Supporting Actor, Ben Hecht nominated for Best Original Screenplay.

ODD COUPLE, THE

PANAVISION & TECHNICOLOR   1968

COMEDY

PARAMOUNT

JACK LEMMON   WALTER MATTHAU

Screenplay by: Neil Simon
Based on: The play by Neil Simon
Directed by: Gene Saks

This is the film version of the popular Broadway play **The Odd Couple**, on which the TV series of the same name was also based. Jack Lemmon is Felix Unger, the irrepressible, fussy neat freak and Walter Matthau is the sloppy, devil-may-care Oscar Madison. The story is simple—both men are divorced and are sharing an apartment, but drive each other nuts. Even if one has already seen the TV series, it is still enjoyable to see how Lemmon and Matthau portrayed the now-familiar characters in their own way.

Academy Award Recognition: Neil Simon nominated for Best Screenplay (based on material from another medium).

OFF LIMITS

BLACK & WHITE   1953

COMEDY/MILITARY

PARAMOUNT

BOB HOPE   MICKEY ROONEY   MARILYN MAXWELL

Story and Screenplay by: Hal Kanter and Jack Sher
Directed by: George Marshall

Bob Hope is Wally Hogan, a boxing manager who joins the Army to keep tabs on his champ fighter who's been called for the draft. However, the champ is rejected on his mental exam, and Wally's stuck in the service alone—that is, until he meets Herbie Tuttle, an aspiring boxer. Herbie talks Wally into taking a chance on him and training him to fight in the ring. The two become best friends, and Wally meets and falls for Herbie's Aunt Connie (Marilyn Maxwell), who doesn't approve of Herbie's fighting. A light comedy with amusing hijinks both in and out of the boxing ring.

OKLAHOMA!

COLOR   1955

MUSICAL
MAGNA THEATRE CORP.

GORDON MacRAE	**SHIRLEY JONES**	**ROD STEIGER**	**GLORIA GRAHAME**
GENE NELSON	**CHARLOTTE GREENWOOD**	**EDDIE ALBERT**	**JAMES WHITMORE**

Screenplay by: Sonya Levien and William Ludwig
Based on: The musical by Richard Rodgers and Oscar Hammerstein II
From: The play *Green Grow the Lilacs* by Lynn Riggs
Directed by: Fred Zinnemann

In this screen adaptation of the hit Broadway musical, the traditional boy-meets-girl story is done in a western pioneer setting. Gordon MacRae is Curly, a young man who falls for the beautiful Laurey (Shirley Jones), but lurking in the shadows is the evil Jud Fry (played by Rod Steiger), a farmhand who wants to have Laurey for himself. This classic musical features great Rodgers and Hammerstein songs, which are done well by the fine voices of MacRae and Jones, with the help of a good supporting cast.

Academy Award Recognition: Robert Russell Bennett, Jay Blackton, and Adolph Deutsch won Best Scoring of a Musical Picture.

ON AN ISLAND WITH YOU

TECHNICOLOR   1948

MUSICAL
MGM

ESTHER WILLIAMS	**PETER LAWFORD**	**RICARDO MONTALBAN**
JIMMY DURANTE	**CYD CHARISSE**	**XAVIER CUGAT** and his orchestra

Screenplay by: Dorothy Kingsley, Dorothy Cooper,
                      Charles Martin and Hans Wilhelm
From: An original story by Charles Martin and Hans Wilhelm
Directed by: Richard Thorpe

Esther Williams is Roz Rennolds, a movie star on location in the Pacific islands. She's engaged to her handsome co-star Ricardo Montez (Ricardo Montalban). Lt. Larry Kingslee (Peter Lawford) is a Navy pilot assigned to the set as technical advisor. He is hopelessly in love with Roz but she won't give him the time of day. When the opportunity presents itself, Larry takes off in a plane with Roz flying her to a remote island so that he can get her undivided attention. Though things don't go exactly according to plan, all involved get a happy ending. A relaxing and pleasant outing with a warm tropical atmosphere.

ON MOONLIGHT BAY

MUSICAL

TECHNICOLOR   1951   WARNER BROTHERS

DORIS DAY	GORDON MacRAE	JACK SMITH
LEON AMES	ROSEMARY DeCAMP	MARY WICKES
ELLEN CORBY	BILLY GRAY	

Screenplay by: Jack Rose and Melville Shavelson
Adapted from: Penrod Stories by Booth Tarkington
Directed by: Roy Del Ruth

This is a story of happenings in a typical family of the early 1900s. Doris Day stars as Marjorie Winfield, a spunky teenage girl, and Billy Gray plays her quite mischievous little brother, Wesley. Each of them is always up to something, much to the consternation of their parents (Rosemary DeCamp and Leon Ames). Gordon MacRae appears as Marjorie's enthusiastic boyfriend, Bill Sherman, who will soon be graduating from high school. Movie veteran Mary Wickes is featured as Stella, the Winfield's house- keeper, and some may recognize Ellen Corby (Grandma on TV's *The Waltons*) as Miss Stevens, Wesley's schoolteacher. A heartwarming and old-fashioned slice of Americana that all generations can enjoy together.

ON THE DOUBLE

COMEDY/MILITARY

PANAVISION & TECHNICOLOR   1961   PARAMOUNT

DANNY KAYE	DANA WYNTER	WILFRED HYDE WHITE
MARGARET RUTHERFORD	DIANA DORS	

Screenplay by: Jack Rose and Melville Shavelson
Directed by: Melville Shavelson

In this comedy set in England during World War II, Danny Kaye is Pfc. Ernest Williams, a funny American GI who does a great imitation of Sir Lawrence Mackenzie-Smith, a prominent British military leader. Williams embarks on a hilarious adventure when the Army puts together a scheme in which he poses as Sir Lawrence in order to trick the Germans. A very witty and unusual story with many surprising twists and turns.

ON THE TOWN
TECHNICOLOR   1949   ## MUSICAL
       MGM

| GENE KELLY | FRANK SINATRA | BETTY GARRETT |
| ANN MILLER | JULES MUNSHIN | VERA ELLEN |

Screenplay by: Adolph Green and Betty Comden
Based on: The musical play, book by Adolph Green and Betty Comden
Directed by: Gene Kelly and Stanley Donen

Music by Leonard Bernstein
Lyrics by Adolph Green, Betty Comden, and Leonard Bernstein

This musical tells the tale of three sailors on a 24-hour leave in New York City, and the women they spend it with. The sailors are Gabey (Gene Kelly), Chip (Frank Sinatra), and Ozzie (Jules Munshin). The gals who show them the town are cab driver Brunhilde Esterhazy (Betty Garrett), anthropologist Claire Huddesen (Ann Miller), and Ivy Smith (Vera Ellen), who is Miss Turnstiles of the New York subway system. A cheerful, light movie with a quick pace and plenty of great musical numbers by the very talented cast.

 Academy Award Recognition: Roger Edens and Lennie Hayton won Best Scoring of a Musical Picture.

OPERATION PACIFIC
BLACK & WHITE   1951   ## DRAMA/MILITARY
       WARNER BROTHERS

| JOHN WAYNE | PATRICIA NEAL | WARD BOND |

Screenplay by: George Waggner
Directed by: George Waggner

John Wayne is Duke Gifford, a naval officer serving in World War II. Patricia Neal is Mary Stuart, a nurse—and Duke's ex-wife. His military career had gotten in the way of their marriage, as he was always away, especially when she needed him most. They now bump into each other 4 years later and still have feelings for one another, though she is dating another man. Will their love get a second chance? Combined with this personal story line is plenty of battle action as Duke cruises in a submarine with buddy "Pop" Perry (Ward Bond). They experience great danger when some of their torpedoes malfunction as they defend themselves against the Japanese. A very interesting and well-done World War II drama.

OPERATION PETTICOAT

EASTMAN COLOR   1959

COMEDY/MILITARY

UNIVERSAL INT'L

CARY GRANT	TONY CURTIS	JOAN O'BRIEN
DINA MERRILL	GENE EVANS	RICHARD SARGENT
GAVIN MacLEOD	MADLYN RHUE	MARION ROSS

Screenplay by: Stanley Shapiro and Maurice Richlin
Suggested by: A story by Paul King and Joseph Stone
Directed by: Blake Edwards

Cary Grant stars as Admiral Matt Sherman, the commanding officer of the Sea Tiger, a World War II submarine, and Tony Curtis is Lieutenant Holden, a handsome wheeler-dealer who's transferred to the sub after a string of cushy assignments. The ship is bombed in port before ever seeing battle, but Sherman and his men manage to patch it together enough to sail to a Pacific repair unit. In its travels, the Sea Tiger picks up a group of female military officers stranded on a Pacific island, and the fun begins as the men and women try to peacefully co-exist in the close confines of a submarine. An excellent comedy with lots of laughs.

 Academy Award Recognition: Paul King, Joseph Stone, Stanley Shapiro and Maurice Richlin nominated for Best Story and Screenplay (written directly for the screen).

OPPOSITE SEX, THE

CINEMASCOPE & METROCOLOR   1956

COMEDY/DRAMA/MUSICAL

MGM

JUNE ALLYSON	JOAN COLLINS	DOLORES GRAY
ANN SHERIDAN	ANN MILLER	LESLIE NIELSEN
AGNES MOOREHEAD	CHARLOTTE GREENWOOD	SAM LEVENE

Screenplay by: Joan Blondell, with Fay and Michael Kanin
Adapted from: A play by Clare Boothe
Directed by: David Miller

This is a remake of *The Women* (1939). The setting is New York City, and the soap-opera story line looks into the lives of a handful of wealthy women. June Allyson is Kay Ashley, a singer married to successful Broadway producer Steve Hilliard (Leslie Nielsen). Kay hears through the grapevine that her husband is having an affair with a chorus girl named Crystal Allen (Joan Collins). Kay finds her way through her predicament, and receives advice from other women she meets along the way. A mixture of comedy and drama, with a few nice songs and good cast.

OUR VERY OWN

DRAMA

BLACK & WHITE   1950   RKO

ANN BLYTH	**FARLEY GRANGER**	**JOAN EVANS**	**JANE WYATT**
ANN DVORAK	**DONALD COOK**	**NATALIE WOOD**	

Screenplay by: F. Hugh Herbert
Directed by: David Miller

Ann Blyth is Gail Macaulay, a teenage girl whose world is turned upside down by her younger sister Joan (played by Joan Evans). In a moment of jealousy, Joan reveals that Gail was adopted. Gail's parents (played by Jane Wyatt and Donald Cook) and her boyfriend Chuck (Farley Granger) try to help her sort through her feelings about her adoption and her new-found birth mother (played by Ann Dvorak). Natalie Wood portrays Gail's youngest sister Penny. A good soap-opera style story about a family handling a crisis.

OUT WEST WITH THE HARDYS

COMEDY

BLACK & WHITE   1938   MGM

MICKEY ROONEY	**LEWIS STONE**	**FAY HOLDEN**
CECELIA PARKER	**ANN RUTHERFORD**	**SARA HADAN**
DON CASTLE	**VIRGINIA WEIDLER**	

Screenplay by: Kay Van Riper, Agnes Christine Johnston and William Ludwig
Based on: The characters created by Aurania Rouverol
Directed by: George B. Seitz

In this installment of the **Andy Hardy** series of movies, Andy Hardy (Mickey Rooney) and his family have a western adventure. They visit the ranch of a family friend who's having difficulties and needs the help of Judge Hardy (Andy's father, played by Lewis Stone). Andy gets busy showing off and trying to be a real cowboy while his sister Marian (Cecelia Parker) has a new romance. A fun and entertaining film for the whole family.

PAGAN LOVE SONG
COLOR   1950   **MUSICAL**
                                                          MGM

ESTHER WILLIAMS   HOWARD KEEL

Screenplay by: Robert Nathan and Jerry Davis
Based on: The book *Tahiti Landfall* by William S. Stone
Directed by: Robert Alton

This pleasant musical is set on the island of Tahiti. Esther Williams is Mimi Bennett, an American woman who lives on her aunt's estate, but the locals consider her a native islander. She meets Hazard Endicott (Howard Keel), a handsome American schoolteacher who has inherited a plantation from his uncle. Hazard and Mimi spend time together as she teaches him the ways of the island and its people, and a romance blossoms between them. Relaxed, light entertainment with beautiful scenery, some nice music and a few of Esther's famous swimming sequences.

PAJAMA GAME, THE
WARNERCOLOR   1957   **MUSICAL/ROMANCE**
                                              WARNER BROTHERS

DORIS DAY   JOHN RAITT   CAROL HANEY   EDDIE FOY, JR.   RETA SHAW

Screenplay by: George Abbott and Richard Bissell
Based on: The play *The Pajama Game*,
                      with book by George Abbott and Richard Bissell
From: The novel *7½ Cents* by Richard Bissell
Directed by: George Abbott and Stanley Donen

Choreography by Bob Fosse

This screen version of the hit Broadway musical is set in the "Sleeptite" Pajama Factory. Doris Day is Kate "Babe" Williams, a shop worker, union activist and the head of the grievance committee. John Raitt (who starred in the play on Broadway) portrays Sid Sorokin, the new factory superintendent. Unexpectedly, Babe and Sid fall deeply in love, but a matter of 7½ cents threatens to keep them apart—the factory's owner keeps refusing to give the union a raise of that amount in their contract. This entertaining musical features good tunes, fine dance numbers, plus an interesting love story.

PALEFACE, THE
COMEDY/WESTERN/MUSICAL

TECHNICOLOR 1948 PARAMOUNT

BOB HOPE   JANE RUSSELL

Screenplay by: Edmund Hartmann and Frank Tashlin;
                  additional dialogue by Jack Rose
Directed by: Norman Z. McLeod

Calamity Jane (Jane Russell) is pardoned by the government from a jail sentence, in return for her help in tracking down some notorious criminals. In order to go undercover as a member of a wagon train, she needs a husband, so Jane gets cowardly dentist Peter Potter (Bob Hope) to marry her. Then, powerful and brave Jane uses the weakling Potter as a decoy while she performs all the tough work. A fun and hilarious Western satire with lots of good action scenes.

Academy Award Recognition: won for Best Song: ***Buttons and Bows***, Music and Lyrics by Jay Livingston and Ray Evans.

PALM BEACH STORY, THE
COMEDY/ROMANCE

BLACK & WHITE 1942 PARAMOUNT

CLAUDETTE COLBERT   JOEL McCREA   MARY ASTOR   RUDY VALLEE

Screenplay by: Preston Sturges
Directed by: Preston Sturges

This story is about the madcap marital difficulties of a young couple, Gerry and Tom Jeffers (Claudette Colbert and Joel McCrea). Gerry likes to live in elegant fashion, but Tom, an idealistic young businessman, doesn't make enough money to support that kind of lifestyle. Gerry decides to leave him and go to Palm Beach, Florida to get a divorce. On the train ride south, she meets an assortment of odd characters, including the wealthy J.D. Hackensacker III (Rudy Vallee), who takes a liking to her and then sets out to win her heart. Tom arrives in Palm Beach to stop the divorce, and Hackensacker's sister, Princess Centimillia, takes a liking to him. Total romantic chaos follows, resulting in a whimsical and zany comedy.

PAPA'S DELICATE CONDITION

TECHNICOLOR   1963   COMEDY/DRAMA/MUSICAL

PARAMOUNT

JACKIE GLEASON	GLYNIS JOHNS	CHARLES RUGGLES	ELISHA COOK, JR.

Screenplay by: Jack Rose
From: A book by Corrine Griffith
Directed by: George Marshall

In this story of a family in the early 1900s, Jackie Gleason plays a free spirited, and good-hearted guy who unfortunately likes to drink a lot. His drinking always gets him into trouble, with bad business deals and the like. His younger daughter doesn't comprehend his "condition" and worships her fun-loving father, while his wife (played by Glynis Johns) and older daughter are exasperated by his antics and try to get him to change. A charming family film about a bygone era, with a happy ending.

 Academy Award Recognition: won Best Song: *Call Me Irresponsible*, Music by James Van Heusen, Lyrics by Sammy Cahn.

PARDNERS

VISTAVISION & TECHNICOLOR   1956   COMEDY/WESTERN/MUSICAL

PARAMOUNT

DEAN MARTIN	JERRY LEWIS	AGNES MOOREHEAD	LON CHANEY

Screenplay by: Sidney Sheldon, screen story by Jerry Davis
Based on: A story by Mervin J. Houser
Directed by: Norman Taurog

Jerry Lewis is Slim Mosely, Jr. the wimpy heir to a huge fortune, and Dean Martin is Wade Kingsley, Jr. a ranch foreman. Despite their obvious differences, the two become "Pardners" and set out to save the ranch that their fathers had once worked together in the distant past. In a next-generation chapter of a major feud, they face off against the sons of the bandits who killed their fathers. An engaging and madcap Western farce with a few nice songs.

PARENT TRAP, THE
TECHNICOLOR   1961

COMEDY
WALT DISNEY

HAYLEY MILLS	**MAUREEN O'HARA**	**BRIAN KEITH**	**CHARLIE RUGGLES**
UNA MERKEL	**LEO G. CARROLL**	**JOANNA BARNES**	

Screenplay by: David Swift
Directed by: David Swift

Hayley Mills plays a double role as two teenage girls who are lookalikes—one from Boston, and the other from California. The two meet at summer camp, and compare notes about their lives, finding that they are actually twins who were separated as babies, when their parents divorced. When their father announces plans to remarry, the girls set out to get their parents (Brian Keith and Maureen O'Hara) back together. A top-notch family-style comedy that people of all ages should enjoy.

PAT AND MIKE
BLACK & WHITE   1952

COMEDY/ROMANCE
MGM

KATHARINE HEPBURN	**SPENCER TRACY**	**ALDO RAY**

Screenplay by: Ruth Gordon and Garson Kanin
Directed by: George Cukor

Katharine Hepburn is Pat Pemberton, a gym teacher who's engaged to a college administrator. Pat is a talented athlete, but doesn't reach her potential because the constant criticism she receives from her fiancé undermines her confidence. At a national golf tournament she meets Mike Conovan (Spencer Tracy), a sports manager and promoter, who turns her career around. But Pat and Mike have trouble getting along, even though they're attracted to one another. An entertaining and enjoyable romantic comedy that's made a little more unique by its sports theme.

 Academy Award Recognition: Ruth Gordon and Garson Kanin nominated for Best Story and Screenplay.

PENNY SERENADE
BLACK & WHITE   1941

DRAMA
COLUMBIA

CARY GRANT   IRENE DUNNE

Screenplay by: Morrie Ryskind
Story by: Martha Cheavens
Directed by: George Stevens

The story of a young couple, Julie and Roger Adams (played by Irene Dunne and
Cary Grant). Julie is injured in an accident, and is left unable to bear children. This is
a major disappointment, because they very much want to start a family. Eventually
they are able to adopt a baby girl, but their happy family life is shattered when the
child later dies from a sudden illness. Somehow, the couple must find a way to go
on. It's a very sentimental drama, so be prepared to cry a few tears.

 Academy Award Recognition: Cary Grant nominated for Best Actor.

PHILADELPHIA STORY, THE
BLACK & WHITE/COLORIZED   1940

COMEDY/ROMANCE
MGM

KATHARINE HEPBURN   CARY GRANT   JAMES STEWART   RUTH HUSSEY

Screenplay by: Donald Ogden Stewart
Based on: A play by Philip Barry
Directed by: George Cukor

The story takes place among the society set in Philadelphia. Tracy Lord (Katharine
Hepburn) and C.K. Dexter Haven (Cary Grant) are a divorced couple who split up
because of his carousing. Tracy is planning to get married again—but this time to
a rather stuffy and boring fellow. James Stewart is Mike Conner, a reporter who's
assigned to get the inside scoop on the big wedding. To annoy Tracy, Dexter Haven
helps Mike and his photographer Liz Imbrie (Ruth Hussey) to get close to the wedding. Confusion builds prior to the ceremony as Dexter Haven, Mike, and the
groom-to-be all compete for Tracy's affections. An extremely sharp comedy that's
executed skillfully by the great cast.

 Academy Award Recognition: James Stewart won Best Actor,
Donald Ogden Stewart won Best Screenplay, nominated for Best Picture,
Katharine Hepburn nominated for Best Actress, Ruth Hussey nominated
for Best Supporting Actress, George Cukor nominated for Best Director.

PILLOW TALK
CINEMASCOPE & EASTMAN COLOR   1959

COMEDY/ROMANCE
UNIVERSAL INT'L

ROCK HUDSON   **DORIS DAY**   **TONY RANDALL**   **THELMA RITTER**

Screenplay by: Stanley Shapiro and Maurice Richlin
Based on: A story by Russell Rouse and Clarence Greene
Directed by: Michael Gordon

Doris Day is Jan Morrow, a single interior decorator with a party line telephone.
Rock Hudson is Brad Allen, a smooth-talking bachelor who shares the line with her.
Jan is disgusted that Brad constantly ties up the line, chatting away the hours with his
many girlfriends. The two absolutely can't stand each other, until they finally meet
face-to-face and he pretends to be someone else—then it's a different story.
An enormously appealing and fun romantic comedy.

Academy Award Recognition: Russell Rouse, Clarence Greene,
Stanley Shapiro and Maurice Richlin won Best Story and Screenplay
(written directly for the screen); Doris Day nominated for Best Actress,
Thelma Ritter nominated for Best Supporting Actress, Frank DeVol
nominated for Best Scoring of a Dramatic or Comedy Picture.

PITTSBURGH
BLACK & WHITE   1942

DRAMA
UNIVERSAL

MARLENE DIETRICH   **RANDOLPH SCOTT**   **JOHN WAYNE**
FRANK CRAVEN   **LOUISE ALLBRITTON**   **SHEMP HOWARD**
THOMAS GOMEZ   **LUDWIG STOSSEL**   **SAMUEL S. HINDS**

Screenplay by: Kenneth Gamet and Tom Reed
Based on: An original story by George Owen and Tom Reed
Additional dialogue by: John Twist
Directed by: Lewis Seiler

Marlene Dietrich is Josie Winters, a coal miner's daughter looking for a better life
than the one her parents had. Pittsburgh Markham (John Wayne) and Cash Evans
(Randolph Scott) are two young coal miners who admire Josie and are inspired by
her to achieve greatness in the mining industry. The rest of the story follows the
trio's triumphs and failures, both professional and personal, over the years. A lively
industrial saga, played out by a talented cast that works well together.

PLEASE DON'T EAT THE DAISIES

COMEDY

CINEMASCOPE & METROCOLOR   1960   MGM

| DORIS DAY | DAVID NIVEN | JANIS PAIGE |
| SPRING BYINGTON | RICHARD HAYDN | |

Screenplay by: Isobel Lennart
Based on: The book by Jean Kerr
Directed by: Charles Walters

Newly appointed drama critic Lawrence Mackay (David Niven), his wife Kate (Doris Day), and their four young sons live a hectic life in a crowded New York City apartment. In search of a better lifestyle, they move to a big old house in the country. Funny things start to happen as the whole family tries to adapt to its new surroundings. A light and genial family comedy, which was also the basis for a 1960s TV series of the same name.

PLEASURE OF HIS COMPANY, THE

COMEDY/DRAMA

COLOR   1961   PARAMOUNT

| FRED ASTAIRE | DEBBIE REYNOLDS | LILLI PALMER | TAB HUNTER |

Screenplay by: Samuel Taylor
Based on: The play by Samuel Taylor and Cornelia Otis Skinner
Directed by: George Seaton

Debbie Reynolds is Jessica Poole, a wealthy young woman who's about to get married. Her parents are divorced, and Jessica's father, Biddeford "Pogo" Poole (played by Fred Astaire), whom she has not seen since childhood, is a playboy who spends his life traveling the globe. Jessica invites him home to give her away at her wedding. Then chaos breaks out as Pogo tries to talk Jessica out of her marriage plans, enticing her to take a trip around the world with him—much to the dismay of her mother, Katharine (Lilli Palmer). An enjoyable, sophisticated comedy with some drama mixed in.

POLLYANNA

TECHNICOLOR   1960

COMEDY/DRAMA

WALT DISNEY

HAYLEY MILLS	JANE WYMAN	RICHARD EGAN
KARL MALDEN	NANCY OLSON	ADOLPHE MENJOU
DONALD CRISP	AGNES MOOREHEAD	KEVIN CORCORAN

Screenplay by: David Swift
Based on: The novel by Eleanor H. Porter
Directed by: David Swift

The story is set in horse-and-buggy days. Hayley Mills plays the part of an orphan girl named Pollyanna, who comes to live with her Aunt Polly (Jane Wyman). Her aunt has a sour disposition and is set in her ways, as are many of the other folks in town. Pollyanna is a naturally radiant and optimistic child who manages to change the lives of many for the better. A charming tale with an excellent cast, that people of all generations can enjoy together.

POOR LITTLE RICH GIRL

BLACK & WHITE/COLORIZED   1936

COMEDY/MUSICAL

20TH CENTURY FOX

| SHIRLEY TEMPLE | ALICE FAYE | GLORIA STUART | JACK HALEY |
| MICHAEL WHALEN | SARA HADEN | JANE DARWELL | |

Screenplay by: Sam Hellman, Gladys Lehman and Harry Tugend
Suggested by: The stories of Eleanor Gates and Ralph Spence
Directed by: Irving Cummings

Shirley Temple is Barbara Barry, the daughter of a very wealthy man—the owner of a major soap company. She has everything a little girl could want, except enough time with the father she adores. Barbara's overprotective governess convinces Mr. Barry that boarding school would be best for her. But while traveling to the boarding school, Barbara is separated from her governess by accident, and decides to embark on a "vacation," to meet new people and have some adventures. Along the way, she becomes part of a song and dance act (with the Dolans, played by Alice Faye and Jack Haley), and is almost kidnaped by a mysterious stranger. An entertaining story, true to the Shirley Temple tradition, in which a little girl spreads cheer and gets a happy ending.

PRIDE OF ST. LOUIS

BLACK & WHITE   1952

DRAMA

20TH CENTURY FOX

DAN DAILEY   JOANNE DRU   RICHARD HYLTON   RICHARD CRENNA

Screenplay by: Herman J. Mankiewicz
Based on: A story by Guy Trosper
Directed by: Harmon Jones

Dan Dailey plays the lead role in this true account of major league baseball star
Jerome Herman "Dizzy" Dean. He began hurling baseballs while a barefoot youth
in the Ozark Mountains in the late 1920s, and went on to become one of the most
famous pitchers in baseball history. The story follows his rise to fame, his courtship and marriage to his wife, Patricia Nash (Joanne Dru), as well as the difficulties
that Dizzy experienced when his career was suddenly ended by a shoulder injury.
Richard Crenna portrays Paul Dean, Dizzy's brother, who was also a major league
pitcher. A good biographical drama, with a happy ending and an important message
about personal growth through adversity.

PRIDE OF THE YANKEES, THE

BLACK & WHITE   1942

DRAMA

RKO

GARY COOPER   TERESA WRIGHT   BABE RUTH   WALTER BRENNAN

Screenplay by: Jo Swerling and Herman J. Mankiewicz
Original Story by: Paul Gallico
Directed by: Sam Wood

This is the true story of Lou Gehrig, one of the most famous baseball players of all
time. Both his career and personal life are shown, beginning in boyhood and continuing until his illness with ALS (amyotrophic lateral sclerosis, also called Lou Gehrig's
Disease) forced him to retire from baseball. Gary Cooper stars in the title role, and
Teresa Wright co-stars as Lou's wife, Eleanor. Both give very fine performances in
this exceptional and moving biographical drama.

 Academy Award Recognition: nominated for Best Picture,
Gary Cooper nominated for Best Actor, Teresa Wright nominated for
Best Actress, Paul Gallico nominated for Best Original Story, Herman J.
Mankiewicz and Jo Swerling nominated for Best Screenplay, Leigh Harline
nominated for Best Scoring of a Dramatic or Comedy Picture.

PRINCESS COMES ACROSS, THE   COMEDY/MYSTERY-SUSPENSE
BLACK & WHITE   1936   PARAMOUNT

CAROLE LOMBARD   **FRED Mac MURRAY**   **DOUGLASS DUMBRILLE**
WILLIAM FRAWLEY   **ALISON SKIPWORTH**   **GEORGE BARBIER**

Screenplay by: Walter DeLeon, Francis Martin, Don Hartman and Frank Butler
Based on: A story by Philip MacDonald
Adapted from: A novel by Louis Lucien Rogger
Directed by: William K. Howard

On a transatlantic ocean voyage the paths of several unusual characters become en-
twined. Carole Lombard plays a beautiful actress who's pretending to be a Swedish
princess named Olga. Fred MacMurray is King Mantell, a musician traveling with his
agent, Benton (William Frawley). A handful of detectives on their way to a convention get word that an escaped murderer is on board ship, and then very strange
occurrences develop as the group tries to identify the guilty party. A very fascinating tale that mystery fans should find very enjoyable.

PRISONER OF ZENDA, THE   DRAMA/ACTION-ADVENTURE
TECHNICOLOR   1952   MGM

STEWART GRANGER   **DEBORAH KERR**   **JAMES MASON**   **LOUIS CALHERN**
JANE GREER   **LEWIS STONE**   **ROBERT DOUGLAS**

Screenplay by: John L. Balderston and Noel Langley
Adaptation by: Wells Root
From: The novel by Anthony Hope and
                         the dramatization by Edward Rose
Directed by: Richard Thorpe

Stewart Granger plays a dual role in this tale that takes place in a European country
in the late 1800s. It begins with the impending coronation of a new king, Rudolph.
A distant lookalike cousin pays an unexpected visit, and is substituted in the coronation at the last minute when Rudolph is drugged by his evil half-brother Michael
(James Mason), who desires the crown for himself. What follows is a swashbuckling
adventure that also involves Rudolph's fiancé Princess Flavia (Deborah Kerr). A very
exciting movie with colorful costumes and good performances by the entire cast.

PRIVATE WAR OF MAJOR BENSON, THE

COMEDY

TECHNICOLOR   1955   UNIVERSAL INT'L

CHARLTON HESTON	JULIE ADAMS	WILLIAM DEMAREST
TIM HOVEY	NANA BRYANT	TIM CONSIDINE
SAL MINEO	MILBURN STONE	

Screenplay by: William Roberts and Richard Alan Simmons
Original story by: Joe Connolly and Bob Mosher
Directed by: Jerry Hopper

Charlton Heston is Major Bernard Benson, a tough-as-nails Army career man.
He gets in trouble with his superiors for making negative comments that end up
printed in a magazine article. As his punishment, Benson is assigned to a boys'
military school to help it regain ROTC accreditation. Once he arrives, he finds that
the boys are much younger than he expected and that the school is managed by
nuns. Major Benson's experiences with the boys and his romance with the school
pediatrician, Dr. Kay Lambert (Julie Adams), change his outlook on life. A very
entertaining and sweet story that the whole family can enjoy together.

 Academy Award Recognition: Joe Connelly and Bob Mosher
nominated for Best Motion Picture Story.

PROUD REBEL, THE

DRAMA

TECHNICOLOR   1958   SAMUEL GOLDWYN/BUENA VISTA

| ALAN LADD | OLIVIA de HAVILLAND | DAVID LADD |

Screenplay by: Joseph Petracca and Lillie Hayward
From: A story by James Edward Grant
Directed by: Michael Curtiz

After the Civil War, a former confederate soldier, John Chandler (Alan Ladd) and his
son David (played by David Ladd, Alan's real-life son) travel north. The father is in
search of a doctor to cure the boy, who became mute from the shock of seeing his
home shattered and his mother killed during the war. When they arrive in a small
town, the two are set upon by a group of hoodlums, but Linnett Moore (played by
Olivia de Havilland), a widow struggling to manage her farm all alone, helps them
out by offering John work. As John and David get to know Linnett, they become
fond of her—and she of them. John never gives up looking for a remedy for his son,
while fighting against the town ruffians who continue to harass them. A moving
story with a happy ending, and the entire cast gives fine performances.

QUIET MAN, THE
TECHNICOLOR   1952   **DRAMA/COMEDY**
                                                               REPUBLIC

JOHN WAYNE   **MAUREEN O'HARA**   **BARRY FITZGERALD**   **WARD BOND**

Screenplay by: Frank S. Nugent
From: The story by Maurice Walsh
Directed by: John Ford

John Wayne is Sean Thornton, an American boxer who returns to his family's homestead in Ireland. Once there, he meets and falls for a beautiful Irish woman named Mary Kate (Maureen O'Hara). Her brother disapproves of their relationship, so Sean goes to the town matchmaker (Barry Fitzgerald) for help in setting up a courtship and marriage deal. Sean and Mary Kate love each other very much, but a secret from his past threatens to ruin their life together. A delightful and enchanting Irish tale with a big action-packed ending.

      Academy Award Recognition: John Ford won Best Director, nominated for Best Picture, Victor McLaglen nominated for Best Supporting Actor, Frank S. Nugent nominated for Best Screenplay.

RACHEL AND THE STRANGER
BLACK & WHITE/COLORIZED   1948   **DRAMA**
                                                               RKO

LORETTA YOUNG   **ROBERT MITCHUM**   **WILLIAM HOLDEN**
SARA HADEN   **TOM TULLY**   **GARY GRAY**

Screenplay by: Waldo Salt
Based on: The stories *Rachel* and *Neighbor Sam* by Howard Fast
Directed by: Norman Foster

William Holden is Davey Harvey, a widower farmer living with his young son on a farm in the wilderness, miles from civilization. He goes to the nearest settlement, a stockade, to find a female to help run the household and raise his son. Davey buys an indentured servant named Rachel (Loretta Young), and marries her just to make things look proper. Davey's friend, Jim Fairways (Robert Mitchum), a hunter, comes to visit occasionally and finds Rachel very attractive. Since there is no love between Davey and Rachel (or so he thinks), Jim begins to court her, and the story continues from there. An unusual frontier drama with a good cast.

RARE BREED, THE

PANAVISION & TECHNICOLOR   1966

DRAMA/WESTERN

UNIVERSAL

| JAMES STEWART | MAUREEN O'HARA | BRIAN KEITH | JULIET MILLS |
| DON GALLOWAY | DAVID BRIAN | JACK ELAM | |

Screenplay by: Ric Hardman
Directed by: Andrew V. McLaglen

The story begins at the 1884 National Stockmen's Exposition in St. Louis. Maureen O'Hara and Juliet Mills portray Martha and Hilary Price, an English widow and her daughter, who are in the cattle breeding business. They have traveled to the exposition to auction a bull that they have bred meticulously, in order to develop a new type of cattle. When the bull is purchased by Alexander Bowen (Brian Keith), a crusty Scotch rancher, they hire cowboy Sam Burnett (James Stewart) to transport the animal west and ensure its safe delivery. The two women follow along, and once the bull has reached its destination, they fight to prove that the offspring of their specially bred specimen can survive the harsh western outdoors. This unique Western is an inspiring tale of personal strength and perseverance.

REAP THE WILD WIND

TECHNICOLOR   1942

DRAMA/ACTION-ADVENTURE

PARAMOUNT

RAY MILLAND	JOHN WAYNE	PAULETTE GODDARD
RAYMOND MASSEY	ROBERT PRESTON	SUSAN HAYWARD
LYNNE OVERMAN	CHARLES BICKFORD	

Screenplay by: Alan Le May, Charles Bennett and Jesse Lasky Jr.
Based on: A *Saturday Evening Post* story by Thelma Strabel
Directed by: Cecil B. DeMille

The setting: the Florida Keys in 1840, where salvage crews, some honest and some unscrupulous, recover goods from ships wrecked by storms or other means. Paulette Goddard is Loxi Claiborne, a strong and spunky young woman trying to carry on her father's legitimate salvage business. She meets the brawny and handsome Captain Jack Stuart (John Wayne) while rescuing him from his sinking vessel. When he is wrongly blamed for the wreck, Loxi attempts to help him save his seafaring career. Ray Milland is Stephen Tolliver, the lawyer for Stuart's shipping company, who investigates the case. An exciting, colorful, action-packed adventure with good special effects.

REAR WINDOW

TECHNICOLOR

DRAMA/MYSTERY-SUSPENSE

1954

UNIVERSAL

JAMES STEWART   GRACE KELLY   WENDELL COREY   THELMA RITTER   RAYMOND BURR

Screenplay by: John Michael Hayes
Based on: The short story by Cornell Woolrich
Directed by: Alfred Hitchcock

James Stewart is L.B. "Jeff" Jeffries, a professional photographer, who's stuck in his apartment for weeks on end while recuperating from a broken leg. From his window, Jeff has a clear view of many neighbors, and watches them to help pass the time. Some of the events he observes lead him to believe that one neighbor (Raymond Burr) has committed a murder, so Jeff tries to solve the case, with the help of his girlfriend Lisa Fremont (Grace Kelly) and his nurse Stella (Thelma Ritter). A fascinating story and interesting characters make this a superior mystery movie.

 Academy Award Recognition: Alfred Hitchcock nominated for Best Director, John Michael Hayes nominated for Best Screenplay.

REBECCA

BLACK & WHITE

DRAMA/MYSTERY-SUSPENSE

1940

UNITED ARTISTS

LAURENCE OLIVIER   JOAN FONTAINE   JUDITH ANDERSON   GEORGE SANDERS

Screenplay by: Robert E. Sherwood and Joan Harrison;
                   adaptation by Philip MacDonald and Michael Hogan.
Based on: The novel by Daphne DuMaurier
Directed by: Alfred Hitchcock

A wealthy widower (Laurence Olivier) and an innocent young woman (Joan Fontaine) meet while on vacation at Monte Carlo, where they quickly fall in love and marry. But when he takes her home to his mansion, called Manderley, she finds herself in an eerie competition with his dead wife's memory, and discovers odd circumstances surrounding the death. An extremely absorbing tale, loaded with suspense.

 Academy Award Recognition: won Best Picture, Laurence Olivier nominated for Best Actor, Joan Fontaine nominated for Best Actress, Judith Anderson nominated for Best Supporting Actress, Alfred Hitchcock nominated for Best Director, Robert E. Sherwood and Joan Harrison nominated for Best Screenplay, Franz Waxman nominated for Best Original Musical Score.

REBECCA OF SUNNYBROOK FARM
BLACK & WHITE/COLORIZED   1938

COMEDY/MUSICAL
20TH CENTURY FOX

SHIRLEY TEMPLE	**RANDOLPH SCOTT**	**JACK HALEY**
GLORIA STUART	**PHYLLIS BROOKS**	**HELEN WESTLEY**
SLIM SUMMERVILLE	**BILL ROBINSON**	**WILLIAM DEMAREST**

Screenplay by: Karl Tunberg and Don Ettlinger
Suggested by: The Kate Douglas Wiggin story
Directed by: Allan Dwan

Randolph Scott is Anthony Kent, an executive in desperate search of a "Little Miss America" for a radio program, but with no success. Shirley Temple is Rebecca Winstead, a talented but motherless little girl who's sent by her irresponsible stepfather (William Demarest) to live with her Aunt Miranda (Helen Westley) at Sunnybrook Farm. By coincidence, Mr. Kent lives next door to the farm and discovers that Rebecca is just the girl he has been looking for. Once it looks like Rebecca is going to be a smash hit, her stepfather decides it would be convenient to take her back. But Rebecca loves life at the farm and needs to find a way to stay there. A very sweet story with entertaining songs and some dances with her well-known partner Bill Robinson, as well as a surprise happy ending.

RELENTLESS
TECHNICOLOR

DRAMA/WESTERN/ACTION-ADVENTURE
1948   COLUMBIA

ROBERT YOUNG	**MARGUERITE CHAPMAN**	**WILLARD PARKER**
AKIM TAMIROFF	**BARTON MacLANE**	**MIKE MAZURKI**
ROBERT BARRAT	**CLEM BEVANS**	

Screenplay by: Winston Miller
Based on: A story by Kenneth Perkins
Directed by: George Sherman

Robert Young stars as Nick Buckley, a traveler with a mare ready to give birth. He stops off in a western town, where he meets a free-spirited young woman named Luella Purdy (Marguerite Chapman), who runs a supply wagon. She is attracted to Nick immediately, but he's a wanderer with no intention of settling down. When Nick is falsely accused of murder, Luella does all she can to help him clear his name. A suspenseful movie with lots of unexpected turns and plenty of action.

REMEMBER THE NIGHT

DRAMA/ROMANCE/CHRISTMAS

BLACK & WHITE   1940   PARAMOUNT

| **BARBARA STANWYCK** | **FRED MacMURRAY** | **BEULAH BONDI** |
| **ELIZABETH PATTERSON** | **STERLING HOLLOWAY** | |

Original Screenplay by: Preston Sturges
Directed by: Mitchell Leisen

Barbara Stanwyck portrays Lee Leander, a woman who's caught shoplifting and goes to trial just before Christmas. Fred MacMurray plays John "Jack" Sargent, the prosecutor on the case. It looks like the jury is going to make an easy acquittal, so Jack gets the case held over until after the holidays. Then Lee is bailed out for Christmas, but has nowhere to go. Jack plans to travel back to his hometown for the holidays, and offers to drop Lee off with her mother on his way. When he sees the home that Lee came from, Jack learns how Lee's life went wrong. As an act of kindness, he takes her along to spend Christmas with his family. She is moved by his family's kindness, and as Lee's true self is revealed, Jack falls in love with her. Now what will they do when the holiday season is over and they have to return to court? A well-done and touching love story that has a Christmas theme, but can be enjoyed any time of year.

RIO GRANDE

DRAMA/WESTERN

BLACK & WHITE   1950   REPUBLIC

| **JOHN WAYNE** | **MAUREEN O'HARA** | **VICTOR McLAGLEN** |
| **CLAUDE JARMAN, JR.** | **BEN JOHNSON** | **HARRY CAREY, JR.** |

Screenplay by: James Kevin McGuinness
Based on: A *Saturday Evening Post* story by James Warner Bellah
Directed by: John Ford

John Wayne plays Lt. Col. Kirby York, a U.S. Cavalry Commander whose son Jeff (Claude Jarman, Jr.) is expelled from West Point. Then Jeff enlists in the Cavalry to prove himself and attempt to meet his father's high expectations, then winds up in his father's unit. York is determined not to show any favoritism toward his son, and is actually extra hard on him. However, York's wife Kathleen (played by Maureen O'Hara) works to soften her husband's unreasonably tough attitude toward their son, who is trying hard to make his father proud. A Western that does a good job of combining a personal story with action.

ROAD TO MOROCCO
BLACK & WHITE   1942

COMEDY/MUSICAL
PARAMOUNT

BING CROSBY   BOB HOPE   DOROTHY LAMOUR   ANTHONY QUINN

Screenplay by: Frank Butler and Don Hartman
Directed by: David Butler

Crosby and Hope are Jeff Peters and Turkey Jackson, two stowaways set adrift on the ocean by a shipwreck. When they reach land, they hitch a ride on a passing camel and wind up heading for Morocco. They arrive there broke and hungry, and sneaky Jeff sells Turkey into slavery for some quick cash. But, in a comic twist, Turkey ends up the new fiancé of the beautiful Princess Shalmar (Dorothy Lamour), who's only using him to escape marriage to another. When Jeff finally meets the Princess, he makes a play for her himself. Then an amusing story unfolds, and eventually Jeff and Turkey are on the run, and try to rescue Princess Shalmar from her original fiancé, the big and powerful Mullay Kasim (played by Anthony Quinn). A very entertaining movie with lots of zany, old-fashioned comedy bits.

 Academy Award Recognition: Frank Butler and Don Hartman nominated for Best Original Screenplay.

ROAD TO RIO
BLACK & WHITE   1947

COMEDY/MUSICAL
PARAMOUNT

**BING CROSBY   BOB HOPE   DOROTHY LAMOUR
GALE SONDERGAARD   FRANK FAYLEN   THE ANDREWS SISTERS**

Screenplay by: Edmund Beloin and Jack Rose
Directed by: Norman Z. McLeod

Bing Crosby and Bob Hope are traveling musicians Scat Sweeney and Hot Lips Barton. They get into trouble and wind up on the run as stowaways on a ship bound for Rio De Janeiro, Brazil. Once on board, they meet a beautiful but distraught young woman, Lucia Maria De Andrade (Dorothy Lamour). She's being hypnotized by her sinister aunt, Catherine Vail (played by Gale Sondergaard), who is trying to force her into a loveless marriage. Scat and Hot Lips leap into action to rescue Lucia from her unhappy fate. An amusing story with lots of funny hijinks.

 Academy Award Recognition: Robert Emmett Dolan nominated for Best Scoring of a Musical Picture.

ROAD TO UTOPIA
BLACK & WHITE   1945

COMEDY/MUSICAL
PARAMOUNT

BING CROSBY   BOB HOPE   DOROTHY LAMOUR

Screenplay by: Norman Panama and Melvin Frank
Directed by: Hal Walker

This is the fourth entry in *The Road to ...* series of movies. Vaudeville entertainers
Duke Johnson and Chester Hooton (Bing Crosby and Bob Hope) head to Alaska
in search of riches, during the gold rush. On the way, they stumble upon a stolen
map that leads to a secret gold mine. The mine is to be inherited by the pretty Sal
Van Hoyden (Dorothy Lamour), who is desperately looking for the missing map.
A group of crooks, pretending to help Sal find it, are actually planning to snatch her
fortune. So Johnson and Hooton are chased for the map across the Yukon tundra
by Sal, the crooks trying to swindle her, and the two brutes who stole the map in
the first place. Light entertainment, with loads of corny jokes and a few songs.

Academy Award Recognition: Norman Panama and Melvin Frank
nominated for Best Original Screenplay.

ROMAN HOLIDAY
BLACK & WHITE   1953

COMEDY/ROMANCE
PARAMOUNT

GREGORY PECK   AUDREY HEPBURN   EDDIE ALBERT

Screenplay by: Ian McLellan Hunter and John Dighton,
Story by: Ian McLellan Hunter
Directed by: William Wyler

Audrey Hepburn is the beautiful Princess Ann, who, weary of being on display at
formal engagements, feels like a prisoner of her own life. While visiting Rome she
escapes from her entourage, and meets handsome American reporter Joe Bradley
(Gregory Peck). He shows her the sights of the great city, and they fall for each
other. Then Bradley has to decide if he should still run his exclusive story about the
princess. A heartfelt, sweet story about true love.

Academy Award Recognition: Audrey Hepburn won Best Actress,
Ian McLellan Hunter won Best Motion Picture Story, nominated for Best
Picture, Eddie Albert nominated for Best Supporting Actor, William Wyler
nominated for Best Director, Ian McLellan Hunter and John Dighton
nominated for Best Screenplay.

ROOM FOR ONE MORE

BLACK & WHITE · 1952

DRAMA/COMEDY
WARNER BROTHERS

CARY GRANT · **BETSY DRAKE** · **LURENE TUTTLE**

Screenplay by: Jack Rose and Melville Shavelson
From: The book by Anna Perrott Rose
Directed by: Norman Taurog

Cary Grant and Betsy Drake co-star as George and Anna Rose, a loving couple with three children. After visiting an orphanage, Anna decides to take in an abandoned and troubled teenage girl. At first, George isn't too crazy about the whole thing, but they work hard and eventually are able to help the girl leave her past behind her. Based on that success, they go on to adopt a boy with both physical and emotional problems and turn his life around, too. An inspiring and heartwarming story of the power of family love.

ROYAL WEDDING

TECHNICOLOR · 1951

MUSICAL
MGM

FRED ASTAIRE · **JANE POWELL** · **PETER LAWFORD**
SARAH CHURCHILL · **KEENAN WYNN** · **ALBERT SHARPE**

Screenplay by: Alan Jay Lerner
Directed by: Stanley Donen

This musical features Fred Astaire and Jane Powell as Tom and Ellen Bowen, a brother and sister dance act. They are invited to perform in England around the time of the wedding of Princess Elizabeth (now Queen Elizabeth). During their trans-Atlantic voyage, Ellen meets an English Lord (played by Peter Lawford) and falls in love. Later, Tom also finds love with an English dancer (Sarah Churchill). Then Tom and Ellen have to decide whether or not to sacrifice their dancing partnership for marriage. There's an abundance of good dance numbers in this movie—including Fred Astaire's famous routine where he dances on the ceiling.

 Academy Award Recognition: nominated for Best Song: *Too Late Now*, Music by Burton Lane, Lyrics by Alan Jay Lerner.

RUN SILENT, RUN DEEP
BLACK & WHITE

DRAMA/MILITARY/ACTION-ADVENTURE
1958

UNITED ARTISTS

CLARK GABLE   BURT LANCASTER   JACK WARDEN   DON RICKLES

Screenplay by: John Gay
Based on: A novel by Commander Edward L. Beach
Directed by: Robert Wise

In this tense World War II drama, submarine Commander Richardson (Clark Gable),
is moved to a new assignment when his old sub is sunk by the Japanese. But he's
met with defiance from the new sub's executive officer, Lt. Jim Bledsoe (played by
Burt Lancaster), who had thought that he would be in line for the new commanding
position. The crew distrusts Richardson as well, but despite personal conflicts, they
all try to achieve their goals. This riveting military drama has loads of suspense and
realistic battle scenes, with a surprise ending. More suitable for teenagers and
adults, not for younger children.

SABOTEUR
BLACK & WHITE

DRAMA/MYSTERY-SUSPENSE
1942

UNIVERSAL

PRISCILLA LANE   ROBERT CUMMINGS

Screenplay by: Peter Viertel, Joan Harrison and Dorothy Parker
Directed by: Alfred Hitchcock

Robert Cummings is Barry Kane, a World War II defense plant worker whose best
buddy is suddenly killed in an enormous and suspicious fire at the factory. In their
search for the saboteur, investigators question the plant employees, and somehow
Kane becomes their prime suspect. Kane is completely innocent, but has no means
of proving it, so he skips town to try and locate the guilty party on his own. In the
meantime, authorities have launched a nationwide manhunt, and the unknown entity
that framed him for the arson is hot on Kane's trail as well, lest he should uncover
the real truth. In his travels, he meets the lovely Patricia Martin (Priscilla Lane),
who at first intends to turn Kane in to the police, but eventually comes to believe
his story and helps him to unravel the mystery. A thrilling story that ends with a
spectacular chase scene atop the Statue of Liberty.

SABRINA

BLACK & WHITE   1954   COMEDY/ROMANCE
                                                         PARAMOUNT

HUMPHREY BOGART   **AUDREY HEPBURN**   **WILLIAM HOLDEN**

Screenplay by: Billy Wilder, Samuel Taylor, and Ernest Lehman
Based on: The play by Samuel Taylor
Directed by: Billy Wilder

The story begins at the Larabee estate on the North Shore of Long Island. Audrey Hepburn is Sabrina, the lovely daughter of the family's chauffeur. The Larabees have two sons: the responsible and serious Linus (Humphrey Bogart), and the irresponsible, devil-may-care David (William Holden). Sabrina longs for David from afar, but he has no interest in her—until she blossoms into a captivating, sophisticated woman after a trip to Europe. Sabrina's father and the Larabees disapprove of this new liaison. Linus sets out to distract Sabrina and break up the romance but to his astonishment, falls in love with her himself. A very enjoyable and enchanting comedy.

 Academy Award Recognition: Audrey Hepburn nominated for Best Actress, Billy Wilder nominated for Best Director; Billy Wilder, Samuel Taylor and Ernest Lehman nominated for Best Screenplay.

SAILOR BEWARE

BLACK & WHITE   1951   COMEDY/MILITARY
                                                         PARAMOUNT

DEAN MARTIN   **JERRY LEWIS**   **CORINNE CALVET**   **MARION MARSHALL**

Screenplay by: James Allardice and Martin Rackin
Based on: A play by Kenyon Nicholson and Charles Robinson
Directed by: Hal Walker

Dean Martin and Jerry Lewis star as Navy recruits Al Crowthers and Melvin Jones. In the usual Martin and Lewis style, Al is the handsome and smooth young gentleman, and Melvin is the clumsy but good-natured fool. As the two pals begin their new life in the Navy, they have their first trip in a submarine, take a chance fighting in the boxing ring, and chase girls. A fun and wacky service comedy.

SALLY AND SAINT ANNE
BLACK & WHITE   1952

COMEDY
UNIVERSAL INT'L

ANN BLYTH   **EDMUND GWENN**   **JOHN McINTIRE**   **FRANCIS BAVIER**

Screenplay by: James O'Hanlon and Herb Meadow
Story by: James O'Hanlon
Directed by: Rudolph Maté

Ann Blyth is Sally O'Mayne, a young Irish-Catholic woman who as a girl discovered that Saint Anne pays special attention to her prayers. Over the years, Sally has prayed for the needs of family, friends and neighbors, no matter how large or small the request. Her unique gift is not a surprise at all to her eccentric family, of which her grandfather (Edmund Gwenn) is the most odd. Trouble brews for the Irish clan when a city alderman, with whom they've had a long-standing feud, tries to put them out of their home. At the same time, Sally attempts to win the heart of a young man who doesn't even know she's alive. Can Saint Anne intervene to help them all? An offbeat and very engaging family comedy.

SAN ANTONIO
TECHNICOLOR   1945

DRAMA/WESTERN
WARNER BROTHERS

ERROL FLYNN   **ALEXIS SMITH**   **S.Z. SAKALL**

Screenplay by: Alan LeMay and W.R. Burnett
Directed by: David Butler

The setting is San Antonio, Texas in 1877. Ranchers are losing their herds to night-time raiders. Errol Flynn is Clay Hardin, a bold rancher who intends to fight back and win. He works diligently to trap the livestock thieves while also romancing pretty traveling singer Jeanne Starr (Alexis Smith). An interesting Western with lots of action.

 Academy Award Recognition: nominated for Best Song: ***Some Sunday Morning***, Music by Ray Heindorf and M.K. Jerome, Lyrics by Ted Koehler.

SAN FRANCISCO

BLACK & WHITE/COLORIZED   1936

DRAMA

MGM

CLARK GABLE   **JEANETTE MacDONALD**   **SPENCER TRACY**

Screenplay by:	Anita Loos
Based on:	The story by Robert Hopkins
Directed by:	W.S. Van Dyke

San Francisco, 1906. Clark Gable is Blackie Norton, a rugged and sometimes unscrupulous character, who owns a popular saloon on the Barbary Coast. Spencer Tracy is Father Mullin, a childhood friend of Blackie's who has tried for years—without success—to reform him. Then along comes Mary Blake (played by Jeanette MacDonald), a refined, proper lady and classical singer. Mary and Blackie fall in love, but since the two come from different worlds, they have a lot of differences to work out. The story climaxes with the great San Francisco earthquake and how all weather the destruction. A good drama with an interesting story line and what were considered impressive special effects in its time.

Academy Award Recognition: nominated for Best Picture, Spencer Tracy nominated for Best Actor, W.S. Van Dyke nominated for Best Director, Robert Hopkins nominated for Best Original Story.

SANDS OF IWO JIMA

BLACK & WHITE/COLORIZED

DRAMA/MILITARY/ACTION-ADVENTURE

1949   REPUBLIC

JOHN WAYNE   **JOHN AGAR**   **ADELE MARA**
FORREST TUCKER   **MARTIN MILNER**

Screenplay by:	Harry Brown and James Edward Grant
Story by:	Harry Brown
Directed by:	Allan Dwan

A story about a Marine Rifle Squad in the Pacific during World War II. John Wayne stars as Sgt. John M. Stryker, the squad's commander. He's a demanding and tough sergeant who disciplines his men strictly to prepare them for battle. He has particular trouble with one of his squad members, Pfc. Al Thomas (Forrest Tucker), with whom he's had conflicts in the past. John Agar is Pfc. Peter Conway, who sees, once the unit faces fierce combat on Iwo Jima, why Stryker was so tough on them. There are lots of intense battle scenes in this action-packed war movie based on the actual historical World War II battle on the Pacific island of Iwo Jima. This movie is more suitable for teenagers and adults, not for young children.

 Academy Award Recognition: John Wayne nominated for Best Actor, Harry Brown nominated for Best Motion Picture Story.

SAVAGE, THE
TECHNICOLOR   1953

DRAMA/WESTERN
PARAMOUNT

CHARLTON HESTON   SUSAN MORROW

Screenplay by: Sydney Boehm
Based on: A novel by L.L. Foreman
Directed by: George Marshall

Photographed in The Black Hills of South Dakota.

In 1868, an 11-year-old white boy is the lone survivor of an Indian raid on a wagon train, and is adopted and raised by the Sioux tribe. Charlton Heston plays this boy as a grown man—now a strong and masterful warrior named Warbonnet. He has no trouble fighting the Indian tribe that killed his father, but has mixed feelings when war erupts between the Sioux and the expanding United States. Plenty of action and an interesting look at the plight of Native Americans at that time.

SAY ONE FOR ME
CINEMASCOPE & DELUXE COLOR   1959

DRAMA/MUSICAL
20TH CENTURY FOX

BING CROSBY	**DEBBIE REYNOLDS**	**ROBERT WAGNER**
RAY WALSTON	**LES TREMAYNE**	**CONNIE GILCHREST**
FRANK McHUGH	**JOE BESSER**	**ALENA MURRAY**

Written by: Robert O'Brien
Directed by: Frank Tashlin
Songs by: Sammy Cahn and James Van Heusen

Bing Crosby is Father Conroy, a parish priest in New York's Theater District. Debbie Reynolds portrays Holly, a young woman aspiring to the stage. When Holly's actor father becomes ill, Father Conroy tries to look out for her best interests. Robert Wagner is Tony Vincent, a fast-talking and womanizing song-and-dance-man. Holly takes a job in his show and Tony romances her, but complications develop because the two come from entirely different backgrounds. A good show business story with some entertaining musical numbers.

 Academy Award Recognition: Lionel Newman nominated for Best Scoring of a Musical Picture.

SCANDAL AT SCOURIE
TECHNICOLOR   1953

DRAMA
MGM

| GREER GARSON | WALTER PIDGEON | DONNA CORCORAN |
| AGNES MOOREHEAD | ARTHUR SHIELDS | PHILIP OBER |

Screenplay by: Norman Corwin, Leonard Spigelgass, and Karl Tunberg
Based on: A story by Mary McSherry
Directed by: Jean Negulesco

The story begins in the late 1800s in French Canada, where a Catholic orphanage burns down. Agnes Moorehead plays Sister Josephine, the nun in charge of the orphanage, who then escorts the children across the countryside to find homes for them. While passing through a predominantly Protestant town, a little girl named Patsy (Donna Corcoran) befriends Mrs. McChesney (Greer Garson), a childless woman who decides to adopt her and agrees to raise the child in the Catholic faith. The problem is that her husband, Patrick McChesney (Walter Pidgeon) is a prominent Protestant politician, and he comes under fire from the community for adopting the Catholic girl. The rest of this touching and heartwarming tale shows how the three work their way toward becoming a family, despite social pressures.

SCARED STIFF

BLACK & WHITE   1953

COMEDY/MYSTERY-SUSPENSE

PARAMOUNT

DEAN MARTIN	**JERRY LEWIS**	**LIZABETH SCOTT**
CARMEN MIRANDA	**GEORGE DOLENZ**	**DOROTHY MALONE**

Screenplay by: Herbert Baker and Walter De Leon;
                             additional dialogue by Ed Simmons and Norman Lear
Based on: A play by Paul Dickey and Charles W. Goddard
Directed by: George Marshall

In this re-make of **The Ghost Breakers** (1940), Dean Martin and Jerry Lewis are buddies Larry Todd and Myron Mertz. They get themselves into quite a mess while trying to help pretty heiress Mary Carroll (Lizabeth Scott), whose life is in danger. A zany and fun mystery, with a few good songs mixed in, that culminates in an amusing romp through an eerie old mansion.

SEA OF GRASS, THE

BLACK & WHITE   1947

DRAMA/WESTERN

MGM

SPENCER TRACY	**KATHERINE HEPBURN**	**MELVYN DOUGLAS**

Screenplay by: Marguerite Roberto and Vincent Lawrence
Based on: A novel by Conrad Richter
Directed by: Elia Kazan
Produced by: Pedro S. Berman

In the late 1800s, cattle baron Jim Brewton (Spencer Tracy), and his wife Lutie (Katherine Hepburn), a lovely woman from St. Louis, live on a huge and isolated ranch, along with their young daughter. But then homesteaders begin moving in and plowing up the prairie, ruining it for cattle. Jim's growing anger and fixation on ridding the territory of homesteaders take their toll on his relationship with Lutie, and the story continues from there. This film is heavier and more dramatic than most of those Tracy and Hepburn made together, but it does have a happy ending. The complexity of the story makes this movie more suitable for people aged pre-teen through adult, rather than very young ones.

SECOND TIME AROUND, THE

CINEMASCOPE & DE LUXE COLOR   1961

COMEDY/WESTERN
20TH CENTURY FOX

DEBBIE REYNOLDS   **STEVE FORREST**   **ANDY GRIFFITH**
JULIET PROWSE   **THELMA RITTER**   **KEN SCOTT**

Screenplay by: Oscar Saul and Cecil Dan Hansen
Based on: A novel by Richard Emery Roberts
Directed by: Vincent Sherman

In 1911 New York, Lucretia Rogers (Debbie Reynolds), a young widow with two children, is pondering her family's future. Offered a job in Arizona by a friend of her deceased husband, she sets out alone, temporarily leaving her children behind with her mother-in-law. After arriving in Arizona, Lucretia finds that the friend has since died, and she is now stranded there with no money. That changes when she lands a job as a ranch hand for a lady rancher named Aggie (Thelma Ritter), who eventually helps Lucretia build a new life. An enjoyable and fun Western comedy that people of all ages can enjoy.

SERGEANT YORK

DRAMA

BLACK & WHITE/COLORIZED   1941

WARNER BROTHERS

GARY COOPER   **WALTER BRENNAN**   **JOAN LESLIE**   **GEORGE TOBIAS**
STANLEY RIDGES   **MARGARET WYCHERLY**   **JUNE LOCKHART**

Screenplay by: Abem Finkel, Harry Chandlee, Howard Koch, John Huston
Based on: The diary of Sergeant York as edited by Tom Skeyhill
Directed by: Howard Hawks

The true story of Alvin York, the decorated World War I sergeant. He began as a rabble-rousing youth in the Cumberland Mountains of Tennessee, but grew into a religious young man. When drafted into the Army, York became a reluctant warrior, but turned into a national hero by capturing 132 prisoners with a team of only eight men. For that incredible feat, he was awarded the Congressional Medal of Honor. An excellent biographical movie with historical significance.

Academy Award Recognition: Gary Cooper won Best Actor, nominated for Best Picture, Walter Brennan nominated for Best Supporting Actor, Margaret Wycherly nominated for Best Supporting Actress, Howard Hawks nominated for Best Director; Harry Chandlee, Abem Finkel, John Huston and Howard Koch nominated for Best Original Screenplay, Max Steiner nominated for Best Musical Scoring of a Dramatic Picture.

SEVEN BRIDES FOR SEVEN BROTHERS
CINEMASCOPE & ANSCO COLOR   1954

MUSICAL/ROMANCE

MGM

JANE POWELL	**HOWARD KEEL**	**JEFF RICHARDS**
RUSS TAMBLYN	**TOMMY RALL**	**HOWARD PETRIE**
VIRGINIA GIBSON	**IAN WOLFE**	

Screenplay by: Albert Hackett, Frances Goodrich, and Dorothy Kingsley
Based on: The story *The Sobbin' Women* by Stephen Vincent Benet
Directed by: Stanley Donen

A frontier musical, set in the Oregon Territory. A brawny backwoodsman named Adam (Howard Keel) heads for town in search of a wife, where he finds Millie (Jane Powell), a pretty woman who is working as a cook at an inn. Glad at the prospect of caring for one man instead of many, she marries him on the spur of the moment. Her husband has big a surprise waiting for her at home, though—his six brothers! Exasperated, Millie sets out to tame the wild bunch of men and teach them how to find women of their own. A superb musical, with great songs and fantastic dance numbers.

Academy Award Recognition: Adolph Deutsch and Saul Chaplin won Best Scoring of a Musical Picture, nominated for Best Picture; Albert Hackett, Frances Goodrich and Dorothy Kingsley nominated for Best Screenplay.

SEVEN LITTLE FOYS, THE
TECHNICOLOR   1955

MUSICAL/DRAMA

PARAMOUNT

BOB HOPE	**MILLY VITALE**	**GEORGE TOBIAS**
ANGELA CLARKE	**HERBERT HEYES**	**RICHARD SHANNON**
BILLY GRAY	**JAMES CAGNEY**	

Screenplay by: Melville Shavelson and Jack Rose
Based on: The life story of Eddie Foy
Directed by: Melville Shavelson

This is the true story of the Foy family, the renowned vaudeville performers. Bob Hope stars as Eddie Foy, who makes the transition from bachelor to married man and eventually, to father of seven children. While Eddie is off on the road perform- ing, his wife raises the children and runs their home. But when she dies, Eddie suddenly has to care for them himself and find a way to keep the family together while he travels to earn a living. His ingenious solution is to revamp his vaudeville act to include all the kids and take them along. A very enjoyable movie that the whole family can enjoy together.

 Academy Award Recognition: Melville Shavelson and Jack Rose nominated for Best Story and Screenplay.

SHADOW OF A DOUBT

BLACK & WHITE

DRAMA/MYSTERY-SUSPENSE

1942

UNIVERSAL

TERESA WRIGHT	**JOSEPH COTTEN**	**MacDONALD CAREY**
HENRY TRAVERS	**PATRICIA COLLINGE**	**HUME CRONYN**

Screenplay by:	Thornton Wilder, Sally Benson and Alma Reville
From:	An original story by Gordon McDonell
Directed by:	Alfred Hitchcock

Teresa Wright is Charlie, a young woman whose Uncle Charlie (for whom she is named) pays an impromptu visit. At first, her whole family is unaware that Uncle Charlie is on the run from the law, but as clues begin to present themselves, young Charlie suspects that her beloved uncle could be the "Merry Widow Murderer." When these suspicions become apparent to Uncle Charlie, her life is suddenly in great danger. An excellent mystery movie with spine-tingling suspense.

 Academy Award Recognition: Gordon McDonell nominated for Best Original Story.

SHADOW OF THE THIN MAN

BLACK & WHITE

COMEDY/MYSTERY-SUSPENSE

1941

MGM

WILLIAM POWELL	**MYRNA LOY**	**BARRY NELSON**	**DONNA REED**	**SAM LEVENE**

Screenplay by:	Irving Brecher and Harry Kurnitz
From:	A story by Harry Kurnitz,
	based on characters created by Dashiell Hammett
Directed by:	W.S. Van Dyke II

Another installment in the *Thin Man* series of movies, in which William Powell and Myrna Loy continue their roles as the famous sleuths, Nick and Nora Charles. This time, Nick and Nora take a trip to the racetrack. When a jockey turns up dead, they have to crack a tough murder case that involves the horse racing world. An intriguing and stylish mystery mixed with a little comedy here and there.

SHAGGY DOG, THE
BLACK & WHITE/COLORIZED   1959

COMEDY/ANIMAL STORIES
WALT DISNEY

| FRED MacMURRAY | JEAN HAGEN | TOMMY KIRK |
| ANNETTE FUNICELLO | TIM CONSIDINE | KEVIN CORCORAN |

Screenplay by: Bill Walsh and Lillie Hayward
Suggested by: ***The Hound of Florence*** by Felix Salter
Directed by: Charles Barton

Fred MacMurray is Wilson Daniels, a mailman who hates dogs, and Jean Hagen is his wife Frieda. Their teenage son Wilby (Tommy Kirk), drives them nuts with his crazy science experiments. Then new neighbors move in with a pretty teenage daughter, Allison (Annette Funicello), and a shaggy sheepdog. When Wilby unexpectedly finds a magic ring, a mystical spell turns him into the neighbor's dog, and so begins a wild adventure. A cute and whimsical family-style comedy.

SHALL WE DANCE
BLACK & WHITE   1937

MUSICAL
RKO

FRED ASTAIRE	GINGER ROGERS	EDWARD EVERETT HORTON
ERIC BLORE	JEROME COWAN	KETTI GALLIAN
WILLIAM BRISBANE	HARRIET HOCTOR	

Screenplay by: Allan Scott and Ernest Pagano, adaptation by P. J. Wolfson
Based on: A story by Lee Loeb and Harold Buchman
Directed by: Mark Sandrich

Music by George Gershwin; Lyrics by Ira Gershwin

Fred Astaire is Petrov, a famous ballet dancer who longs to try tap dancing. Ginger Rogers is Linda Keene, a contemporary singing and dancing star. When they meet, Linda finds Petrov attractive, but he pretends to be married in order to keep her from getting serious. Petrov's plan backfires when rumors fly that he is secretly married to Linda. When no one believes the truth, the two decide to end the scandal by actually marrying and then getting a planned divorce. To add to the confusion, they end up really falling in love. Will they stay together or not? A charming musical with the fine and elegant dancing that was the trademark of the Astaire and Rogers team.

 Academy Award Recognition: nominated for Best Song: *They Can't Take That Away from Me*, Music by George Gershwin, Lyrics by Ira Gershwin.

SHANE
COLOR   1953   DRAMA/WESTERN
                                                                        PARAMOUNT

ALAN LADD   **JEAN ARTHUR**   **VAN HEFLIN**
BRANDON de WILDE   **JACK PALANCE**

Screenplay by: A.B. Guthrie, Jr. and Jack Sher
Based on: The novel by Jack Schaefer
Directed by: George Stevens

Alan Ladd is Shane, a former gunfighter who's trying to put his past behind him and live a peaceful life. He takes a job as a farm hand, but gets pulled into an ongoing battle between homesteaders and the cattle ranchers who bully them. Jean Arthur co-stars as Marion Starrett, the woman who hires Shane to work on her farm. This tense and riveting story takes many suspenseful turns as Shane helps the homesteaders stand up for themselves. A strong drama more suitable for ages pre-teen through adult, not for very young children.

 Academy Award Recognition: nominated for Best Picture, George Stevens nominated for Best Director, Brandon de Wilde and Jack Palance both nominated for Best Supporting Actor, A.B. Guthrie, Jr. nominated for Best Screenplay.

SHE WORE A YELLOW RIBBON

TECHNICOLOR   1949

DRAMA/WESTERN

RKO

JOHN WAYNE	**JOANNE DRU**	**JOHN AGAR**
BEN JOHNSON	**HARRY CAREY, JR.**	**VICTOR McLAGLEN**
MILDRED NATWICK	**GEORGE O'BRIEN**	**ARTHUR SHIELDS**

Screenplay by: Frank Nugent and Laurence Stallings
Story by: James Warner Bellah
Directed by: John Ford

John Wayne is Nathan Brittles, a U.S. Cavalry Captain in the wild west who is about to retire in several days. A very able leader, he is admired greatly by his men. He heads out on his last patrol, which includes the escort of two women on one leg of their trip back East. His last assignment proves to be a dangerous one, as he and his men clash with Native American tribes in the wake of the massacre of General Custer's troops. A very good Western, and considered by many fans to be among Wayne's best movies.

SHEEPMAN, THE

CINEMASCOPE & METROCOLOR   1958

COMEDY/WESTERN

MGM

GLENN FORD	**SHIRLEY MacLAINE**	**LESLIE NIELSEN**
MICKEY SHAUGHNESSY	**EDGAR BUCHANAN**	**WILLIE BOUCHEY**
PERNELL ROBERTS	**SLIM PICKENS**	

Screenplay by: Buzz Henry, William Bowers and James Edward Grant
Based on: A story by James Edward Grant
Directed by: George Marshall

Glenn Ford is Jason Sweet, a man who arrives in a western town with enough sheep to start a ranch, but there's a problem—it's a cattle town. He meets up with his old enemy, Johnny Bledsoe (Leslie Nielsen), who happens to be the most prominent cattle rancher in the area, and the two lock horns once again over their new opposing interests. Shirley MacLaine is Dell Payton, Johnny's fiancé, who's also involved in all the commotion. A hearty Western comedy with a happy ending.

Academy Award Recognition: James Edward Grant, William Bowers nominated for Best Story and Screenplay (written directly for the screen).

SHOW BOAT
TECHNICOLOR   1951   MUSICAL/DRAMA
                                               MGM

KATHRYN GRAYSON	AVA GARDNER	HOWARD KEEL
JOE E. BROWN	MARGE CHAMPION	GOWER CHAMPION
ROBERT STERLING	AGNES MOOREHEAD	LEIF ERIKSON
WILLIAM WARFIELD		

Screenplay by: John Lee Mahin
Based on: The musical play *Show Boat* by Jerome Kern and
                  Oscar Hammerstein, from Edna Ferber's novel
Directed by: George Sidney

In this musical portrayal of life on a river boat, Kathryn Grayson is Magnolia Hawks, the daughter of the boat's owner Captain Andy Hawks (Joe. E. Brown). Though her parents warn against it, she marries gambler Gaylord Ravenal (Howard Keel), who brings her nothing but misery. Ava Gardner plays Julie LaVerne, a woman of mixed race who endures the sting of racial prejudice. A colorful screen production of this classic American stage show, featuring its fine, time-honored songs.

Academy Award Recognition: Adolph Deutsch and Conrad Salinger nominated for Best Scoring of a Musical Picture.

SILK STOCKINGS
CINEMASCOPE & METROCOLOR   1957   MUSICAL
                                               MGM

| FRED ASTAIRE | CYD CHARISSE | JANIS PAIGE |
| PETER LORRE | GEORGE TOBIAS | JULES MUNSHIN |

Screenplay by: Leonard Gershe and Leonard Spigelgass
Suggested by: *Ninotchka* by Melchior Lengyel
Directed by: Rouben Mamoulian

Music and Lyrics by Cole Porter

A musical remake of *Ninotchka* (1939). Fred Astaire is Steve Canfield, an American movie producer making a film in Paris. When he schemes to secure the services of a well-known Russian composer, a beautiful Communist envoy named Ninotchka (Cyd Charisse) is sent to straighten out the situation. Steve falls for her, but has his work cut out for him—he has to break through Ninotchka's tough exterior. A sleek, sophisticated musical with an unusual story line.

SINGIN' IN THE RAIN

TECHNICOLOR   1952

MUSICAL

MGM

GENE KELLY	DEBBIE REYNOLDS	DONALD O'CONNOR
JEAN HAGEN	MILLARD MITCHELL	CYD CHARISSE
RITA MORENO	DOUGLAS FOWLEY	

Screenplay by: Adolph Green and Betty Comden
Suggested by: The song *Singin' in the Rain*
Directed by: Gene Kelly and Stanley Donen

The setting is Hollywood, and talking pictures are beginning to replace silent films. Silent film stars Don Lockwood (Gene Kelly) and Lena Lamonte (Jean Hagen) run into big trouble when they begin production on their first talkie. Lena has a terrible speaking voice and can't sing. Then Don meets aspiring singer/actress Kathy Selden (Debbie Reynolds), and with the help of his buddy Cosmo Brown (Donald O'Connor), they use Kathy's voice to cover Lena's for the film. Don falls in love with Kathy, and his first talking picture is saved. But what will Don do about egotistical Lena, who now expects all of her films to be made the same way? A cheerful movie, with great music and dancing, providing excellent entertainment for the whole family.

 Academy Award Recognition: Jean Hagen nominated for Best Supporting Actress, Lennie Hayton nominated for Best Scoring of a Musical Picture.

SMALL TOWN GIRL

TECHNICOLOR   1953

MUSICAL

MGM

JANE POWELL	FARLEY GRANGER	ANN MILLER
S.Z. SAKALL	ROBERT KEITH	BOBBY VAN
BILLIE BURKE	FAY WRAY	NAT KING COLE

Screenplay by: Dorothy Cooper and Dorothy Kingsley
Story by: Dorothy Cooper
Directed by: Leslie Kardos

Rick Livingston (Farley Granger) is a slick young man from New York City who is arrested and thrown in jail for a minor offense while passing through a small country town. Rick's engaged to New York dancer Lisa Bellmount (Ann Miller), but falls for Cindy Kimbell (Jane Powell) the daughter of the town's judge. However, Cindy is currently dating the local shopowner's son, Ludwig Schlemmer (Bobby Van). The story continues from there, with S.Z. "Cuddles" Sakall stealing many scenes as Eric Schlemmer, Ludwig's lovable father. An engaging and genial musical that has some very entertaining dance numbers.

 Academy Award Recognition: nominated for Best Song: *My Flaming Heart*, Music by Nicholas Brodszky, Lyrics by Leo Robin.

SNOWBALL EXPRESS
TECHNICOLOR   1972

COMEDY
WALT DISNEY

DEAN JONES	**NANCY OLSON**	**HARRY MORGAN**
KEENAN WYNN	**JOHNNY WHITAKER**	**MICHAEL McGREEVEY**
GEORGE LINDSEY	**KATHLEEN CODY**	**MARY WICKES**

Screenplay by: Don Tait and Jim Parker, and Arnold Margolin
Based on: The book *Chateau Bon Vivant* by Frankie and John O'Rear
Directed by: Norman Tokar

Dean Jones is Johnny Baxter, a frustrated office worker who inherits a hotel in Colorado from his recently deceased uncle. Excited about the opportunity to start a new life, he quits his job to move there with his wife Sue (Nancy Olson) and their children. When they arrive, they find that the old ski lodge is falling apart, but decide to try and fix it up, hopefully turning it into a money-making operation. A fun-filled comedy for the whole family, with great scenery filmed at Crested Butte, Colorado.

SOME LIKE IT HOT
BLACK & WHITE   1959

COMEDY
UNITED ARTISTS

MARILYN MONROE	**TONY CURTIS**	**JACK LEMMON**
GEORGE RAFT	**PAT O'BRIEN**	**JOE E. BROWN**

Screenplay by: Billy Wilder and I.A.L. Diamond
Suggested by: A story by R. Thoeren and M. Logan
Directed by: Billy Wilder

The story begins in 1929 Chicago, where gangsters threatened to rule the streets. Tony Curtis and Jack Lemmon are two unemployed musicians named Joe and Jerry, who accidentally witness the St. Valentine's Day Massacre. Fleeing angry mobsters, they go into hiding by disguising themselves as women and going on the road with an all-female band. Joe and Jerry compete for the most voluptuous band member, Sugar Kane (Marilyn Monroe), while also fending off the advances of the men who are falling in love with them. A marvelous and hilarious comedy with a great cast.

 Academy Award Recognition: Jack Lemmon nominated for Best Actor, Billy Wilder nominated for Best Director, Billy Wilder and I.A.L. Diamond nominated for Best Screenplay (based on material from another medium).

SOMEBODY UP THERE LIKES ME

DRAMA

BLACK & WHITE/COLORIZED   1956   MGM

PAUL NEWMAN	PIER ANGELI	EVERETT SLOANE
EILEEN HECKART	SAL MINEO	HAROLD J. STONE

Screenplay by:	Ernest Lehman
Based on:	The autobiography of Rocky Graziano, written with Rowland Barber
Directed by:	Robert Wise

The true life story of middle-weight boxing champion Rocky Graziano, starring Paul Newman. As a youth, Rocky was always in some sort of trouble, but turned his life around to become one of the boxing world's great champions. Eileen Heckart plays Rocky's mother and Pier Angeli portrays his wife, Norma. A well-done and inspiring biographical drama.

SON OF FLUBBER

COMEDY

BLACK & WHITE   1963   WALT DISNEY

FRED MacMURRAY	NANCY OLSON	KEENAN WYNN
TOMMY KIRK	ED WYNN	CHARLIE RUGGLES
LEON AMES	WILLIAM DEMAREST	PAUL LYNDE

Screenplay by:	Bill Walsh and Don DaGradi
Based on:	A story by Samuel M. Taylor and the Danny Dunn Books
Directed by:	Robert Stevenson

In this sequel to *The Absent-Minded Professor* (1961), Fred MacMurray continues his role as Professor Ned Brainard. This time, he attempts to use "Flubber" gas to control the weather, while his young assistant Biff Hawk (Tommy Kirk) tries to use it to win football games for their college team. When an old flame of Dr. Brainard's shows up and upsets his wife Betsy, he's got some domestic problems to solve as well. A very good and funny follow-up to the first movie.

SON OF FURY
BLACK & WHITE

DRAMA/ACTION-ADVENTURE

1942

20TH CENTURY FOX

TYRONE POWER	GENE TIERNEY	GEORGE SANDERS	FRANCES FARMER
ELSA LANCHESTER	KAY JOHNSON	JOHN CARRADINE	HARRY DAVENPORT
DUDLEY DIGGES	RODDY McDOWELL		

Screenplay by: Philip Dunne
Based on: The novel *Benjamin Blake* by Edison Marshall
Directed by: John Cromwell

Tyrone Power is Benjamin Blake, a man whose birthright to wealth and power has been stolen by his ruthless uncle, Sir Arthur Blake (George Sanders). As a boy, Ben (played by young Roddy McDowall) is forced into indentured servitude and treated terribly by Sir Arthur, but endures and grows to manhood determined to regain his rightful place in the world. What follows is the story of Ben's quest to prove that he is the rightful master of the family estate. Gene Tierney plays a tropical island girl whom Ben falls for along the way. An interesting and action-packed story of adventure and perseverance.

SON OF LASSIE
TECHNICOLOR

DRAMA/ANIMAL STORIES

1945

MGM

PETER LAWFORD	DONALD CRISP	JUNE LOCKHART	NIGEL BRUCE
LEON AMES	LASSIE	LADDIE	

Screenplay by: Jeanne Bartlett
Based on: Some characters from the book
                          Lassie Come Home by Eric Knight
Directed by: S. Sylvan Simon

A sequel to *Lassie Come Home* (1943), where Peter Lawford portrays the now grown-up Joe Carraclough. Donald Crisp repeats the role of his father Sam, and June Lockhart continues the role of Joe's friend Priscilla, which was originated by

Elizabeth Taylor in the first movie. Joe is in uniform now, attending flight school to prepare for World War II. Lassie's mischievous pup, Laddie, grows up while Joe's away at training. Then they go on to share exciting wartime adventures together. A noble tale of the faithful bond between man and dog.

SON OF PALEFACE
TECHNICOLOR

1952

COMEDY/WESTERN/MUSICAL
PARAMOUNT

BOB HOPE　　　　**JANE RUSSELL**　　　　**ROY ROGERS**

Screenplay by:　　Frank Tashlin, Robert I. Welch, and Joseph Quillan
Directed by:　　　Frank Tashlin

Bob Hope plays the son of Peter Potter and Calamity Jane in this sequel to 1948's *The Paleface*. He is a spoiled young man from the East who goes out West to claim his inheritance. When he gets there, he finds out that the inheritance was secretly hidden by his father, who owed money to everybody in town. Potter must locate the treasure and pay off the debts before the angry townspeople get hold of him. Along the way, he meets a feisty female outlaw named Mike (Jane Russell), who attempts to use Potter as her alibi. A fun Western with lots of action.

 Academy Award Recognition: nominated for Best Song: *Am I in Love*, Music and Lyrics by Jack Brooks.

SONG OF THE THIN MAN
BLACK & WHITE

1947

COMEDY/MYSTERY-SUSPENSE
MGM

WILLIAM POWELL	MYRNA LOY	KEENAN WYNN	DEAN STOCKWELL
PHILIP REED	PATRICIA MORRISON	GLORIA GRAHAME	JAYNE MEADOWS
DON TAYLOR	LEON AMES		

Screenplay by:　　Steve Fisher and Nat Perrin;
　　　　　　　　　additional dialogue by James O'Hanlon and Harry Crane
Story by:　　　　Stanley Roberts
Based on:　　　　The characters created by Dashiell Hammett
Directed by:　　　Edward Buzzell

This is the last entry of the *Thin Man* series of films. Famous sleuths Nick and Nora Charles (William Powell and Myrna Loy) work to solve the murder of a bandleader that occurs while they are enjoying an evening of music and dancing aboard the pleasure boat S.S. Fortune. The circumstances of the crime are very complex and there is no shortage of possible suspects. A touch of comedy is thrown in here and there with the antics of their son, Nick Jr. (Dean Stockwell) and their dog, Asta. A fascinating mystery, where the identity of the killer is concealed right up to the very end.

SONS OF KATIE ELDER, THE

COLOR   1962

DRAMA/WESTERN

PARAMOUNT

JOHN WAYNE	DEAN MARTIN	MARTHA HYER
EARL HOLLIMAN	JOHN ANDERSON, JR.	PAUL FIX
DENNIS HOPPER	GEORGE KENNEDY	JAMES GREGORY

Screenplay by: William Wright
Directed by: Henry Hathaway
Produced by: Hal Wallis

John, Tom, Matt, and Bud (played by John Wayne, Dean Martin, Earl Holliman and John Anderson, Jr.), the four sons of a woman named Katie Elder, attend her Texas funeral. While in town to lay their mother to rest, they investigate how she has lost the family's ranch at the time of their father's death. In stirring up old secrets, the brothers find plenty of trouble—including being framed for the murder of the town's sheriff. An exciting story with lots of action.

SOUND OF MUSIC, THE

DELUXE COLOR   1965

MUSICAL

20TH CENTURY FOX

JULIE ANDREWS	CHRISTOPHER PLUMMER	RICHARD HAYDN
PEGGY WOOD	ELEANOR PARKER	

Screenplay by: Ernest Lehman
Based on: The stage musical with Music and Lyrics by
                  Richard Rodgers and Oscar Hammerstein II,
                  and book by Howard Lindsay and Russell Crouse
Directed by: Robert Wise

This story takes place during the Nazi occupation of Austria in World War II. Julie Andrews stars as Maria, the young governess who comes to the aid of an Austrian family of motherless children. She brings warmth, music and love back into the children's lives, as well as that of their overly-strict military father, Captain Von Trapp (Christopher Plummer). One of the most loved family movies of all time, with a fabulous musical score. Based on a true story.

 Academy Award Recognition: won Best Picture, Robert Wise won Best Director, Irwin Kostal won Best Scoring of Music (adaptation or treatment), Julie Andrews nominated for Best Actress, Peggy Wood nominated for Best Supporting Actress.

SOUTH PACIFIC
TECHNICOLOR   1958

MUSICAL
SAMUEL GOLDWYN

| **MITZI GAYNOR** | **ROSSANO BRAZZI** | **JOHN KERR** |
| **JUANITA HALL** | **RAY WALTON** | **FRANCES NUYEN** |

Screenplay by: Paul Osborn
Based on: The Broadway musical, from the book
                    Tales of the South Pacific by James Michener
Directed by: Joshua Logan

Music by Rodgers and Hammerstein

Mitzi Gaynor is Nellie Forbush, a Navy nurse on a South Pacific island during World War II, who meets Emile De Becque (Rossano Brazzi) an older, widowed plantation owner, and falls in love with him. There are barriers to their relationship though, as he is reluctant to make changes in his life and already has children. In a second story line, a young serviceman, Lt. Cable (played by John Kerr) loves a beautiful island girl named Liat (played by France Nuyen) but their racial differences stand in their way. There are funny accessory characters who round out the stories as well—Ray Walston as Luther Billis, and Juanita Hall as Bloody Mary. The famous tunes of Rodgers and Hammerstein, combined with the lovely tropical photography, make this movie an enjoyable experience.

 Academy Award Recognition: Alfred Newman and Ken Darby nominated for Best Scoring of a Musical Picture.

SPOILERS, THE
BLACK & WHITE   1942

DRAMA/WESTERN
UNIVERSAL

JOHN WAYNE	**MARLENE DIETRICH**	**RANDOLPH SCOTT**
MARGARET LINDSAY	**HARRY CAREY**	**SAMUEL HINDS**

Screenplay by: Lawrence Hazard and Tom Reed
Based on: Rex Beach's novel
Directed by: Ray Enright

It's the year 1900 in Nome, Alaska. The Gold Rush is on and claim jumping
and crooked deals are the order of the day. Marlene Dietrich is Cherry Malotte,
a saloon owner who is in love with gold miner Roy Glennister (John Wayne).
Glennister is co-owner of a mine whose claim is being challenged, in a fraudulent
conspiracy, by Gold Commissioner McNamara (Randolph Scott) and Judge Stillman
(Samuel Hinds). The story unfolds from there, with a bit of mystery and plenty
of action.

STAGECOACH
BLACK & WHITE   1939

DRAMA/WESTERN
UNITED ARTISTS

CLAIRE TREVOR	**JOHN WAYNE**	**ANDY DEVINE**
JOHN CARRADINE	**THOMAS MITCHELL**	**LOUISE PLATT**

Screenplay by: Dudley Nichols
Original story by: Ernest Haycox
Directed by: John Ford

John Wayne is The Ringo Kid, a fugitive whose mission is to avenge the murders of
his father and brother. On his way, he catches a ride on a stagecoach, filled with
passengers, which is being escorted by the Cavalry to protect it from Indian attacks.
When the Cavalry unit is ordered to turn back, the passengers decide to proceed
with the coach anyway. The rest of the story chronicles the group's journey, and
how they conquer the dangers that await them. Claire Trevor portrays a passenger
named Dallas, a woman of ill-repute who was run out of her town by a group of
angry wives. Andy Devine plays Buck Rickabough, the stagecoach driver, in this
exciting and action-packed Western.

 Academy Award Recognition: Thomas Mitchell won Best Supporting
Actor; Richard Hageman, Frank Harling, John Leipold and Leo Shuken
won Best Musical Score, nominated for Best Picture, John Ford nominated
for Best Director.

STARS AND STRIPES FOREVER

TECHNICOLOR   1952   MUSICAL
                                                       20TH CENTURY FOX

| CLIFTON WEBB | DEBRA PAGET | ROBERT WAGNER | RUTH HUSSEY |
| FINLAY CURRIE | ROY ROBERTS | TOM BROWNE HENRY | |

Screenplay by: Lamar Trotti; screen story by Ernest Vajda
Based on: *Marching Along* by John Philip Sousa
Directed by: Henry Koster

Clifton Webb stars as John Philip Sousa, the great marching band leader and composer of *Stars and Stripes Forever*, which is often played on patriotic occasions such as the Fourth of July. Sousa worked with the Marine Corps Band and later formed his own band, which traveled far and wide, playing to large crowds. Ruth Hussey portrays Sousa's wife Jennie. Robert Wagner plays Willie, Sousa's lifelong friend from his Marine days, who was the first-ever sousaphone player. Debra Paget is Lily, a young and aspiring singer. Excellent family entertainment that's educational as well, painting a picture of a bygone era.

STATE FAIR

TECHNICOLOR   1945   MUSICAL
                                                       20TH CENTURY FOX

JEANNE CRAIN	DANA ANDREWS	DICK HAYMES	VIVIAN BLAINE
CHARLES WINNINGER	FAY BAINTER	DONALD MEEK	FRANK McHUGH
PERCY KILBRIDE	HENRY MORGAN		

Screenplay by: Oscar Hammerstein II
From: A novel by Philip Stong; adapted by Sonya Levien and Paul Green
Directed by: Walter Lang

Music and Lyrics by Richard Rogers and Oscar Hammerstein II

This popular musical revolves around the adventures of a farm family at their annual state fair. While Mr. and Mrs. Frake (Charles Winninger and Fay Bainter) compete for blue ribbons (he for his prized hog, she for her canned goods), their son (Dick Haymes) and daughter (Jeanne Crain) are busy looking for the true loves that they have long dreamed of. A quaint and tuneful portrayal of American rural traditions.

Academy Award Recognition: won Best Song: *It Might As Well Be Spring*, Music by Richard Rodgers, Lyrics by Oscar Hammerstein II; Charles Henderson and Alfred Newman nominated for Best Scoring of a Musical Picture.

STATE OF THE UNION

DRAMA

BLACK & WHITE   1948   MGM

SPENCER TRACY	KATHERINE HEPBURN	VAN JOHNSON
ANGELA LANSBURY	ADOLPH MENJOU	LEWIS STONE
HOWARD SMITH	CHARLES DINGLE	MAIBEL TURNER

Screenplay by: Anthony Veiller and Myles Connolly
Based on: The play by Howard Lindsay and Russell Crouse
Directed by: Frank Capra

This is the story of Grant Matthews (Spencer Tracy), a wealthy man who is prompted by Kay Thorndyke (Angela Lansbury), a powerful newspaper publisher with whom he is having an affair, to run for President of the United States. Katharine Hepburn is Mary Matthews, Grant's wife, from whom he has been separated quite some time, and who knows of his affair with Kay. If his personal life becomes public, he has no chance of nomination—so Mary reluctantly agrees to join Grant on the campaign trail. As they spend time together, they reconsider their marriage. Then Grant's integrity is tested, as he is advised by Kay and political leader Jim Conover (Adolph Menjou) to make compromises on his ideals for the good of the candidacy. Van Johnson portrays reporter Spike McManus, who handles publicity for the campaign. A well-done and intelligent political drama.

STORY OF SEABISCUIT

DRAMA/ANIMAL STORIES

TECHNICOLOR   1949   WARNER BROTHERS

SHIRLEY TEMPLE	BARRY FITZGERALD	LON McCALLISTER

Screenplay by: John Taintor Foote
Directed by: David Butler

Maggie O'Hara, a student nurse, and her Uncle Sean, an expert horse trainer, arrive in the United States to start a new life. They left Ireland to escape their grief over the accidental death of Maggie's brother, a jockey. Much to the dismay and ridicule of his skeptical bosses, Sean puts his faith in a young colt named Seabiscuit and enlists the aid of a young and talented jockey named Ted Knowles (Lon McCallister). Maggie and Ted fall in love, but there is a major obstacle in their relationship— Maggie is still haunted by her brother's death and can't bear to risk losing Ted the same way. The rest of the story follows Sean and Ted's efforts to transform Seabiscuit into a champion racehorse while Maggie and Ted work on their relationship. A pleasant and heartwarming tale.

STORY OF VERNON AND IRENE CASTLE, THE

MUSICAL/DRAMA

BLACK & WHITE   1939   RKO

FRED ASTAIRE	GINGER ROGERS	EDNA MAY OLIVER	WALTER BRENNAN

Screenplay by: Richard Sherman;
                   adaptation by Oscar Hammerstein II and Dorothy Yost
Based on: The stories *My Husband* and
                   My Memories of Vernon Castle by Irene Castle
Directed by: H.C. Potter

The true story of the famous husband and wife ballroom dance team of the early 1900s. Vernon Castle (Fred Astaire) works in vaudeville as a comic, but his real talent is dancing. Then he meets Irene Foote (Ginger Rogers), an aspiring dancer, who convinces Vernon that he's been wasting his natural dancing ability. The two form a dance act, fall in love and marry. They struggle to find their niche in show business, but eventually become a huge hit. The dance numbers in this movie are re-creations of the Castles' style from years ago, done in excellent fashion by the Astaire–Rogers team. A good biographical portrait that has a bittersweet ending, since Vernon Castle died in a World War I plane crash.

STOWAWAY

COMEDY/DRAMA/MUSICAL

BLACK & WHITE/COLORIZED   1936   20TH CENTURY FOX

SHIRLEY TEMPLE	ROBERT YOUNG	ALICE FAYE
EUGENE PALLETTE	HELEN WESTLEY	ARTHUR TREACHER

Screenplay by: William Conselman, Arthur Sheekman and Nat Perrin
Story by: Samuel G. Engel
Directed by: William A. Seiter

Shirley Temple stars as a little orphan girl named Barbara (her Chinese name is Ching-Ching) whose missionary parents were killed in China. She is befriended by Tommy Randall (Robert Young), a wealthy and kind American bachelor. Barbara stows away on the ocean liner which Tommy is taking back to the United States. Once on board ship, Barbara also meets Susan Parker (Alice Faye), a beautiful young woman who is engaged, but not particularly happy about her impending marriage. Barbara charms both Tommy and Susan and changes both of their lives for the better—in Shirley Temple's usual cheery style.

STRATEGIC AIR COMMAND
VISTAVISION & TECHNICOLOR　　　　　1955

DRAMA/MILITARY
PARAMOUNT

JAMES STEWART	JUNE ALLYSON	FRANK LOVEJOY
BARRY SULLIVAN	ALEX NICHOL	BRUCE BENNETT
ROSEMARY DeCAMP	HENRY MORGAN	

Screenplay by:　　Valentine Davies and Beirne Lay, Jr.
Story by:　　　　Beirne Lay, Jr.
Directed by:　　Anthony Mann

The Strategic Air Command (SAC) was a Global Bombing unit of the Air Force during the post-World War II period. Its purpose was to provide defensive atomic strike power anywhere in the world. For this they needed mature, experienced pilots, to execute the long flights and to carefully transport the sensitive atomic bombs. In this movie, James Stewart is Dutch Holland, a professional baseball player who is called back to service in SAC because of his extensive World War II experience. The story follows his new Air Force experiences and their effect on his personal life with wife Sally (co-star June Allyson). An interesting Air Force drama with good flight scenes.

 Academy Award Recognition: Beirne Lay, Jr. nominated for Best Motion Picture Story.

STRATTON STORY, THE
BLACK & WHITE/COLORIZED　　　　　1949

DRAMA
MGM

| JAMES STEWART | JUNE ALLYSON | FRANK MORGAN | AGNES MOOREHEAD |

Screenplay by:　　Douglas Morrow and Guy Trosper
Story by:　　　　Douglas Morrow
Directed by:　　Sam Wood

Technical adviser:　Monty Stratton

This is the inspirational, true story of professional baseball player Monty Stratton, with James Stewart in the starring role. Monty begins his baseball career pitching in sandlot games for three dollars a game, and works his way up to a position with the Chicago White Sox ball club. Then tragedy strikes—he loses a leg in a hunting accident, but perseveres and works his way back to playing pro baseball again. June Allyson co-stars as Monty's wife, Ethel, and Agnes Moorehead portrays Monty's mother. A very touching drama about overcoming great odds to achieve success.

 Academy Award Recognition: Douglas Morrow won Best Motion Picture Story.

STRIKE UP THE BAND
BLACK & WHITE   1940   MGM

JUDY GARLAND	**MICKEY ROONEY**	**JUNE PREISSER**
WILLIAM TRACY	**PAUL WHITEMAN and his orchestra**	

Screenplay by: John Monks, Jr. and Fred Finklehoffe
Directed by: Busby Berkeley

The tale of a group of high schoolers who form a dance band and try to raise enough money to travel to Chicago for a big audition. Mary Holden (Judy Garland) and Jimmy Connors (Mickey Rooney) are the leaders of the group. Mary loves Jimmy, and works hard to get him to consider her a girlfriend, rather than just a buddy. An enjoyable, youthful musical with good production numbers.

 Academy Award Recognition: Georgie Stoll and Roger Edens nominated for Best Score, nominated for Best Song: *Our Love Affair*, Music and Lyrics by Roger Edens and Georgie Stoll.

SUMMER STOCK
TECHNICOLOR   1950   MGM

JUDY GARLAND	**GENE KELLY**	**EDDIE BRACKEN**
GLORIA De HAVEN	**MARJORIE MAIN**	**PHIL SILVERS**

Screenplay by: George Wells and Sy Gomberg
Story by: Sy Gomberg
Directed by: Charles Walters

Jane Falbury (Judy Garland) is an industrious young woman who has fallen on hard times, while trying to run her family's farm single-handedly. Then, without her approval, Jane's sister Abigail (Gloria De Haven) promises the barn to her boyfriend

Joe (Gene Kelly), an aspiring actor, to use as a summer theater for his latest show. Reluctantly, Jane agrees to let the theater troupe stay, as long as the whole crew pitches in to work the farm. Various mishaps and romantic mixups occur among the group of young people, with good songs sprinkled in between. A delightful and fun musical.

SUMMERTIME

DRAMA/ROMANCE

TECHNICOLOR   1955   UNITED ARTISTS

KATHARINE HEPBURN   ROSSANO BRAZZI

Screenplay by:	H.E. Bates and David Lean
Based on:	The Original play *The Time of The Cuckoo* by Arthur Laurents
Directed by:	David Lean

Katharine Hepburn is Jane Hudson, an American spinster on vacation in Venice, Italy. She's not only there to see the sights, but is also longing for a magical romance. Jane meets a handsome shopowner named Renato (Rossano Brazzi). He falls for her, and together they fulfill her fantasy. This film was made with an unusual kind of artistry, and its beautiful photography of Venice gives the feeling of actually being there.

 Academy Award Recognition: Katharine Hepburn nominated for Best Actress, David Lean nominated for Best Director.

SUN VALLEY SERENADE

MUSICAL

BLACK & WHITE   1941   20TH CENTURY FOX

SONJA HENIE	**JOHN PAYNE**	**GLENN MILLER and his orchestra**	**MILTON BERLE**
LYNN BARI	**JOAN DAVIS**	**THE NICHOLAS BROTHERS**	

Screenplay by:	Robert Ellis and Helen Logan
Story by:	Art Arthur and Robert Harari
Directed by:	H. Bruce Humberstone

John Payne is Ted Scott, a pianist and lead singer with a struggling but talented band (portrayed by Glen Miller and his Orchestra). Milton Berle plays Nifty Allen, the band's pushy publicist, who talks Ted into sponsoring a war refugee as a publicity stunt. They expect the refugee to be a small child but are shocked to receive a pretty young woman from Norway named Karen Benson (played by world-famous skating star Sonja Henie). Karen decides almost immediately that Ted is the man she will marry. Despite the fact that he already has a girlfriend, singer Vivian Dawn (played by Lynn Bari), Karen is determined to win Ted over and tags along on the band's trip to Sun Valley, Idaho. Since she's from Norway, the cold weather in Sun Valley is just her style and there's lots of skating and skiing to be done. Several Glenn Miller favorites are featured in this cheerful movie with happy music.

 Academy Award Recognition: Emil Newman nominated for Best Scoring of a Musical Picture, nominated for Best Song: *Chattanooga Choo Choo*, Music by Harry Warren, Lyrics by Mack Gordon.

SUNRISE AT CAMPOBELLO

DRAMA

TECHNICOLOR   1960   WARNER BROTHERS

RALPH BELLAMY	**GREER GARSON**	**HUME CRONYN**
JEAN HAGAN	**ANNE SHOEMAKER**	**ALAN BUNCE**
TIM CONSIDINE	**ZINA BETHUNE**	

Screenplay by: Dore Schary
Directed by: Vincent J. Donehue

Ralph Bellamy and Greer Garson star as Franklin D. and Eleanor Roosevelt in this true story of FDR's triumph over polio and the rebuilding of his political career, which all took place in the 1920s, before he became President. Hume Cronyn co-stars as Louie Howe, Franklin's good friend, who worked with Eleanor to preserve FDR's public image, despite his physical disability. The modern viewer should bear in mind that in those times any physical impairment was looked upon as a great stigma—unlike today—when people with disabilities are admired for facing special challenges and are encouraged to fully participate in life. A very intelligent biographical drama with a talented cast.

SUPPORT YOUR LOCAL GUNFIGHTER
COLOR BY DELUXE   1971

COMEDY/WESTERN
UNITED ARTISTS

JAMES GARNER	**SUZANNE PLESHETTE**	**HARRY MORGAN**	**JOAN BLONDELL**
JOHN DEHNER	**HENRY JONES**	**DUB TAYLOR**	**MARIE WINDSOR**
JACK ELAM	**ELLEN CORBY**		

Screenplay by: James Edward Grant
Directed by: Burt Kennedy

James Garner is Latigo Smith, an unlucky gambler who sneaks off a train to escape from his fiancé, and lands in a western mining town called Purgatory. Smith's real challenge begins when the townspeople mistake him for Swifty Morgan, a master gunfighter who was supposed to have gotten off the train the very same night. Suzanne Pleshette co-stars as Patience, a rough-and-tumble frontier woman who longs to go back East to college. This movie is not a sequel to *Support Your Local Sheriff* (1969), but was made as a follow-up due to that film's popularity. A very boisterous and fun Western comedy.

SUPPORT YOUR LOCAL SHERIFF!
COLOR   1969

COMEDY/WESTERN
UNITED ARTISTS

JAMES GARNER	**JOAN HACKETT**	**WALTER BRENNAN**	**HARRY MORGAN**
JACK ELAM	**HENRY JONES**	**BRUCE DERN**	

Screenplay by: William Bowers
Directed by: Burt Kennedy

A gold rush at a mining camp turns it into a wild and wooly boom town, rampant with outlaws. James Garner stars as Jason McCullough, a drifter with plans to go to the Australian Frontier. The town is in dire need of a strong and brave sheriff, and since he's broke, McCullough takes the job. He tames the outlaws with his quick wit and courage rather than with brawn. Somehow, McCullough also finds time to court Prudy Perkins (Joan Hackett), the outspoken daughter of Mayor Olly Perkins (Harry Morgan). Walter Brennan appears as Pa Danby, the head of the town's most notorious outlaw family. A very funny and rousing Western comedy with a great cast of characters.

SUSAN SLEPT HERE
TECHNICOLOR   1954   RKO

COMEDY/CHRISTMAS

DICK POWELL	**DEBBIE REYNOLDS**	**ANNE FRANCIS**
GLENDA FARRELL	**ALVY MOORE**	**HORACE McMAHON**

Screenplay by: Alex Gottlieb
Based on: A play by Steve Fisher and Alex Gottlieb
Directed by: Frank Tashlin

Dick Powell is Mark, a middle-aged Hollywood comedy writer who's trying to come up with an idea for a serious drama to change the direction of his career. Mark's policeman friend brings a pretty 17-year-old delinquent girl named Susan (Debbie Reynolds) to his doorstep, asking him to let her spend the Christmas holidays in his apartment instead of jail—and possibly giving him inspiration for a new script. As Mark and Susan get to know each other, both of their lives are changed for the better.   A pleasant and sweet holiday comedy with a happy ending.

 Academy Award Recognition: nominated for Best Song: *Hold My Hand*, Music and Lyrics by Jack Lawrence and Richard Meyers.

SUSPICION
BLACK & WHITE/COLORIZED   1941   RKO

DRAMA/MYSTERY-SUSPENSE

CARY GRANT	**JOAN FONTAINE**	**SIR CEDRIC HARDWICKE**
NIGEL BRUCE	**DAME MAY WHITTY**	

Screenplay by: Samson Raphaelson, Joan Harrison and Alma Reville
From: The novel **Before The Fact** by Francis Iles
Directed by: Alfred Hitchcock

Joan Fontaine is Lina McLaidlaw, a wealthy heiress headed for spinsterhood—until she meets popular playboy Johnnie Aysgarth (Cary Grant), who marries her in a whirlwind romance. After their honeymoon, she begins to discover some secrets about him, and through various turns of events, suspects that he could be a cold-blooded murderer. An excellent mystery with loads of suspense.

 Academy Award Recognition: Joan Fontaine won Best Actress, nominated for Best Picture, Franz Waxman nominated for Best Musical Scoring of a Dramatic Picture.

SWAN, THE

CINEMASCOPE & EASTMAN COLOR   1956

COMEDY/DRAMA/ROMANCE

MGM

GRACE KELLY	ALEC GUINNESS	LOUIS JOURDAN
AGNES MOOREHEAD	JESSIE ROYCE LANDIS	BRIAN AHERNE
LEO G. CARROLL	ESTELLE WINWOOD	

Screenplay by: John Dighton
From: The play *The Swan* by Ferenc Molnar
Directed by: Charles Vidor

In Central Europe in 1910, Grace Kelly is Princess Alexandra—a descendant of a royal family which was ousted from its kingdom by Napoleon. Her cousin, Prince Albert (Alec Guinness), who is destined to be king, considers taking Alexandra as his wife. Alexandra's mother (played by J.R. Landis) works feverishly to get her married to Albert so that the family will have a crown once again. Meanwhile, Albert's mother (Agnes Moorehead) is very eager for him to marry as well. There is one minor complication, though—Alexandra is in love with her tutor, the dashing Nicholas Agi (Louis Jourdan). A humorous tale of romance, done with very colorful costumes.

SWISS FAMILY ROBINSON

PANAVISION & TECHNICOLOR   1960

DRAMA/ACTION-ADVENTURE

WALT DISNEY

| JOHN MILLS | DOROTHY McGUIRE | JAMES MacARTHUR | JANET MUNRO |

Screenplay by: Lowell S. Hawley
Based on: The novel *Swiss Family Robinson* by Johann Wyss
Directed by: Ken Annakin

This is the saga of a family on their way to New Guinea to settle new land. When they are stalked by pirates, their ship is forced into a storm and they end up ship-wrecked on a tropical island. There, they set up a home for themselves, living off the land and using what little resources they can find to prepare a defense against the sinister pirates, who continue to threaten them. A colorful story of adventure and survival, filmed on the beautiful island of Tobago in the West Indies.

TAKE A LETTER, DARLING
BLACK & WHITE   1942

COMEDY/ROMANCE
PARAMOUNT

| ROSALIND RUSSELL | FRED MacMURRAY | MacDONALD CAREY |
| CONSTANCE MOORE | ROBERT BENCHLEY | CECIL KELLAWAY |

Screenplay by: Claude Binyon
Story by: George Beck
Directed by: Mitchell Leisen

Rosalind Russell is A.M. MacGregor, a sharp-minded advertising executive who always has things under control. She hires a new personal secretary, Tom Verney (Fred MacMurray), who's a handsome, independent fellow. Tom needs a steady salary very badly and is willing to do just about anything to earn it. In the past, Ms. MacGregor had made a habit of using male secretaries to help her in business deals—to ward off clients who are romantically inclined and to ease the suspicions of their sometimes jealous wives. But she gets more than she bargained for by hiring Verney—she falls in love with him. A pleasant and amusing romantic comedy.

 Academy Award Recognition: Victor Young nominated for Best Scoring of a Dramatic or Comedy Picture.

TAKE ME OUT TO THE BALL GAME
TECHNICOLOR   1948

MUSICAL
MGM

| FRANK SINATRA | ESTHER WILLIAMS | GENE KELLY |
| BETTY GARRETT | EDWARD ARNOLD | JULES MUNSHIN |

Screenplay by: Harry Tugend and George Wells
Story by: Gene Kelly and Stanley Donen
Directed by: Busby Berkeley

Music and Lyrics by Betty Comden, Adolph Green and Roger Edens

Gene Kelly and Frank Sinatra are baseball players Eddie O'Brien and Dennis Ryan, in the early years of the sport. In the off-season they work together in a vaudeville song and dance act. When they arrive at spring training one year, they find that their team has a new owner, Kathleen Higgins (Esther Williams). She's an unusual woman with a great knowledge of and interest in baseball. Both fellows court Katherine while Dennis is hotly pursued by enamored fan Shirley Delwyn (played by Betty Garrett). Very genial and breezy entertainment, with good songs.

TALL IN THE SADDLE

BLACK & WHITE/COLORIZED · 1944

RKO

JOHN WAYNE	**ELLA RAINES**	**WARD BOND**
GEORGE "GABBY" HAYES	**AUDREY LONG**	**ELISABETH RISDON**

Screenplay by: Michael Hogan and Paul P. Fix
Original story by: Gordon Ray Young
Directed by: Edwin L. Marin

A cowboy named Rocklin (John Wayne) is set to begin a new job, but upon arrival, discovers that the ranch's owner has died. Rocklin has little use for women, but that soon changes. He gets help from the capable and attractive Arly Harolday (Ella Raines) when he becomes entangled in a mystery involving the suspicious circumstances of the ranch owner's death. Gabby Hayes plays Rocklin's sidekick Dave, an out-of-work stagecoach driver. A fast moving and exciting Western.

TAMMY AND THE BACHELOR

COLOR · 1957

COMEDY/ROMANCE

UNIVERSAL INT'L

DEBBIE REYNOLDS	**LESLIE NIELSEN**	**WALTER BRENNAN**
MALA POWERS	**SIDNEY BLACKMER**	**MILDRED NATWICK**
FAY WRAY	**PHILIP OBER**	

Screenplay by: Oscar Brodney
Based on: A novel by Cid Ricketts Sumner
Directed by: Joseph Pevney

Debbie Reynolds is Tammy Tyree, a young woman living on a country riverbank with her Grandpa (Walter Brennan). One day, they rescue a young man named Peter Brent (Leslie Nielsen) from the river's whirlpool, and Tammy falls love with him while nursing him back to health. In gratitude, Peter offers that should anything ever happen to Grandpa, Tammy can rely on his wealthy family for support. When Grandpa's arrested for moonshining, he sends Tammy off to live with Peter's family. Tammy finds them to be rather stuffy people, but her optimism and purity of spirit changes the lives of all for the better. Light entertainment—a sweet story.

Academy Award Recognition: nominated for Best Song: *Tammy*, Music and Lyrics by Ray Evans and Jay Livingston.

TEACHER'S PET

VISTAVISION & BLACK & WHITE   1958   COMEDY/ROMANCE

                                                                                        PARAMOUNT

| CLARK GABLE | DORIS DAY | GIG YOUNG | MAMIE VAN DOREN |
| NICK ADAMS | MARION ROSS | JACK ALBERTSON | |

Screenplay by: Fay and Michael Kanin
Directed by: George Seaton

Jim Gannon (Clark Gable) is City Editor for a major New York newspaper, and Erica Stone (Doris Day) teaches journalism at an evening college. Gannon worked his way up through the school of hard knocks, and believes that most college learning is useless. He's invited to speak to Erica's class but in a mixup, is mistaken for a student. Gannon finds Erica rather attractive, and is reluctant to insult her, so he continues the charade. Over time, they fall in love and he changes his mind about the value of a good education. A humorous story of unexpected romance.

Academy Award Recognition: Gig Young nominated for Best Supporting Actor, Fay and Michael Kanin nominated for Best Story and Screenplay (written directly for the screen).

TEAHOUSE OF THE AUGUST MOON, THE

CINEMASCOPE & METROCOLOR   1956   COMEDY/MILITARY

                                                                                        MGM

| MARLON BRANDO | GLENN FORD | MACHIKO KYO |
| EDDIE ALBERT | PAUL FORD | HENRY (HARRY) MORGAN |

Screenplay by: John Patrick
Based on: A book by Vern J. Sneider and the play by John Patrick
Directed by: Daniel Mann

This story takes place on the island of Okinawa during the U.S. occupation after World War II. Glenn Ford plays the inept Captain Fisby, who is assigned to a small village to help the natives rebuild and improve their lives. Marlon Brando is Sakini, the irreverent Okinawan interpreter who assists him. Fisby is commissioned to build a schoolhouse, but the men of the community talk him into creating a fancy Japanese teahouse for them instead. A very amusing military comedy with an unusual story.

TEN GENTLEMEN FROM WEST POINT

DRAMA/MILITARY/ACTION-ADVENTURE

BLACK & WHITE   1942   20TH CENTURY FOX

| GEORGE MONTGOMERY | MAUREEN O'HARA | JOHN SUTTON |
| LAIRD CREGAR | WARD BOND | |

Screenplay by: Richard Maibaum;
                  additional dialogue by George Seaton
Suggested by: A story by Malvin Wald
Directed by: Henry Hathaway

A dramatization of the founding of West Point, the first military academy in the United States. The story follows the progress of the first graduating class and how they hold up under the pressure from their demanding and tough commanding officer. George Montgomery and Maureen O'Hara are the central characters— he's a cadet, originally from the woods of Kentucky; she's a New York socialite and enthusiastic supporter of the Academy. An inspiring story with a good mix of drama and action.

TENDER TRAP, THE

COMEDY/ROMANCE

CINEMASCOPE & EASTMAN COLOR   1955   MGM

| FRANK SINATRA | DEBBIE REYNOLDS | DAVID WAYNE |
| CELESTE HOLM | CAROLYN JONES | |

Screenplay by: Julius Epstein
Based on: The play by Max Shulman and Robert Paul Smith
Directed by: Charles Walters

The setting: New York City. Charlie Y. Reader (Frank Sinatra) is a bachelor talent agent who has a steady parade of girls marching through his life, one of whom, Sylvia Crewes (Celeste Holm), wishes he would marry her. Then he meets the young and pretty Julie Gillis (Debbie Reynolds) when she auditions for a show. Charlie is interested in her, but she won't date him because he is not her type. But much to Julie's surprise, as they spend time working together, she falls for him. She then attempts to tame Charlie's wild ways and convince him to settle down with her. Standing on the sidelines observing all the action is Charlie's married but separated pal, Joe McCall (David Wayne). A cute romantic comedy done with sophistication and glamor.

 Academy Award Recognition: nominated for Best Song: *(Love Is)*
The Tender Trap, Music by James Van Heusen, Lyrics by Sammy Cahn.

TEST PILOT

BLACK & WHITE   1938   **DRAMA**

MGM

| CLARK GABLE | MYRNA LOY | SPENCER TRACY | LIONEL BARRYMORE |

Screenplay by: Vincent Lawrence and Waldemar Young
Based on: An original story by Frank Wead
Directed by: Victor Fleming

The story opens with test pilot Jim Lane (Clark Gable) working on setting a coast-to-coast speed record. He is an arrogant sort of character who works and plays hard. Gunner Sloane (Spencer Tracy) is Jim's assistant, and Howard B. Drake (Lionel Barrymore) is his sponsor. During his flight, Jim's plane experiences mechanical failure and makes an emergency landing on a farm in Kansas. There, he meets Ann Barton (Myrna Loy), a wisecracking farmer's daughter who knows how to put Jim in his place. They fall in love, get married, and set up housekeeping in New York. All goes well until one of Jim's close friends dies in the National Air Races. This makes the risks that Jim is taking every day seem more real to Ann and puts stress on their marriage. An excellent aviation tale with superb flight scenes.

 Academy Award Recognition: nominated for Best Picture, Frank Wead nominated for Best Original Story.

TEXAS

BLACK & WHITE   1941   **COMEDY/WESTERN**

COLUMBIA

| WILLIAM HOLDEN | GLENN FORD | CLAIRE TREVOR | EDGAR BUCHANAN |
| GEORGE BANCROFT | DON BEDDOE | WILLARD ROBERTSON | |

Screenplay by: Horace McCoy, Lewis Meltzer, Michael Blankfort
Directed by: George Marshall

At the end of the Civil War, Dan Thomas and Todd Ramsey (William Holden and Glenn Ford) are two former Confederate soldiers heading west to find work. They get into plenty of scrapes before finally reaching Texas, and eventually end up on opposite sides of the law—Thomas as a cattle rustler, Ramsey as a cowboy. But the two will still have one thing in common. They both fall in love with "Mike" King (Claire Trevor), a rancher's daughter. An engaging story with lots of action and a talented cast.

TEXAS CARNIVAL

TECHNICOLOR   1951

MUSICAL

MGM

| ESTHER WILLIAMS | RED SKELTON | HOWARD KEEL | ANN MILLER |
| KEENAN WYNN | PAULA RAYMOND | TOM TULLY | |

Screenplay by: Dorothy Kingsley
Story by: George Wells and Dorothy Kingsley
Directed by: Charles Walters

Esther Williams and Red Skelton are Debbie Telford and Cornie Quinell, partners in a carnival dunking booth. Cornie runs into inebriated Texas millionaire Dan Sabinas (Keenan Wynn) who gives him his big luxury car by mistake. When Debbie and Cornie show up later at a Dan's hotel to return the car, they are mistaken for Dan and his sister Marilla (Paula Raymond). Debbie and Cornie go along with the charade, and while masquerading as millionaires, they both find romance. Cornie flips for Sunshine Jackson (Ann Miller), the sister of the town sheriff, and Debbie falls in love with Slim Selby (Howard Keel), Dan's cattle foreman. A bright and breezy movie with a slender plot—meant just for fun.

THAT DARN CAT

COMEDY/MYSTERY-SUSPENSE/
ANIMAL STORIES

TECHNICOLOR   1965

WALT DISNEY

HAYLEY MILLS	DEAN JONES	DOROTHY PROVINE
RODDY McDOWALL	NEVILLE BRAND	ELSA LANCHESTER
WILLIAM DEMAREST	FRANK GORSHIN	ED WYNN

Screenplay by: The Gordons and Bill Walsh
Based on: *The Undercover Cat* by the Gordons
Directed by: Robert Stevenson

The cat of the title, a Siamese named D.C. (which stands for Darn Cat), follows a man home from the fish market. The man turns out to be one of a pair of bank robbers who is holding a bank teller hostage, intending to kill her if necessary. The hostage cleverly replaces the cat's collar with her wristwatch and turns him loose. When D.C. returns home to his teenage owner, Patti Randall (Hayley Mills), she picks up on the signal and goes to Zeke Kelso (Dean Jones), the FBI Agent who's assigned to the case. Patti then assists Zeke while he tries to follow D.C. around town and track down the criminals. A fun Disney family comedy with lots of action.

THAT FORSYTE WOMAN

TECHNICOLOR   1949   DRAMA/ROMANCE
                                                     MGM

ERROL FLYNN   **GREER GARSON**   **WALTER PIDGEON**
ROBERT YOUNG   **JANET LEIGH**   **HARRY DAVENPORT**
AUBREY MATHER

Screenplay by: Jan Lustig, Ivan Tors and James B. Williams;
                  additional dialogue by Arthur Wimperis
Based on: Book I. of *The Forsyte Saga* by John Galsworthy
Directed by: Compton Bennett

A soap opera style drama about upper crust English society. Greer Garson is
Irene Forsyte, who married the wealthy Soames Forsyte (Errol Flynn) for financial
security—not for love. Trouble erupts when her niece, June (Janet Leigh), intro-
duces Irene to her handsome fiancé Philip (Robert Young). Philip falls in love with
Irene, and she with him. Meanwhile, Jolyon Forsyte (Walter Pidgeon), June's father
and the outcast of the Forsyte family, also admires Irene from afar. A very exquisite
romantic drama, with colorful costumes and a fine cast.

THERE'S NO BUSINESS LIKE SHOW BUSINESS   MUSICAL

CINEMASCOPE & DELUXE COLOR   1954   20TH CENTURY FOX

ETHEL MERMAN   **DONALD O'CONNOR**   **MARILYN MONROE**
DAN DAILEY   **JOHNNIE RAY**   **MITZI GAYNOR**

Screenplay by: Phoebe and Henry Ephron
From: A story by Lamar Trotti
Directed by: Walter Lang

Lyrics and Music by Irving Berlin

The saga of vaudeville troupers The Donahues (Ethel Merman and Dan Dailey),
which begins in 1919 and continues through World War II. The couple goes on to
have three children (played by Donald O'Connor, Johnnie Ray, and Mitzi Gaynor)
who all join their act, which changes over the years. They have some family
squabbles along the way, with entertaining Irving Berlin tunes sprinkled here and
there. A winning musical with a talented cast and a happy ending.

 Academy Award Recognition: Lamar Trotti nominated for Best
Motion Picture Story, Alfred Newman and Lionel Newman nominated for
Best Scoring of a Musical Picture.

THEY DIED WITH THEIR BOOTS ON
BLACK & WHITE/COLORIZED   1941

DRAMA/ACTION-ADVENTURE
WARNER BROTHERS

ERROL FLYNN	**OLIVIA de HAVILLAND**	**ARTHUR KENNEDY**	**CHARLEY GRAPEWIN**
GENE LOCKHART	**ANTHONY QUINN**	**HATTIE McDANIEL**	

Screenplay by: Wally Kline and Aeneas Mackenzie
Directed by: Raoul Walsh

Errol Flynn stars as General George Custer in this dramatization of a true story. In 1857, Custer arrives at West Point as a new cadet. Later, the Civil War breaks out and, despite a poor record, he is graduated early to help fill a shortage of officers. He uses unorthodox methods in combat, and is always in trouble with his superiors, but goes on to become a General, achieving great victories. After the war, Custer is given assignments out west, battling with Native American tribes. Olivia de Havilland co-stars as Mrs. Custer in this huge, robust saga that ends with Custer's famous last stand at Little Big Horn. Some may prefer to watch this movie in more than one sitting, as it is rather long.

THEY WERE EXPENDABLE
BLACK & WHITE/COLORIZED   1945

DRAMA/MILITARY/ACTION-ADVENTURE
MGM

ROBERT MONTGOMERY	**JOHN WAYNE**	**DONNA REED**
JACK HOLT	**WARD BOND**	

Screenplay by: Frank Wead Comdr. U.S.N. (Ret)
Directed by: John Ford

The setting is 1941 in Manila Bay, The Philippines, during World War II. The small P.T. boats (motor torpedo boats) are making their first appearance in the Navy, though the top brass are not impressed by their capabilities, and still put their faith in the bigger ships. Lt. John Brickley (Robert Montgomery) and Lt. Rusty Ryan (John Wayne) command their own squadron of P.T. boats. They are tired of being given only routine assignments, when they know that their unit could be doing great things in the war effort. In the face of many obstacles, Brickley and Ryan do all they can to prove the strength and usefulness of the P.T. boats and their crews. This movie is a salute to all of the Americans who fought so bravely in the Philippines. When U.S. forces were driven out by the Japanese in the early days of the war, many Americans were left behind, facing a very uncertain fate. A top-notch war drama with realistic battle scenes and an exciting story.

THIN MAN GOES HOME, THE

COMEDY/MYSTERY-SUSPENSE

BLACK AND WHITE   1944   MGM

WILLIAM POWELL	MYRNA LOY	LUCILE WATSON
GLORIA De HAVEN	ANN REVERE	HELEN VINSON
HARRY DAVENPORT	LEON AMES	EDWARD BROPHY

Screenplay by: Donald Meek, Robert Riskin and Dwight Taylor
From: An original story by Robert Riskin and Harry Kurnitz;
Based on: The characters created by Dashiell Hammett
Directed by: Richard Thorpe

William Powell and Myrna Loy continue their roles as super sleuths Nick and Nora
Charles in another entry of the *Thin Man* series of films. This time, they take a trip
to visit Nick's parents, and Nora wants Nick to have a chance to show off his crime-
solving talent and impress his father, who is a doctor. So she starts a false rumor
that Nick is in town to crack a big case, as bait to attract a real one. Nora's efforts
are successful, and they get into a mystery involving a local artist's murder. A fun
whodunit with lots of unexpected turns and a surprise ending.

THIRTY SECONDS OVER TOKYO

DRAMA/MILITARY

BLACK & WHITE/COLORIZED   1944   MGM

| VAN JOHNSON | ROBERT WALKER | SPENCER TRACY |
| DON DeFORE | ROBERT MITCHUM | |

Screenplay by: Dalton Trumbo
Based on: The book and *Collier's* story by
                  Captain Ted W. Lawson and Robert Considine
Directed by: Mervyn Leroy

This is the true account of what happened to a group of men who made the first
bombing raid on Japan, 131 days after the Japanese attack on Pearl Harbor.
Lt. Colonel James H. Doolittle (played by Spencer Tracy) was in charge of preparations for the retaliatory bombing. Because of the long-distance flight involved,
the risky mission was performed by B-25 bombers that took off from an aircraft
carrier. But because these planes were too large to come back and land on the
carrier, the pilots had to finish their assignment by proceeding to China (which was
held by the Japanese at the time) and getting to safety whatever way they could.
Van Johnson portrays Captain Ted Lawson, who was one of these American pilots
and the author of the book on which this movie was based. A very powerful drama,
with fine acting, that clearly depicts the distinguished bravery of these men.

36 HOURS
BLACK & WHITE/COLORIZED

DRAMA/MILITARY/MYSTERY-SUSPENSE
1965   MGM

JAMES GARNER   **EVA MARIE SAINT**   **ALAN NAPIER**
ROD TAYLOR   **WERNER PETERS**

Screenplay by: George Seaton
Directed by: George Seaton

James Garner is Major Pike, an Intelligence Officer with the Allied High Command in London, in the days preceding the D-Day attack in June of 1944. He is sent to Lisbon on a spy mission, but he is drugged and apprehended by the enemy. Since Pike knows all of the details of the invasion plan, he is taken to Germany to be interrogated. There, he becomes the victim of an elaborate scheme by the Germans to make him think that six years have passed and that he is an amnesia patient in an American hospital. Rod Taylor plays German Maj. Walter Gerber, who perfectly impersonates an American doctor, and Eva Marie Saint portrays Anna Hedler, a nurse who poses as Pike's wife. A stirring drama with an extremely clever plot and top-notch acting by the entire cast.

THIS EARTH IS MINE
CINEMASCOPE & TECHNICOLOR

DRAMA/ROMANCE
1959   UNIVERSAL INT'L

ROCK HUDSON   **JEAN SIMMONS**   **DOROTHY McGUIRE**
CLAUDE RAINS   **CINDY ROBBINS**

Screenplay by: Casey Robinson
From: The novel *The Cup and The Sword* by Alice Tisdale Hobart
Directed by: Henry King

This is a tale of a prosperous family dynasty in the California wine country during Prohibition. Jean Simmons is Elizabeth Rambeau, who is sent to the California vineyards by her father to follow through with an arranged marriage. But then things become complicated when John Rambeau (Rock Hudson), a handsome cousin (related by marriage), falls for her. This dramatic soap opera has a rather interesting story line and is performed well by the talented cast.

THIS LAND IS MINE

BLACK & WHITE   1943   RKO

DRAMA

| CHARLES LAUGHTON | MAUREEN O'HARA | GEORGE SANDERS |
| WALTER SLEZAK | KENT SMITH | UNA O'CONNOR |

Screenplay by: Dudley Nichols
Directed by: Jean Renoir

A fictional drama about events that occur in a small European country during World War II, when it becomes occupied by the Nazis. Charles Laughton portrays Arthur Lory, a cowardly bachelor school teacher who's dominated by his mother. He likes his beautiful neighbor and co-worker, Louise Martin (Maureen O'Hara), but his controlling mother prevents him from courting her. Arthur finds the courage and bravery he didn't think he had when he must ultimately stand up against the Nazis to defend his fellow citizens. A riveting story that explores how different types of people respond in such threatening situations, but with a serious theme that may be inappropriate for some fearful younger children.

THOUSANDS CHEER

TECHNICOLOR   1943   MGM

MUSICAL

GENE KELLY	KATHRYN GRAYSON	JOSÉ ITURBI	MICKEY ROONEY
ELEANOR POWELL	JUNE ALLYSON	GLORIA De HAVEN	ANN SOTHERN
LUCILLE BALL	MARSHA HUNT	FRANK MORGAN	KAY KYSER
LENA HORNE	RED SKELTON	MARGARET O'BRIEN	JUDY GARLAND

Screenplay by: Paul Jarrico and Richard Collins;
                   based on their story *Private Miss Jones*
Directed by: George Sidney

Kathryn Jones (played by Kathryn Grayson), a pretty operatic soprano, tags along with her father, who's a Colonel, to entertain the troops during World War II. She's also trying to get her parents, who have been separated for many years, back together again. In her travels, she meets an enthusiastic young soldier named Eddie Marsh (played by Gene Kelly). At first, Eddie's only reason for getting friendly with Kathryn is to secure a favor from her father, but ultimately he falls in love with her. This movie becomes a show within a show, featuring many cameo appearances by major stars of the time. The story about Kathryn and Eddie is not as important as the parade of stars across the screen, which was meant to boost the morale of the wartime audience.

 Academy Award Recognition: Herbert Stothart nominated for Best Scoring of a Musical Picture.

THREE LITTLE WORDS   MUSICAL
TECHNICOLOR   1950   MGM

FRED ASTAIRE	**RED SKELTON**	**VERA-ELLEN**
ARLENE DAHL	**KEENAN WYNN**	**GALE ROBBINS**
GLORIA De HAVEN	**PHIL REGAN**	**HARRY SHANNON**

Screenplay by: George Wells
Based on: The lives and songs of Bert Kalmar and Harry Ruby
Directed by: Richard Thorpe

Technical Adviser: Harry Ruby

The story begins in the year 1919. Bert Kalmar (Fred Astaire) is a successful vaudeville song and dance man, along with his partner, Jessie Brown (Vera Ellen). When a knee injury ends Kalmar's dancing career, he begins working as a lyricist, teaming up with Harry Ruby (Red Skelton), a songwriter who composes great tunes but has trouble writing the words. The movie continues from there, tracing the ups and downs of the sometimes volatile Kalmar–Ruby partnership. A very entertaining musical, with good songs and good dance numbers.

 Academy Award Recognition: Andre Previn nominated for Best Scoring of a Musical Picture.

THREE MUSKETEERS, THE
COLOR   1948

DRAMA/ACTION-ADVENTURE
MGM

LANA TURNER	GENE KELLY	JUNE ALLYSON
VAN HEFLIN	ANGELA LANSBURY	FRANK MORGAN
VINCENT PRICE	KEENAN WYNN	JOHN SUTTON
GIG YOUNG	ROBERT COOTE	IAN KEITH
REGINALD OWEN	PATRICIA MEDINA	

Screenplay by: Robert Ardrey
Based on: The novel by Alexander Dumas
Directed by: George Sidney

Gene Kelly is the agile swordsman D'Artagnan, who joins the Three Musketeers (Van Heflin is Athos, Gig Young is Porthos, and Robert Coote is Aramis) in protecting the honor of their Queen Anne (Angela Lansbury). Countess Charlotte de Winter (Lana Turner) and Prime Minister Richelieu (Vincent Price) are trying to overthrow King Louis XIII (Frank Morgan). The brave and loyal Musketeers will stop at nothing to defend the Crown, with the valuable help of the lovely Constance Bonacieux (June Allyson). This is a superb movie version of the classic novel, with an all-star cast, beautiful photography, colorful costumes, and plenty of exciting swashbuckling action.

THREE SMART GIRLS
BLACK & WHITE   1936

COMEDY/MUSICAL
UNIVERSAL

DEANNA DURBIN	NAN GREY	BARBARA READ
BINNIE BARNES	ALICE BRADY	RAY MILLAND
CHARLES WINNINGER	MISCHA AUER	

Story and Screenplay by: Adele Comandini
Directed by: Henry Koster

In Switzerland, three sisters receive the news that their divorced father is about to remarry. The "three smart girls," named Penny (Deanna Durbin), Joan (Nan Grey), and Kay (Barbara Read) decide to head for New York to halt the wedding and pave the way for a possible reconciliation of their parents. The cute story line, along with a few songs by Deanna, make this movie pleasant and enjoyable.

Academy Award Recognition: Adele Commandini nominated for Best Original Story.

THREE STRIPES IN THE SUN

BLACK & WHITE   1955   **DRAMA/MILITARY**

COLUMBIA

| ALDO RAY | PHIL CAREY | DICK YORK |
| CHUCK CONNORS | CAMILLOE JANCLAIRE | MITSUKO KIMURA |

Screenplay by:	Richard Murphy, adaptation by Albert Duffy
Based on:	*The New Yorker* magazine article, entitled
	The Gentle Wolfhound by E.J. Kahn, Jr.
Directed by:	Richard Murphy

Technical Advisor: Master Sergeant Hugh O'Reilly

Aldo Ray plays the lead role in this true story of Master Sergeant Hugh O'Reilly. O'Reilly was an American serviceman who fought in World War II and then was assigned to duty in Japan during the post-war occupation. This brawny, tough guy harbored lots of bad feeling toward the Japanese because of the war, but that all changed when he fell in love with a beautiful Japanese interpreter (played by Mitsuko Kimura). Then, when he befriended a group of children in a Japanese orphanage, O'Reilly became dedicated to improving their living conditions. A very sweet and heartwarming story, with some amusing moments mixed in with the drama.

THRILL OF IT ALL, THE

COLOR   1963   **COMEDY**

UNIVERSAL INT'L

| DORIS DAY | JAMES GARNER | ARLENE FRANCIS |

Screenplay by:	Carl Reiner
Based on:	A story by Larry Gelbart and Carl Reiner
Directed by:	Norman Jewison

Beverly Boyer (Doris Day), the dedicated suburban wife of obstetrician Gerald Boyer (James Garner), is a traditional, full-time homemaker and mother to their two children. But then, Beverly is offered a job in TV commercials. The fun begins as the family's quiet and routine lifestyle is jolted into high gear by her rise to TV fame. A frivolous and frothy family-style comedy.

THUNDERHEAD, SON OF FLICKA
TECHNICOLOR   1945

DRAMA/ANIMAL STORIES
20TH CENTURY FOX

RODDY McDOWALL   **PRESTON FOSTER**   **RITA JOHNSON**

Screenplay by: Dwight Cummins and Dorothy Yost
Based on: The novel by Mary O'Hara
Directed by: Louis King

In this sequel to **My Friend Flicka** (1943), Roddy McDowall stars again as Ken McLaughlin, the son of rancher Rob McLaughlin (Preston Foster). One of their mares, Flicka, comes home with a beautiful white colt which they aptly name Thunderhead. The colt grows into a headstrong, renegade horse, but Ken works hard to train him. Then a wild horse steals away the McLaughlin's best mares to begin creating his own herd, putting the family's living in jeopardy, but faithful Thunderhead comes to the rescue. A lively and interesting animal story.

TICKLISH AFFAIR, A
PANAVISION & METROCOLOR   1963

COMEDY/ROMANCE
MGM

SHIRLEY JONES   **GIG YOUNG**   **RED BUTTONS**
CAROLYN JONES   **EDGAR BUCHANAN**   **EDDIE APPLEGATE**
EDWARD PLATT   **BILLY MUMY**

Screenplay by: Ruth Brooks Flippen
Based on: The story **Moon Walk** by Barbara Luther
Directed by: George Sidney

A Navy ship receives an SOS from shore. But when the crew responds, they find that the message is a false alarm, and that it was sent by one of the mischievous young sons of Navy widow Amy Martin (Shirley Jones). The ship's commanding officer, Key Weedon (played by Gig Young), takes an interest in Amy, and before long they start dating. But, standing in the way of their relationship are her nervous misgivings about marrying a Navy man again. A genial and amusing romantic comedy.

TIME OF THEIR LIVES, THE

BLACK & WHITE   1946

COMEDY
UNIVERSAL

| BUD ABBOTT | LOU COSTELLO | MARJORIE REYNOLDS |
| BINNIE BARNES | JOHN SHELTON | GALE SONDERGAARD |

Screenplay by: Val Burton, Walter De Leon and Bradford Ropes;
                     additional dialogue by John Grant
Directed by: Charles Barton

The story begins at an estate called Danbury Manor during the American Revolution. Bud Abbott is Cuthbert Greenway, the butler, and Lou Costello is Horatio Primm, a tinker (mender of tin utensils, such as pots and pans). One night, Primm and Melody Allen (played by Marjorie Reynolds), who is the pretty fiancé of Master Danbury, are mistaken for traitors and shot dead. Upon their death, their ghosts are required to roam the Danbury Manor grounds until they can prove their innocence. Eventually, the original mansion burns down, but in 1946 a new one is rebuilt. The restless spirits then try to get the Manor's new inhabitants to help them earn their freedom. It just so happens that Ralph Greenway (also played by Bud Abbott), a descendant of the original Danbury Manor butler, is visiting the new home and lends a hand. A very enjoyable comedy with good special effects.

TIN STAR, THE

VISTAVISION & BLACK & WHITE   1957

DRAMA/WESTERN
PARAMOUNT

| HENRY FONDA | ANTHONY PERKINS | BETSY PALMER |
| MICHEL RAY | NEVILLE BRAND | JOHN McINTIRE |

Screenplay by: Dudley Nichols
Based on: A story by Barney Slater and Joel Kane
Directed by: Anthony Mann

Henry Fonda is Morgan Hickman, a bounty hunter who rides into a western town with a recent catch. Anthony Perkins plays the town's young and inexperienced sheriff, Ben Owens. Shunned by the townspeople, Hickman finds shelter outside of town at a farm inhabited by a woman and her young son. During his stay, Hickman befriends the naive Sheriff Owens and teaches him how to survive confrontations with dangerous criminals. A good Western that tells an interesting personal story.

 Academy Award Recognition: Barney Slater, Joel Kane and
Dudley Nichols nominated for Best Story and Screenplay (written directly
for the screen).

TO CATCH A THIEF
VISTAVISION & TECHNICOLOR 1955

COMEDY/MYSTERY-SUSPENSE
PARAMOUNT

CARY GRANT GRACE KELLY

Screenplay by: John Michael Hayes
Based on: The novel by David Dodge
Directed by: Alfred Hitchcock

In France, a jewel thief is running rampant and the police are searching for him. John Robie (Cary Grant), a notorious former jewel thief, is a prime suspect but is innocent. He concludes that the crook they are looking for must be someone who is imitating his techniques. Robie decides that the only way to clear his name is to apprehend the guilty party himself. Along the way, he romances Frances Stevens (Grace Kelly), a captivating and wealthy American woman. Smooth and classy entertainment, with plenty of suspense and beautiful scenery of the French Riviera.

TO EACH HIS OWN
BLACK & WHITE 1946

DRAMA
PARAMOUNT

OLIVIA de HAVILLAND JOHN LUND MARY ANDERSON
ROLAND CULVER PHILIP TERRY GRIFF BARNETT

Screenplay by: Charles Brackett and Jacques Théry
Directed by: Mitchell Leisen

Olivia de Havilland stars as Josephine Norris, a young woman who has a love affair with an airplane pilot (John Lund) and is left alone and pregnant when he is killed. She bears an illegitimate son and when her plans to keep him fall through, she spends many years trying to somehow remain a part of his life. A very touching drama with an interesting story line and a superb performance by Miss de Havilland.

 Academy Award Recognition: Olivia de Havilland won Best Actress, Charles Brackett nominated for Best Original Story.

TO HAVE AND HAVE NOT

BLACK & WHITE   1944

DRAMA

WARNER BROTHERS

HUMPHREY BOGART	**WALTER BRENNAN**	**LAUREN BACALL**
DOLORES MORAN	**HOAGY CARMICHAEL**	**SHELDON LEONARD**

Screenplay by: Jules Furthman and William Faulkner
Directed by: Howard Hawks

It's the summer of 1940 on the Caribbean isle of Martinique, after the fall of France to Nazi Germany. Harry Morgan (Humphrey Bogart) is an American fishing boat operator and Eddie (Walter Brennan) is his shipmate. When Morgan meets an attractive young woman named Marie Browning (Lauren Bacall), he becomes part of a caper involving local politics and the French Resistance. A complex story of intrigue that slowly unfolds. This was Lauren Bacall's movie debut.

TO HELL AND BACK

CINEMASCOPE & TECHNICOLOR

DRAMA/MILITARY/ACTION-ADVENTURE

1955

UNIVERSAL INT'L

AUDIE MURPHY	**MARSHALL THOMPSON**	**CHARLES DRAKE**
JACK KELLY	**GREGG PALMER**	**PAUL PICERNI**
DAVID JANSSEN	**DENVER PYLE**	

Screenplay by: Gil Doud
Based on: Audie Murphy's autobiography **To Hell and Back**
Directed by: Jesse Hibbs

Audie Murphy portrays himself in this biographical film, which chronicles his early life and then his World War II achievements. He was the most decorated soldier of World War II and winner of the Congressional Medal of Honor—all accomplished by the age of 19. A top-notch war movie that depicts many acts of heroism in combat, with lots of exciting action.

TO SIR, WITH LOVE

DRAMA

TECHNICOLOR   1967   COLUMBIA

| SIDNEY POITIER | CHRISTIAN ROBERTS | JUDY GEESON |
| SUZY KENDALL | LULU | |

Screenplay by: James Clavell
From: The novel by E.R. Braithwaite
Directed by: James Clavell

Sidney Poitier is Mark Thackeray, an unemployed engineer who takes a job teaching high school in a tough London neighborhood. Slowly but surely, this fine man turns his class of defiant teenagers into responsible, well-mannered young adults ready to face the world that awaits them. A very inspiring and touching movie with important messages about growing up.

TOBY TYLER

DRAMA/COMEDY

TECHNICOLOR   1960   WALT DISNEY

| KEVIN CORCORAN | HENRY CALVIN | GENE SHELDON |
| BOB SWEENEY | RICHARD EASTHAM | JAMES DRURY |

Screenplay by: Bill Walsh and Lillie Hayward
Based on: The book by James Otis Kaler
Directed by: Charles Barton

Kevin Corcoran is Toby Tyler, an orphan boy who feels unwanted by his aunt and uncle. He runs away to join the circus, and makes lots of new friends, most notably Mr. Stubbs, the chimpanzee. Toby has various new adventures, starting out as a food concessionaire's helper but eventually becoming a performer in the show. An excellent family movie with just the right mixture of things that most kids enjoy.

TOO HOT TO HANDLE

BLACK AND WHITE   1938

COMEDY/ACTION-ADVENTURE

MGM

CLARK GABLE   MYRNA LOY   WALTER PIDGEON

Screenplay by:	Laurence Stallings and John Lee Mahin
Based on:	Story by Len Hammond
Directed by:	Jack Conway

Clark Gable is Chris Hunter, a newsreel cameraman for Union Newsreel Syndicate. Walter Pidgeon plays Bill Dennis, a cameraman for Union's chief rival, Atlas Newsreel Corporation. They are in a heated competition for stories about a war in China. Hunter meets an attractive lady aviator named Alma Harding (Myrna Loy), who could become Union's star reporter by filming stories from the air. He promises to help Alma find her brother who is lost in the Amazon, but only as a friendly gesture toward the business deal. But to Hunter's surprise, he begins to fall in love with Alma and then really puts his heart into locating her brother. There's plenty of action in this robust story of adventure in far away places.

TOP HAT

BLACK & WHITE   1935

MUSICAL

RKO

FRED ASTAIRE   GINGER ROGERS   EDWARD EVERETT HORTON
ERIK RHODES   ERIC BLORE   HELEN BRODERICK

Screenplay by:	Dwight Taylor and Allan Scott
Story by:	Dwight Taylor
Directed by:	Mark Sandrich

Lyrics and Music by Irving Berlin

Dale Tremont (Ginger Rogers) is a single girl whose married friend Madge (played by Helen Broderick) plans to set Dale up with her husband 's pal Jerry Travers (Fred Astaire). By accident, Dale and Jerry meet before the intended formal introduction, and Dale mistakes Jerry for Madge's husband Horace (Edward Everett Horton). Dale and Jerry fall for each other and now poor Dale thinks that she is having a love affair with her friend's husband. A classy, elegant musical with great songs and fabulous dances by Fred and Ginger.

Academy Award Recognition: nominated for Best Picture; nominated for Best Song: ***Cheek to Cheek*** Music and Lyrics by Irving Berlin.

TOPPER

BLACK & WHITE/COLORIZED   1937   COMEDY

MGM

| CONSTANCE BENNETT | CARY GRANT | ROLAND YOUNG |
| BILLIE BURKE | ALAN MOWBRAY | EUGENE PALLETTE |

Screenplay by: Jack Jevne, Eric Hatch and Eddie Moran
Based on: The novel by Thorne Smith
Directed by: Norman Z. McLeod

Cary Grant and Constance Bennett are George and Marion Kerby, a wealthy couple who live in the finest style. Cosmo Topper (Roland Young) is a mild-mannered man leading a boring life, henpecked by his wife Henrietta (Billie Burke). Topper is the chief executive of the bank in which the Kerbys are the major stockholders. The Kerbys are killed in a car accident and are transformed into ghosts who make it their mission to change Topper's life. With lots of supernatural antics, they teach Topper and his wife Henrietta how to have fun and enjoy life again. A cute, old-fashioned comedy that children should enjoy.

 Academy Award Recognition: Roland Young nominated for Best Supporting Actor.

TOPPER RETURNS

BLACK & WHITE   1941   COMEDY/MYSTERY-SUSPENSE

UNITED ARTISTS

JOAN BLONDELL	ROLAND YOUNG	CAROLE LANDIS
BILLIE BURKE	DENNIS O'KEEFE	PATSY KELLY
H.B. WARNER	EDDIE (ROCHESTER) ANDERSON	

Screenplay by: Jonathan Latimer and Gordon Douglas;
                   additional dialogue by Paul Gerard Smith
Based on: The fictional characters conceived by Thorne Smith
Directed by: Roy Del Ruth

This movie is the second sequel to *Topper* (1937). Ann Carrington (Carole Landis) and her friend, Gail Richards (Joan Blondell), arrive at a spooky old mansion. It was left to Ann by her mother, who died a mysterious death. Very suspicious and weird things begin to happen, then Gail is murdered—by mistake. Ann was really the intended target. Gail becomes a ghost, and sets out to solve her own murder in order to save Ann's life, which is still in danger. Gail gets some help from Ann's neighbor Cosmo Topper (Roland Young). Once again, Billie Burke plays the role of Topper's nagging wife Henrietta. A funny mystery with lots of surprises.

TORPEDO RUN
CINEMASCOPE & METROCOLOR

DRAMA/MILITARY/ACTION-ADVENTURE
1958   MGM

GLENN FORD	**ERNEST BORGNINE**	**DIANE BREWSTER**
DEAN JONES	**L.Q. JONES**	**PHILIP OBER**

Screenplay by: Richard Sale and William Wister Haines
Based on: Stories by Richard Sale
Directed by: Joseph Pevney

The setting is the South Pacific in 1942, during World War II. Glenn Ford is
Lt. Commander Barney Doyle, a submarine skipper whose wife and child have
been taken as prisoners by the Japanese in the Philippines. Doyle and his crew
are dispatched to destroy a Japanese ship that participated in the attack on Pearl
Harbor. To make the mission more complicated, Doyle's wife and child are on
board on a prisoner transport ship that is being used to screen their target.
Fortunately, Doyle's buddy and second in command, Lt. Archer Sloan (played
by Ernest Borgnine), is there to help him through the crisis. An exciting and
suspenseful submarine war drama.

TROUBLE WITH ANGELS, THE
COLOR BY PATHÉ

COMEDY
1966   COLUMBIA

ROSALIND RUSSELL	**HAYLEY MILLS**	**JUNE HARDING**	**BINNIE BARNES**
GYPSY ROSE LEE	**CAMILLA SPARV**	**MARY WICKES**	

Screenplay by: Blanche Hanalis
Based on: The novel by Jane Trahey
Directed by: Ida Lupino

Teenager Mary Clancy (Hayley Mills) has been placed in a Catholic convent school
because she's very troublesome. She and her best friend, Rachel Devery (played by
June Harding), are the most mischievous girls in their class and drive the Mother
Superior (Rosalind Russell) crazy. But with the Mother's help, they eventually
mature and realize the error of their ways. A sweet movie, with a surprise ending,
that girls should especially enjoy.

TWO TICKETS TO BROADWAY

MUSICAL

TECHNICOLOR   1951   RKO

TONY MARTIN   **JANET LEIGH**   **GLORIA De HAVEN**
EDDIE BRACKEN   **ANN MILLER**

Screenplay by: Sid Silvers and Hal Kanter
Based on: A story by Sammy Cahn
Directed by: James V. Kern

This is a story about young people in New York City trying to break into show business. Janet Leigh plays young hopeful Nancy Peterson, and Tony Martin portrays singer Dan Carter. The plot is very slender, but includes everything necessary for pleasant musical entertainment—comedy, romance, and good songs.

TWO WEEKS WITH LOVE

MUSICAL

TECHNICOLOR   1950   MGM

JANE POWELL   **RICARDO MONTALBAN**   **LOUIS CALHERN**
ANN HARDING   **PHYLLIS KIRK**   **CARLETON CARPENTER**
DEBBIE REYNOLDS   **CLINTON SUNDBERG**

Screenplay by: John Larkin and Dorothy Kingsley
Story by: John Larkin
Directed by: Roy Rowland

This story takes place around the turn of the century. Patty Robinson (Jane Powell) is a 17-year-old young lady whose mother insists on treating her like a child. All the other girls her age are dating and wearing corsets—things that she is not yet allowed to do. The family goes on summer vacation to the Catskills, where she meets and falls for handsome, dashing bachelor Demi Armendez (Ricardo Montalban). Now Patty tries harder than ever to convince her parents to let her be more grown up. Debbie Reynolds plays the role of Patty's cute and spunky younger sister, Melba. A delightful and cheery portrayal of simpler times that the whole family can enjoy.

UGLY DACHSHUND, THE

TECHNICOLOR   1966

COMEDY/ANIMAL STORIES

WALT DISNEY

DEAN JONES   **SUZANNE PLESHETTE**   **CHARLIE RUGGLES**

Screenplay by: Albert Aley
Based on: The book by G.B. Stern
Directed by: Norman Tokar

Dean Jones and Suzanne Pleshette are Mark and Fran Garrison, a childless couple raising their pet dachshund's new litter of pups. Fran adores the little dogs and fusses over them as if they were children. But then their veterinarian gives Mark a Great Dane puppy, whose mother is unable to nurse him, hoping that the mother dachshund will feed him. Mark, who loves bigger dogs, becomes attached to the Great Dane and wants to keep him, and Fran agrees, even though she's not crazy about the idea. The huge and lovable hound is good-natured enough, but the mischievous little dachshunds always get him into trouble. The rest of the story goes on to show how the friendly Great Dane proves himself to Fran as a valuable and faithful companion. A sweet and appealing animal tale, enjoyable for people of all ages.

UNINVITED, THE

BLACK & WHITE   1944

DRAMA/MYSTERY-SUSPENSE

PARAMOUNT

RAY MILLAND   **RUTH HUSSEY**   **DONALD CRISP**
CORNELIA OTIS SKINNER   **ALAN NAPIER**   **GAIL RUSSELL**

Screenplay by: Dodie Smith and Frank Partos
Based on: The novel by Dorothy MacArdle
Directed by: Lewis Allen

Ray Milland and Ruth Hussey are Roderick and Pamela Fitzgerald, a brother and sister who purchase an old mansion on the shoreline of England, despite being warned of strange occurrences there. When they find out for themselves that the lovely house they have bought is haunted, the Fitzgeralds set out to solve the mystery of the ghostly goings-on. A good, spooky ghost story that's suitable for children who have already outgrown nighttime fears.

UNSINKABLE MOLLY BROWN, THE

MUSICAL

PANAVISION & METROCOLOR   1964   MGM

DEBBIE REYNOLDS   **HARVE PRESNELL**   **ED BEGLEY**
JACK KRUSCHEN   **HERMIONE BADDELEY**

Screenplay by: Helen Deutsch
Based on: The musical play *The Unsinkable Molly Brown*;
                   Music and Lyrics by Meredith Willson, Book by Richard Morris
Directed by: Charles Walters

Debbie Reynolds stars as Molly, a girl who was abandoned as a baby, but was found
and raised by an all-male backwoods household. As she grows to womanhood, she
dreams of a great life in the civilized world, with education and wealth. Molly eventually leaves home to seek her fortune, and meets a miner named Johnny Brown
(Harve Presnell) who strikes it rich with gold and then marries her. Molly travels
to Europe to become educated and refined, but Johnny becomes concerned that
he's losing the spunky and down-to-earth girl that he originally fell in love with.
An engaging story about a woman achieving her wildest dreams, done with lively
musical numbers and songs.

Academy Award Recognition: Debbie Reynolds nominated for Best
Actress; Robert Armbruster, Leo Arnaud, Jack Elliott, Jack Hayes, Calvin
Jackson and Leo Shuken nominated for Best Scoring of Music (adaptation
or treatment).

VALLEY OF DECISION, THE

DRAMA

BLACK AND WHITE   1945   MGM

GREER GARSON   **GREGORY PECK**   **DONALD CRISP**
MARSHA HUNT   **LIONEL BARRYMORE** **PRESTON FOSTER**

Screenplay by: John Meehan and Sonya Levien
Based on: The novel by Marcia Davenport
Directed by: Tay Garnett

In Pittsburgh, the town of big steel mills, Mary Rafferty (Greer Garson) is an Irish
immigrant who finds employment as a domestic in the home of the well-to-do
Scott family. The Scotts own a large steel mill where Mary's father, Patrick (Lionel
Barrymore), worked until he was crippled by an accident on the job. Because of

this, Patrick hates the Scotts and is upset that Mary is now working on their staff. The Scott children are spoiled and unkind to Mary, except for son Paul (Gregory Peck), who befriends her and makes her feel more welcome. As time goes by, Mrs. Scott becomes very fond of her, and Mary becomes almost like part of the family. Eventually, Paul falls in love with Mary, but they have some problems to work out regarding their different backgrounds. Their love is put to the ultimate test when a major labor strike hits the steel mills, and Mary is torn between her loyalties to both the Scott family and the mill workers. An exceptionally good tale of conflicting social classes, acted out by a very strong cast.

 Academy Award Recognition: Greer Garson nominated for Best Actress, Herbert Stothart nominated for Best Scoring of a Dramatic or Comedy Picture.

VERTIGO

DRAMA/MYSTERY-SUSPENSE

TECHNICOLOR   1958   UNIVERSAL

JAMES STEWART	KIM NOVAK	BARBARA BEL GEDDES
TOM BELMORE	HENRY JONES	RAYMOND BAILEY
ELLEN CORBY	KONSTANTIN SHAYNE	LEE PATRICK

Screenplay by: Alec Coppel and Samuel Taylor
Based on: The novel *D'entre Les Morts* by
                   Pierre Boileau and Thomas Narcejac
Directed by: Alfred Hitchcock

James Stewart is retired police detective John "Scottie" Ferguson. He had a bad experience on the job that left him with a fear of heights, which causes attacks of vertigo. Ferguson is hired by an old friend who suspects that his wife Madeleine (Kim Novak) is possessed by the spirit of a dead person. He is to follow Madeleine and protect her from danger. Ferguson not only does that, but falls in love with her as well. A very haunting mystery movie done with director Hitchcock's usual flair. The intricacy of the plot makes this film more appropriate for teenagers and adults, rather than young children.

VIRGINIA CITY
BLACK & WHITE   1940

DRAMA/WESTERN
WARNER BROTHERS

| ERROL FLYNN | MIRIAM HOPKINS | RANDOLPH SCOTT |
| HUMPHREY BOGART | FRANK McHUGH | ALAN HALE |

Screenplay by: Robert Buckner
Directed by: Michael Curtiz

This movie employs fictional characters, but is based on a true story that occurred during the Civil War. A plan was devised to smuggle some gold (that was owned by southerners) from Virginia City, Nevada back to the South. This gold would replenish the funds needed by the Confederate government to continue fighting the war. In this fictionalized saga, Randolph Scott portrays Vance Irby, the Confederate officer in charge of the smuggling operation, and Errol Flynn plays Kerry Bradford, the Union Spy whose mission it is to halt the operation. Miriam Hopkins also stars as Julia Hayne, a Confederate co-conspirator who unwittingly falls in love with Bradford. An entertaining Western with an interesting and historical story, plus plenty of action.

VIRGINIAN, THE
COLOR   1946

DRAMA/WESTERN
PARAMOUNT

| JOEL McCREA | BRIAN DONLEVY | SONNY TUFTS | BARBARA BRITTON |
| FAY BAINTER | HENRY O'NEILL | WILLIAM FRAWLEY | |

Screenplay by: Frances Goodrich, Albert Hackett,
                Edward E. Paramore and Howard Estabrook
Based on: The novel by Owen Wister and the play by
                Owen Wister and Kirk La Shelle
Directed by: Stuart Gilmore

This is an update of the original film version from 1929. Joel McCrea plays a cowboy called "The Virginian." His best friend, Steve (Sonny Tufts), runs afoul of the law by getting involved with a cattle rustler named Trampas (Brian Donlevy). The Virginian warns Steve that he will be obligated to turn him in if he continues down this wrong path. His warning goes unheeded, and Steve is hanged for his crimes. This causes trouble between The Virginian and his girlfriend Molly (played by Barbara Britton), who doesn't understand his need to uphold the law against his buddy. Ultimately, The Virginian is forced to take a stand against the villain Trampas as well. A good Western that teaches important lessons about right and wrong.

VIVA LAS VEGAS

PANAVISION & METROCOLOR   1964   **MUSICAL**

MGM

| **ELVIS PRESLEY** | **ANN-MARGRET** | **CESARE DANOVA** |
| **WILLIAM DEMAREST** | **NICKY BLAIR** | |

Screenplay by: Sally Benson
Directed by: George Sidney

Elvis Presley is Lucky Jackson, a race car driver who's preparing to compete in the Las Vegas Grand Prix. He needs to raise enough money to buy the new engine his car needs for the race. Then Lucky meets the gorgeous and talented Rusty Martin (Ann-Margret), who is saving up to buy her father a boat so that he can set up his own business. Lucky and Rusty fall in love, but end up competing against each other for the cash prize that's being offered in a talent contest. A colorful, fun movie with lots of singing and dancing, as well as a happy ending.

WACKIEST SHIP IN THE ARMY, THE

CINEMASCOPE & EASTMAN COLOR   1961   **COMEDY/MILITARY**

COLUMBIA

JACK LEMMON	**RICKY NELSON**	**JOHN LUND**
CHIPS RAFFERTY	**TOM TULLY**	**JOBY BAKER**
WARREN BERLINGER	**PATRICIA DRISCOLL**	**RICHARD ANDERSON**

Screenplay by: Richard Murphy;
                 screen story by Herbert Margolis and William Raynor
Based on: A story by Herbert Carlson,
                 originally published by Popular Publications, Inc.
Directed by: Richard Murphy

The story takes place in the South Pacific during World War II. Navy Lt. Rip Crandall (Jack Lemmon) is overwhelmed when he's put in command of an old sailing sloop with an inexperienced and inept crew. Crandall and his second in command, Ensign Tommy Hanson (Ricky Nelson), have an important assignment—to sail through enemy waters and place a watchman, who will track the maneuvers of Japanese troops, on a remote island. Naturally, many funny things happen to them along the way. An amusing military comedy with good performances by the whole cast.

WAIT 'TIL THE SUN SHINES, NELLIE

TECHNICOLOR   1952

DRAMA

20TH CENTURY FOX

DAVID WAYNE	JEAN PETERS	HUGH MARLOWE
ALBERT DEKKER	HELENE STANLEY	TOMMY MORTON
JOYCE MacKENZIE	ALAN HALE, JR.	RICHARD KARLAN

Screenplay by: Allan Scott
Adaptation by: Allan Scott and Maxwell Shane
Based on: A novel by Ferdinand Reyher
Directed by: Henry King

David Wayne stars as Ben Halper, a barber who arrives in a small Illinois town in the 1890s with his new bride, Nellie (Jean Peters). The young couple starts out with nothing, but before long, they start a family while both Ben's business and the town begin to grow. This heartfelt saga continues for 50 years, and shows how Ben's spirit triumphs despite many setbacks and sorrows. A well-done and inspiring story.

WAR OF THE WILDCATS

BLACK & WHITE   1943

DRAMA/WESTERN

REPUBLIC PICTURES

| JOHN WAYNE | MARTHA SCOTT | ALBERT DEKKER | GEORGE "GABBY" HAYES |

Screenplay by: Ethel Hill and Eleanor Griffin;
                   original story and adaptation by Thomson Burtis
Directed by: Albert S. Rogell

Catherine Allen (Martha Scott) is a school teacher and author of romance stories. She decides to travel and experience more of the world, and meets oil man James L. Gardener (Albert Dekker) on board the train out of town. Catherine finds James attractive because he is just like one of the characters from her stories. Then they meet up with a wandering cowboy and former soldier named Summers (John Wayne). The three go on to have exciting real-life adventures just like those that Catherine has so far only written about. Summers and Gardner compete intensely, both in the oil business and for Catherine's affections, in this entertaining and action-packed tale.

WELCOME STRANGER

BLACK & WHITE   1947   COMEDY/DRAMA

PARAMOUNT

BING CROSBY	JOAN CAULFIELD	BARRY FITZGERALD
WANDA HENDRIX	FRANK FAYLEN	ELIZABETH PATTERSON
PERCY KILBRIDE	CHARLES DINGLE	

Screenplay by: Arthur Sheekman;
                 adaptation by Arthur Sheekman and N. Richard Nash
Story by: Frank Butler
Directed by: Elliott Nugent

Bing Crosby is Dr. Jim Pearson, a young physician who is sent to fill in for elderly small-town doctor Joseph McRory (Barry Fitzgerald), who plans to take a much-needed vacation. However, Dr. Pearson is not exactly the type of replacement that Dr. McRory had expected, and at first they don't get along, but various events oblige them to work things out. Add to the mix a pretty schoolteacher named Trudy (Joan Caulfield), who is engaged to the town pharmacist but in love with Dr. Pearson. Now, there are lots of reasons that Dr. Pearson's temporary situation should turn into a permanent one. But will he decide to stay or move on? A nicely spun and endearing tale of small-town American life.

WEST POINT STORY, THE

BLACK & WHITE   1950   MUSICAL

WARNER BROTHERS

| JAMES CAGNEY | VIRGINIA MAYO | DORIS DAY | GORDON MacRAE |
| GENE NELSON | ALAN HALE, JR. | ROLAND WINTERS | |

Screenplay by: John Monks, Jr., Charles Hoffman and Irving Wallace
From: A story by Irving Wallace
Directed by: Roy Del Ruth

Elwin Bixby (James Cagney), a tyrannical and demanding Broadway director, is on the skids because he's so difficult that no one will work with him any more. Even his girlfriend Eve Dillon (Virginia Mayo) is just about finished with him. Then show-biz producer Harry Eberhardt (Roland Winters), whose nephew Tom (Gordon MacRae) attends the West Point Military Academy, asks Bixby to oversee the student show in which Tom is starring. Eberhardt wants Bixby to entice Tom, who's very talented, to leave West Point behind for the Broadway stage. As part of his plan, Bixby imports pretty movie star Jan Wilson (Doris Day) to appear in the production. As things get underway, Tom falls for Jan, and considers leaving the Army to get married, while the incorrigible Bixby wreaks havoc upon the Academy. A pleasant musical with some nice songs and an unusual story.

 Academy Award Recognition: Ray Heindorf nominated for Best Scoring of a Musical Picture.

WEST SIDE STORY

PANAVISION & TECHNICOLOR	1961	MUSICAL
		UNITED ARTISTS

NATALIE WOOD	RITA MORENO	RICHARD BEYMER
GEORGE CHAKIRIS	RUSS TAMBLYN	

Screenplay by:	Ernest Lehman
From:	The Broadway musical by Leonard Bernstein, Stephen Sondheim, and Arthur Laurents
Based on:	A story by Jerome Robbins, suggested by Shakespeare's *Romeo and Juliet*
Directed by:	Robert Wise and Jerome Robbins

In this story of forbidden love, Maria (Natalie Wood) is a Puerto Rican girl, and Tony (Richard Beymer) is an Italian boy. When the two fall desperately in love, they are headed for trouble, as each has loyalties to different New York City street gangs. Sometimes, when Broadway musicals are translated into movies, something is lost, but not in this case—the entire cast provides excellent performances, with superb music and dancing.

 Academy Award Recognition: won Best Picture, Jerome Robbins and Robert Wise won Best Directors, Rita Moreno won Best Supporting Actress, George Chakiris won Best Supporting Actor; Saul Chaplin, Johnny Green, Sid Ramin and Irwin Kostal won Best Scoring of a Musical Picture, Ernest Lehman nominated for Best Screenplay (based on material from another medium).

WESTERN UNION

TECHNICOLOR

DRAMA/WESTERN/ACTION-ADVENTURE

1941

20TH CENTURY FOX

ROBERT YOUNG	RANDOLPH SCOTT	DEAN JAGGER
VIRGINIA GILMORE	JOHN CARRADINE	SLIM SUMMERVILLE
CHILL WILLS	BARTON MacLANE	VICTOR KILIAN

Screenplay by: Robert Carson
Directed by: Fritz Lang

The year is 1861, and the Civil War is raging, while a crew is stringing the Western Union telegraph line across miles of wilderness. Dean Jagger is Edward Creighton, the chief of the project; Robert Young and Randolph Scott are his assistants, Richard Blake and Vance Shaw. The telegraph crew faces interference from various Indian nations and vandalism committed by Confederate saboteurs. Meanwhile, Blake and Shaw compete for the affections of Creighton's sister, Sue (Virginia Gilmore). A very exciting tale with an abundance of action.

WESTERNER, THE

BLACK & WHITE

1940

DRAMA/WESTERN

UNITED ARTISTS

GARY COOPER	WALTER BRENNAN	DORIS DAVENPORT	FRED STONE

Screenplay by: Jo Swerling and Niven Busch
From: The story by Stuart N. Lake
Directed by: William Wyler

Gary Cooper is Cole Hardin, a stranger who arrives in a western town where there is a continuing battle between cattle ranchers and homesteading farmers. When he befriends Judge Roy Bean (a legend of the old West, played by Walter Brennan) and develops a romantic interest in a farmer's daughter, Hardin is reluctantly pulled into the conflict. A great movie that is admired by many die-hard Western fans, but it does have a somewhat dark mood. More appropriate for teenagers and adults than young children.

 Academy Award Recognition: Walter Brennan won Best Supporting Actor, Stuart N. Lake nominated for Best Original Story.

WHEELER DEALERS, THE
PANAVISION & METROCOLOR   1963    COMEDY/ROMANCE
MGM

JAMES GARNER	LEE REMICK	PHIL HARRIS
CHILL WILLS	JIM BACKUS	LOUIS NYE
JOHN ASTIN	PAT HARRINGTON, JR	

Screenplay by: Patricia Crowley, George J.W. Goodman and Ira Wallach
Based on: A novel by George J.W. Goodman
Directed by: Arthur Hiller

Henry Tyrone (James Garner), a wealthy oil baron, gets into financial trouble when he hits a lengthy run of dry wells. He goes to New York to raise enough money to keep from going broke. Once there, he meets Molly Thatcher (Lee Remick), an energetic and attractive businesswoman who's trying make it big on Wall Street. Together, they get busy wheeling and dealing to boost her career and amass the funds that he needs, while also starting a little romance. A pleasant comedy for light enjoyment.

WHITE CHRISTMAS
VISTAVISION & TECHNICOLOR   1954    MUSICAL/CHRISTMAS
PARAMOUNT

BING CROSBY	DANNY KAYE	ROSEMARY CLOONEY
VERA ELLEN	DEAN JAGGER	MARY WICKES
JOHN BRASCIA	ANNE WHITFIELD	

Screenplay by: Norman Krasna, Norman Panama, Melvin Frank
Directed by: Michael Curtiz

Lyrics and Music by Irving Berlin

The story begins on Christmas Eve, 1944, and Army buddies Bob Wallace (Bing Crosby) and Phil Davis (Danny Kaye) are busy entertaining their fellow GIs near the front lines of World War II. When the war is over, Bob and Phil become a hit entertainment team, and marry a pair of singing sisters, Betty (Rosemary Clooney) and Judy (Vera Ellen). The rest of the tale tells of the ups and downs of their friendship over the years, and their attempt to resurrect a failing ski resort. A cheerful holiday treat, suitable for the whole family.

 Academy Award Recognition: nominated for Best Song: ***Count Your Blessings Instead of Sheep***, Music and Lyrics by Irving Berlin.

WHO DONE IT?
BLACK & WHITE   1942

UNIVERSAL

BUD ABBOTT	**LOU COSTELLO**	**PATRIC KNOWLES**
WILLIAM GARGAN	**LOUISE ALLBRITTON**	**THOMAS GOMEZ**
WILLIAM BENDIX	**DON PORTER**	**JEROME COWAN**
MARY WICKES	**LUDWIG STOSSELL**	

Screenplay by: Stanley Roberts, Edmund Joseph and John Grant
Original Story by: Stanley Roberts
Directed by: Erle C. Kenton

Abbott and Costello play soda jerks who are hoping to get into radio showbiz.
They witness the murder of a network executive on the set of a radio mystery show
and set out to solve the crime. The result is a very fast-paced comedy where Bud
and Lou are chased by both the bad guys and the police. A fun movie with lots of
slapstick and Abbott and Costello's trademark word-play routines.

WHO'S MINDING THE MINT?
COLOR BY PATHÉ   1967

COMEDY

COLUMBIA PICTURES

JIM HUTTON	**DOROTHY PROVINE**	**MILTON BERLE**
JOEY BISHOP	**BOB DENVER**	**WALTER BRENNAN**
VICTOR BUONO	**JACK GILFORD**	**JAMIE FARR**

Screenplay by: R.S. Allen and Harvey Bullock
Directed by: Howard Morris

Harry Lucas (Jim Hutton) is a handsome young bachelor working in a U.S. mint.
Verna Baxter (Dorothy Provine) is a pretty and sweet co-worker who's interested
in Harry, but he is only interested in playing the field and living for the moment.
One day, by mistake, Harry takes home a $50,000 stack of bills in a paper lunch bag.
Then he accidentally shreds the cash in his garbage disposal. In order to fix things,
he hatches a plot with retired mint worker Pop Gillis (Walter Brennan). They
decide to sneak into the plant at night and print up replacement bills for the ruined
ones. Harry and Pop get help from an assortment of characters who become
partners in the deal, and in no time, their simple plan has become a major
operation. A zany, madcap comedy with a very amusing story.

WILD AND THE INNOCENT, THE

CINEMASCOPE & EASTMAN COLOR   1959

DRAMA/WESTERN

UNIVERSAL INT'L

| AUDIE MURPHY | JOANNE DRU | GILBERT ROLAND |
| JIM BACKUS | SANDRA DEE | |

Screenplay by: Sy Gomberg and Jack Sher
Story by: Sy Gomberg
Directed by: Jack Sher

Audie Murphy is Yancey, the nephew of a backwoods fur trapper. He is traveling to the city (the first time he has done so alone) to trade in a load of furs. Along the way, he meets Marcy Howard (Sandra Dee), the daughter of a no-good thief, who wants to go to the city to get a job and escape her dismal life. Yancey agrees to let Marcy travel with him, and along their journey, the two young people learn a lot about the dangers of the world that neither has experienced before. A very unusual Western that tells an important story about growing up.

WINCHESTER '73

BLACK & WHITE   1950

DRAMA/WESTERN

UNIVERSAL INT'L

| JAMES STEWART | SHELLEY WINTERS | DAN DURYEA | STEPHEN McNALLY |
| MILLARD MITCHELL | WILL GEER | ROCK HUDSON | |

Screenplay by: Robert L. Richards and Borden Chase
From: A story by Stuart N. Lake
Directed by: Anthony Mann

In Dodge City, the Centennial is being celebrated, and part of the festival is a shooting competition, for which the prize is a valuable gun—the Winchester '73, "the gun that won the west." James Stewart is Lin McAdam, a stranger who comes to town and enters the contest. As luck would have it, his toughest competitor is Dutch Henry Brown (Stephen McNally), with whom McAdam has had a long-standing grudge. Will Geer (Grandpa of TV's **The Waltons** series) appears as legendary sheriff Wyatt Earp in this top-notch Western with loads of action.

WINGS OF EAGLES
COLOR   1957   DRAMA/MILITARY
                                                                       MGM

JOHN WAYNE   DAN DAILEY   MAUREEN O'HARA   WARD BOND

Screenplay by: Frank Fenton and William Wister Haines
Based on: The life and writings of Commander Frank W. "Spig" Wead
Directed by: John Ford

This film is dedicated to the men who brought air power to the U.S. Navy in the
Post World War I period. One such man was Commander Frank "Spig" Wead
(John Wayne). He was among the first Navy flyers, a free-spirited and adventurous
man who broke aviation records. Maureen O'Hara portrays his wife Minnie, who
had to cope with all the difficulties that went along with military life. Wead worked
to create Navy flying power that rivaled that of the Army. During his long recovery
from an accidental fall, Wead became a writer of plays and movie scripts about the
Navy. He later went back to the military to help out during World War II. A rather
inspiring biographical drama about a man of great achievement.

WITH A SONG IN MY HEART
TECHNICOLOR   1952   DRAMA/MUSICAL
                                                                 20TH CENTURY FOX

SUSAN HAYWARD   DAVID WAYNE   RORY CALHOUN
THELMA RITTER   ROBERT WAGNER   HELEN WESTCOTT
UNA MERKEL

Screenplay by: Lamar Trotti
Directed by: Walter Lang

This is the true life story of singer Jane Froman, starring Susan Hayward. Jane was a
famous entertainer who rose to fame in the mid-1930s, and went on the road to
entertain the troops during World War II. On one such trip, her plane crashed into
the ocean. She survived, but lost one leg and endured many surgeries to save the
other. During her own recuperation period, she still reached out to entertain
wounded soldiers. With grit and determination, Jane Froman triumphed over her
physical limitations and eventually resumed her singing career. A very inspiring and
moving drama.

 Academy Award Recognition: Alfred Newman won Best Scoring of a
Musical Picture, Susan Hayward nominated for Best Actress, Thelma
Ritter nominated for Best Supporting Actress.

WITHOUT LOVE
BLACK & WHITE   1945

COMEDY/ROMANCE
MGM

SPENCER TRACY   **KATHARINE HEPBURN**   **LUCILLE BALL**   **KEENAN WYNN**

Screenplay by: Donald Ogden Stewart
Based on: The play by Philip Barry
Directed by: Harold S. Bucquet

A scientist named Pat Jamieson (Spencer Tracy) arrives in Washington, D.C. to begin research on a special secret project. Due to World War II, there's a shortage of available space, so he sets up a basement laboratory in the home of widow Jamie Rowan (Katharine Hepburn). Jamie has shut the door on her feelings since her beloved husband's death, and Pat, who's been unlucky in love, has vowed never to get involved with a woman again. They eventually decide to get married as an arrangement of convenience only, without love—or so they think! An offbeat and very charming story.

WITNESS FOR THE PROSECUTION
BLACK & WHITE   1957

DRAMA/MYSTERY-SUSPENSE
UNITED ARTISTS

TYRONE POWER   **CHARLES LAUGHTON**   **MARLENE DIETRICH**   **ELSA LANCHESTER**

Screenplay by: Billy Wilder and Harry Kurnitz
Directed by: Billy Wilder

Charles Laughton is Sir Wilfrid Robarts, an elderly English barrister with a heart condition, who's looked after by his over-protective nurse, Miss Plimsoll (played by Elsa Lanchester). Despite his health problem, Robarts is determined to remain active, and takes on the nearly hopeless defense of Leonard Vole (Tyrone Power), a man accused of murdering a wealthy woman. Vole's sole alibi is provided by his wife Christine (Marlene Dietrich) and as the case develops, an interesting story unfolds. An exceptionally suspenseful tale of mystery with no violence and a surprise ending.

Academy Award Recognition: nominated for Best Picture, Charles Laughton nominated for Best Actor, Elsa Lanchester nominated for Best Supporting Actress, Billy Wilder nominated for Best Director.

WIZARD OF OZ, THE
TECHNICOLOR   1939

MUSICAL
MGM

JUDY GARLAND	FRANK MORGAN	RAY BOLGER
BERT LAHR	JACK HALEY	BILLIE BURKE
MARGARET HAMILTON	CHARLEY GRAPEWIN	THE MUNCHKINS

Screenplay by: Noel Langley, Florence Ryerson and Edgar Allan Woolf
From: The book by L. Frank Baum, adaptation by Noel Langley
Directed by: Victor Fleming

This is the well-known story of the fantastic adventure of a girl named Dorothy.
Judy Garland is in the starring role, with Ray Bolger as the Scarecrow, Jack Haley as
the Tin Man, and Bert Lahr as the Cowardly Lion. Each member of this group has
an unusual problem, and their common goal is to visit the Wizard in the Land of Oz
to get help. However, the diabolical Wicked Witch of the West (played expertly by
Margaret Hamilton) has different plans for them. For many years, this has been a
popular family favorite, with great songs, impeccable costumes and scenery, as well
as a perfect cast.

Academy Award Recognition: Herbert Stothart won Best Original
Musical Score; won Best Song: *Over the Rainbow*, Music by Harold
Arlen, Lyrics by E.Y. Harburg; nominated for Best Picture.

WOMAN OF THE YEAR
BLACK & WHITE/COLORIZED   1942

COMEDY/ROMANCE
MGM

| KATHARINE HEPBURN | SPENCER TRACY | FAY BAINTER | REGINALD OWEN |
| WILLIAM BENDIX | ROSCOE KARNS | DAN TOBIN | |

Screenplay by: Ring Lardner, Jr. and Michael Kanin
Directed by: George Stevens

Spencer Tracy is Sam Craig, a sportswriter, and Katharine Hepburn is Tess Harding,
an international columnist. Both work for the same newspaper and, despite their
obvious differences, they fall in love and marry. Then new conflicts erupt between
Sam and Tess as they attempt to manage their dual-career marriage. The Hepburn-
Tracy team is perfectly suited to this very appealing romantic comedy.

Academy Award Recognition: Michael Kanin and Ring Lardner, Jr.
won Best Original Screenplay, Katharine Hepburn nominated for
Best Actress.

WORLD IN HIS ARMS, THE
TECHNICOLOR   1952

DRAMA/ACTION-ADVENTURE
UNIVERSAL INT'L

GREGORY PECK	ANN BLYTH	ANTHONY QUINN

Screenplay by:	Borden Chase;
	additional dialogue by Horace McCoy
Based on:	The novel by Rex Beach
Directed by:	Raoul Walsh

The story begins in 1850 San Francisco, at a time when seal hunting was legal and a major industry. Gregory Peck stars as Captain Jonathan Clark, a seal hunter whose ship is named The Pilgrim of Salem, and whose chief rival is the scurvy character named Portugee (Anthony Quinn). Clark meets Russian Countess Marina Selanova (Ann Blyth), who is on the run from an arranged marriage. Her only hope is to make it to Alaska, where she can be protected by her uncle, a Russian General. While Marina makes arrangements with Clark (who doesn't know her true identity) to take her to Alaska aboard The Pilgrim, the two fall madly in love. But before they set sail, Marina is stolen away by her fiancé, and so the story continues, leading up to a risky mission by Clark to rescue his beloved. A colorful and exciting tale of adventure with lots of action.

YANKEE DOODLE DANDY
BLACK & WHITE/COLORIZED   1942

MUSICAL
WARNER BROTHERS

JAMES CAGNEY	JOAN LESLIE	WALTER HUSTON
RICHARD WHORF	IRENE MANNING	GEORGE TOBIAS
ROSEMARY DeCAMP	JEANNE CAGNEY	FRANCES LANGFORD

Screenplay by:	Robert Buckner and Edmund Joseph;
	original story by Robert Buckner
Based on:	The life story of George M. Cohan
Directed by:	Michael Curtiz
Lyrics and Music by:	George M. Cohan.

James Cagney stars in the true life story of George M. Cohan. Cohan's show business career is traced from childhood, when he performed in vaudeville with his family, all the way to his receiving the Congressional Medal of Honor for his songs

Over There and *Grand Old Flag*. Excerpts from the many well-known shows that Cohan wrote are featured throughout this excellent and lively musical.

 Academy Award Recognition: James Cagney won Best Actor, Ray Heindorf and Heinz Roemheld won Best Scoring of a Musical Picture, nominated for Best Picture, Walter Huston nominated for Best Supporting Actor, Michael Curtiz nominated for Best Director, Robert Buckner nominated for Best Original Story.

YEARLING, THE
TECHNICOLOR   1946

DRAMA/ANIMAL STORIES
MGM

GREGORY PECK	JANE WYMAN	CLAUDE JARMAN, JR.
CHILL WILLS	CLEM BEVANS	MARGARET WYCHERLY
HENRY TRAVERS	FORREST TUCKER	

Screenplay by: Donn Gift and Paul Osborn
Based on: The Pulitzer Prize novel by Marjorie Kinnan Rawlings
Directed by: Clarence Brown

In 1878 Florida, the Baxters (Gregory Peck and Jane Wyman) are a hard-working but poor couple struggling to build a life for themselves and their son Jody (Claude Jarman, Jr.). About to approach young manhood, Jody faces a dilemma when the fawn he befriends grows into an adult deer that destroys his family's crops. A very moving drama about growing up and making tough decisions, with a rather bittersweet ending.

 Academy Award Recognition: nominated for Best Picture, Gregory Peck nominated for Best Actor, Clarence Brown nominated for Best Director.

YOU GOTTA STAY HAPPY

BLACK & WHITE   1948

COMEDY/ROMANCE

UNIVERSAL INT'L

JOAN FONTAINE   JAMES STEWART   EDDIE ALBERT

Screenplay by: Karl Tunberg
From: The *Saturday Evening Post* Serial by Robert Carson
Directed by: H.C. Potter

The story begins in New York City, where Dee Dee Dillwood (Joan Fontaine), a bored and fickle socialite, marries a man whom she does not love. When she flees from her wedding night, Dee Dee crosses paths with Marvin Payne (James Stewart), an aviator trying to get his own cargo airline off the ground. In an odd chain of events, he ends up taking her with him on a cross-country flight. Poor Marvin really has his hands full, carrying a weird conglomeration of cargo and putting up with Dee Dee's crazy antics, as well as those of his wacky business partner, Bullets Baker (Eddie Albert). Along the way on this strange adventure, Dee Dee finds meaning in life and a man she truly loves. An amusing and offbeat comedy.

YOUNG MR. LINCOLN

BLACK & WHITE   1939

DRAMA

20TH CENTURY FOX

HENRY FONDA   ALICE BRADY   MARJORIE WEAVER
ARLEEN WHELAN   DONALD MEEK   WARD BOND

Screenplay by: Lamar Trotti
Directed: John Ford

Henry Fonda stars as President Abraham Lincoln in this biographical drama of Lincoln's young adult years. It depicts the beginning of his interest in law and his first major court case as a lawyer, defending two young men set to be hanged for murder. Henry Fonda gives an impressive performance portraying the younger Lincoln whom many of us don't know much about.

Academy Award Recognition: Lamar Trotti nominated for Best Original Story.

YOUNG TOM EDISON
BLACK & WHITE   1940

DRAMA
MGM

| MICKEY ROONEY | FAY BAINTER | GEORGE BANCROFT |
| VIRGINIA WEIDLER | EUGENE PALLETTE | VICTOR KILIAN |

Screenplay by: Bradbury Foote, Dore Schary, and Hugo Butler
Based on: Material by H. Alan Dunn
Directed by: Norman Taurog

Tom Edison (Mickey Rooney) and his family endure a great amount of ridicule in their small hometown. Because of his inquisitiveness and his love of scientific experiments, many people think that Tom is crazy. This true story shows how Tom Edison's intelligence and ingenuity helped his family and others in difficult situations, eventually endearing him to the community that had once rejected him. A very interesting, and at times amusing, portrayal of the famous inventor's boyhood. An excellent family film that's educational as well as fun.

YOURS, MINE AND OURS
DELUXE COLOR   1968

COMEDY
UNITED ARTISTS

| HENRY FONDA | LUCILLE BALL | VAN JOHNSON |
| TOM BOSLEY | TIM MATTHIESON | |

Screenplay by: Melville Shavelson and Mort Lachman
Story by: Madelyn Davis and Bob Carroll, Jr.
Directed by: Melville Shavelson

This movie is based on a true story. Lucille Ball is Helen North, a nurse and Navy widow with 8 children. Henry Fonda is Frank Beardsley, a Navy career man and a widower with 10 children. When Helen and Frank start dating, they are each shocked to find out how many children the other has, but they don't let it stand in the way of their love. Somehow, they manage to overcome the pandemonium to create a large, unified family.   A top-notch and funny family comedy.

ZEBRA IN THE KITCHEN   COMEDY/ANIMAL STORIES

METROCOLOR   1965   MGM

JAY NORTH   **MARTIN MILNER**   **ANDY DEVINE**
JOYCE MEADOWS   **JIM DAVIS**

Screenplay by: Art Arthur
Based on: A story by Elgin Ciampi
Directed by: Ivan Tors

Chris Carlyle (Jay North) is a boy who lives in the country and has a pet mountain
lion named Sunshine. When his family moves to the city, he decides to put Sunshine
in a zoo, because the big cat has no skills to survive in the wild. The zoo is run by
Dr. Hartwood (Martin Milner), who is constantly urging city officials to improve the
quality of the animals' lives. Chris dislikes seeing all of the animals penned up in the
zoo, and when the opportunity arises, he opens their cages and sets them all free.
Then total disorder erupts as the animals spread out and wander throughout the
city. This movie uses fun and adventure to teach a lesson about the proper care of
our animal friends.

THE STARS

ABBOTT & COSTELLO

William "Bud" Abbott was born on October 2, 1895 in Asbury Park, New Jersey. His parents worked for the Barnum and Bailey Circus, and he began his show business career in childhood as a carnival worker. Bud grew up to serve as a box-office cashier and manager of several theaters across the United States, and then started to perform as a "straight man" in vaudeville comedy acts. Bud married his wife, Betty Smith, in 1918 and they had two adopted children.

Lou Costello was born Louis Francis Cristillo on March 6, 1906 in Paterson, New Jersey. His father was an Italian immigrant and an insurance salesman; his mother was Irish. Lou worked at odd jobs after finishing high school and then went to Hollywood to try getting into show business. He did carpentry work at the MGM and Warner Brothers studios and also worked as a stunt man. Since a big break in films didn't seem likely, he became a vaudeville comedian. Costello married Anne Battlers, a dancer, in 1934, and they had three children: Carole, Patricia, and Lou Jr. (who drowned accidentally in the family swimming pool at the age of 2).

In 1931, at a theater in Brooklyn, New York, Bud Abbott filled in one day for Lou Costello's "straight man," who was ill—and the rest is history. The two formed a comedy team that played in burlesque shows, vaudeville and movie theaters. The contrast between the roly-poly, zany Costello and the tall, thin, wise-cracking Abbott was the basis for one of the best comedy acts ever. In 1938, they earned nationwide recognition when they appeared on radio in "The Kate Smith Hour." In 1939, their performance in a Broadway revue led to a movie contract with Universal studios. They made their first film in 1940. During the 1940s, the duo enjoyed simultaneous success in both their long string of popular Universal films and their own radio show—The Abbott and Costello Program. They made the Box Office Top Ten list from 1941 through 1944 (placing first in 1942), and again from 1948 through 1951. They went to television in 1952 with the series "The Abbott and Costello Show," which lasted only one season. They continued making films well into the 1950s. Their long partnership was dissolved in 1957 because of their often stormy off-screen relationship. There were also financial disputes after the break-up. In 1959, Abbott made a brief, unsuccessful attempt to continue the act with a new partner, named Candy Candido. Abbott also performed voice record-ings for the television cartoon series "The Abbott and Costello Show" in 1966.

Both are now deceased; Costello died in 1959 and Abbott passed away in 1974.

ALLYSON, JUNE

Born Ella Geisman in the Bronx, New York on October 7, 1917, June Allyson grew up the hard way. Her father abandoned the family and her mother worked in a print shop to make it by. As a young girl, due to an injury, June wore a corrective back brace and got involved in swimming to build her strength. She went on to win a New York free-style swimming championship. June chose dancing as her path into show business, and worked as a chorus girl and understudy on Broadway. Getting a starring role in the 1941 Broadway show "Best Foot Forward" led to her movie career, as she was sent to Hollywood to recreate the role on film in 1943. June Allyson was under contract with MGM from 1943 to 1953, usually playing the clean-cut girl-next-door. In the 1950s, she began portraying devoted and suppor- tive wives. From 1959 to 1961, she hosted "The Dupont Show" on television, and during the '60s and '70s occasionally appeared on TV, in movies, and in nightclubs. Her first husband was actor Dick Powell; their daughter Pam was adopted, and then they had a son, Richard Keith. Powell passed away in 1963. Afterwards, she went on to marry and divorce barber Glenn Maxwell and then married Dr. David Prince Ashrow in 1976. She became a grandmother in 1984, and in recent years has appeared in television commercials.

AMECHE, DON

Domenico Felix Amici, the second of eight children in a large Italian family, was born in Kenosha, Wisconsin on May 31, 1908. He grew up to study law, and while attending the University of Wisconsin in Madison, began acting on stage. He subse- quently left college to try show business. In 1929, Don appeared on Broadway and worked in vaudeville. In 1930, he began acting in radio series such as "The Empire Builder" and became very well known. In 1936, 20th Century Fox signed him for movies and he became one of their biggest stars—Ameche's friendly smile and sincere portrayals of nice guys endeared him to audiences. He starred in comedies, musicals, and dramas. Don's best-known dramatic performance during these years was in the title role of the biographical film **The Story of Alexander Graham Bell**. After his contract with Fox ended in 1944, he worked freelance, but his popularity as a movie star waned by the end of the 1940s. In the '50s, he returned to the Broadway stage in successful shows such as "Silk Stockings" and "Holiday for Lovers." Ameche was married only once, in 1932, to his childhood sweetheart, Honore Prendergast. They had a family of 6 children: four sons (Dominic, Ronald, Thomas and Lawrence) and two adopted daughters (Barbara and Cornelia). In 1983, he took his career back to the movies, with a role in the comedy **Trading Places**. In 1985, he won the Academy Award for Best Supporting Actor for his performance in the film **Cocoon**. He continued to appear in films through the late '80s and early '90s, including: **Cocoon: the Return** (1988), **Oscar** (1991), and **Homeward Bound: The Incredible Journey** (1993). Having made a phenomenal comeback late in life, Don Ameche passed away in 1993.

AMES, LEON

He was born Leon Waycoff in Portland, Indiana on January 20, 1903, the child of Russian immigrants. In 1925, he started performing on the stage, and worked his way toward his first substantial movie role in 1932. In 1933, he helped to found the Screen Actors Guild. Over the years, Ames became one of the best-known character actors. He played a wide array of roles, but eventually settled into the niche of play- ing dependable and kindly fathers. His most notable role is probably that of the family patriarch in the MGM classic **Meet Me in St. Louis** (1944). In the '50s, in addition to occasional movie work, he began starring in such series as "Life With Father," "Frontier Judge," and "Father of the Bride." Ames also appeared in a supporting role on the '60s TV series "Mr. Ed." More recently, he played a role in the popular 1986 movie **Peggy Sue Got Married**. Leon Ames died in 1993.

ANDREWS, DANA

Carver Dana Andrews was born on January 1, 1909 in Collins, Mississippi, the son of a Baptist minister. He attended Sam Houston College, and after a stint as a book-keeper for the Gulf Oil Company, headed for California to start a show business career. During the '30s, he studied singing and got acting experience with the Pasadena Playhouse, while also working at various jobs. His first wife, Janet Murray, died shortly after giving birth to their son, David (who later died also). In 1939, he married again, to actress Mary Todd, and they had three children: Kathryn, Stephen and Susan. Andrews finally got a break in the movie business, and from 1939 until 1950 worked under a contract that was shared by two studios: Samuel Goldwyn and 20th Century Fox. He was one of the first film actors to have a shared contract. He made his movie debut in 1940, but didn't get really important roles until the mid-'40s, in movies such as **Laura** (1944) and **The Best Years of Our Lives** (1946). Dana Andrews played many different types of roles over the years, giving solid performances. In 1958, he started to make guest appearances on television. He starred in a television soap opera called "Bright Promise" from 1969 to 1972.

ARTHUR, JEAN

Jean Arthur was born Gladys Georgianna Greene on October 17, 1905 in New York City. As a child she modeled for her father, who was a photographer. In 1923 after a talent scout for the Fox studio spotted one of her photos, Jean made her first screen appearance in a silent movie. Her film career did not progress as quickly as she had hoped, so in 1932 she went back East to try the stage. After getting some stage experience, she finally landed a movie contract with Columbia. Jean got a big break in 1935 with her role in the John Ford film **The Whole Town's Talking**. Her comedic talent, aided by her rather unique speaking voice, stood out on the screen and she became a popular leading lady. She usually played female heroes with somewhat offbeat personalities. Famous director Frank Capra, with whom she made some of her best-known movies (including **Mr. Deeds Goes to Town** in 1936, and **Mr. Smith Goes to Washington** in 1939), dubbed Jean Arthur his favorite actress. She made 72 films in all, and was nominated for the Best Actress Academy Award for her performance in **The More the Merrier** (1943). Her movie career ended in the mid-'40s, amidst conflict with Columbia executives. She made only two movies after that: **A Foreign Affair** (1948) and **Shane** (1953). During the '50s, Arthur starred in "Peter Pan" on Broadway and tried her hand at TV in "The Jean Arthur Show." Later on, she taught drama at both Vassar and the

North Carolina School of the Arts. She was married and divorced twice: her first husband was photographer Julian Anker, the second was producer Frank Ross. Jean Arthur died in California in 1991.

ASTAIRE, FRED

Born Frederick Austerlitz, Jr. in Omaha, Nebraska on May 10, 1899, Fred Astaire studied at the Alvienne School of the Dance and the Ned Wayburn Studio of Stage Dancing. In 1906, Fred began dancing in vaudeville with his older sister Adele. As a team, they starred in hit shows both on Broadway and in London. When his sister married and retired from show business, he started to work in movies. He got a contract with RKO and appeared in his first film in 1933. Fred hit it big when he teamed with Ginger Rogers in **Flying Down to Rio** that same year. They went on to thrill depression-era audiences in a series of elegant musicals. Astaire's trademark was his sophisticated and smooth style of dance, and from 1935 to 1937, he was among the Box Office Top Ten stars. In 1949, Fred Astaire was given an Honorary Academy Award for his contributions to film, and in 1981 received the American Film Institute's Life Achievement Award. He was known to be a perfectionist about his work and was involved in every aspect of his dance numbers, including his behind-the-scenes decision making. Though he had many on-screen dance partners, his most famous achievements as part of a team were made when paired with Ginger Rogers. Their last movie together was 1949's **The Barkleys of Broadway**. One of his most innovative solo dance numbers came in the 1951 film **Royal Wedding**, where he danced on the walls and ceiling of a room, with the help of a specially built set. He was later successful on television as well—his first TV special in 1958 earned 9 Emmy Awards. Fred hosted the "Alcoa Premiere" TV drama series from 1961 to 1963, and occasionally appeared in the series "It Takes a Thief" between 1967 and 1970. He and his wife Phyllis Baxter Potter married in 1933 and had two children, Fred Jr. and Ava. Phyllis passed away in 1954, and in 1980, Astaire married female jockey Robyn Smith (they met through their common interest in race horses). Fred Astaire passed away in 1987.

BACALL, LAUREN

Born Betty Joan Perske in the Bronx, New York on September 16, 1924. Lauren Bacall studied at Julia Richman High School and the American Academy of Dramatic Arts. In the early 1940s, she worked as a model and got some small roles on Broadway. Her image on the cover of *Harper's Bazaar* magazine in 1943 captured the interest of Hollywood director Howard Hawks, with whom she signed a movie contract that was later sold to Warner Brothers. Her first film was 1944's **To Have and Have Not**, in which she co-starred with Humphrey Bogart. She impressed moviegoers and critics alike with her on-screen charisma and unusual combination of toughness and glamor. In 1945, Lauren married Humphrey Bogart and they had two children: a son, Steven Humphrey and a daughter, Leslie Howard. Bogart and Bacall had a popular on-screen chemistry, and made three more films together during the '40s. While holding out for better roles and refusing to play the ones offered her, she was fined and suspended by the Warner Brothers studio in the late '40s. In 1950, Bacall left Warner Brothers, but continued to make movies for other studios, trying all different kinds of roles. Then her husband, Humphrey Bogart, died of cancer in 1957. In 1961, she married actor Jason Robards. They had a son, Sam Prideaux, but eventually divorced. In 1959, Bacall starred in Broadway's "Goodbye Charlie" and since then has continued to appear on stage. Bacall was well-received in the Broadway play "Cactus Flower" in the late '60s, won the Tony Award for her role in "Applause" in 1970, and had yet another Broadway success in "Woman of the Year" in 1981. In 1979, she published her autobiography, *Lauren Bacall by Myself*, to which she wrote a sequel entitled, *Now* (1994). Bacall also co-authored a book about Humphrey Bogart entitled, *Bogart; In Search of My Father* with her son, Stephen Humphrey Bogart, and Gary Provost. She has made appearances on television as well, in series such as "The Rockford Files" and in movies made for TV. Recently, she received an Academy Award nomination for her supporting role in the Barbara Streisand film **The Mirror Has Two Faces**. Lauren Bacall is one of the 1997 honorees of the Kennedy Center for the Performing Arts.

BALL, LUCILLE

Lucille Desiree Ball was born in Jamestown, New York on August 6, 1911. Her father, a linesman with the Anaconda Copper Company, died when Lucille was only 4 years old. Her mother raised her in Celoron, New York, where she became an avid movie fan and dreamed of a showbiz career. At the age of 19 she went to New York City, studied acting at the John Murray Anderson-Robert Milton drama school, and worked as a model and a chorus girl in musicals. In 1933, she was selected to be a "Goldwyn Girl" and went to Hollywood to start her movie career. She was first under contract to Columbia and then signed with RKO. Until 1938, when she got her first lead part, Lucille appeared in small roles. From 1943 to 1946, she was under contract with MGM and from 1947 to 1951, she did freelance movie work and acted on radio's "My Favorite Husband" series. Although she had worked in films for many years, somehow she never seemed to get roles that fully displayed her talent and was not considered one of the great movie stars. Lucille ascended to superstardom when she and husband Desi Arnaz (they married in 1940 and had two children, Lucie Desiree and Desi, Jr.) went to television in 1951 with their "I Love Lucy" series, produced by their own company, Desilu Productions. In 1957, they started to produce other TV series as well, after purchasing the RKO studios and lot. Through the '50s and '60s, Lucy still made an occasional movie, such as **Fancy Pants** (1950) and **The Long, Long, Trailer** (1954), but TV was her main venue. In 1960, she and Desi Arnaz divorced. That same year, she appeared on Broadway in the show "Wildcat." Lucy married Gary Morton in 1961. In 1962, she purchased Desi's portion of Desilu Productions and went back to television, first in "The Lucy Show," and later in "Here's Lucy" (1966-1974). In 1967, Lucy sold Desilu to Gulf & Western. In 1977 she received the Life Achievement Award from the Friar's Club. In 1985, Lucy performed a dramatic role in a TV movie called "Stone Pillow," portraying a homeless woman. She died in 1989, but left her millions of fans lots of TV reruns and movies to remember her by. Lucille Ball also published an autobiography entitled, *Love, Lucy*.

BERGMAN, INGRID

Ingrid Bergman, born in Stockholm, Sweden on August 29, 1915, was orphaned as a young child, and was raised by relatives. She studied at The Royal Dramatic Theater School in Stockholm and became a Swedish movie star in the 1930s before making her first U.S. film in 1939. After World War II began in Europe, Bergman moved to the United States and became one of the biggest movie stars of the '40s. She won the Academy Award for Best Actress for her role in 1944's **Gaslight** and was nominated for the award three other times during that decade—**For Whom the Bell Tolls** (1943), **The Bells of St. Mary's** (1945) and **Joan of Arc** (1948). Ranked among the Box Office Top Ten from 1946 to 1948, Ingrid Bergman was rejected by the moviegoing public for a number of years after having an out-of-wedlock pregnancy by director Roberto Rossellini while still married to Dr. Peter Lindstrom (they had wed in 1937 and subsequently divorced in 1950). She and Lindstrom had a daughter named Pia, who's now a well-known theater critic. Bergman and Rossellini married in 1950 and had three children: son Robertino and twin daughters Isotta and Isabella (who is now a famous actress). Eventually, the scandal that surrounded her love affair subsided, and she returned to popularity in film with **Anastasia** in 1956, for which she won a second Best Actress Academy Award. The marriage to Rossellini was formally annulled, and in 1958 she married stage producer Lars Schmidt, but their marriage ended in divorce in 1974. Ingrid Bergman won the Academy Award for Best Supporting Actress in 1974 for her performance in **Murder on the Orient Express**, and was nominated for Best Actress in 1978 for **Autumn Sonata**. In 1980, she published her autobiography, *Ingrid Bergman: My Story*. She brought excellence to television in 1982 when she starred in the miniseries "A Woman Called Golda," a biographical drama about Israel's much-admired Prime Minister, Golda Meir. In 1982, Ingrid Bergman passed away after a long battle with cancer.

BOGART, HUMPHREY

Humphrey De Forest Bogart was born in 1899 in New York City. His father was a wealthy surgeon and his mother was Maud Humphrey, a well-known magazine illustrator. He attended school at both Trinity and Andover, but was expelled from the latter for bad behavior. During World War I, he served in the Navy where he received an injury that slightly paralyzed his upper lip and created a speech pattern which later became his trademark. Bogart then worked at a few different jobs before making his way to the Broadway stage. He started in movies in 1930, but it wasn't until 1941 that he became a major star, thanks to the films **High Sierra** and **The Maltese Falcon**. He almost always played tough guys, some of whom occasionally revealed their deep-down softheartedness and sense of honor. Under contract with Warner Brothers, he was listed in the Box Office Top Ten every year between 1943 and 1949, as well as in 1955. He made 75 films in all, winning Best Actor at the Academy Awards in 1951 for his role in **The African Queen**, and nominated for Academy Awards for **Casablanca** (1943) and **The Caine Mutiny** (1954). He was married four times. His fourth and most notable marriage was to sometime co-star Lauren Bacall. They remained married until his death from cancer in January of 1957. Bogart and Bacall had two children: a son, Stephen Humphrey and a daughter, Leslie Howard.

BOND, WARD
Ward Bond was born on April 9, 1905 in Denver, Colorado. He played football while attending U.S.C. Ward and teammate John Wayne were chosen by John Ford to appear in the film **Salute**. From then on, in addition to a professional relation-ship, the three (Ford, Wayne and Bond) enjoyed a lifelong friendship. Bond became a solid character actor and had supporting roles in approximately 200 films. His roles ranged from villain, to lawman, to hero's friend. In his later years, he went on to star in TV's "Wagon Train." In 1936, Ward Bond married Doris Sellers and in 1954 he married Mary Lou (Bond). He died in Texas in November 1960.

BRENNAN, WALTER
Walter Brennan was born in Swampscott, Massachusetts on July 25, 1894. In his teen years, he worked as a lumberjack and bank clerk. Trained to be an engineer, he chose acting instead and started playing in vaudeville and stock theater. In 1923, he began his movie career as an extra and stuntman. Although he was actually far younger, he usually played crusty old-timers. Brennan won the Academy Award for Best Supporting Actor an unprecedented three times within five years: **Come and Get It** (1936), **Kentucky** (1938) and **The Westerner** (1940). In 1941, he was nominated as Best Supporting Actor for **Sergeant York**. He entered the medium of television with the long-running series "The Real McCoys" (1957-63) playing the irascible, but lovable Granpappy Amos McCoy. Brennan then went on to do more TV. From 1964-65 he played in the series "Tycoon"; from 1967-69, the series "The Guns of Will Sonnett"; and from 1970-71, the series "To Rome with Love." He married his childhood sweetheart, Ruth Wells, in 1920 and they had three children: Arthur, Walter and Ruth. Brennan was able to continue acting in TV movies until the time of his death, at the age of 80, in 1974.

BYINGTON, SPRING
Born on October 17, 1886 in Colorado Springs, Colorado, Spring Byington was orphaned at an early age. A perennial favorite, her career spanned Broadway, the movies and television. Spring made her stage debut at 14 with a Denver stock

company, and in 1924, she made her Broadway debut in "Beggar on Horseback."
She then went on to appear in 20 more plays. Her film debut was in 1934's **Little
Women** and from there she went on to play in at least 92 more movies. Byington's
bright, cheerful and sweet personality made her perfect for maternal supporting
roles. From 1936-1940, she enjoyed success appearing in the "Jones Family" movie
series. She won the Best Supporting Actress Academy Award in 1938 for **You Can't
Take It With You**. Eventually, her acting talents led her to television, where she
was a regular on "Laramie." She is best remembered by TV audiences for her role
as Lily Ruskin in the CBS series "December Bride." A divorced mother of two
daughters, Spring died in 1971.

CAGNEY, JAMES

James Francis Cagney, Jr., was born in New York City on July 17, 1899. He started
off in show business as a child, performing in productions at the Lenox Hill Settlement House. In 1919, he moved on to the vaudeville stage, and in the 1920s to
Broadway. He and his wife Frances Willard Vernon were married in 1922 and had
two adopted children, James Jr. (son) and Casey (daughter). In 1927, James and
Frances established the Cagney School of Dancing. Due to his success on Broadway
in a show called **Penny Arcade**, Warner Brothers chose him to re-create his role
on film which led to a contract with the Warner Brothers studio. The film that
made him a star was **The Public Enemy** in 1931, where he was originally cast as a
supporting actor but was promoted to the starring role once filming was under way.
In 1936, Cagney sued Warners for breach of contract, but was re-signed by them in
1938. From 1939 to 1943, Cagney was part of the Box Office Top Ten stars. He
was nominated twice for the Best Actor Academy Award (1938 and 1955) and won
Best Actor in 1942 for his performance in **Yankee Doodle Dandy**, which was his
favorite movie. In 1943, he formed William Cagney Productions with his brother.
He served as both vice president (1934-1939) and president (1942-1943) of the
Screen Actors Guild. Cagney also received Lifetime Achievement Awards, in 1974
from the American Film Institute and later, in 1980, from the Kennedy Center for
Performing Arts. An exceptionally talented actor with a broad range of ability, he
appeared in all kinds of movies, from musicals to Westerns. His autobiography was
published in 1976, and in 1981, he came out of retirement (since 1961) to appear in
the movie **Ragtime**. After a career of outstanding show business achievement,
James Cagney died in 1986.

CHARISSE, CYD

Born Tula Ellice Finklea on March 8, 1921 in Amarillo, Texas, Cyd Charisse started
ballet lessons at the age of 6 and joined the Ballet Russe at 13. In 1933, she married
her dance teacher, Nico Charisse; they had a son named Nicky. During the late
'30s and early '40s, she toured Europe with the Ballet Russe until World War II
broke out. After adding acting to her repertoire, she went to Hollywood in 1943 as
a bit player. In 1946, she was signed by MGM, and began her rise to stardom as a

movie dancer. Cyd combined her ballet style with contemporary dance, and presented it all beautifully with her exquisite tall and lean figure. Among the highlights of her career were dances with Gene Kelly in 1952's **Singin' In the Rain** and 1954's **Brigadoon**, and with Fred Astaire in **The Band Wagon** (1953) and **Silk Stockings** (1957). She and Nico Charisse divorced in 1947, and in 1948 she married singer Tony Martin (they had a son, Tony, Jr.). As movie musicals faded in the late '50s, Cyd tried some dramatic roles, and in the '60s appeared in European films. In addition, she and husband Tony Martin formed a successful nightclub act together. In 1972, Cyd Charisse appeared on stage in Australia in a production of "No, No, Nanette." In 1976, Cyd and Tony published their combined biography, **The Two of Us**. She performed on Broadway in 1992 in the show "Grand Hotel." In 1997, Charisse and Martin were among the stars participating in a salute to MGM movie musicals at Carnegie Hall in New York.

COBURN, CHARLES

Charles Coburn was born on June 19, 1877 in Savannah, Georgia. He became a well-known character actor whose roles ranged from comedic to villainous, and whose monocle and cigar eventually became his trademark. In his youth, he took to the stage and became manager of a movie theater at 17. In 1901, he made his Broadway debut. He married his first wife, Ivah Wills, in 1906 and they starred together in a Shakespearean company that they founded, known as the Coburn Players. They then went on to act together in Broadway plays. By the mid-'30s, Coburn began playing character roles in films. He won a Best Supporting Actor Academy Award for **The More the Merrier** (1943) and was nominated twice in that category for **The Devil and Miss Jones** (1941) and **The Green Years** (1946). He married Winifred Natzka in 1959 (his first wife, Ivah had died in 1937). Charles Coburn passed away in 1961.

COLBERT, CLAUDETTE

Claudette Colbert was born Claudette Lily Chauchoin in Paris, France on September 13, 1903, and moved to New York with her family at age nine. She worked her way through drama studies at the Art Students League with a job in a dress shop. Colbert appeared in many Broadway productions during the 1920s, and after that experience, embarked on a movie career. She made her first movie (a silent picture) in 1927, and in 1928 landed a contract with Paramount, which lasted until 1944. After that, she worked freelance, and became known for her keen business instincts in guiding her own career. She starred in 62 films, won the Best Actress Oscar for **It Happened One Night** in 1934, and was nominated for two Academy Awards—**Private Worlds** (1935) and **Since You Went Away** (1944). Noted for her classy demeanor, Colbert played every part with a combination of spirit and smooth sophistication. She had a wide range of talent—excelling at both comedy and drama—and was one of the highest paid actresses of her time. In the early 1950s, she appeared in films and theater in Europe and in 1956 worked on

Broadway in "Janus." She returned to American films with her last movie, **Parrish**, in 1961, and continued to make occasional appearances on Broadway up until 1985, including "The Kingfisher" (1978) and "Aren't We All?" (1984). In 1984, Colbert was honored by the Film Society of Lincoln Center. In 1987, she was in the television production of "The Two Mrs. Grenvilles." She was married twice: first to actor Norman Foster from 1928 to 1935, and then to Dr. Joel Pressman, from 1935 until his death in 1968. When she retired, Claudette Colbert settled on the island of Barbados, where she died in 1996 at the age of 92.

COOPER, GARY
Gary Cooper (Frank James Cooper) was born on May 7, 1901 in Helena, Montana. His parents were British, and they sent him to Dunstable, Bedfordshire, England for his education. He then returned to Montana to study agriculture and put in some time as a ranch hand. He later moved to Los Angeles and worked as an extra and stunt rider in movie Westerns. He got a contract with Paramount in 1926 and became a star in the late 1920s. Tall and handsome with a shy kind of charm, Cooper was a favorite of female movie fans. As talkies took over, he remained a star, becoming one of the top Hollywood stars of the 1930s. The New York Times deemed him the highest paid entertainer of 1937. That same year, he contracted with Samuel Goldwyn, and later, in 1947, with Warner Brothers. Gary Cooper won the Academy Award for Best Actor twice—for **Sergeant York** in 1941, and for **High Noon** in 1952. He received nominations for that award three other times, as well— for **Mr. Deeds Goes to Town** (1936), **Pride of the Yankees** (1942), and **For Whom the Bell Tolls** (1943). Cooper was also given a Special Academy Award in 1961 for "his many memorable screen performances and the international recognition he, as an individual, has gained for the motion picture industry." Cooper and his wife Veronica Balfe, a socialite, had only one child, a daughter named Maria. Before his death from cancer at the age of 60 in May 1961, his last project was the narration of an episode of the TV program "Project 20."

COTTEN, JOSEPH
Joseph Cotten was born on May 15, 1905 in Petersburg, Virginia. He studied acting at the Hickman School of Expression in Washington, DC. As a struggling young actor, he supported himself by selling paint, advertising space and sometimes writing drama reviews for the Miami Herald. In 1930, the Belasco Theatre hired him to work as an understudy and assistant manager, which then led to Broadway. In 1937, Cotten joined Orson Welles' Mercury Theater. In 1939, he left the Mercury Theater to take on the lead role in "The Philadelphia Story," opposite Katherine Hepburn. Welles took him to Hollywood in 1941 where Cotten made his film debut in a lead role in **Citizen Kane**. During the '40s and '50s, playing romantic leads, he also appeared in thriller movies—namely Alfred Hitchcock's **Shadow of a Doubt** (1942) and Carol Reed's **The Third Man** (1949). Over the years, he worked under a number of contracts, with RKO, David O. Selznick,

Warner Brothers, and 20th Century Fox. He won Best Actor at the Venice Festival for **Portrait of Jennie** (1948). In 1953, Cotten appeared on Broadway in "Sabrina Fair." During the late '50s and early '60s, his career shifted to television where he hosted several shows: "The 20th Century Fox Hour," "On Trial," "The Joseph Cotten Show," and "Hollywood and the Stars." After the death of his first wife Lenore Kipp Lamont in 1960 (with whom he had a stepdaughter), Cotten married actress Patricia Medina. He appeared in the 1977 television miniseries "Aspen." Joseph Cotten's autobiography, **Vanity Will Get You Somewhere**, was published in 1987; he died in 1994.

CRAIN, JEANNE
The daughter of two teachers, Jeanne Crain was born in Barstow, California on May 25, 1925, and grew up near Hollywood. In high school she was named "Inglewood High Grid Queen of 1941," and also won the title "Miss Long Beach" in the Miss America contest. Becoming a model after graduation, she was dubbed "Camera Girl of 1942." After making the movie studio rounds without any success, Jeanne was discovered quite accidentally by a talent scout as a member of the audience at the Max Reinhardt Playhouse. She made her screen debut in 1946 and so began a film career that continued into the '60s. Two of her most well-known movies are **State Fair** (1945) and **Margie** (1946). She is also a professional painter, whose works (mainly portraits) have been exhibited in the Westwood Art Association galleries and at the Mascagni d'Italy. In 1945, she married actor Paul Brinkman who left the film industry to manufacture missile parts and radar sets, which made him a millionaire. They have seven children: Paul, Michael, Timothy, Jeanine, Lisabette, Maria and Christopher. Until recently, she still appeared in summer stock or city playhouses in revivals of "The Philadelphia Story" and "Claudia."

CROSBY, BING
Harry Lillis Crosby was born in Tacoma, Washington on May 2, 1903 (some sources also indicate 1901 or 1904). At seven years of age, he was nicknamed "Bing" after his favorite comic strip, "The Bingville Bugle." He came from a musical family, and dropped out of college to try show business. In 1926, he began singing with the Paul Whiteman Band and in 1927 became part of a trio called The Rhythm Boys. They sang on the road and on the radio, and then Bing struck out on his own in a series of musical movie shorts. In Los Angeles in 1930, he worked on nightly radio broadcasts from the Cocoanut Grove, and in 1931 broadcasted for CBS. Also in 1931, he began an association with Paramount movie studios that would last 25 years. He landed his first starring role in **The Big Broadcast of 1932**, and so began his long and illustrious film career. He spent lots of time in the Box Office Top Ten, including a long stretch of consecutive years between 1943 and 1954. For many years he enjoyed simultaneous success in movies, on radio (Kraft Music Hall), and on records, becoming one of the wealthiest people ever in American show business. Bing won The Best Actor Academy Award in 1944 for his role as a priest

in **Going My Way** and was nominated for the same award for the continuation of that role in **The Bells of St. Mary's** (1945) and another performance in **The Country Girl** (1954). Crosby also teamed with Bob Hope and Dorothy Lamour seven times to make the popular series of **The Road to...** movies. In the 1960s, he moved to television with a sitcom, "The Bing Crosby Show." This show lasted only one season, but he went on to make annual musical specials which were enjoyed by many. He owned a production company that made TV series, such as "Ben Casey," "The Wild, Wild West" and "Hogan's Heroes." Crosby became a multi-millionaire by investing in what later became the Minute Maid Orange Juice Corporation, and also appeared in its TV commercials. His first wife, actress Dixie Lee, died of cancer in 1952. They had four sons. With his second wife, actress Kathryn Grant, he had two sons and one daughter. Bing Crosby died in 1977, ending an enduring show business career.

DAILEY, DAN
Born on December 14, 1914, in New York City, Dan Dailey performed in a minstrel show as a child. Later, while appearing with Minsky's burlesque troupe, he took a number of everyday jobs—shoe salesman, grocery clerk, etc. He was also a band leader aboard a cruise ship and a social director at a resort in the Catskills. In the '30s, he made his way to the Broadway stage, which led to a 1939 MGM movie contract. He was drafted into military service during World War II, and when he returned to civilian life found it difficult to resume his Hollywood career. In 1947, he fortunately landed a co-starring role with Betty Grable in the 20th Century Fox film, **Mother Wore Tights** which revived his career—and remained with the Fox studio for 11 years. His personal life was rather difficult. He was married, unsuccessfully, four times and his only child, son Dan III, committed suicide at 29. When Hollywood musicals were no longer popular, Dailey went back to the stage and appeared in Las Vegas nightclubs. He also did television—starring in the series "The Governor and J.J." and "Faraday and Company." Dan Dailey died in 1978.

DAVIS, BETTE
Born Ruth Elizabeth Davis in Lowell, Massachusetts on April 5, 1908, she was educated in Massachusetts' Cushing Academy and studied dancing at the Mariarden School. Later, in New York, she attended the Robert Milton-John Murray Anderson School of the Theatre. In the late 1920s, she acted in stock theater and Broadway stage productions. In 1930, she got a contract with Universal, but they turned her loose in 1932 when her films did not do well. But, that same year Warner Brothers signed her. Her performance in the 1934 movie **Of Human Bondage** established her as a major star, and she went on to make a string of very successful films. Over her entire career she made a variety of films, including comedies, but was best known for portraying especially evil women. Her relationship with the Warner Brothers studio was a rocky one—in 1936 she was suspended without pay for her refusal to perform in films that she considered to be of inferior quality. Davis took

the studio to court but lost. She won two Academy Awards for Best Actress for her roles in: **Dangerous** (1935) and **Jezebel** (1938). She was nominated for that award four other times: for **Dark Victory** (1939) , **The Letter** (1940), **Now Voyager** (1942), and **Mr. Skeffington** (1944). In 1941, Davis became the president of The Academy of Motion Pictures Arts and Sciences, and helped to establish the Hollywood Canteen, which she also presided over. Davis founded her own production company, called B.D. Inc., in 1947. Due to the waning popularity of her films, her contract with Warners was dissolved in 1949 by mutual agreement. During the '50s, she still made some movies, and also did stage and TV work. In the '60s, she made a series of horror films. In the '70s and '80s, she worked in the television miniseries "The Dark Secret of Harvest Home" and the weekly series "Hotel." Married four times, Bette had three children: Barbara Davis Sherry (with William Grant Sherry), Margo and Michael (both adopted with Gary Merrill). In 1977, she received the American Film Institute's Life Achievement Award. She also wrote two autobiographies—*The Lonely Life* (1962) and *This 'n' That* (1987). Bette Davis passed away in October 1989 in Neuilly sur Seine, France.

DAY, DORIS

Doris Day was born Doris von Kappelhoff on April 3, 1924 in Cincinnati, Ohio and grew up to study at the Fanchon and Marco Dance School in Los Angeles. By 1940, she was singing with Bob Crosby's band and from 1940 to 1946 went on to sing with Les Brown's Band, becoming a successful and popular recording artist. The year 1948 was a busy one for her—she appeared in her first movie, **Romance on the High Seas**, got a contract with Warner Brothers, and worked on the radio and in concert tours with Bob Hope. During the early '50s, most of her movies were musical comedies. Doris expertly portrayed the quintessential girl-next-door: kind, smart, spunky and optimistic. Later in the decade, she began to move into more serious roles with films such as **Love Me or Leave Me** (1955) and Alfred Hitchcock's **The Man Who Knew Too Much** (1956). Her contract with Warner Brothers ended in 1955, and that same year she formed her own company, Arwin Productions. From 1959's **Pillow Talk** (for which she received an Academy Award nomination for Best Actress) and heading into the early 1960s, she began portraying either the single working woman or devoted wife. Doris Day enjoyed a great degree of success—she was a top box office attraction throughout most of her movie career, and was hugely popular with audiences. She was married three times and had a son, Terry with first husband, Al Jorden. After the death of her third husband, Martin Melcher in 1968, she found out that all of her income had been squandered and embezzled. In 1974, she won her lawsuit against the couple's former lawyer for $22 million. She became an activist for the rights and needs of animals in the late 1960s. She continued her career on television from 1968 to 1973 in her own series "The Doris Day Show" and again in 1985 as host of "Doris Day and Friends."   In recent years, she has not made many public appearances, choosing to lead a more private life. She has published her autobiography, *Doris Day: Her Own Story*.

De HAVEN, GLORIA

Gloria De Haven, the daughter of Carter De Haven and Flora Parker (who were stars of the stage and silent movies) was born on July 23, 1924 in Los Angeles. As a child, she accompanied them on the vaudeville circuit. At age 11, she started in films as an extra in Charlie Chaplin's **Modern Times**, which her father directed, and then went on to play bit parts. She graduated from Ken-Mar Professional School. During her teens, De Haven sang with bands (including Bob Crosby's), and joined MGM at age 18 where she starred in very popular musicals. In the '50s Gloria moved on to television and the stage. She was married to actor John Payne from 1944-50 and they had two children: Kathleen and Thomas. In 1953, she had a short-lived marriage to businessman Martin Kimmel. She married her third husband, Richard Fincher, twice (1957-62 and 1964-68) and they had two children: Harry and Faith. In 1997, she appeared in a supporting role in the Jack Lemmon-Walter Matthau comedy **Out to Sea**.

de HAVILLAND, OLIVIA

Born of English parents in Tokyo, Japan on July 1, 1916, Olivia Mary de Havilland began her movie career when she was spotted on stage at the age of 19 in Shakespeare's **Midsummer's Night Dream**, and was chosen to play the same role on film. In 1934, she signed a contract with Warner Brothers where de Havilland became known for asserting herself to obtain quality roles, for which she frequently received suspensions from the studio. In 1941, she became a citizen of the United States. Between 1943 and 1945, she was involved in legal battles with the Warner studio and made no movies, but instead appeared with the USO entertaining troops (World War II) and on radio programs. In 1945, the courts ruled in de Havilland's favor and she was released by Warner Brothers to continue her film career elsewhere. Olivia won Best Actress Academy Awards twice: for **To Each His Own** (1946) and **The Heiress** (1949). She was nominated for Best Supporting Actress for **Gone With the Wind** (1939). She has also won awards from the New York Film Critics and the Venice Festival. In 1951, she appeared in "Romeo and Juliet" on the New York stage. By the late '50s Olivia began to spend most of her time in France. In 1962, she wrote her memoir, titled *Every Frenchman Has One*. During the '60s and '70s, de Havilland appeared occasionally in both films and TV, most notably in the television miniseries "Roots: The Next Generation." Olivia and her sister, actress Joan Fontaine, had a long-standing rift between them. She was married twice: to writer Marcus Goodrich (they had a son, Benjamin) and to editor Pierre Galante (they had a daughter, Gisele). Olivia de Havilland presently resides in France.

DIETRICH, MARLENE

Born Maria Magdalene Dietrich in Berlin, Germany on December 27, 1901, she was educated at Augusta Victoria School in Berlin, boarding schools in Weimar and Hochschule für Musik. After appearing as a chorus girl in Germany's revue circuit, she joined Max Reinhardt's Deutsche Theaterschule in 1920 and then went on to appear in German films. American director Josef von Sternberg discovered her while filming **The Blue Angel** in Germany, and cast her in that movie. In 1930, after the film's completion, he brought Dietrich to Hollywood and she signed a contract with Paramount. Her husband, Rudolf Sieber, and their daughter, Maria, remained in Germany. Von Sternberg was responsible for creating Marlene's image and they had a long personal/professional relationship. Dietrich went on to make many films, usually playing seductive and glamorous women. During World War II she entertained U.S. troops, took part in war bond drives and broadcasted anti-Nazi propaganda in German. Awarded the Medal of Freedom for performing while risking her life, she was also named Chevalier of the French Legion of Honor. When her daughter, Maria, gave birth to a son in 1948, Marlene was named "the world's most glamorous grandmother." In the '50s, she began appearing in cabarets and making recordings. She drew record crowds while appearing in London, Paris, Moscow, Las Vegas and New York. She was still a popular and glamorous star well into the '70s. She created a trend in American style with her preference for wearing slacks. In 1984, Dietrich narrated a screen biography produced by Maximilian Schell called simply *Marlene*; she died in 1992.

DONLEVY, BRIAN

Born in Ireland, Brian Donlevy came to the U.S. as a child. He went into the military, serving under General Pershing against Pancho Villa, and becoming a World War I pilot. After the war, he became a well-known male model due to his good looks. Brian began acting on Broadway in 1924. In 1935, he became a film star after appearing in the Hollywood film **Barbary Coast**. This was the beginning of a successful movie career that spanned four decades. While In his private life he was actually a very soft-spoken and easygoing person, his roles consisted primarily of villains, heroes, drunks and gangsters. Brian was nominated for Best Supporting Actor in 1939 for his performance in the film **Beau Geste**. Divorced from his first wife in his 20s, Brian married again in 1936 to singer Marjorie Lane and they had a daughter, Judith. In 1966, he married for the third time to Bela Lugosi's widow, Lillian. Brian Donlevy died in 1972.

DOUGLAS, KIRK

Born to Russian immigrants as Issur Danielovitch on December 9, 1916, Kirk Douglas worked as a waiter to pay for his education at St. Lawrence University. There he tried his hand at school dramatics and also excelled in wrestling. To pay for his education at the American Academy of Dramatic Arts, he wrestled professionally, in addition to working as an usher and bell-hop. In 1941, he made his Broadway debut, but his acting career was interrupted by his World War II service in the Navy. He resumed his Broadway career in 1945 and also acted on radio. His 1949 role in **Champion**, for which he received an Academy Award nomination for Best Actor, established him as a Hollywood star. Kirk Douglas was also nominated two other times for Best Actor at the Academy Awards, for **The Bad and the Beautiful** (1952) and **Lust for Life** (1956). He won The New York Critics Best Actor Award for **Lust for Life**, in which he portrayed artist Vincent Van Gogh. In 1955, he began to produce films by establishing his own company (Bryna Productions), and in the '70s, while still playing leading men, Douglas began to direct films as well. In the '80s, in addition to continuing his acting career, he became involved in civic causes, testifying before Congress on discrimination and abuse of the elderly. Kirk became a Goodwill Ambassador for the State Department and the USIA. In 1981, he became the first person to receive the Presidential Medal of Freedom, a private citizen's highest honor. In 1983, Kirk received another private citizen's award for public service, the Jefferson Award. In 1984, he was elected to the Cowboy Hall of Fame. In 1985, the Chevalier of the Legion of Honor was awarded him by the French government. His other awards include: American Cinema Award (1987), German Golden Kamera Award (1988), National Board of Review's Career Achievement Award (1989). Married twice, Kirk has four sons—two (Michael and Joel) with first wife Diana Dill and two (Peter and Eric) with second wife Anne Budyens. Son Michael followed in his father's footsteps and has achieved fame in Hollywood as an actor-director. Kirk Douglas received a Special Academy Award in 1996 for "50 years as a creative and moral force in the motion picture community." He heads his own charitable foundation, which has provided help to Cedars-Sinai Medical Center, The Los Angeles Mission (which includes the Anne Douglas Center for Women), and the Access Theater for the Handicapped. He also raised about $2 million for the Alzheimer's Unit at the Motion Picture Hospital and Country Home in Woodland Hills.

DUNNE, IRENE

Irene Marie Dunne was born in 1898 (some sources also indicate 1901, 1904, or 1907) in Louisville, Kentucky. She got her early education at Loretta Academy in St. Louis, a Catholic convent school, and went on to graduate from Chicago Musical College in 1919. In 1923, she performed her first starring role on Broadway. In 1930, Dunne appeared in her first film launching a movie career that spanned 20 years and 40 movies of all kinds. In **Cimarron** (1930) the character she played aged from 17 to 80 years old, and her fine performance made her a star. She was nominated five times for Best Actress at the Academy Awards: for **Cimarron** (1930), **Theodora Goes Wild** (1936), **The Awful Truth** (1937), **Love Affair**, (1939), and **I Remember Mama** (1948). From 1940 to 1951, she made appearances on Lux Radio Theatre, recreating some of her screen roles. In 1952, she left the movie business and worked in television. In 1957 and 1958, she served as alternate delegate to the 12th General Assembly of the United Nations, and in 1965 became a member of the Board of Directors of Technicolor, Inc. Her husband was a dentist, Dr. Francis D. Griffin, and they had an adopted daughter, Mary Frances. Irene was noted and admired for maintaining high standards in her personal lifestyle, despite the Hollywood temptations that surrounded her. She passed away in September 1990, but re-makes of her best movies continue to be done—most recently, **Love Affair** (starring Warren Beatty and Annette Bening).

DURANTE, JIMMY

James Francis Durante was born in New York City on February 10, 1893, to poor immigrant parents. His father was a sideshow barker. At 16, Jimmy was a ragtime piano player in the Bowery. In the early 1920s, he owned his own nightclub. Then he successfully teamed with Lou Clayton and Eddie Jackson to play in vaudeville and nightclubs. In 1928, the team played New York's Palace Theater, and in 1929 they appeared in Ziegfeld's "Show Girl." Durante went solo in 1930 when he won an MGM contract and made his film debut in **Roadhouse Nights**. Throughout the '30s, he worked on Broadway, on the radio, and in Hollywood. Known as "The Schnozzola" for his unmistakably large nose, Durante always directed his jokes at himself, and disliked humor that was crude or insulting to others. His other trademarks were his malapropisms (humorous misuse of words), the song "Inka Dinka Doo" and his usual sign-off "Goodnight Mrs. Calabash, wherever you are." His first wife, Jeanne Olsen, whom he married in 1916, died in 1943. During the '50s and '60s, he made many guest appearances on television shows, and even hosted his own series "The Jimmy Durante Show" from 1954-56. He featured his old partners, Clayton and Jackson, on that show. In 1950, Durante received the Peabody Award for Entertainment. In 1960, he married Margie Little and they adopted a daughter, CeCe Alicia. He became a philanthropist, donating money to many worthy causes. Making appearances in Las Vegas nightclubs and TV specials into the '70s, Jimmy Durante died in 1980.

DURBIN, DEANNA

Deanna Durbin was born Edna Mae Durbin on December 4, 1921 in Winnipeg, Canada. When she was a youngster, her family moved to Los Angeles because her father needed a warmer climate for his health. A talented singer with a classical style, Deanna became popular on the Eddie Cantor Radio Hour. She made her first movie at 15 with Judy Garland at MGM before landing a contract with Universal. At the Universal studio, she made her best known movies, beginning in 1936 with **Three Smart Girls**, and followed by **One Hundred Men and a Girl** in 1937. Deanna also won a special Oscar (special because of her young age) in 1938. She was an overnight sensation with moviegoers and it is said that she rescued Universal Pictures from bankruptcy. Deanna was a favorite of Sir Winston Churchill, Prime Minister of England. Durbin made 21 films before choosing to end her film career at the age of 27. She was married three times: at 19 to studio executive Vaughn Paul, at 23 to producer Felix Jackson (they had a daughter Jessica), and in 1950 to director Charles David (with whom she had a son Peter). Deanna Durbin retired from the movies in 1948, later moved to France with her third husband, and has resided there ever since.

DURYEA, DAN

Born on January 23, 1907 in White Plains, New York, Dan Duryea worked his way through Cornell University by waiting on tables. He played the lead role in many of the school's theater productions. For six years, he worked in advertising, but illness forced him to find a less stressful occupation. In 1935, Duryea made his Broadway debut, and in 1939 became famous for his role in **The Little Foxes**. He later went to Hollywood to recreate the role for his 1941 film debut and began a career that spanned approximately 60 movies. Having started out on Broadway playing nice guys, Duryea eventually became famous as one of Hollywood's greatest villains (his private demeanor, however, was quiet and reserved). Two of his best known films were made in the '40s—**The Woman in the Window** (1944) and **Scarlet Street** (1945). His first venture into television was in the series "China Smith" (1952-55), then from 1967-68 he appeared in TV's "Peyton Place." His only marriage was in 1931, to Helen Bryan; they had two sons: Peter and Richard. Dan Duryea died of cancer in 1968.

FAYE, ALICE

Alice Faye was born Alice Jeanne Leppert, a policeman's daughter, on May 5, 1912 in New York City. She started out in show business as a dancer and chorus girl. She later sang with Rudy Vallee's orchestra and appeared on his radio show, then went to Hollywood with him when he got a movie role with the Fox movie studio. At first, she was supposed to sing only one song in the film, but because of problems with the movie's original leading lady, Faye was given the starring role. In 1934, she signed a contract with Fox and the rest is history, as she rose to become their top musical star. Many of the songs she performed in her movies became standards that are still heard today. She made 32 movies and was a major star for 11 years, being listed in the Box Office Top Ten for 1938 and 1939. She was married to sometime co-star Tony Martin from 1937 to 1940, and in 1941 married Phil Harris, an orchestra leader with whom she had two daughters, Alice Jr. and Phyllis. Alice Faye quit the movie business in 1945, and until the mid-1950s did a radio sitcom (a spin-off of the Jack Benny Show) with her husband Phil Harris. She returned to make one film each in the years 1962 and 1978 and went back to Broadway with John Payne (one of her film screen co-stars) in "Good News" in 1974. In 1990, she wrote a book entitled, ***Growing Older, Staying Young***. Most recently, she appeared in an in-depth interview for the American Movie Classics cable TV channel.

FITZGERALD, BARRY

Born William Joseph Shields in Dublin, Ireland on March 10, 1888, Barry Fitzgerald did not begin his acting career until 20 years after he graduated from college. He started as an extra in nighttime productions at London's Abbey Theater, and later acted full time. He came to the U.S. with the Abbey players in the late '20s and worked on Broadway. John Ford brought Fitzgerald to Hollywood in 1936 to recreate the role he played in Broadway's **The Plough and the Stars**. Fitzgerald became a popular supporting actor; his quaint and amusing characters with heavy Irish brogues made him quite a scene stealer. Even while he did very well in Hollywood, he continued to act on Broadway. He had the distinction of receiving two Academy Award nominations for the same performance in the 1944 movie, **Going My Way**: Best Actor and Best Supporting Actor (which he won). Though he had become an American citizen years before, he retired to Ireland in 1958. His brother was actor Arthur Shields. Barry Fitzgerald died in 1961.

FLYNN, ERROL

Errol Leslie Flynn was born in Tasmania on June 20, 1909. Before entering show business, he worked at many different jobs. He then went to England to try acting on the stage. Warner Brothers brought him to Hollywood, where he was given the 1935 starring role in the movie **Captain Blood**, and his career took off from there. The dashing and handsome actor is best known for his roles in action-oriented or swashbuckling movies such as **The Adventures of Robin Hood** (1938). For the movie **Gentleman Jim** (1942), where he portrays boxer Jim Corbett, Flynn did his own boxing scenes and trained hard to reproduce Corbett's actual style. World War II provided material for many of Flynn's movies as well, where he performed many on-screen acts of heroism. Flynn was known to be quite a ladies' man. By the 1950s, his popularity had diminished, but he did go on to make a few more films of a more dramatic nature. Errol was married three times and had three daughters and one son. He died in October of 1959, but has left fans of action-adventure movies plenty to remember him by.

FONDA, HENRY

Henry Jaynes Fonda was born on May 16, 1905 in Grand Island, Nebraska. He grew up in Omaha, Nebraska; his father owned a print shop. He started by acting in community theater and eventually made his way to Broadway. In 1934, he appeared in his first movie, the film version of **The Farmer Takes a Wife**, in which he had starred on stage. And so began a long and noteworthy film career, spanning 80 movies. That career was interrupted briefly by World War II when he served in the United States Navy, rising to the rank of lieutenant and earning the Bronze Star and Presidential Citation. Nominated for an Academy Award for **The Grapes of Wrath** (1940), Fonda received a special Academy Award in 1981 for his many years of contributions to motion pictures. The American Film Institute presented him with its Life Achievement Award in 1978. His finest and most remembered roles were those where he portrayed the strength of the American Spirit. Over the years, he also continued to work on the Broadway stage and did some TV as well (series: The Deputy, The Smith Family; miniseries: Captains and the Kings, Roots: The Next Generation). He was married five times and had three children, Jane and Peter with wife Frances Brokaw, and Amy, adopted with wife Susan Blanchard. One of America's most respected actors, Henry Fonda finally won Best Actor at the 1982 Academy Awards for **On Golden Pond**, just months before he died.

FONTAINE, JOAN

Born on October 22, 1917 in Tokyo, Japan, of English parents, Joan de Beauvoir de Havilland grew up in California. She assumed her stepfather's name Fontaine, and acted on the stage before making her first film in 1935. She appeared in several more films before hitting it big with her role in **Rebecca** in 1940, for which she was nominated for an Academy Award. First under contract with Jesse Lasky in 1935, her contract was later transferred to RKO, and then in 1940 she signed with David O. Selznick. In 1941, she won Best Actress at the Academy Awards for her perform-ance in **Suspicion**. On screen, she usually portrayed very delicate females, but in real life enjoyed such varied pursuits as fishing and golf, as well as piloting planes and balloons. Her sister was another famous actress, Olivia de Havilland, but they had a long-standing rift between them. She was married and divorced four times between 1939 and 1969, and had a daughter, Deborah, with her second husband, producer William Dozier. In 1948, she and Dozier formed their own production company, Rampart Productions. She appeared on Broadway in 1954 in "Tea and Sympathy." Her autobiography, **No Bed of Roses** was published in 1978.

FORD, GLENN

Born in Quebec, Canada, on May 1, 1916, Gwyllyn Samuel Newton Ford adopted his professional name from Glenford, the Canadian town where his father owned a paper mill. As a youngster, he moved to California with his family, and in his teens he worked on Will Rogers' ranch as a stableboy. Glenn began acting in Santa Monica High School plays. Prior to trying his hand at professional acting, he became the manager of a small theater. He played juvenile supporting parts and then lead parts with a variety of West Coast stage companies. In 1939, Columbia Pictures gave him a contract and during the early '40s he became established as a young leading man in films. Ford served in the Marines during World War II (1942-45). Upon his return to films in 1946, he became a major star, appearing in the film **Gilda** opposite Rita Hayworth, and then opposite Bette Davis in **A Stolen Life**. A very versatile actor, he was able to master all kinds of roles in all types of movies, ranging from comedies, to Westerns, to thrillers. He generally played strong, silent types who could leap into action when necessary, such as his roles in **The Blackboard Jungle** (1955) and **The Fastest Gun Alive** (1956). Glenn's first marriage, in 1943, to dancer Eleanor Powell lasted for 16 years (they had a son, Peter). He married two more times—to television actress Kathryn Hays in 1966 and then to actress-model Cynthia Hayward in 1977. Ford served as a Colonel in the Marines in the Vietnam War (1967-68). In 1970, he published his autobiography, **Glenn Ford, R.F.D. Beverly Hills**. During the '70s, he worked mostly on television, in the series "Cade's County" (1971-72) and "The Family Holvak" (1975), as well as made-for-TV movies and miniseries. On the big screen, Ford's more recent credits include **Midway** (1976), and **Superm**an (1978).

FOSTER, PRESTON

Preston Foster was born on August 24, 1900 in Ocean City, New Jersey. He started out as a singer in the entertainment business, playing lead roles with the Grand Opera Company of Philadelphia. Later, he became a radio and vaudeville singer. From 1928-32 he got dramatic roles on Broadway. In 1932, his appearance in the film **The Last Mile** propelled him to stardom. When Foster became a movie star, he was seldom cast as a singer. A big man, he usually played heroes, but at times also portrayed villains. He worked at almost every Hollywood studio and made a total of about 95 movies. In the '50s, he starred in the television series "Waterfront." As a singer/guitar player, he and his wife, actress Sheila D'Arcy, developed a road act in which they toured 28 weeks a year. Preston Foster died in July of 1970.

FRAWLEY, WILLIAM

William Frawley was born in Burlington, Iowa on February 26, 1887. He toured as a vaudeville performer, and started a movie career in the early 1930s. Frawley became a well-known character actor, and appeared in roughly 150 films. He usually played somewhat crusty characters, which many claimed were similar to his true self. To the TV generation, though, William Frawley will always be remembered as the grumpy but lovable Fred Mertz on the "I Love Lucy" series from 1951 to 1957. From 1960 to 1964, he played Bub, the caring uncle of the motherless family in Fred MacMurray's "My Three Sons" series. William Frawley passed away in 1966.

GABLE, CLARK

Clark William Gable was born in Cadiz, Ohio on February 1, 1901. He went to school in Hopedale, Ohio and attended evening classes at Akron University. While getting started in acting in the early 1920s with repertory companies, theater groups, and stock companies, he held various jobs, including telephone lineman and Oklahoma oil field worker. In 1928, he appeared on Broadway and then continued in other stage roles in New York. In 1931, Gable began to make some movies. In 1934, he finally got a contract with MGM, which lasted for 20 years. Gable spent plenty of time on the Box Office Top Ten list: 1932-1943, 1947-1949, and 1955. He was a favorite among female moviegoers for his unusual combination of charm and powerful masculinity. He won the Best Actor Academy Award in 1934 when he was loaned to Columbia Pictures for **It Happened One Night**. Probably his best-known role is that of Rhett Butler in 1939's **Gone With The Wind**. In World War II, he enlisted in the Air Force as a private, even though he was well past the age to be drafted, and rose to the rank of Major by the time he was discharged. He resumed his film career after the war, still retaining his popularity. He was a co-founder of the Russ-Field Gabco production company in 1956. Gable was married five times. With fifth wife Kay Williams, he had one son, John Clark Gable (born after Clark Gable died), who is a race car driver. Famous actress Carole Lombard was Clark Gable's third wife; she died prematurely in a plane crash in 1942. Clark Gable remained a major movie star right up until his death from a heart attack in November of 1960, co-starring with Marilyn Monroe in **The Misfits**.

GARDNER, AVA

Ava Lavinia Gardner was born on December 24, 1922, near Smithfield, North Carolina, the youngest of six children. At Atlantic Christian College, she learned secretarial skills. Ava went to New York to visit her sister and look for an office job. During the visit, her brother-in-law, a photographer, took some pictures of her and forwarded them to MGM executives. She got a movie contract with MGM in 1941 and played bit parts until getting her first substantial movie role in 1944. Ava's performance in **The Killers** (1946) and **The Hucksters** (1947) made her a star and glamor queen. She was nominated for Best Actress at the Academy Awards in 1953 for her work in **Mogambo**. Gardner continued making films for MGM until 1958, after which she worked freelance. She lived in Spain for a number of years, and then in London. Ava was married three times: first to actor Mickey Rooney, second to bandleader Artie Shaw, and third to singer/actor Frank Sinatra. In 1985, she appeared in the television mini-series "A.D.," the TV movie "The Long Hot Summer," and the weekly series "Knots Landing." While working on her autobiography, Ava Gardner died in London in 1990.

GARLAND, JUDY

Judy Garland was born Frances Ethel Gumm on June 10, 1922 in Grand Rapids, Minnesota, to vaudevillians Jack and Virginia Lee. She grew up in Los Angeles, and had two older sisters, Virginia and Suzanne, with whom she began singing at age 3. In 1929, they made their screen debut as the Gumm Sisters and also toured with their act, later changing their name to the Garland Sisters. By 13, Judy had a Hollywood agent. She finally got a contract with MGM in 1935 after being rejected by RKO, Columbia, and Paramount Pictures. Many of her most successful movies during her early teen years were those where she was paired with Mickey Rooney, MGM's popular male teenage star. While working together, they forged a strong lifelong friendship. In **The Wizard of Oz** (1939), she got the chance to prove herself as a mature musical star. As Judy grew into adulthood, she continued to entertain audiences in major movie musicals such as **Meet Me In St. Louis** (1944) and **The Harvey Girls** (1946). She received two Academy Award nominations, one for Best Actress in **A Star Is Born** (1954), and one for Best Supporting Actress in **Judgment at Nuremberg** (1961), both of which were dramatic films. Judy also performed on radio during its heyday, and made records as well. In 1950, MGM failed to renew her contract due to her health problems, but Judy went on to appear in her own very popular stage concerts (in such venues as the London Palladium and New York's Palace Theatre), and an occasional film. From 1963 to 1964, she had her own TV program called "The Judy Garland Show." Married five times, she had three children: daughter Liza Minnelli (with second husband, movie director Vincente Minnelli), daughter Lorna Luft and son Joey Luft (both with third husband Sid Luft). Unfortunately, personal problems had taken their toll on her career before she died in 1969 of a drug overdose, but she lives on in film as one of the greatest entertainers of all time.

GARNER, JAMES

James Garner was born James Scott Bumgarner on April 7, 1928 in Norman, Oklahoma. He joined the Merchant Marines at age 16 after dropping out of high school, was wounded in the Korean War, and received the Purple Heart. Upon his discharge, he worked as a traveling salesman, carpet layer, and male model. His first try at acting was a non-speaking role in the 1954 Broadway production of "The Caine Mutiny Court-Martial." From then on, he began to land small film and television parts. In 1957, he established the starring role in TV's "Maverick." This led to starring roles in Hollywood, where in the mid-1960s, he was one of the highest paid leading men. Garner established a production company and then invested the earnings in oil and real estate. He later starred in another television series, "The Rockford Files," which ran from 1974-1980 and won him an Emmy Award in 1977. In 1985, Garner received an Academy Award nomination for Best Actor for his performance in the film **Murphy's Romance**. He continues to do TV work; his most recent film is **My Fellow Americans** (1997) with co-star Jack Lemmon. Married to Lois Clarke since 1956, they have two daughters.

GARSON, GREER

Greer Garson was born in County Down, Ireland on September 29, 1903. Her first name is a contraction of Gregor—her mother was descended from the Scottish clan McGregor. Greer's father died when she was just four months old, and subsequently she and her mother moved to London. They had a difficult time because she was a sickly child. She got a scholarship and graduated from London University with Honours, and then pursued graduate studies at the University of Grenoble in France. She worked for an advertising firm in London, trying acting on her own time (doing a lot of light comedy), and working her way from repertory theater to the London stage. In 1938, after seeing her work in a play, Louis B. Mayer of MGM studios brought her to Hollywood. Her first movie was 1939's **Goodbye, Mr. Chips**, for which she received the first of six Academy Award nominations. She won Best Actress at the 1942 Academy Awards for her role in **Mrs. Miniver**. From 1942 to 1946 she was rated among the Box Office Top Ten, and nine of her first eleven films premiered at Radio City Music Hall in New York, setting a record by playing for 64 weeks in total. Her screen roles were generally dramatic ones where she portrayed dignified women of great inner strength. Leading man Walter Pidgeon was her frequent film co-star. Garson made 24 movies in a 28-year career, and performed often on the radio as well, but her popularity dropped off quickly in the late forties. In 1955, she made her last movie for MGM, **Her Twelve Men**, but went on to make an occasional film through the '60s, most notably **Sunrise at Campobello**, where she portrayed First Lady Eleanor Roosevelt. In 1958, she performed on Broadway in "Auntie Mame," and in 1978 worked in the TV miniseries "Little Women." Garson was married three times, the second time to actor Richard Ney, who portrayed her son in the film **Mrs. Miniver**. Her third husband was wealthy oil baron Elijah "Buddy" Fogelson, and they lived on a ranch in New Mexico. Together, they donated millions to the arts, including theater scholarships at Southern Methodist University. Fogelson died in 1987, but Garson still supported the school, donating $10 million to build a theater which was named for her. She also donated 12 of her films from her private collection to the University. In her later years, she suffered from heart problems, having a heart attack in 1980 and quadruple bypass surgery in 1988. Greer Garson died in 1996 at the age of 92.

GLEASON, JAMES
Born on May 23, 1886 in New York City, to actor parents who operated a theater, James Gleason appeared on the stage as a child. Later, after serving in the Spanish-American War, he and wife Lillian (whom he married in 1905), joined his parents in their stock company. He also served in World War I, which interrupted his acting career, but he resumed it playing on Broadway in "The Five Million." After his Hollywood debut in 1922, he spent the next six years as a Broadway director/playwright/actor. Some of the plays and musicals he wrote or collaborated on in the late '20s through the '30s were made into films. Jimmy's film career as a scriptwriter/actor and occasional director continued from 1928 to 1958, during which time he made over 150 movies. As an actor, Gleason's roles were primarily those of tough-talking, but good-hearted characters. He was nominated for the Best Supporting Actor Academy Award in **Here Comes Mr. Jordan** (1941). Gleason and his wife Lillian had one son, Russell (also an actor) who died in 1945, then Lillian died in 1947. James Gleason passed away in 1959.

GODDARD, PAULETTE
Paulette Goddard was born Pauline Marion Goddard Levee in Whitestone Landing, New York on June 3, 1905, and attended Mount Saint Dominic's Academy in Caldwell, New Jersey. She made her film debut with a bit part in the Laurel and Hardy film **Berth Marks**. In 1926, Paulette made her stage debut in Ziegfeld's "No Foolin'." She had roles in many forgettable films until 1936, when she was cast by and co-starred with Charles Chaplin in **Modern Times**. This made her a star, and she maintained her stardom through the mid-1940s. She was considered one of Hollywood's great beauties. Her career as a comedic actress was launched by her role opposite Rosalind Russell in **The Women** (1939). For her part in the war drama, **So Proudly We Hail** (1943), Paulette was nominated for a Best Supporting Actress Academy Award. In 1944, she made a 5-month USO tour of the Far East. In 1947, she appeared at the Abbey Theatre, Dublin in "Winterset." During the

'50s, Goddard made occasional television appearances. In 1964, she had a supporting role in the film **Time of Indifference** with Claudia Cardinale. Her final acting appearance was in the 1972 television movie, "The Snoop Sisters." Paulette Goddard was married four times: Edgar James (1931), Charlie Chaplin (1933), Burgess Meredith (1944) and Erich Maria Remarque (1958). She died in 1990, leaving her $20 million fortune to New York University, although she never attended the school.

GRABLE, BETTY

Ruth Elizabeth Grable was born in St. Louis, Missouri on December 18, 1916. Her mother prepared Betty for stardom from an early age, having her study ballet, tap dancing, and acrobatics. She also arranged for Betty to go to Hollywood at age 13 by telling the movie studio she was older, which got her a part in the chorus of a musical at Fox. However, the studio canceled her contract when they discovered her true age. While getting her movie career started during the 1930s (contracts with Goldwyn, RKO and Paramount), she also sang with Ted Fiorita's band and appeared on Broadway. Her big break came when Alice Faye became ill, was unable to film **Down Argentine Way** (1940), and 20th Century Fox studios gave Betty the part in Faye's place. From then on, Betty Grable was a major movie star, being listed in the Box Office Top Ten every year between 1942 and 1951 (a record among female stars), and ranking number one in 1943. With blonde hair and very blue eyes, she made quite a spectacle on Technicolor film. Due to the phenomenal popularity of her pin-up posters with the GIs in World War II, her shapely legs (gams, as they were called in those days) were probably the most famous in the entire world. She made 55 films over her entire career, and was under contract with 20th Century Fox from 1940 through 1953. She was married twice: first, from 1937 to 1940 to actor Jackie Coogan, and second, to bandleader Harry James, whom she met on the set of **Springtime in the Rockies** (1942). She and Harry James had two daughters, Victoria and Jessica, and remained married for 22 years until their divorce in 1965. After her film career ended, Betty made appearances in Las Vegas, performing many of the songs from her movies. During the 1960s, she starred on stage in various shows, of which "Hello, Dolly!" was the most notable. Almost all of the income she had earned over the years went to pay off husband Harry James' gambling debts, so Betty kept working. She even worked right through most of her illness with cancer (many did not realize just how ill she was) until she passed away on July 2, 1973. Many of Betty Grable's Hollywood co-stars and friends still say what a truly nice person she was and that her tremendous fame never changed her.

GRANT, CARY

Cary Grant was born Archibald Alexander Leach on January 18, 1904 in Bristol, England. He had a difficult childhood—when he was ten years old his mother was placed in an institution due to a nervous breakdown and he did not see her again for over 20 years. He received a scholarship to the Fairfield Academy, but left school as a teenager to join the Bob Pender Troupe, a group of comedians and acrobats. When the troupe came to New York, he decided to stay in the United States and try his hand at show business. He performed in Broadway musicals during the '20s and early '30s, still using his original name, Archie Leach. The Fox movie studio turned him down for a film contract, but Paramount took him aboard—he assumed the name "Cary" from a Broadway show he starred in, and the studio executives came up with "Grant." In 1932, he made his first movie, and eventually became the king of romantic comedy in the American film industry. He was under contract with Paramount between 1932 and 1937, and thereafter worked freelance. His screen presence expertly combined smooth sophistication and a comic zaniness that endeared him to many female fans. He worked with a long list of top Hollywood leading ladies, including Katharine Hepburn, Irene Dunne, Myrna Loy, and Deborah Kerr. Grant was given an Honorary Academy Award in 1969 for "his unique mastery of the art of screen acting with the respect and affection of his colleagues," and also received the Lifetime Achievement Award of the American Film Institute. He was married five times, first to Virginia Cherrill, second to Barbara Hutton, third to actress Betsy Drake (with whom he co-starred in some films), fourth to actress Dyan Cannon (with whom he had his daughter Jennifer), and last, until his death from a stroke on November 29, 1986, to British journalist Barbara Harris. He has left fans a very large number of movies to enjoy, as he continued working in films right through the 1960s. He also published his autobiography, entitled *Evenings With Cary Grant*.

GRAYSON, KATHRYN

Kathryn Grayson was born Zelma Kathryn Hedrick on February 9, 1922 in Winston-Salem, North Carolina. She studied music and took voice lessons as a teenager. Kathryn sang on Eddie Cantor's radio show in 1940, and was discovered by MGM studios, who signed her to a movie contract. A pretty young lady with an operatic singing voice, she made her film debut in 1941 and went on to star in many musicals during the '40s and early '50s. A few of her best-known movies were: **Thousands Cheer** (1943), **Show Boat** (1951), and **Kiss Me Kate** (1953). She was married and divorced twice: her first husband was actor John Shelton, and her second was singer Johnny Johnston. When singer Mario Lanza (one of her movie co-stars) and his wife both died at young ages, Kathryn Grayson brought their children to live with her. In the '60s, she started to do stage work, which included the shows "Camelot," "Kiss Me Kate," and "Show Boat." In 1966, Kathryn performed in a television production of the opera "Die Fledermaus." In 1990, she appeared on the popular television series "Murder, She Wrote."

GREENWOOD, CHARLOTTE

Frances Charlotte Greenwood was born in Philadelphia, Pennsylvania, on June 25, 1890. She had reached her full height of 5' 10" at age 11! In her early teens she performed in vaudeville and on Broadway. She played some parts in silent films, but then returned to the stage. In the late '20s, Charlotte had lead roles in "B" comedies and supporting parts in musicals. She created the role of Aunt Eller in Broadway's "Oklahoma." She was noted for her incredible flexibility and practically vertical high kicks and the 1940's musical era was when she reached the peak of her popularity. Greenwood was married twice and her second marriage to husband Martin Broones lasted until his death. She died in 1978.

GWENN, EDMUND
Born in Wales on September 26, 1875, Gwenn became a British stage star as a youth. He made his film debut in Britain in 1916, and performed in many George Bernard Shaw plays. Gwenn's Broadway debut was in the 1920 production of "The Skin Game." In 1935, he made his Hollywood debut in **The Bishop Misbehaves**. From the '20s through the '40s he was very popular both on Broadway and in Hollywood playing kindly, lovable elders, and stealing many scenes with his charm. He was nominated for Best Supporting Actor three times: for **Miracle on 34th Street** (1947), **Mister 880** (1950) and **The Trouble with Harry** (1955). Divorced from his wife, Minnie Terry, Edmund Gwenn died in 1959.

HALEY, JACK
John Joseph Haley was born on August 10, 1899 in Boston, Massachusetts. In the '20s, Jack started in vaudeville, then graduated to Broadway appearing in "Good News" and "Gay Paree." In 1933, he played in Hollywood's **Sitting Pretty**. Jack stole the show from co-stars Alice Faye and Walter Winchell in **Wake Up and Live** (1936). His most famous film role was The Tin Man in 1939's **The Wizard of Oz**. His many charitable contributions led the Catholic Church to honor him with the Knight of Malta. Son, Jack Haley, Jr. is a Hollywood director. Jack Haley, Sr. died in June of 1979.

HENIE, SONJA
Born April 8, 1913 in Oslo, Norway, Sonja Henie was the daughter of a well-known Norwegian skater, Wilhelm Henie. She started dancing at four, skating at eight. She became an award-winning skater—at ten she won the Open Championship of Norway and at 15 became the World Champion. For three consecutive Winter Olympics (1928, 1932, 1936) Sonja set world records and won gold medals. While touring the U.S. with a professional ice show, she was noticed by Darryl F. Zanuck who cast her in **One in a Million**, her film debut. That same year, she was bestow- ed with the Knight of the Order of St. Olaf. Sonja became one of the 20th Century Fox studios leading stars acting mainly in light, entertaining movies that included musical skating production numbers. In 1937, 1938 and 1939 she was in the Box Office Top Ten. In the early '40s, Sonja became the producer and star of the Hollywood Ice Revue, performing in Madison Square Garden and other national

arenas. In 1945 she visited American army hospitals as a USO entertainer. She married three times: Dan Topping (1940), Winthrop Gardiner (1949), and Niels Onstad (1949). Sonja Henie died in October of 1969.

HEPBURN, KATHARINE

Katharine Houghton Hepburn was born in Hartford, Connecticut in November 1907, the daughter of a wealthy couple, her father a surgeon and her mother a women's activist. She was an adventurous and spirited child. When she grew up, Katherine went to college at Bryn Mawr. She embarked upon her professional acting career in 1928, and made her mark on the Broadway stage before going to Hollywood and getting her first movie role and a contract with RKO in 1932. The 1933 film **Morning Glory** made her a star. In 1938, she bought out her RKO contract so that she couldn't be forced to make the movie **Mother Cary's Chickens**, which she found distasteful, and returned to Broadway to star in the play "The Philadelphia Story," which was written specifically for her. In 1940, Hepburn resumed her movie career with the film version of that play. She made more than 40 films in her career and holds records for the most Academy Award nominations—12 in all—and the most Academy Awards won—at four—**Morning Glory** (1933), **Guess Who's Coming to Dinner** (1967), **The Lion in Winter** (1968), and **On Golden Pond** (1982). The on-screen chemistry between Katherine Hepburn and Spencer Tracy was a hit with audiences, and over the years they starred together in a total of nine films. It was revealed in recent years that they had an off-screen love affair for many years as well. She was married just once, when she was young—a short-lived marriage to Ludlow Ogden Smith, a well-to-do Philadelphian. Hepburn has always maintained that her career consumed most of her energy, so she was not well-suited to marriage and motherhood. During the 1950s, she toured in Shakespearean plays and continued to do stage work through the early 1980s. In the past several years, she occasionally came out of retirement to make films for television. She also published an autobiography, *Me: Stories of My Life*. Until very recently, she lived in the brownstone home in New York City that she bought when she first became famous, but now resides at the family home in Old Saybrook, Connecticut. Hepburn is admired by many, as much for her spirit of self-determination as for her achievements.

HEPBURN, AUDREY

Audrey Hepburn was born Edda van Heemstra Hepburn-Ruston on May 4, 1929 in Brussels, Belgium; her mother was Dutch and her father, British. She was a student of ballet at both the Arnhem Conservatory of Music in Amsterdam and the Marie Rambert School in London. During the horrors of World War II, she lived in Arnhem, experiencing many difficulties—her dancing is what kept her life together. In 1949, she appeared in the chorus of a London stage production and studied acting. In 1951, she got several small movie roles in England and that same year was selected for the lead role in "Gigi," the Broadway show in New York that became a huge hit. In 1953, she made her first American movie, **Roman Holiday**, for which she won the Academy Award for Best Actress. Her movie roles made perfect use of her European flair and regal presence. In between films she did other work as well, starring on Broadway in 1957 in "Ondine," and appearing in the production of "Mayerling" for television. She retired from the movies between 1967 and 1976 to raise her two sons, Sean (from her first marriage to actor Mel Ferrer) and Luca (from her second marriage to Andrea Dotti). When she returned to work, she made movies for both the big screen and television. In recent years, she became involved in humanitarian causes, becoming Special Ambassador for UNICEF in 1988. She was very successful in utilizing her fame to bring attention to the plight of starving children around the world. Unfortunately, Audrey Hepburn died of cancer in 1993.

HESTON, CHARLTON

Born Charles Carter on October 4, 1923, in Evanston, Illinois, Charlton Heston studied speech and drama at Northwestern University. In 1943, he appeared in the amateur student film "Peer Gynt." He also performed on radio in Chicago. After a three-year stint in the Air Force, he returned to civilian life and worked in stock theater. He made his 1947 debut on Broadway in Katherine Cornell's "Anthony and Cleopatra." Heston played lead roles in television specials, which eventually led him to a Hollywood film career. His imposing presence made him well-suited for movie epics—playing Moses, Michelangelo, etc. In 1959, he won a Best Actor Academy Award for **Ben Hur**. A six-term president of the Screen Actors Guild, he was a conservative political activist, and also served as Chairman of the American Film Institute. In 1977, Heston received the Jean Hersholt Humanitarian Award at the Academy Award ceremonies. Heston has been married to wife, Lydia, whom he met at Northwestern University, since 1944. They have two children—daughter Holly, and son Fraser, who is a film director. He recently wrote his autobiography, **In the Arena** and another book by Heston, **To Be a Man: Letters to My Grandson** was published in 1997. This second book consists of advice for his grandson about honesty, friendship, sportsmanship, etc. Also in 1997, Charlton Heston has been honored by The Kennedy Center for the Performing Arts and bestowed the French title, Commander in the Order of Arts and Letters.

HOLDEN, WILLIAM

William Holden was born William Franklin Beedle, Jr. in O'Fallon, Illinois on April 17, 1918. His father was a chemist and his mother was a former schoolteacher. He grew up in South Pasadena, California, studied chemistry at a junior college, and tried his hand at acting at the Pasadena Playhouse. At age 20, he got a contract with Paramount (this contract was later shared with Columbia), made his first screen appearance in the Betty Grable movie **Million Dollar Legs**, and went on to the lead role in the 1939 film **Golden Boy**. Over the years, Holden portrayed various types of characters, but the vast majority of his screen roles were dramatic ones. He served in the Army Air Corps as a lieutenant during World War II, but three movies released during his absence kept his career alive. During the 1950s, he also appeared on television as both an actor and a narrator for documentaries. He won the Academy Award for Best Actor in 1953 for **Stalag 17**, and was nominated two other times: for **Sunset Boulevard** (1950), and **Network** (1976). Holden married actress Brenda Marshall in 1941, became stepfather to her daughter Virginia, and then father to his and Brenda's two sons, Peter Wesley and Scott. Eventually, though, Holden and Marshall divorced. William Holden died in 1981, while still working at starring roles in movies and television.

HOLLIDAY, JUDY

Born Judith Tuvim in New York City on June 21, 1922, she graduated from Julia Richman High School in 1938. That same year, she became a switchboard operator for Orson Welles' Mercury Theater. Along with Betty Comden, Adolph Green, John Frank and Alvin Hammer, she formed a sketch group known as "The Revuers." They performed in New York clubs and on radio from 1938 to 1944. In 1944, she got a movie contract with 20th Century Fox. The following year, she made her stage debut in "Kiss Them for Me." On Broadway in 1946, Judy replaced actress Jean Arthur in "Born Yesterday" as the dumb, but crafty Billie Dawn. In 1949, she made a big impression in the film **Adam's Rib** in which she played a scatter-brained suspect in an attempted murder. Given a contract by Columbia Pictures in 1950, Judy achieved her greatest success playing Billie Dawn again, in the movie version of **Born Yesterday** and won a Best Actress Academy Award. Her gift of comedic timing, exaggerated New York accent, and enthusiasm were her trademarks and endeared her to audiences. Cast in the Betty Comden-Adolph Green play "Bells Are Ringing" on Broadway in 1956, she repeated that role in the 1960 film version. Married to David Oppenheim in 1948, she divorced him in 1957; they had a son, Jonathan. At only 42 years of age, Judy Holliday died of cancer in 1965.

HOPE, BOB

He was born Leslie Townes Hope in Eltham, England, in May of 1903, the son of an English stonemason, and moved with his family to Cleveland, Ohio at the age of 4. He became a U.S. citizen in 1920. After high school, Hope set his sights on show business, learning to dance. He got into vaudeville, touring with Fatty Arbuckle's show, doing comedy, singing, and dancing. Hope continued in vaudeville with two different partners, Lloyd Durbin and George Byrne, until he became a solo stand-up comedian and then a headliner. He also got work on Broadway, starring in "Roberta" in 1933 and, that same year, made his radio debut as a guest on Rudy Vallee's show. In 1938, Bob Hope made his first film, **The Big Broadcast of 1938**, where he sang what was to become his theme song: "Thanks for the Memory." From 1939 until 1948, he had his own radio program, "The Bob Hope Pepsodent Show." He simultaneously built a legendary movie career, starring in a total of 55 movies, spending each year from 1941 to 1953 in the Box Office Top Ten (holding the number one spot in 1949). The series of **The Road to...** movies Hope made with Bing Crosby and Dorothy Lamour are among his best known. He later took his talent to television, hosting "Chesterfield Sound Off Time" (1951-1952), "The Colgate Comedy Hour" (1952-1953), and "Bob Hope Presents the Chrysler Theatre" (1963-1967). His TV variety specials were popular for years, right through to the '90s. The effort that has made him the most famous though, has been his entertaining of American troops around the world through four wars: World War II, the Korean War, the Vietnam War, and most recently, the Gulf War. He has been bestowed with over 800 awards, among them, three Honorary Academy Awards (1940, 1952, and 1965), as well as the Congressional Gold Medal. He has been married since 1934 to singer Dolores Reade, and they raised four adopted children: Linda, Anthony, Nora and Kelly. Three books that Bob has written are: *Dear Prez, I Wanna Tell Ya; Bob Hope's Presidential Joke Book*, *Don't Shoot, It's Only Me*, and *I Was There*.

HORTON, EDWARD EVERETT

Born in Brooklyn, New York on March 18, 1886, Edward Everett Horton's father was a New York Times proofreader. Horton played in more than 120 films during the '30s and '40s. His characters were noted for their nervous and high-strung personalities. In the early 1900s, he began working on Broadway and in other stage productions in Philadelphia and Los Angeles. He made his first movie in 1922. In 1932, he starred on stage in "Springtime for Henry," in a role that he made famous and repeated many times in the years to come. His best known performances are in Ginger Rogers-Fred Astaire musicals such as **Top Hat** (1935) and **Shall We Dance** (1937), as well as **Here Comes Mr. Jordan** (1941). In 1950, he went to TV in the series "Holiday Hotel." In 1960, he toured in the stage production of "Once Upon a Mattress." During the '60s, besides making an occasional movie, he performed narrations for the TV cartoon shows "Rocky and His Friends" and "The Bullwinkle Show," as well as making guest appearances on the comedy series "F Troop," (as Indian medicine man Roaring Chicken). Horton made occasional television appearances in the '60s. He worked right up until 1970, within a few weeks of his death at age 84.

HUDSON, ROCK

Rock Hudson was born Roy Harold Scherer, Jr. in Winnetka, Illinois on November 17, 1925. His father was an auto mechanic and his mother was a telephone operator; they divorced when he was eight years old. After high school graduation, he became a mail carrier; during World War II, he served in the Navy as an airplane mechanic. When he returned to civilian life, before entering films, he spent some time as a truck driver. Hudson made his film debut in **Fighter Squadron** (1948). Without prior acting experience, he learned his craft on the job. He mainly appeared in adventure films, but after starring in **Magnificent Obsession** (1954), Hudson became established as a romantic leading man. In 1956, he was nominated for a Best Actor Academy Award for his role in **Giant**. Rock also enjoyed great popularity co-starring in light comedies with Doris Day. His 1955 marriage to Nancy Gates lasted three years. In 1958, *LOOK* magazine gave him the Star of the Year Award and he was designated Hollywood's top box-office draw. He later did TV, starring in the series "McMillan and Wife" (1971-1977) and from 1984-85 making guest appearances in the series "Dynasty." Rock died in October 1985 of complications from AIDS. He was one of the first major celebrities to publicly announce that he had AIDS, which led to a national campaign to fight the disease. In 1986, his autobiography was published: **Rock Hudson, His Own Story**.

JOHNSON, VAN

Charles Van Dell Johnson was born in Newport, Rhode Island on August 28, 1916. His father was a plumbing contractor; his mother deserted the family when Van was only 3 years old. In his hometown, Van acted with the drama society at the Trinity Church, and after high school worked as an office clerk. He then left for New York at the age of 19. He eventually sang and danced his way to the Broadway stage, where he understudied such greats as Eddie Bracken, Desi Arnaz, and Gene Kelly. His start in movies was a bumpy one—he was screen tested and rejected by RKO and Columbia, then was signed by Warner Brothers but released from the contract. Subsequently, friend Lucille Ball convinced MGM to give him a chance, and he finally got a lasting contract with that studio in 1942. He started at MGM in small parts, but when he got his first major film role (co-starring with Lionel Barrymore) Johnson became an overnight hit with movie fans. His boyish good looks, complete with red hair and freckles, made him a favorite of "bobby-soxers." In his first three years as a star, the studio worked him hard; he made 13 movies, at times working on three simultaneously. In 1943, he was in a serious car accident; Spencer Tracy and Irene Dunne, scheduled to star with him in **A Guy Named Joe** helped save his career during his months-long recuperation by refusing to film without him. The accident left him with a metal plate in his forehead, which made him ineligible for military service in World War II. That fact partly contributed to his popularity during the war years, as many other male box office stars were off to war and unable to make films. He spent 12 years at MGM, and was listed among the Box Office Top Ten in 1945 and 1946. By the mid-1950s his popularity as a leading man had dropped off as quickly as it had risen, but he continued to work in supporting roles. He was married to Evie Abbott Wynn (ex-wife of actor Keenan Wynn); they had a daughter, Schuyler, and eventually divorced. He moved to New York in the 1960s and has continued to appear in movies, on TV (including the miniseries "Rich Man, Poor Man" in 1976), on Broadway, and in dinner theater.

JONES, SHIRLEY

Shirley Jones was born in Smithton, Pennsylvania on March 31, 1934. She began singing as a child, and started studying voice formally at the age of 12. As a young lady, she was crowned Miss Pittsburgh. After high school, she got work in the chorus of the Broadway musical "South Pacific," and from there went straight to

Hollywood. Her fine singing voice and wholesome brand of beauty made Shirley a perfect choice for movie musicals, such as **Oklahoma** (1955), **Carousel** (1956), and **The Music Man** (1962). On television, she got a chance to try drama on the program "Playhouse 90." In a departure from her usual screen characters, she got a dramatic role in the 1960 film **Elmer Gantry** for which she received a Best Supporting Actress Academy Award. Jones' movie career was cut short by the disappearance of movie musicals in the '60s, but she went on to success in television, stage and nightclubs. She is probably best known to the TV generation as Shirley Partridge, mother of the singing "Partridge Family" (the popular series that ran from 1970-74). Her co-star in that series was David Cassidy, who is also her stepson, as Shirley was married to singer Jack Cassidy. She and Jack had three sons, Shaun, Patrick and Ryan. Jones also starred in another, short-lived series entitled "Shirley Miller" (1979-80). After Jack Cassidy's death, Shirley married actor/comedian Marty Ingels. She has served as the National Chairman of the Leukemia Foundation. Recently, she hosted the critically acclaimed TV special for the A&E Channel, "Rodgers & Hammerstein: The Sound of Movies." Currently, Shirley Jones appears on stage, in both concerts and musical productions such as "The King and I."

KAYE, DANNY

Danny Kaye was born David Daniel Kaminski to immigrant parents in Brooklyn, New York, on January 18, 1913. A tailor's son, he left school at age 15 to work in an insurance office, and at 17 worked as a clowning busboy on the "Borscht Circuit" in the New York Catskills. He then toured the Orient with a musical group, learning to use pantomime and facial expressions to win laughs. When he returned to the Catskills, he met his future wife, Sylvia Fine. (She was a songwriter and pianist who later wrote many of his songs and much of his comedy material.) As he made his way up in vaudeville and nightclubs, Kaye continued to work at various jobs—insurance agent, soda jerk, etc. In 1939, he made his Broadway debut in "The Straw Hat Revue." In 1941, he appeared in the play "Lady in the Dark" where he stopped the show every night singing "Tchaikovsky"—which contained the names of 54 Russian composers, real and otherwise—in 38 seconds flat. Danny Kaye's uncanny ability to deliver tongue twisting dialogue became his trademark. In 1943, Samuel Goldwyn signed him for a movie contract. In 1944, he starred in **Up in Arms**, the first of a string of very successful films. Danny's comedic versatility helped him rise to great popularity in the late '40s—one of his best movies was **The Secret Life of Walter Mitty** in 1947. In 1948 and 1949, his appearances at the London Palladium broke entertainment records, and Danny was asked to appear at the Royal Palace. In the late '50s, he began to devote more of his time to traveling for UNICEF and entertaining children in developing countries. From 1963-1967, he starred in "The Danny Kaye Show" TV variety program, winning an Emmy and a Peabody Award. In 1970, he returned to Broadway in the musical, "Two by Two." Kaye received a special Academy Award "for his unique talents, his service to the Academy, the motion picture industry, and the American people." In 1981, he received the Jean Hersholt Humanitarian Award. Over the years, his talent as a musician allowed him to conduct the New York Philharmonic and other symphony orchestras in concert appearances. Danny Kaye died in 1987.

KEEL, HOWARD

Howard Keel was born Harold Clifford Leek in Gillespie, Illinois on April 13, 1917. He worked as an aviation mechanic and then, briefly, as a singing busboy. Keel later worked at Douglas Aircraft, studying singing at night and performing in shows put on by the company. In 1945, he made his stage debut in the West Coast production of "Carousel," and appeared in "Oklahoma" in London in 1948. That same year, he had a small role in a British film. In 1950, back in the United States, Keel made the movie **Annie Get Your Gun** and signed a contract with MGM studios. He went on to star in many movie musicals during the '50s, which showcased his fine baritone singing voice and handsome good looks. In the late '50s he appeared in nightclubs and concerts, and served as president of The Screen Actors Guild. In 1958, Keel starred on Broadway in a revival of "Carousel." In 1968, he and former movie co-star Kathryn Grayson performed together in a nightclub act. Howard Keel toured in "Man of La Mancha" in 1970, and joined the cast of the popular television series "Dallas" in 1981.

KELLY, GENE

Eugene Curran Kelly was born in Pittsburgh, Pennsylvania on August 23, 1912. His father was a salesman for Columbia Gramophone and his mother acted in stock theater. He began taking dancing lessons as a child, performed in a dance act with his brother Fred and played football in high school. He then pumped gas and ran his own dance classes to work his way through the University of Pittsburgh. For seven years after that, he continued to teach dancing. Hoping to become a dance director, Gene then went to New York and wound up getting roles on the stage. He became a Broadway star with the lead in "Pal Joey." That success brought a movie contract with David O. Selznick, but Selznick didn't use Kelly in any films and sold his contract to MGM. In 1942, he made his first movie, co-starring with Judy Garland in **For Me and My Gal**. Gene's athletic and casual dancing style, combined with his creative talent for choreography, produced some of the finest dance numbers in film history. One such number, in **Anchors Aweigh** (1945) where he hoofs with cartoon characters Tom and Jerry, took two months of filming. Kelly served in the Photographic Section of the Navy in World War II. With Stanley Donen, he directed his first movie, **On The Town** in 1950. Kelly received an Honorary Academy Award in 1951 "in appreciation of his versatility as an actor, singer, director and dancer, and specifically for his brilliant achievements in the art of choreography on film." In 1952 he created his best-known dancing performance, the title musical number of the film **Singin' In the Rain**. In 1957, he shattered his kneecap while skiing. His dancing days were over, but he went on to direct both movies (including **Hello, Dolly** in 1969) and Broadway musicals. On television, he starred in the 1962 series "Going My Way," which was based on the 1944 film. Kelly also made occasional television appearances through the mid-'80s (including the miniseries "North and South" in 1985). He received the Lifetime Achievement Award from the American Film Institute in 1985, and the Screen Actors Guild Achievement Award in 1988. He was married to and divorced from actress Betsy Blair (they had a daughter, Kerry). His second marriage, to his dance assistant Jeanne Coyne, lasted 13 years, until she died (they had two children, Timothy and Bridget). In 1990 he married writer Patricia Ward. He appeared in the 1980 film **Xanadu** and the 1994 film **That's Entertainment Part III**. A show business legend, Gene Kelly passed away in 1996 at the age of 83.

KERR, DEBORAH

Deborah J. Kerr-Trimmer was born in Helensburgh, Scotland on September 30, 1921. Deborah was a dance student at Hicks-Smale Drama School, which was managed by her aunt, in Bristol, England. After winning a scholarship and training at the Sadler's Wells ballet school, she made her stage debut in "Prometheus," produced in London by the corps de ballet. In 1941, she made her British film debut in **Major Barbara**. In 1945, she appeared in the play "Gaslight" touring France, Belgium and Holland, performing for the Allied forces. In 1946, she signed a movie contract with MGM and made her first American film, **Black Narcissus**. Based on her fine performance in that movie, she was given the lead female role in **The Hucksters** (1947). In most of her movie work, Deborah Kerr portrayed refined women of strong character. However, she broke out of her ladylike image in 1953 when she played an adulteress in Columbia's **From Here to Eternity**. In 1956, she performed another memorable and classy movie role opposite Yul Brynner, as Anna in **The King and I**. Kerr received six Academy Award nominations for Best Actress: **Edward My Son** (1949), **From Here to Eternity** (1953), **The King and I** (1956), **Heaven Knows, Mr. Allison** (1957), **Separate Tables** (1958), and **The Sundowners** (1960). She also won four New York Film Critics' Awards. In the 1970s, she turned her attention to the stages of Broadway in ("Tea and Sympathy," "Seascape") and London ("Candida"). She has two daughters, Melanie and Francesca from her 1945 marriage to Anthony Bartley. In 1959, she married writer Peter Viertel. They make their home in Switzerland.

LADD, ALAN

Alan Walbridge Ladd was born in Hot Springs, Arkansas on September 3, 1913. He grew up in poverty, as he was only 4 when his father, an accountant, died. Alan and his mother moved to California. He became a champion swimmer and diver at North Hollywood High School, where he also began to perform on stage. Later, he acted on radio programs such as "Lux Radio Theater." When he was 25, he was discovered by high-powered agent Sue Carol. He played minor movie roles for a number of years, but eventually got a contract with Paramount in 1941. In 1942, he became a star with the movie **This Gun For Hire**. That same year, he and Sue Carol were married—he had divorced his first wife Midge Harrold the year before (they had a son, Alan Jr., who grew up to become a movie studio executive). Sue continued to manage Ladd's career, and they had two children, Alana and David. At only 5'6" tall, Alan Ladd was an unlikely movie hero, but the strength and power with which he portrayed his characters made up for his compact physical stature. Generally playing tough men who had a bit of a dark side, Alan became one of Hollywood's most popular leading men. He spent 1947, 1953 and 1954 in the Box Office Top Ten. He and actress Veronica Lake had a very effective on-screen chemistry, and she frequently appeared as his co-star. In 1943, like many other stars, he went into the Army, but received a medical discharge in 1944. He founded his own radio production company in 1948, and later founded Jaguar Productions in 1954. He signed a movie contract with Warner Brothers in 1954 that lasted until 1959, after which he started producing programs for television. He also made an occasional movie during the early '60s. Alan Ladd died in January of 1964.

LAMOUR, DOROTHY
Born Mary Leta Dorothy Slaton on December 10, 1914, in New Orleans, Louisiana, Dorothy was crowned Miss New Orleans of 1931. After working in Chicago as an elevator operator, she became a singer. In 1935, she went to Hollywood where she landed a contract with Paramount. Her first movie was **The Jungle Princess** (1936) and she became known as the "Sarong Girl" because she usually played beautiful and exotic women in tropical locales. From there Dorothy graduated to her best-known roles in the **The Road to...** series of movies with Bing Crosby and Bob Hope. Dorothy was a pinup queen during World War II and made many USO tours, raising $300 million in war bonds. She worked with various bands for Herbie Kaye, Rudy Vallee and Eddie Duchin. On radio, she appeared in the show "The Dreamer of Songs," as well as "The Chase and Sanborn Show" and "The Sealtest Variety Theatre." In 1950, she worked on TV in shows such as "The Colgate Comedy Hour," "Damon Runyon Theatre," and "The Arthur Murray Party." She debuted on stage in 1951 in "Roger the Sixth" and went to Broadway in 1958 in "Oh! Captain." In 1961, she traveled with her own nightclub show. Dorothy also toured in stage productions of "DuBarry Was a Lady" (1963) and "Hello, Dolly!" (1967). During the '60s and '70s, she toured on the Dinner Theater circuit. Her first marriage in 1935 to bandleader Herbie Kaye ended in divorce (1939). In 1943, she married William Ross Howard III (who died in 1977). In addition to her stepson with Ross, she had two more sons. They lived in Baltimore and she commuted to Hollywood. Her autobiography, *My Side of the Road*, was published in 1980. Dorothy Lamour passed away in 1996.

LANCHESTER, ELSA
Elizabeth Sullivan Lanchester was born on October 28, 1902 in Lewisham, London. She danced and acted as a child, studied with Isadora Duncan, and made her stage

debut in 1920. From then on, Elsa acted on the stage and in films, both in England and the United States. In 1939, she became a permanent resident of the U.S. and in 1950 was sworn in as a U.S. citizen. She was a prominent character actress who played a wide variety of roles, though she was best known for the eccentric and humorous characters. Lanchester was nominated for the Best Supporting Actress Academy Awards for her performances in **Come To the Stable** (1949) and **Witness for the Prosecution** (1958). From 1951-61, she toured in a one-woman show entitled, "Elsa Lanchester—Herself." She also worked on television, in "The John Forsythe Show" from 1965-66, and in "Nanny and the Professor" in 1971. Elsa Lanchester was married to actor Charles Laughton, and published two autobiographies, *Charles Laughton and I* (1968) and *Elsa Lanchester Herself* (1983); she died in 1986.

LANSBURY, ANGELA

Angela Lansbury was born in London on October 16, 1925. Her mother was British stage and screen actress, Moyna MacGill, and Angela began studying drama at 12. She studied at Webber-Douglas School of Singing and Dramatic Art in London and Feagin School of Drama and Radio in New York. Coming to the U.S. from London after the German blitz, she worked as a salesgirl in New York while continuing her studies. In 1943 she got a 7-year MGM contract. Her first role was that of the housemaid in the 1944 movie **Gaslight** when she was only 18. Angela had supporting roles in many popular movies—**National Velvet** (1944), **The Harvey Girls** (1946), and **The Three Musketeers** (1948). Known as the "youngest character actress," she generally played parts older than her years—and was often cast as the "heavy." She was nominated for the Best Supporting Actress Academy Award three times: **Gaslight** (1944), **The Picture of Dorian Gray** (1945), and **The Manchurian Candidate** (1962). Over the years, Angela Lansbury has also enjoyed great popularity on the Broadway stage winning four Tony Awards: "Mame" (1966), "Dear World" (1969), "Gypsy" (1975) and "Sweeney Todd" (1979). She has also done work on television doing made-for-TV movies ("The Shell Seekers," "The Love She Sought") and appearing in the very popular, long-running series, "Murder, She Wrote," from 1984-96. In 1988, she did an exercise video for older adults called "Positive Moves." She has also gracefully hosted the Tony and Emmy Awards. In 1996 she was honored by the American Foundation for AIDS Research for her staunch support, performing without compensation at fund-raising benefits and donating money, as well. That same year, Angela appeared in a holiday TV special, a musical called "Mrs. Santa Claus" and won the 1996 Television Critics' Association Career Achievement Award. Still married to Peter Shaw (her manager) whom she wed in 1949, Angela has three children.

LAUGHTON, CHARLES

Charles Laughton was born in Scarborough, England on July 1, 1899. His father was a hotel proprietor, and Charles eventually went to London to learn the hotel business by working as a reception clerk. He served in the military during World War II, and upon his return, took up acting. He later studied at the Royal Academy of Dramatic Art, where he won a gold medal. He made his London stage debut in 1926 and established himself as a professional actor. In 1929, he made his first feature film, and married actress Elsa Lanchester. In 1931, he got a movie contract with Paramount, marking the beginning of his American movie career, which lasted until the early '60s. Laughton won the Academy Award for Best Actor in 1933 for **The Private Life of Henry VIII**. A heavyset man, he played a wide variety of roles, ranging from the disfigured Quasimoto in **The Hunchback of Notre Dame** (1939) to the distinguished barrister in **Witness for the Prosecution** (1957). Over the years, Charles Laughton also performed on radio and television. He died in 1962.

LAWFORD, PETER
Born on September 7, 1923 to a privileged family in London (his father was a knighted World War I general), Peter became a romantic leading man due to his natural good looks. In 1931, he made his British film debut, and got his big break in the 1940s Hollywood movies when they began producing "British" films such as **Mrs. Miniver** (1942). His role in **The White Cliffs of Dover** (1944) made him an American movie star. At the height of his popularity, he appeared in **Meet Me in St. Louis** (1944) and **Little Women** (1949). In the 1950s, Lawford ventured into television in the series "Dear Phoebe" (1954-55). His next series was "The Thin Man" (1957-59). He also was a regular on "The Doris Day Show." From the '60s on, he played character roles in films and also became a television executive producer for the shows: "Johnny Cool" (1963), "Billie" (1965), "Salt and Pepper" (1968) and "One More Time" (1970). Lawford's first marriage was to Patricia Kennedy (daughter of Mr. and Mrs. Joseph P. Kennedy) and they had four children: Christopher, Sydney, Victoria and Robin. From 1971-73, he was married to Mary Rowan (daughter of comedian Dan Rowan). In 1976 he married Deborah Gould, and at the time of his death in 1984, he was married to Patricia Seaton.

LEIGH, JANET
Janet Leigh was born Jeanette Helen Morrison on July 6, 1927. She studied music at the College of the Pacific. Janet was discovered by actress Norma Shearer, whose agent got her an MGM contract. She made her movie debut in 1947 in **The Romance of Rosy Ridge**. In her early film career, she was cast as sweet and nice young ladies, but over time, progressed to stronger and edgier roles. Janet Leigh made three films while on loan to RKO, and worked at Columbia and Universal in the '50s. She also worked on television, beginning in 1957, in "The Schlitz Playhouse of Stars." She was nominated for Best Supporting Actress at the Academy Awards in 1960 for her performance in the Alfred Hitchcock thriller **Psycho**. In 1962, she traveled through South America, promoting the Peace Corps. In 1975, Leigh appeared on Broadway in "Murder Among Friends." She has two

daughters, Kelly and Jamie Lee, from her third marriage to actor Tony Curtis. Daughter Jamie Lee Curtis is now a famous actress as well, and Janet appeared with her in the 1980 film **The Fog**. Janet Leigh published her autobiography *There Really Was a Hollywood* in 1984, and also published a novel, entitled *House of Destiny* in 1995. She currently makes occasional public appearances, and is enjoying being a grandmother.

LEMMON, JACK

John Uhler Lemmon III was born in Boston, Massachusetts on February 8, 1925 and was educated in Rivers Country Day School and Phillips Academy. He went on to Harvard, where he participated in the Naval Reserve and was a member of the Harvard Dramatic Club. After graduation from college, he played piano in New York City's Old Nick Saloon. With his first wife, Cynthia (they had a son, actor Christopher Lemmon) Jack acted in radio soap operas. He was also a producer and actor in several television series. His Broadway debut in "Room Service" led to a Columbia Pictures contract. In his first two films, he co-starred with Judy Holliday. Next came his Academy Award winning performance (Best Supporting Actor) as Ensign Pulver in **Mister Roberts** (1955). He married for the second time in 1962 to actress Felicia Farr and they have two children. His incredible versatility ranges from broad comedy to intense drama, and he has achieved a total of eight Academy Award nominations. In 1971, he made his directorial debut with the film **Kotch**, starring Walter Matthau. Odd Couple Lemmon and Matthau have made several movies together and continue to make more. In 1973, Jack Lemmon won the Academy Award for Best Actor in **Save The Tiger**. In 1985, Jack Lemmon appeared on Broadway in a revival of Eugene O'Neil's "Long Day's Journey Into Night." His many international awards include: Best Foreign Actor, British Academy - **Some Like It Hot**, (1959); Best Foreign Actor, British Academy - **The Apartment** (1960); Best Actor, British Academy and Best Actor, Cannes Festival - **The China Syndrome** (1979); Best Actor, Berlin Festival - **Tribute** (1981); Best Actor, Cannes Festival - **Missing** (1982). Jack Lemmon also received the American Film Institute Lifetime Achievement Award in 1988. One of the 1996 honorees at The Kennedy Center Honors, that same year he received the Golden Bear Award at the Berlin Film Festival for his life's work. He co-starred with James Garner in **My Fellow Americans** (1996). In recent years he and Walter Matthau teamed up for the movies **Grumpy Old Men** and **Grumpier Old Men** and in 1997 they worked together again in the film **Out to Sea**.

LOY, MYRNA

Born Myrna Williams in August of 1905 in Raidersburg, Montana, Myrna Loy danced as a young girl and then taught dancing while in high school in Los Angeles. A photographer discovered her while she was working as a chorus girl at Graumann's Chinese Theater. She made her first appearance in a bit part, and in 1926, Warner Brothers gave her a contract. At that time, she was most often cast as mysterious

Asian women. Loy worked to establish herself as a leading lady and got a contract with MGM in 1932. In 1934, she really hit it big when she co-starred with William Powell in **The Thin Man**. Loy and Powell went on to make a series of these movies, but she got roles in many other comedies as well, frequently cast as the perfect wife. She was listed in the Box Office Top Ten in 1937 and 1938. Her status as a top leading lady continued over many years, and evolved into more motherly roles in the '40s as she matured. She spent time working for the Red Cross in 1942. In 1945, Loy attended United Nations sessions in San Francisco and in 1985 began her service as U.S. representative to UNESCO, which lasted for more than 3 years. When she reached her late 50s, she fashioned a new career for herself on the American stage. In 1985, Myrna Loy was honored with a tribute at Carnegie Hall by the Motion Picture Academy; she also received an Honorary Academy Award in 1990. She was married four times. Her autobiography, **Myrna Loy; Being and Becoming** was published in 1987. One of the most famous American actresses, Myrna Loy passed away in 1993.

MacMURRAY, FRED

Frederick Martin MacMurray was born in Kankakee, Illinois on August 30, 1907. His mother was later divorced from his musician father. As a teenager, he did factory work and earned a football scholarship to college. He sang and played the saxophone with various bands and orchestras, and eventually earned the lead role in the Broadway show "Roberta." Based on that performance, Fred got a contract with Paramount Pictures in 1934, and stayed on for 11 years. In 1945, he signed up with 20th Century Fox. MacMurray's down-to-earth, all-American demeanor was very popular with movie fans, and he performed well in both comedic and dramatic roles. He usually played nice guys, but he surprised many with his expertly evil portrayal in **Double Indemnity** (1944). In the 1950s, he made several Westerns, and in the 1960s moved on to Disney films. MacMurray starred for many years (1960-1972) on television as one of America's favorite fathers on the weekly series "My Three Sons." He was married twice: first to "Roberta" chorus girl Lillian Lamont, who died in 1953, then to actress/singer June Haver in 1954. He had four children, Susan and Robert with Lillian Lamont, then adopted twins Laurie and Kathryn with June Haver. Having enjoyed one of the most enduring acting careers in America, Fred MacMurray passed away on November 5, 1991.

MacRAE, GORDON

Gordon MacRae was born in East Orange, New Jersey on March 12, 1921. The son of musical parents, he sang and played musical instruments during his school years. He graduated from Deerfield Academy, and then headed for New York City to start his show business career. At the 1939-40 World's Fair, he sang in an amateur contest and won. He then worked as a band singer for two years. MacRae served in the military during World War II, as an Air force navigator. After that, he sang on radio shows and landed a role on Broadway in "Three to Make Ready." His performance in that show led to a career as a leading man in movie musicals. MacRae had clean-cut good looks and a very impressive voice, making him the perfect choice for such films as **On Moonlight Bay** (1951), **By the Light of the Silvery Moon** (1953), **Oklahoma!** (1955), and **Carousel** (1956). Also in 1956, MacRae had his own television show. With the fading of movie musicals, he went back to the stage in touring companies, stock theater, and night clubs. He was married to actress Sheila MacRae from 1941 to 1967; they had four children, two sons and two daughters. Their daughters Meredith and Heather later became actresses as well. In 1983, he became Honorary Chairman of the National Council on Alcoholism, after revealing his own battle with alcoholism. Gordon MacRae died of cancer in 1986, at the age of 64.

MAIN, MARJORIE

Marjorie Main was born Mary Tomlinson on February 24, 1890, in Acton, Indiana. She was educated at Franklin College and the Hamilton School of Expression in Kentucky. She went on to study drama in both Chicago and New York, taught drama at Bourbon College and played the Chautauqua circuit doing Shakespeare. To avoid embarrassing her father, a minister who disapproved of her show business career, she changed her name to Marjorie Main. In 1916, she made her stage debut and was active on Broadway throughout the '20s. Her first movie roles were not great ones, but she eventually found her niche when she recreated her role in Broadway's **The Women** in the 1939 film version. Because of her brusque, crusty style, Main was cast in many comedies—teaming six times with the equally gruff Wallace Beery. She went on to work with Percy Kilbride (another excellent character actor) in 1947's **The Egg and I**, which led to their very popular **Ma and Pa Kettle** movie series. She was married to psychologist/author Dr. Stanley LeFevre Krebs from 1921 until his death in 1935. Marjorie Main died in April 1975.

MARTIN & LEWIS

Dean Martin was born Dino Paul Crocetti in June of 1917 in Steubenville, Ohio. He was an amateur boxer and worked in a steel mill before trying show business. Dean became a nightclub singer, at first using the name Dino Martino. He was married three times and had eight children (son Dino was killed in a military plane crash). After the breakup of his partnership with Jerry Lewis, he resumed his singing career and started a solo movie career. He hosted his own variety series on television, "The Dean Martin Show," which ran from 1965 to 1974. Dean recorded more than 100 musical albums; some of his biggest hits were "That's Amore," "Memories Are Made of This," "Volare," and "Everybody Loves Somebody Sometime," which became his theme song. His relaxed and mellow singing style was his trademark. Into the '90s, he put on very successful stage shows, sometimes appearing with

Sammy Davis, Jr. and Liza Minnelli. He turned his show business earnings into a sizable fortune in real estate. Dean Martin died in 1995 at the age of 78.

Jerry Lewis was born Joseph Levitch on March 16, 1926 in Newark, New Jersey, the son of traveling entertainers. During the school year, he stayed with relatives, but during the summer went with his parents to the Catskills, where they worked on the "Borscht Circuit," and he occasionally joined them on stage. As a teenager, Lewis developed his own comedy act. In 1944, he married Patty Palmer, who was a singer with Jimmy Dorsey's band; they had six sons. After the split of the Martin-Lewis team, Jerry signed a solo movie contract with Paramount in 1959. He made a number of comedy films (acting, producing, and directing) during the '60s. These films were big hits in France, where his celebrity became larger than it had been in the United States. Lewis stopped making movies for a while during the '70s, but returned to the screen in 1982 in **The King of Comedy**. That same year, he published his autobiography, *Jerry Lewis in Person*. In 1983, he married Sandra Pitnick; they have an adopted daughter. In France in 1984, Lewis received two awards: The Commander of the Order of Arts and Sciences, and Commander of the Legion of Honour. For years, Jerry Lewis has devoted most of his time to The Muscular Dystrophy Association. Its annual Labor Day Telethon, hosted by Lewis, has become an American tradition.

In 1946, Dean Martin and Jerry Lewis teamed up on stage at the 500 Club in Atlantic City. They were a big hit and took their act to nightclubs and theaters across the country, and to radio as well. Lewis played zany funny man to Martin's sophisticated straight man. In 1948, the duo got a movie contract with Paramount studios and made their first screen appearance in 1949's **My Friend Irma**. They went on to make 16 films together and hosted "The Colgate Comedy Hour" on television from 1950-55. Their partnership broke up in 1956.

McCREA, JOEL

Born in South Pasadena, California on November 5, 1905, Joel McCrea was the son of a utility executive. One of his grandfathers was a Pacific Southwest stagecoach driver who had fought Apache Indians, and the other, a gold prospector. At a very young age, he raised and cared for his own horses. When he was nine years old, the family moved to Hollywood and Joel became drawn to the film industry, where he held horses for his film heroes, William S. Hart and Tom Mix. After graduating from Pomona College, McCrea performed at the Pasadena Community Playhouse. He began his movie career in 1922, performing as a silent movie extra and stuntman. In 1929, he began to land featured roles and then lead roles. His popularity as a leading man during the '30s and '40s spanned dramas, urbane comedies, and adventure stories. The high point of his career was working with directors Hitchcock, Sturges, Stevens and Wellman during the 1940s. From about 1946 on, he starred most often in Westerns. All told, he made about 90 films in his career. McCrea's television credits included "Four Star Playhouse" and the series "Wichita Town." He was married to actress Frances Dee; they had a son, Jody. Because of his wise investments in livestock and real estate, Joel became one of Southern California's wealthiest ranchers. He passed away in 1990, but his ranch in Thousand Oaks, California has been nominated for inclusion in The National Register of Historic Places, and his family has donated much of the land for public parkland.

McDANIEL, HATTIE
Hattie McDaniel was born on June 10, 1895, in Wichita, Kansas, to a Baptist preacher father and spiritual singer mother. Although she won a drama medal at 15, Hattie began her career as a band singer. In 1932, she got a break in the movie business and during the 1930s and 1940s, Hattie made many films (38 of them) before her Award-winning role in 1939's **Gone With The Wind**. Throughout her acting career she was limited to roles as domestics because of the racism that prevailed at that time. However, she took her roles as far as she could, starting as the quiet, loyal servant and growing to become a sassy, outspoken helpmate. Her characters became more socially equal. For example, her character in **Gone With the Wind** was the glue that held the family together. Hattie McDaniel has an important place in history. She was the first African-American to sing on U.S. radio, appearing on both "Amos 'n Andy" and "The Eddie Cantor Show." For her part in **Gone With the Wind**, she was the first black player to: (1) be nominated for an Academy Award, (2) win the Award for Best Supporting Actress, and (3) be invited to take part in an Academy Awards dinner. In 1947, she began starring in her own radio series called "Beulah" which moved to television in 1951. Hattie McDaniel, an American trailblazer, died in 1952.

McDOWALL, RODDY
Born in London on September 17, 1928, Roderick Andrew McDowall became a British child actor of the 1930s. During the 1940 London Blitz, Roddy and his family were evacuated to the United States. He became a very popular child star, appearing in **How Green Was My Valley** in 1941 and **Lassie Come Home** in 1942. Having become typecast because of his extremely youthful looks, Roddy left Hollywood in 1952 for New York and took to the stage, acting in 22 plays. He also went into television winning a supporting Emmy for "Not Without Honor." In 1955, he performed at the Shakespearean Festival in Stratford, Connecticut, in the plays "Julius Caesar" and "The Tempest." In 1960, he returned to Hollywood to play character roles in movies. In 1967, he starred in **Planet of the Apes**, and its popularity led to sequels. In all, Roddy made over 100 movies. The owner of an excellent collection of old motion pictures and memorabilia, he is also a highly regarded photographer. He published a book of photographs of some of his friends (among them Mary Martin and Judy Garland) titled, **Double Exposure**. Roddy has also served as a Screen Actors Guild representative to the National Film Preservation Board. In 1996, he returned to the stage after a 12-year absence to star in a production of "Dial 'M' for Murder."

McGUIRE, DOROTHY

Dorothy Hackett McGuire was born in Omaha, Nebraska on June 14, 1918. At the age of 13, Dorothy McGuire worked on stage at the Omaha Community Playhouse (co-starring with Henry Fonda). She was educated at Ladywood Convent in Indianapolis and Pine Manor Junior College in Wellesley, Massachusetts. She later went to New York and landed a lead role in "Big Sister," a radio soap opera, as well as parts in several plays. Dorothy became understudy to Martha Scott, the star of "Our Town," and in 1938 got the chance to handle the role herself. Her refreshing, clean-cut personality was the key to her success—she usually played "appealing" and kind characters in dramas. She won out over 208 candidates for the lead in Broadway's "Claudia" (1941), and became a big hit when she recreated that role in the 1943 film version. She went on to appear in many films such as **A Tree Grows in Brooklyn** (1945) and **The Enchanted Cottage** (1945). In 1947, Dorothy was nominated for Best Actress at the Academy Awards her performance in the film **Gentlemen's Agreement**. As she got older, she moved to supporting character roles. Married to John Swope (*LIFE* magazine photographer and theatrical producer) from 1943 until he passed away in 1979, they had two children: Mary and Mark. In 1976, she went back to Broadway in "The Night of the Iguana." Through the '80s, she performed in many television dramas such as "Rich Man, Poor Man" and "The Runaways."

MILLAND, RAY

Ray Milland was born in Wales on January 3, 1907 (some sources indicate 1905). He attended King's College in Cardiff and served as a Royal Household Cavalry guardsman in London. In 1929, he entered British films, but left for Hollywood in 1930, where he started with small parts and then graduated to leading man roles in the mid-'30s. His movie roles were varied—he did comedy, suspense and military drama. Milland's Academy Award winning role as an alcoholic in **Lost Weekend** (1945) left him in a severe depression from which he nearly did not recover. He also won the New York Film Critics and Cannes Festival Awards for this role. In the 1950s, Ray Milland began to direct some of the movies in which he acted. From 1953-55, he starred in the comedy television series, "The Ray Milland Show," and from 1959-60 starred in the television drama "Markham." At age 60, he made his Broadway debut in the play "Hostile Witness" and later played the role in the movie as well. Married to wife Muriel since 1932, they had two children—son Daniel and daughter Victoria. Ray Milland died in 1986.

MILLER, ANN

Born Johnnie Lucille Collier on April 12, 1919 in Houston, Texas, Ann Miller was a professional dancer as a child. When her parents divorced, Ann's mother took her to Hollywood, where she worked as an extra. She made her screen debut as a dancer in 1936, and in 1937 she won an RKO contract that lasted until 1940. She also went to Broadway appearing in the 1939 show "George White's Scandals." From 1941-46, Ann was under contract to Columbia playing leads in "B" movies.

Due to the success of her performance in the film **Easter Parade** (1948), she got a contract with MGM Studios which lasted until 1956. At MGM, she finally got good roles in major musicals and became one of the top stars of movie dancing. Among her best roles were those in **On the Town** (1949) and **Kiss Me Kate** (1953). In the mid-1950s her film career ended so she made the transition to nightclub acts, as well as TV and stage productions. In the 1960s, she went on tour in stage musicals such as "Can Can." Returning to Broadway, she replaced Angela Lansbury in "Mame" from 1969-70. In St. Louis in 1972, she did "Anything Goes" and then went on tour with that show, as well. Later, Ann played opposite Mickey Rooney on the stage in "Sugar Babies" which started in Los Angeles, ran on Broadway (1979-1982), and then went on tour across the U.S. (1982-1985). She was married three times: to Consolidated Steel heir Reese L. Milner (1946-47); and Texas oil magnates Bill Moss (1958-61) and Arthur Cameron (1961-62). She also published her autobiography, *Miller's High Life* (1972). In 1997, she appeared in a salute to MGM musicals at New York's Carnegie Hall.

MIRANDA, CARMEN

Maria do Carmo Miranda da Cunha was born near Lisbon, Portugal on February 9, 1909. The family moved to Rio de Janeiro, Brazil, where she served an apprentice-ship from age 14 to 19 to a French dressmaker. This experience enabled her to eventually help design her own costumes in later years. During her 20s, Carmen sang professionally, in clubs and on records. Between 1934 and 1938 she made Brazilian films. New York producer Lee Shubert discovered her when she was appearing at Rio's Casino and he cast her in Broadway's "Streets of Paris" in 1939. From there Shubert took Carmen and her extended family to Hollywood, where 20th Century Fox billed her as "The Brazilian Bombshell." A very petite person, she was only 5 feet tall, so she used 6" platform shoes and sky-scraper, fruit-laden hats (which were coupled with outlandish costumes) to add to her height. These, combined with her fractured English, happy-go-lucky personality and South American musical numbers appealed to the American World War II audiences who were looking for light-hearted entertainment. In 1947, Carmen married producer David Sebastian. She made occasional TV appearances. She died very suddenly of a heart attack in August 1959. In Rio de Janeiro, the Carmen Miranda Museum draws interest from many tourists; it houses many of her movie costumes and memorabilia.

MITCHUM, ROBERT

Born in Bridgeport, Connecticut on August 6, 1917, Robert Mitchum had a rough childhood. His father, who worked for the railroad, was killed in a trainyard acci-dent, and the family was plunged into poverty. Robert (only 2 years old)—along with his brother and sister—spent the following ten years living in the homes of relatives. A problem student in school, he hit the road when he was 14 and be-came a drifter, sailing to Europe as a freighter ship workman and wandering across the United States, holding various jobs. In the late 1930s, he joined the Long Beach Civic Theatre. In the early 1940s, he worked for Lockheed aircraft. In 1942, through an agent, he started to get some villain roles in a string of **Hopalong Cassidy** movies, as well as small parts in other feature films. These led to a 1944 contract with RKO which was later shared with David O. Selznick and eventually purchased by Howard Hughes. In 1945, he was nominated for an Academy Award as Best Supporting Actor for **The Story of G.I. Joe**. He was drafted by the Army for World War II, but the interruption didn't damage his career at all—his popularity continued to grow. Mitchum made a total of over 100 movies, usually playing the rough-and-ready type of man, but in a way that appealed to both male and female moviegoers. He was so popular that his career even survived his 1954 arrest for possession of marijuana. That same year, Mitchum founded his own production company, DRM Productions, which later became Talbot Productions. He was married only once, to Dorothy Spence, and they had three children: Jim, Chris, and Petrine. In recent years, he appeared in made-for-TV films and mini-series, including: "The Winds of War," "North and South," and "A Family for Joe." Robert Mitchum died from emphysema and lung cancer in July 1997.

MONTGOMERY, ROBERT

Born Henry Montgomery, Jr., on May 21, 1904 in Beacon, New York, Robert Montgomery was the son of a rubber company president. Although educated at private schools, his father's death in 1920 reduced the family to poverty, and Montgomery had to work as a railroad mechanic and oil tanker deckhand. When his attempts at writing short stories failed, his friends encouraged him to try his hand at acting. In 1924, he made his stage debut in New York and very quickly became an established Broadway actor. In 1929, he got an MGM contract, appearing in talking films, and enjoyed a long run as a leading man. Then playing psychotic characters in two films, he changed his acting image. Montgomery was instrumental in founding the Screen Actors Guild and, beginning in 1935, served as its president for four terms. He also helped to expose labor racketeering in the movie industry. During World War II, Montgomery served in the Navy. For his service aboard a destroyer on D-Day, he received a Bronze Star and later was inducted as a Chevalier of the French Legion of Honor. After the war he returned to Hollywood and continued acting, but also tried directing. In his first directorial effort, **Lady in the Lake** (1946), he introduced an unusual filming technique—using the camera to project the view through the lead character's eyes. On television, from 1950-1957, he was the producer/director/host (and occasional star) of "Robert Montgomery Presents." In 1955, his direction of the Broadway play "The Desperate Hours" earned him a Tony Award. From 1969-70, Montgomery was president of Lincoln Center's Repertory Theater. His daughter, Elizabeth Montgomery, became an actress and was also very successful in films and on television, most notably in the series "Bewitched." Robert Montgomery died in September of 1981.

MOOREHEAD, AGNES

Agnes Robertson Moorehead was born on December 6, 1906 in Clinton, Massachusetts, the daughter of a Presbyterian minister. She graduated from Muskingum College in Ohio, earned an M.A. in English and public speaking from the University of Wisconsin at Madison, and achieved a Ph.D. in literature at Bradley University. Agnes taught high school public speaking classes, became a singer on radio in St. Louis, and performed with the St. Louis Municipal Opera. She also taught drama classes and attended the American Academy of Dramatic arts. In 1928, she started to play small parts on Broadway. In the '30s, Moorehead became a radio actress and toured in vaudeville with Phil Baker. Then she joined Orson Welles' Mercury Theatre, and got a role in his 1941 film **Citizen Kane**. Following that, she had movie contracts with both Warner Brothers and MGM. Over the years, Moorehead played a wide variety of characters on the screen, ranging from neurotic spinster to hero's friend. She was nominated numerous times at the Academy Awards for Best Supporting Actress: for **The Magnificent Ambersons** (1942), **Mrs. Parkington** (1944), **Johnny Belinda** (1948), and **Hush, Hush Sweet Charlotte** (1964). In 1942, she won the Best Actress award from the New York Film Critics for her role in **The Magnificent Ambersons**. She toured in theater productions in the early '50s, including her own one-woman show. The TV generation probably remembers Moorehead best for her role as a witch named Endora in the long-running series "Bewitched" (1964-71). She also appeared on Broadway in "Gigi" in 1973. She was married and divorced twice, and had a son, Sean. Agnes Moorehead died of lung cancer in 1974.

NIVEN, DAVID

James David Niven was born in Scotland on March 1, 1909. Descended from two generations of professional soldiers, he was educated at the Royal Military College in Sandhurst and served in the Highland Light Infantry in Malta. After this stint in the service, he became an international drifter, working at such jobs as laundry messenger, bartender, lumberjack, news reporter, and gunnery instructor to Cuban revolutionists. In 1934, Niven traveled to Los Angeles and entered the movie industry. He began as an extra, then played a Mexican in **Hopalong Cassidy** (1935). This was the role that made him a success, and Niven quickly became a second lead actor. In 1939, he starred in **Wuthering Heights**. During World War II, he returned to the military as a Second Lieutenant in the Rifle Brigade, then served with the Commandos in the top-secret Phantom Reconnaissance Regiment. Promoted to Colonel, he was transferred to the British Liberation Army until Germany's surrender. After appearing in two British war propaganda films, he often commuted between Hollywood and London, acting in many American and British films. Along with Charles Boyer and Dick Powell, he co-founded television's Four Star Playhouse, and also appeared in some of the productions. Also on TV, Niven hosted "The David Niven Show," and performed in the "Alcoa Theatre," "The Rogues" series, and "A Man Called Intrepid" miniseries. In 1958, Niven received the Best Actor Academy Award and the New York Critics Best Actor Award for his performance in the movie drama **Separate Tables**. In 1980, he received the London Evening Standard Special Award. He had two sons with his first wife, Primula Rollo, who died in 1940: David (a film and production executive) and James. He married Hjordis Tersmeden in 1948 and they had two daughters, Fiona and Kristina. David Niven also authored two novels and an autobiography; he had ALS and died in Switzerland in 1983.

O'BRIEN, MARGARET

She was born Angela Maxine O'Brien in Los Angeles, California on January 15, 1937. Her father died just months before she was born and her mother raised her alone. Starting as a model at the age of 3, she broke into movies at the age of 4. She got her screen name "Margaret" from her first leading role on film in **Journey for Margaret** (1942). O'Brien ranked among the Box Office Top Ten in 1945 and 1946. When she was 7, she received a special Academy Award (Outstanding Child Actress) for her part as Judy Garland's baby sister in **Meet Me In St. Louis** (1946). O'Brien had a waif-like personality and was cast in roles that displayed her vulnerability. Unable to make the transition from child actress to adolescent actress, she almost completely retired from the screen in 1951. After that, she concentrated on stage and television work, including the popular TV series "Marcus Welby, MD" and the 1979 TV miniseries "Testimony of Two Men." In 1979, she became a civilian aide to Clifford Alexander, Secretary of the Army. Margaret O'Brien was married twice and has one daughter, Mary.

O'BRIEN, PAT

William Joseph Patrick O'Brien was born in Milwaukee, Wisconsin on November 11, 1899. He was a childhood friend of Spencer Tracy, and the two attended military school together. They even joined the Navy together during World War II. Following their stint in the service, they both attended the American Academy of Dramatic Arts. Pat started out as a song-and-dance man, then played dramatic roles on Broadway. Although he played the lead role in a 1921 silent film Western, his movie career did not begin in earnest until the advent of talking pictures. In the 1930s, the Warner Brothers studio cast him as heroes, co-starring many times with James Cagney. His most memorable starring role was in **Knute Rockne–All American** (1940), where he portrayed the famous football coach. Throughout the '40s O'Brien enjoyed great popularity in both lead and supporting roles and in the '50s began to play character roles. He also became a favorite St. Patrick's Day guest on television. In 1981, he was reunited with James Cagney in the film **Ragtime**. Married to actress Eloise Taylor from 1931 until his death in 1983, they had four children: Mavourneen, Sean, Terence Kevin and Kathleen.

O'CONNOR, DONALD

Donald O'Connor was born to show business parents on August 28, 1925 in Chicago, Illinois. He made his debut in vaudeville as a very young child in "The O'Connor Family" circus and vaudeville act. In 1937 he made his movie debut with a tap dance number in **Melody for Two**. From 1938-39 he worked under contract with Paramount, playing many juvenile roles. After that, he went back on the road with his family's act. Then in 1941 he was signed by Universal, where he starred in very popular teen musicals (Peggy Ryan a frequent co-star). During World War II, O'Connor served in the U.S. Army's entertainment division. In 1950, he made the first in a popular series of **Francis** films, in which he played sidekick to a talking mule. One of his most notable performances, while on loan to MGM, was his "Make 'Em Laugh" dance routine in the popular musical **Singin' in the Rain** (1952). In 1953, Donald received an Emmy as a rotating host for "The Colgate Comedy Hour." In 1954 and 1955, he starred in television's "The Donald O'Connor Texaco Show." Donald O'Connor was also a composer of music: in 1956, his first symphony, "Reflexions d'un Comique," was performed by the Los Angeles Philharmonic. He retired from the movies in 1965, but returned to the screen in 1981's **Ragtime**. That same year, he made his Broadway debut in "Bring Back Birdie." Donald was married to Gwendolyn Carter in 1944; they had a daughter, Donna. He has been married since 1956 to former starlet Gloria Noble; they have three children: Don, Alicia and Kevin. Donald O'Connor's made his most recent screen appearance in the Jack Lemmon-Walter Matthau film **Out to Sea** (1997).

O'HARA, MAUREEN

Born Maureen FitzSimmons in Milltown, Ireland on August 17, 1920, she came by her talent naturally from her mother, who was an opera singer and actress. At 12 years old, she acted in plays on the radio in Dublin, and at 14 became a member of the Abbey Players, Ireland's national theater group. She studied at Dominican College, Burke's School of Elocution, Abbey Theatre School, and London's Guildhall School of Music. At 17, she won a beauty contest, which led to her first movie role in England, appearing with Charles Laughton. Laughton brought her along with him to America to make **The Hunchback of Notre Dame** (1939), and so began a stellar movie career that would generate 52 films (five of them co-starring with John Wayne). In 1939, she contracted with 20th Century Fox and RKO, and in 1953 entered into contract with Columbia. O'Hara's beautiful red hair (which was done true justice in Technicolor films) dazzled audiences, while she entertained them with graceful characters of great inner strength. Over the years, she has also been much admired for her real-life confidence and spunk. Her first marriage was annulled, and her second marriage to Will Price (they had a daughter, Bronwyn) ended in divorce in 1953. She was married a third time (after Price died) to Charles F. Blair Jr., a retired Air Force brigadier general. He was killed in a plane crash, ending their 10-year union. In 1991, Maureen O'Hara co-starred with John Candy in the film **Only the Lonely**. She has been appearing occasionally on television: most recently, in the critically acclaimed holiday TV movie "The Christmas Box" (1995) and as a favorite guest of viewers on Tom Snyder's late night talk show.

PAYNE, JOHN

John Payne was born to well-to-do parents in Roanoke, Virginia, on May 23, 1912. His mother was an opera singer and he was a direct descendent of John Howard Payne, the composer of "Home Sweet Home." When his family lost its fortune in the Great Depression of the 1930s, John had to take menial jobs to pay for his education. After graduating from Roanoke College, he studied drama at Columbia University and voice at Julliard, then became a radio and band singer. Noticed by Sam Goldwyn for his bit part in Broadway's "At Home Abroad" with Beatrice Lillie and Reginald Gardner, he was given a Hollywood contract. In 1936, Payne made his movie debut in **Dodsworth**. Dropped by Goldwyn in 1938, he went on to Warner Brothers and landed better roles. Then he hit it big at 20th Century Fox, where he remained for seven years, becoming a popular star of the '40s Technicolor musicals with such stars as Alice Faye and Betty Grable. In 1973, he appeared on the Broadway stage with Faye in a revival of "Good News." He was married first to actress Anne Shirley in 1937 (they had a daughter named Julie), and then to actress Gloria De Haven in 1944 (they had a daughter, Kathie and a son, Thomas). In 1953, he married Alexandra Curtis. John Payne made wise investments in real estate, which made him a very wealthy man; he passed away in 1989.

PECK, GREGORY

Eldred Gregory Peck was born on April 5, 1916 in La Jolla, California. He attended the University of California at Berkeley; he started out in Pre-Med studies but later chose to pursue an English major. He took part in a play during his senior year of college and discovered his acting talent. Peck then went to New York, studied at the Neighborhood Playhouse Theatre school, and worked at various jobs until he got some theatrical roles and made his way to the Broadway stage. He had trouble getting into the movie business because studio executives thought he was too tall and lanky, and not handsome enough. Peck was finally offered a contract and a film role by independent filmmaker Casey Robinson, got the chance to prove himself, and before long the major studios (MGM, Fox, RKO, and David O. Selznick) were sharing his contract. He was nominated for a Best Actor Academy Award four times: for **The Keys of the Kingdom** (1944), **The Yearling** (1946), **Gentleman's Agreement** (1947), and **Twelve O'Clock High** (1949) before winning the fifth time in 1962 for **To Kill A Mockingbird**. He was on the Box Office Top Ten List in 1947 and again in 1952. Peck also gave back to the arts: in 1948, he co-founded the La Jolla Playhouse, in 1965 became a charter member of the National Arts Council, and served as the Chairman of the Board of Trustees of the American Film Institute from 1967 to 1969. He was married twice: first to Greta Rice, a makeup artist (they had three sons—Jonathan, Stephen and Carey—and later divorced), second to Veronique Passani (they have a son, Anthony, and a daughter, Cecelia). In more recent years, Gregory Peck appeared in the 1982 television miniseries "The Blue and The Gray," and received the Lifetime Achievement Award from the American Film Institute in 1989. Still one of the most admired American actors, Peck recently filmed a TV miniseries entitled, "Moby Dick," for the USA Network.

PIDGEON, WALTER

Walter Davis Pidgeon was born in New Brunswick, Canada, on September 23, 1897. He came from a financially prosperous background; his father owned a chain of stores. He served in the Canadian Army during World War I, and studied at the University of New Brunswick. Then, while working for a bank in Boston, he studied singing at The New England Conservatory of Music. At a party, Fred Astaire heard him sing, and helped Pidgeon to get an audition. That led to a musical career which took Pidgeon to both Europe and the Broadway stage. He also sang for Victor Records. He made his first movie in 1926 and for several years appeared in both silents and talkies for various studios and finally got an MGM contract in 1937. In 1941, Walter Pidgeon became a major movie star after making two important films: **Manhunt** and **How Green Was My Valley**. Both of these were made while he was on loan to Fox. That same year, he also filmed **Blossoms in the Dust**, which marked the beginning of his very successful eight-movie pairing with leading lady Greer Garson. They developed a longtime friendship off-screen, as well. Pidgeon made over 100 films in all and was nominated twice for Best Actor at the Academy Awards—in 1942 for **Mrs. Miniver** and in 1943 for **Madame Curie**. His screen characters were usually strong and distinguished gentlemen. In 1943, he became a U.S. citizen. He also served 33 years on the Board of Directors of the Screen Actors Guild. In 1956, Walter Pidgeon hosted the "MGM Parade" television series. He left MGM in 1957, and worked on Broadway, in films for other studios, and in television movies right through the '70s. His first wife, Edna Pickles, was his childhood sweetheart; she died after the birth of their daughter, Edna. He was married again, in 1930, to Ruth Walker. Walter Pidgeon died in 1984.

POITIER, SIDNEY

Sidney Poitier was born in Miami, Florida on February 20, 1924. His parents were from the Bahamas; Sidney was raised and educated in Nassau. He served in the U.S. Army as a physiotherapist and later joined the American Negro Theater, where he made his 1949 debut in the production of "Lysistrata." He began his film career in the '50s and quickly rose in popularity to become the number one African-American actor in Hollywood. In 1958, Poitier was nominated for the Best Actor Academy Award for his performance in **The Defiant Ones**, for which he also won Berlin Festival and British Academy awards. In 1959, he acted on Broadway in **Raisin in the Sun** and made the film version in 1961. For his role in **Lilies of the Field** (1963), Poitier won Best Actor at both the Academy Awards and the Berlin Festival. In 1967, he made three very successful films: **To Sir, With Love**, **Guess Who's Coming to Dinner?** and **Heat of the Night**. In the '70s, he turned his attention to directing films, some of which he acted in as well. In 1950, he married Juanita Hardy and they had three daughters: Beverly, Pamela and Sherry. They later divorced, and in 1976 he married actress Joanna Shimkus. In the 1991 film **Separate But Equal**, he portrayed Supreme Court Justice Thurgood Marshall, and became the first African-American to receive the American Film Institute's Life Achievement Award. He made a TV movie, the sequel "To Sir, With Love II" in 1996. In 1997, he played South African hero Nelson Mandela in **Mandela and de Klerk**, a movie made for the Showtime cable channel. That same year Poitier was sworn in as the Bahamas' Ambassador to Japan.

POWELL, JANE

Born Suzanne Burce in Portland Oregon on April 1, 1929, Jane Powell became a teenage singing star and went on to become a leading lady in MGM musicals. She adopted the screen name Jane Powell from the part she played in her first movie, **Song of the Open Road** (1944). In 1951, she played her first adult role as Fred Astaire's sister, and Peter Lawford's girl friend in **Royal Wedding**. Through the mid-1950s, Jane continued to enjoy great popularity with MGM. After making her final film in 1958, she performed in night clubs, summer stock, concerts and television. In 1974, she replaced Debbie Reynolds in Broadway's "Irene." She married Geary Steffen in 1949 and they had two children—son Geary Jr. and daughter Suzanne. She married for the second time in 1954 to Pat Nerney and they had a daughter, Lindsay. She married twice more: in 1965 to manager James Fitzgerald and in 1979 to writer David Parlour. Jane Powell still performs in dinner theater productions and summer musicals.

POWELL, WILLIAM

William Horatio Powell was born in Pittsburgh, Pennsylvania on July 28, 1892. He studied at the American Academy of Dramatic Arts in New York, with the help of a wealthy aunt, after it became apparent that his effort to pay his way on his own, by working for a telephone company, would take too long. Even though it took him 13 years to do so, he eventually paid his aunt back. Powell worked on Broadway and in various theatrical companies before appearing for the first time on the silver screen in 1919. He then embarked on a 33-year Hollywood career that included 34 silent pictures and 62 talking pictures. He was contracted with Paramount from 1925 to 1931, with Warner Brothers from 1931 until 1934, when he went to MGM. During the 1920s, he usually played villains as a supporting actor. When talking pictures evolved, he became a star due to the high quality of his speaking voice and his comic talent. One of his most famous roles was that of Nick Charles in the popular series of **Thin Man** movies. That series, which co-starred Myrna Loy, began in 1934 and consisted of six films. Over the years, Powell and Loy made seven other movies together. Powell's characters were usually sophisticated but roguish gentlemen. He was nominated three times for a Best Actor Academy Award—**The Thin Man** (1934), **My Man Godfrey** (1936), and **Life With Father** (1947). Powell retired from acting after the 1955 movie **Mr. Roberts**. William Powell never did receive an Academy Award for any of his vast number of films, but in 1947 he did receive the New York Film Critics Best Actor Award for **Life With Father** and **The Senator Was Indiscreet** (1947). He was married three times, first to actress Eileen Wilson (they had a son, William David), second to movie star Carole Lombard, and third, from 1940 until his death in 1984, to actress Diana Lewis.

POWER, TYRONE

Tyrone Edmund Power was born in Cincinnati, Ohio on May 5, 1914; he came from a bloodline of actors in Tyrone County, Ireland on his father's side. His father, also named Tyrone Power, was a well-known actor of stage and film. Young Tyrone was prepared for the acting profession from an early age by his mother, Patia Powell, an actress and drama teacher. After high school, he did stage work in Chicago and New York, some radio acting, and also had bit parts in a couple of movies. By 1936, he was under contract with 20th Century Fox, where he became a major star and remained until 1955. He was a handsome and dashing leading man, a romantic favorite of the ladies. Tyrone performed in various types of movies: musicals, Westerns, action/adventures, as well as dramas. From 1938 to 1940, he was listed in the Box Office Top Ten. His movie career was interrupted for three years during World War II, when he served in the Marines—working his way up from private to pilot (and first lieutenant) of C-46 transport planes. His first marriage was to French actress Annabella; he adopted her daughter Anne. Second, he married actress Linda Christian, with whom he had two daughters, Romina and Taryn. He married a third time to Debbie Minardos (not an actress), and they had a son, Tyrone IV, who was born after Power's death from a heart attack in November of 1958.

RAINS, CLAUDE

William Claude Rains was born in London, England on November 10, 1889. He started in show business as a child, appearing on the London stage. In 1911, he got his first adult role, and began touring the United States in 1912 in "Androcles and the Lion." The years 1915 through 1919 found Rains in World War I military service, where he rose from the rank of private to captain. During the '20s and '30s, he worked on stage in many productions. In 1933, at the age of 43, he made his U.S. movie debut in **The Invisible Man**. After that, he acted in a long list of films over three decades, playing a wide variety of lead and supporting roles. Rains was nominated four times for Best Supporting Actor at the Academy Awards: for **Mr. Smith Goes to Washington** (1939), **Casablanca** (1943), **Mr. Skeffington** (1944), and **Notorious** (1946). Rains' trademark was his fine and distinguished speaking voice and his sophisticated manner. He was married six times and had one daughter, Jennifer. Claude Rains passed away in 1967.

REAGAN, RONALD

Born in Tampico, Illinois on February 6, 1911, Ronald Reagan played football and acted in high school plays in Dixon, Illinois. During his years at Eureka College, he played football and was on the debate and swim teams. He won an award in a Northwestern University School of Speech contest for his performance in a one-act play. After graduation, from 1932-37, Reagan was a radio sportscaster in Davenport, Iowa. For a time, he also announced the Chicago Cubs' baseball games. In 1937, after signing a contract with Warner Brothers, he played romantic lead roles in some 50 "B" movies. In 1940, he played his most memorable role, that of George Gipp, the dying Notre Dame halfback in **Knute Rockne–All American**. Serving as a captain with the USAAF in World War II, Reagan was assigned to produce training films. After his return to Hollywood and civilian life, he served as president of the Screen Actors Guild from 1947-1952 and again in 1959. From 1953-54, when he entered the realm of television, his first job was hosting "The Orchid Awards." From 1954-62, he hosted and occasionally starred in "General Electric Theater." During 1965 and 1966, he hosted "Death Valley Days." Reagan then became politically active and was elected Governor of California for two terms (1966-74). In 1980, he was elected President of the United States and served two terms (surviving an assassination attempt in the first term). During his presidency, he published a book entitled, **Ronald Reagan Talks to America**. Married to actress Jane Wyman in 1940, they had two children, daughter Maureen and adopted son Michael. His second marriage was to actress Nancy Davis in 1952 and they also had two children: daughter Patti and son Ron. Recently, it was announced that former President Reagan is suffering from Alzheimer's Disease.

REED, DONNA

Donna Reed was born Donna Belle Mullenger on January 27, 1921 in Denison, Iowa. She grew up on a farm, and was elected Queen in her high school's beauty contest. After graduation, she went to live with an aunt in Los Angeles to attend college. She worked at several jobs to pay for her tuition, and studied to be a teacher. Donna acted in two college plays and when she was chosen as Campus Queen, her picture appeared in the newspaper and she was noticed by MGM talent scouts. In 1941, she got a contract with MGM and by the mid-'40s became a well-known leading lady. She generally portrayed very nice, wholesome women, most notably in **It's a Wonderful Life** (1946). After leaving MGM, she worked for Columbia, then went on to freelance. In 1953, she won Best Supporting Actress at the Academy Awards for her role in **From Here to Eternity**, which was a character that greatly departed from those she usually played. She continued making movies through the late '50s, but went to TV in 1958 with "The Donna Reed Show," which was very popular and enjoyed a long run until 1966. She dropped out of sight for a while, but made TV movies in 1979 and 1983. She was married three times: first to MGM makeup artist William Tuttle (1943-45), second to producer Tony Owen (1945-71, they had four children), and third to retired U.S. Army Colonel Grover Asmus (in 1974). Donna replaced the ailing Barbara Bel Geddes as Miss Ellie in the series "Dallas" in 1984. When Bel Geddes returned to the show the following year, Reed sued the show for breach of contract. Donna received a $1 million settlement in that suit before she died of cancer in 1986.

REYNOLDS, DEBBIE

Born Mary Frances Reynolds in El Paso, Texas on April 1, 1932, Debbie Reynolds attended high school in Burbank, California. In 1948, she entered and won the "Miss Burbank" contest, which resulted in a Warner Brothers contract and her film debut in **June Bride**. In 1950, she moved to MGM, where her bubbly personality and charm made her very popular in their light-hearted musicals. Two of Debbie's most memorable roles were in 1952's **Singin' in the Rain**, and the 1964 movie

The Unsinkable Molly Brown. In 1961, she developed her own nightclub act. From 1969-70, she starred on television in "The Debbie Reynolds Show," and in the early '70s, she appeared in "Irene" on the Broadway stage. In 1955, she married singer Eddie Fisher and they had two children: daughter Carrie (now a well-known screen writer) and son Todd (a TV director). They later divorced, and over the years she married two more times: her second husband died (leaving Debbie with tremendous debts, which she worked hard to repay), and her third marriage ended in divorce. In the '80s, she recorded two exercise videos. Debbie owns an extensive collection of movie memorabilia and costumes. Her collection, as well as her stage act, are showcased in her Las Vegas hotel, which opened in 1992; it is managed by her son, Todd. In 1989, Debbie published her autobiography, **Debbie, My Life**. She made a movie comeback with the 1997 Albert Brooks film **Mother**, playing the title role, and received a Golden Globe nomination for that performance. Debbie Reynolds also received the Lifetime Achievement Award at the 1997 American Comedy Awards.

RITTER, THELMA

Thelma Ritter was born on February 14, 1905 in Brooklyn, New York. Her movie career didn't start until mid-life, when she was in her forties. She studied at the American Academy of Dramatic Arts in New York, and performed on the road in vaudeville and stock theater. She then left show business for a while, but returned to perform in a radio series in 1944. She made her movie debut in 1947, in a supporting role in **Miracle on 34th Street**. Ritter landed a contract with 20th Century Fox in 1949, which lasted until 1955. For years she was a Hollywood mainstay, expertly playing wisecracking and outspoken supporting characters. She was nominated for Best Supporting Actress at the Academy Awards six times: for **All About Eve** (1950), **The Mating Season** (1951), **With a Song in My Heart** (1952), **Pickup on South Street** (1953), **Pillow Talk** (1959), and **The Birdman of Alcatraz** (1962). In 1955, she went to television in the play "The Catered Affair" (which was written specifically for her by Paddy Chayevsky), and in 1957 appeared on Broadway in the musical "New Girl in Town." Thelma Ritter made her last movie in 1968 and passed away in 1969.

ROGERS, GINGER

Ginger Rogers was born Virginia Katherine McMath in Independence, Missouri on July 16, 1911. She got her start as a child star in vaudeville with Eddie Foy's troupe (her mother Lela was her manager). Her parents were divorced, and after she was adopted by her stepfather she took his last name. When she grew up, she worked her way to the Broadway stage. In 1930, she got a contract with Paramount and made her first movie. Ginger didn't make it big at Paramount, but was later signed up with RKO. When they paired her with Fred Astaire in **Flying Down to Rio** in 1933, her dancing talent was finally fully recognized, and she became a star. Besides being an excellent dancer, she was also a very capable dramatic actress and won the Academy Award for Best Actress in 1940 for **Kitty Foyle**. Ginger made 73 films in all, and worked diligently to ensure that she was known as a star in her own right and not only as Fred Astaire's dance partner. From the 1950s through the early 1970s, she worked mostly on the stage, in productions such as "Love and Let Love," "Hello Dolly!," "Mame," and "Coco." In 1971, she served as fashion consult-ant to the J.C. Penney department stores, and in 1976 performed in a nightclub act. She was married and divorced 5 times. Rogers also published her autobiography, **Ginger, My Story**, in 1992 Prior to her death in 1995 at the age of 83, Ginger Rogers appeared in the 1994 film "That's Entertainment III."

ROONEY, MICKEY

Born Joe Yule, Jr. in Brooklyn, New York on September 23, 1920, he began in show business at the age of 2, appearing on the vaudeville stage with his parents Joe Yule and Nell Brown. He continued to work on the stage through childhood, and in 1926 made his first movie. Under the name Mickey McGuire, he had his own series of comedy shorts. In 1932, he took the name Mickey Rooney, and in 1934 got a contract with MGM. There his role as the high-spirited teenager in the small American town of Carvel in the **Andy Hardy** movie series elevated him to stardom. From 1937 to 1946, Mickey made 15 "Andy Hardy" movies and then one more in 1958. Known for his small stature (he was only 5'1" tall), Rooney was amazingly multi-talented—he could sing, dance, and play musical instruments, and his acting ability had a wide range, from drama to comedy. He received a special Academy Award in 1938 (special because of his young age), and was on the Box Office Top Ten list between 1938 and 1943, holding the number one spot for 1939, 1940, and 1941. He was nominated for Best Actor at the Academy Awards for **Babes in Arms** (1939) and **The Human Comedy** (1943), and for Best Supporting Actor for **The Bold and the Brave** (1956) and **The Black Stallion** (1979). During World War II, from 1944 to 1946, he served in the United States Army. Since his long run at MGM ended, he has done work both on the stage and in television. In 1963, he appeared in summer stock in "The Tunnel of Love," in 1964 worked in nightclubs with dancer Bobby Van, and thereafter went on tour in various other shows. In 1964 and 1965, he appeared on television in two series: "Mickey" and "NBC Follies." From 1979 until 1985, he starred in "Sugar Babies" (co-star Ann Miller), a stage show that began in Los Angeles, enjoyed a long Broadway run, and subse-quently went on the road nationally. He was nominated for a Tony Award for his Broadway "Sugar Babies" performance and received a second special Academy Award in 1982 for his lifetime of contributions to the movies. Over the years, he has married eight times and has had seven children. In 1991, he published his autobiography, **Life is Too Short**. Most recently, he starred in the critically acclaimed television series "The Black Stallion" on the Family Channel.

RUSSELL, ROSALIND

Born on June 4, 1908 in Waterbury, Connecticut, Rosalind Russell was the daughter of a wealthy lawyer and a fashion editor. She attended Marymount College in Tarrytown, New York and later studied at the American Academy of Dramatic Arts, after which she toured in summer stock. In the '30s, she appeared in New York's Garrick Gaieties and went on tour with the shows "Roar China," "Talent" and "Second Man." Rosalind made her film debut in 1934's **Evelyn Prentice**. While she played mostly dramatic parts in her early career, she later emerged as a comedian, and this remained her forte for years to come. Her Broadway successes include "Wonderful Town" (1953) and "Auntie Mame" (1956). In 1958 she recreated her stage role of Auntie Mame on film for which she received a Best Actress Academy Award nomination. She was nominated for that award three other times: **My Sister Eileen** (1942), **Sister Kenny** (1946), **Mourning Becomes Electra** (1947) and **Auntie Mame** (1956). Because she was active in approximately 94 civic associations, Rosalind Russell was given the Jean Hersholt Humanitarian Award in 1972. She was married to producer Frederic Brisson from 1941 until her death in 1976, and they had a son, Carl Lance. She published an autobiography, entitled, *Life is a Banquet*.

SAKALL, S.Z.

Szdke Szakall was born on February 2, 1884 (some sources indicate 1883) in Hungary. After graduating from the University of Hungary, he wrote plays and became a stage director. He then found a niche on the European stage. Sakall starred successfully in a British film and then came to America in 1940, embarking on a very prolific film career. He was aptly nicknamed "Cuddles" because of his chubby-cheeked, lovable face. The excitability and flustered, fractured English of his screen characters were his trademarks. In 1922 he married his wife, Boeszike and they remained married until his death in 1955.

SCOTT, RANDOLPH

Descended from Virginia pioneers, George Randolph Scott was born in Orange, Virginia on January 23, 1903. He attended the Georgia Institute of Technology and earned an engineering degree from the University of North Carolina. He tried working in a textile manufacturing business with his father, but his real love was acting. In 1925, he set out for California and joined the Pasadena Playhouse to study his craft. Scott began in films by acting in minor Westerns, which he did for many years. His big success came after he signed separate agreements with two studios in 1938—20th Century Fox and Universal—from then on, he got major roles. He made about 66 films altogether through the '30s and '40s; most of them Westerns. Two of his more prominent movies were **The Spoilers** (1942) and **Pittsburgh** (1942), both co-starring Marlene Dietrich and John Wayne. Scott really hit his stride in the '50s, when he was ranked among the Box Office Top Ten from 1950-53. With Harry Joe Brown, Scott had formed a production company in 1950 and was able to create his own, new style of Westerns, which were very successful. In 1956, he began making a series of seven Westerns with director Budd Boetticher. From 1936-39, Scott was married to socialite Ariana duPont Somerville. In 1944, he married Patricia Stillman and they adopted two children, son Christopher and daughter Sandra. He wisely invested his movie earnings in real estate and oil wells, and became a very wealthy man. Randolph Scott retired from the movies in 1962; he died in 1987.

SINATRA, FRANK

Francis Albert Sinatra, the son of an immigrant fireman, was born in Hoboken, New Jersey on December 12, 1915. He attended high school in Hoboken and in his first job he was a copyboy at a local newspaper. The organizer of "The Hoboken Four" singing group, Frank won first prize on the "Major Bowes Amateur Hour" radio show. He earned $15 at his first job as a singer-emcee in Englewood, New Jersey's Rustic Cabin. In 1939, he sang with Harry James' Band, and from 1940-42, with Tommy Dorsey's Band. From 1943-44 and again from 1947-49, he sang on radio's "Your Hit Parade." He also had his own radio program, "Songs by Sinatra" (1945-47). During 1950-52, he appeared on television in his own musical show, called "The Frank Sinatra Show." In 1953, he won a Best Supporting Actor Academy Award for his first dramatic role in **From Here to Eternity**. In 1955, at the Academy Awards, he was nominated for Best Actor when he starred in **The Man with the Golden Arm**. In 1957-58, he again appeared on television in a musical/drama series, "The Frank Sinatra Show." Sinatra also founded a record company, Reprise Records. In 1965, he tried his hand at directing **None But the Brave**. He won the Jean Hersholt Humanitarian Award in 1970 and received Kennedy Center honors for life achievement in 1983. In 1985, he was given America's highest honor, the Medal of Freedom. He married first wife, Nancy Barbato, in 1939, and they have three children: Nancy, Frank Jr. and Christina. He was married the second time to actress Ava Gardner in 1951 and next, in 1966, to actress Mia Farrow. In 1976, he married Barbara Marx, his current wife.

SKELTON, RED

Richard Bernard Skelton was born in Vincennes, Indiana, on July 18, 1913. Because his circus clown father died before his birth and his mother had to work at a low-paying job as a charwoman to support her four sons, Skelton grew up in poverty. Singing for pennies on the streets at age 10 and quitting school at age 12, Red joined a medicine show and spent the rest of his youth entertaining on show boats, in circuses, vaudeville and burlesque. Doing one-night stands as a comic, he was not terribly successful until the early '30s, when his popular doughnut-dunking routine earned him a booking at the Paramount Theater in New York City. He made successful appearances on radio, and in 1938, Red made his movie debut in **Having Wonderful Time** with Ginger Rogers. In 1940, he was put under contract by MGM, finding film success in 1941's **Whistling in the Dark**. While assigned to

Special Services in the Army from 1943-45, Red crossed the Atlantic and Mediterranean, performing in approximately 3,800 shows on hospital ships and troop carriers. At the same time, he had a successful radio program, which led to television's "The Red Skelton Show" in 1951—which earned high Nielsen ratings for two decades. Among his most beloved characters were Freddie the Freeloader, Clem Kadiddlehopper, Cauliflower McPugg and the Seagulls, Heathcliff and Gertrude. In the late '60s, he performed in clubs and comedy concerts. In 1991, at age 80, Red brought his act to Carnegie Hall. His clown paintings, once merely a hobby, became quite famous and have sold for as much as $40,000 each. Red's first wife Edna Stilman (whom he married in 1931) became his vaudeville partner, writer and manager. She remained his chief writer after their 1943 divorce. He had two children with second wife, model Georgia Davis (married in 1945): a daughter Valentina, and a son, Richard Freeman (who died of leukemia at age 9). He was married to his third wife, Lothian Toland, when he died in September of 1997 at the age of 84.

STANWYCK, BARBARA

Barbara Stanwyck was born Ruby Stevens on July 16, 1907 in Brooklyn, New York. The last of five children, she was left an orphan at only 4 years old and she grew up in foster homes. Barbara went to work at the age of 13 and held various jobs. When she was a little older, she performed as a dancer in nightclubs, and toured with The Ziegfield Follies. At 19, she became a Broadway star with a dramatic role in the hit play "The Noose." She made her first movie appearance (in a silent film) in 1927 in New York. She moved to Hollywood in 1928 when she married actor Frank Fay, but movie success did not come right away. In 1930, she finally got a break when she was chosen for a film by Frank Capra. That role launched her long and successful movie career. She contracted with Warner Brothers in 1931, but in 1935 began to work freelance. In 1936, she also started acting on radio in the "Lux Radio Theatre" program. Stanwyck had a wide range of talent, excelling at comedy as well as heavy drama. Her characters usually had a tough edge to them, but often they had a good heart. A hard worker who was admired by directors, she was a four-time Best Actress nominee at the Academy Awards: for **Stella Dallas** (1937), **Ball of Fire** (1941), **Double Indemnity** (1944), and **Sorry, Wrong Number** (1948). She was divorced from her first husband in 1935 and married actor Robert Taylor in 1939; they divorced in 1952. In 1956 she founded a production company, the Barwyk Corporation. Stanwyck made the move to television with "The Barbara Stanwyck Show" (1960-1961) and "The Big Valley" (1965-1969). She later worked in the miniseries "The Thorn Birds" (1983), and both the "Dynasty" and "The Colbys" series. Though she never won at the Academy Awards for any single performance, in 1981 she received a Special Academy Award for "superlative creativity and unique contribution to the art of screen acting." After a long and full acting career, Barbara Stanwyck died in January of 1990.

STEWART, JAMES

James Maitland Stewart was born in Indiana, Pennsylvania on May 20, 1908. His father owned a hardware store. Stewart studied architecture at Princeton, but after graduating in 1932, decided to try an acting career instead. He worked with Joshua Logan's University Players in Massachusetts, and made his way to the Broadway stage. He then became a major movie star shortly after signing an MGM contract in 1935. Stewart won a Best Actor Academy Award for his performance in **The Philadelphia Story** (1940) and was nominated for that award on four other occasions: **Mr. Smith Goes to Washington** (1939), **It's a Wonderful Life** (1946), **Harvey** (1951), and **Anatomy of a Murder** (1959). The overwhelming sincerity of his screen portrayals touched audiences and made him a long-time favorite. He served in the Air Force during World War II, flying 25 missions over Europe and receiving honors: the Distinguished Service Medal, the Air Medal, and DFC with Oak Leaf Clusters. Later, in the Air Force Reserve, he became a Brigadier General. In 1947, he returned to the Broadway stage in "Harvey," and later made the movie version in 1951. He remained a bachelor for many years until 1949, when he married Gloria McLean and became stepfather to her two sons, Michael and Ronald. He and Gloria then became the parents of twin daughters, Judy and Kelly in 1951. Although his acting was acclaimed for many previous years, he achieved his highest box office numbers in the 1950s, making the Box Office Top Ten every year of the decade except 1951. In 1961, he appeared in a stage revival of "Harvey" with Helen Hayes. Unfortunately, his son Ronald was killed in the Vietnam War in 1969. Stewart continued making movies for the both the big and small screens through to the early 1980s. He also did TV series work in the 1970s: "The Jimmy Stewart Show" (1971-1972) and "Hawkins" (1973-1974). In 1980, he received the Life Achievement Award from the American Film Institute, and in 1985 was given a Special Academy Award for "his 50 years of meaningful performances, for his high ideals, both on and off the screen, with the respect and affection of his colleagues." He also was awarded the Presidential Medal of Freedom by President Reagan. As recently as 1991, he was still working, doing a voice role for the animated feature "An American Tail 2: Fievel Goes West." His wife Gloria died in 1994. A very fine man who was considered a great American institution, James Stewart died in July of 1997 at the age of 89.

STONE, LEWIS

Lewis Stone was born on November 15, 1879 in Worcester, Massachusetts. He made his film debut in 1915. He then served in the Spanish-American War and in the World War I cavalry. He also trained Chinese troops in the Boxer Rebellion. He resumed his movie career after completing his military service. His popularity continued into the "talkies" and onto Broadway, where he played more mature parts, then character parts. All of his war experience imparted Stone with a military bearing that influenced many of his acting roles. In 1928, Lewis was nominated for the Best Actor Academy Award in **The Patriot**. One of his best known characters is Judge Hardy, the father in the **Hardy Family** series. Stone appeared in over 200 films altogether. After his first wife, Margaret Langham died, he married Florence Oakley and they had two daughters, Virginia and Barbara. He remained married to third wife, Hazel Wolf from 1930 until he passed away in 1953.

TAYLOR, ELIZABETH

Elizabeth Rosemond Taylor was born in London on February 27, 1932, to American parents. Her father was an art dealer and her mother was a former Broadway ingenue, known professionally as Sara Sothern. She took ballet lessons and when she was three, danced with her class before the Royal Family. When war threatened England in 1939, the family returned to the U.S. and her father opened an art gallery at the Beverly Hills Hotel. In 1941, Elizabeth made her movie debut playing in a bit part in "B" comedy at Universal Studios. In 1943, she got a contract with MGM and a prime role in **Lassie Come Home**. After making that movie together, she and Roddy McDowall became lifelong friends. She remained at MGM until the early '60s, and as she grew up, Elizabeth Taylor made the transition from child star to adolescent to mature woman very easily. Her stunning beauty led many to dub her "the most beautiful woman in the world." Coinciding with her 1950 film **Father of the Bride**, she married hotel heir Nicky Hilton. This film was followed shortly by a sequel, **Father's Little Dividend**. In 1960, Elizabeth received the Best Actress Academy Award for **Butterfield 8**. In 1966, she received the Best Actress Academy Award, as well as Best Actress Awards from the British Academy and New York Film Critics for her performance **Who's Afraid of Virginia Woolf?** Her first marriage ended in divorce, and she subsequently married seven more times. She has four children, sons Michael and Christopher (with husband Michael Wilding) and daughters Liza (with husband Mike Todd) and Maria (adopted with husband Richard Burton). 1981, she appeared in Broadway in "The Little Foxes." After the death of her friend, Rock Hudson, Taylor co-founded the American Foundation for AIDS Research in 1985. In 1987, Elizabeth was awarded the French Legion d'Honeur and also marketed her own line of perfumes. During the '80s, she did quite a bit of television work, appearing in made-for-TV movies, and the miniseries "North and South." She has made guest appearances on the soap opera "General Hospital," as well as sitcoms, and has provided the voice of "Baby Maggie" for the cartoon series "The Simpsons." In 1993, Taylor received the American Film Institute's Lifetime Achievement Award, as well as the Jean Hersholt Award from the Motion Picture Academy of Arts and Science. That same year, she created the Elizabeth Taylor Foundation for AIDS. Recently, Liz Taylor has overcome bouts of serious illness, including double hip replacement and brain surgery. She has also published two books: her 1965 autobiography, *Elizabeth Taylor—Her Own Story*, and 1988's *Elizabeth Takes Off on Self-Esteem and Self-Image*.

TEMPLE, SHIRLEY

Shirley Jane Temple was born in Santa Monica, California on April 23, 1928. She began training for show business when she was only a toddler. At four years old, she had parts in movie shorts called "Baby Burlesks" and "Frolics of Youth." Next, she began to get small roles in feature films, and got a chance to sing in "Stand Up and Cheer" (1934), which landed her a contract with 20th Century Fox. Her first starring role was in Paramount's **Little Miss Marker** (1934). Shirley was bestowed with a special Academy Award (special because of her young age) that same year for her outstanding contribution to screen entertainment. Many of her adult co-stars still marvel at the intelligence and professionalism that she possessed at such a young age. Her singing and dancing, presented with her curly locks and dimpled smile, cheered moviegoers in the depths of the Great Depression. From 1935 through 1938, Shirley was the number one Box Office draw. At the peak of her popularity, Shirley Temple dolls and books were hot items. Frequently, her dance partner was Bill "Bojangles" Robinson, and together they broke through the color barriers in place at the time. It was almost unheard of for an African-American man to be seen dancing or holding hands with a white female. When Shirley became a teenager, she still made a few movies, but after marrying actor John Agar in 1945 retired to raise their daughter, Linda Susan. Shirley and Agar divorced in 1949. In 1950, she married businessman Charles A. Black, and they had a son, Charles and a daughter, Lori. From 1958 to 1960, she hosted the television series "Shirley Temple Storybook." She also brought attention to the plight of women with breast cancer when she herself survived the ordeal. In the 1960s, known then by her married name, Shirley Temple Black, she became politically active. She was appointed U.S. Representative to the United Nations in 1968, and later served as U.S. Ambassador to Ghana from 1974 to 1976. Shirley was U.S. Chief of Protocol from 1976 to 1977 (the first woman in 200 years to hold that position). In 1980, she became a grandmother for the first time, but her image as a little girl lives on in her films for new generations to enjoy. Shirley Temple Black has published **Child Star: an Autobiography**, and currently resides in California.

TRACY, SPENCER

Spencer Tracy was born in Milwaukee, Wisconsin on April 5, 1900. Among the schools he attended were Northwestern Military Academy in Wisconsin and the American Academy of Dramatic Arts in New York. He worked as a stage actor for quite some time before becoming a Broadway star. Tracy made his first movie in 1930, which launched a legendary career that spanned 76 films. He first worked under contract with Fox and then got an MGM contract in 1935. He won two Academy Awards for Best Actor, in 1937 for **Captains Courageous** and in 1938 for **Boys' Town**, becoming the first male actor to win the award in consecutive years. He also set a record by being nominated for Best Actor on seven other occasions. In his acting roles, Tracy could achieve great intensity, but in an easy fashion that seemed so natural. He usually portrayed men who were burly but diamonds-in-the-rough. Tracy worked under contract with MGM for 20 years, until they let him go in 1955, due to problems on the set. That year, he won Best Actor at the Cannes Festival for **Bad Day at Black Rock**. He married Louise Treadwell in 1923 and they had two children, John (who was born deaf) and Suzy, before separating in the 1930s. With Spencer's help, Louise founded the John Tracy Clinic at USC to aid the deaf. In recent years, it was revealed that Tracy had a long-time relationship with frequent co-star Katharine Hepburn. He and Louise were never divorced and at his death on June 10, 1967, he provided for his family by leaving everything to Louise, their children, and his brother. In 1968, he was awarded Best Actor by the British Academy for his performance in **Guess Who's Coming to Dinner?**

TREVOR, CLAIRE

Born Claire Wemlinger on March 8, 1909 in Bensonhurst, Long Island, Claire Trevor was educated at Columbia University and the American Academy of Dramatic Arts. In 1929, she made her stage debut in Ann Arbor, Michigan with Robert Henderson's Repertory Players. In 1930, she appeared in St. Louis with the Warner Brothers stock company and in Southampton with the Hampton Players stock company. In 1932, Trevor made her Broadway debut in "Whistling in the Dark." The following year she was signed with Fox Studios and appeared mainly in "B" pictures, becoming typecast in roles of gang molls or floozies. From 1937 to 1940 she acted on radio opposite Edward G. Robinson in the show "Big Town." From 1938-43, Claire had a contract with Warner Brothers. Nominated for a Best Supporting Actress Academy Award for her roles in **Dead End** (1937) and **The High and the Mighty** (1954), Claire won that award for **Key Largo** in 1948. In 1947, Trevor appeared on Broadway in "The Big Two." In the mid-1950s, she entered the world of television. In 1981, she returned to Fox Studios in Hollywood, appearing as Sally Field's mother in the film **Kiss Me Goodbye**. Her first marriage was to radio producer Clark Andrews in 1938. Her second marriage was to Navy Lt. Cylos Dunsmoore and their son, Charles, was born in 1943. In 1948, she married movie producer Milton Bren; they had a son, Peter.

VERA-ELLEN

She was born Vera-Ellen Westmeyer Rohe in Cincinnati, Ohio on February 16, 1926, the daughter of a piano salesman father and a mother who dreamed of her child's stardom. Because she was a frail child, Vera-Ellen was given dancing lessons to build her strength. At age 13, she made her dancing debut at the Chicago World's Fair. A winner on radio's "Major Bowes Amateur Hour," Vera-Ellen went on to become a Rockette, and then a chorus dancer in Billy Rose's Casa Mañana Club (New York). In 1939, she made her Broadway debut in the Broadway musical "Very Warm for May," and went on to play in the shows "Higher and Higher" and "Panama Hattie." Vera-Ellen went to Hollywood in the mid-1940s , where she was highly regarded by her peers—most notably Gene Kelly—for her dancing excellence. Her most famous movie role was in **On the Town** (1949); her other important films are **Call Me Madam** (1953) and **White Christmas** (1954). Married from 1945-46 to dancer Robert Hightower, she was married again from

1954-66 to oil millionaire Victor Rothschild. After her two-month old daughter from her second marriage died, she became a recluse, and never appeared publicly again. Suffering from various physical ailments (including anorexia), Vera-Ellen died of cancer in August 1981.

WAGNER, ROBERT

Robert John Wagner, Jr. was born on February 10, 1930 in Detroit, Michigan, the son of a successful steel executive. He attended the Black-Foxe Military Institute and The Harvard School. Wagner set his mind on acting while he was in high school, got a movie contract with 20th Century Fox in 1950, and made his screen debut in **The Happy Years** (1950). He appeared in many movies through the '50s and '60s. Wagner started out as a youthful leading man who appealed to the "bobby-soxer" generation, and grew to become a solid actor, co-starring with such Hollywood greats as Spencer Tracy and Bing Crosby. He later took his career to television, starring in four different series: "It Takes a Thief" (1968-70), "Switch" (1975-78), "Hart to Hart" (1979-84), and "Lime Street" (1985). Wagner also appeared in the popular 1978 mini-series "Pearl." He married actress Natalie Wood in 1957 after a much-publicized romance; they divorced in 1962 and married each other again in 1972. In between marriages to Natalie, Wagner tied the knot with actress Marion Marshall. He has three daughters: Natasha (Natalie Wood's daughter from her marriage to British producer Richard Gregson), Katie (Wagner's daughter from his marriage to Marion Marshall), and Courtney (born to Wagner and Natalie Wood during their second marriage). Natalie Wood died tragically in an accidental drowning in 1981. Since then, in addition to continuing his acting career, Wagner has been busy raising his three daughters and has married actress Jill St. John, a close friend of the family.

WAYNE, JOHN

Born Marion Michael Morrison in Winterset, Iowa on May 26, 1907, he attended high school in Glendale, California and went on to become a USC football player. He started in the movie business in 1927 with a job in the property department of 20th Century Fox studios. Wayne made his first on-screen appearance in 1928, but he did not ascend to stardom right away—he appeared mostly in low-budget Westerns for several years. His performance in John Ford's **Stagecoach** (1939) gave him a good, serious role and the boost he needed to become a star. John Ford also directed many of Wayne's most popular films in future years. His strong, brave, and honorable film characters made John Wayne America's ultimate hero of the silver screen for many years—whether in Westerns or war movies. In addition to film work, Wayne also worked on the radio from 1942 to 1943 in the series "Three Sheets to the Wind." He co-founded the Motion Picture Alliance for the Preservation of American Ideals in 1944, and in 1947 started Wayne-Fellows Productions and the Batjac Production Company. In 1960, Wayne served as director on the movie **The Alamo**. He finally received an Academy Award for Best Actor in 1969 for his performance in **True Grit**. John Wayne died in 1979, but through his many films continues to entertain millions.

WEBB, CLIFTON

Clifton Webb was born Webb Parmallee Hollenbeck in Indianapolis, Indiana on November 19, 1981. He spent his early childhood studying dancing and acting. By the age of 10, he was quite a seasoned performer and at 17, sang lead opera roles in "Madame Butterfly" and "La Boheme." In 1914, he played the Palace Theatre, while teamed with Mae Murray. In 1917, Webb began to perform in musical comedies, then moved on to dramatic roles in London, on Broadway, and in some silent films of the '20s. In 1944, he started making movies again after a 20 year absence from the screen. That year, he landed a role in the film **Laura** when he was spotted by 20th Century Fox while starring in the Broadway play "The Man Who Came to Dinner." Webb was nominated for a Best Supporting Actor Academy Award for **Laura**, and two years later he was nominated for that award again, this time for his performance in **The Razor's Edge.** Two years after that he was nominated for Best Actor in **Sitting Pretty** (which led to the **Mr. Belvedere** series of movies). Another of his most notable roles was in the popular film **Cheaper by the Dozen** (1950). Clifton Webb died in 1966.

WICKES, MARY

Born Mary Isabelle Wickenhauser in St. Louis, Missouri on June 13, 1916, Mary Wickes graduated from Washington University in St. Louis, which in later years bestowed her with an honorary doctorate degree. In the late '30s, she took to the stage, working in stock theater and eventually on Broadway. Mary became famous for her role as the nurse, Miss Preen, in the Broadway play **The Man Who Came to Dinner**. Her movie career began when she repeated that role on film in 1941. She grew to become one of Hollywood's most popular character actresses— her tall, lanky figure and her angular facial features made her stand out from the crowd. Wickes generally played outspoken, wisecracking supporting characters who, though beleaguered, interjected humor into various situations. Some of her better known films were: **June Bride** (1948), **On Moonlight Bay** (1951), **By the Light of the Silvery Moon** (1953), **The Music Man** (1962), and **The Trouble With Angels** (1966). In addition to her movie work, Wickes continued to make occasional stage appearances. From the '50s right through to the '80s, she became a fixture on television as well, performing in many series, including "Make Room for Daddy," "The Halls of Ivy," "Dennis the Menace," "Julia," "Sigmund the Sea Monster," "Doc," and "The Father Dowling Mysteries." She also appeared in a "Studio One" production of "Mary Poppins," and was nominated for an Emmy Award for her role in the series "Mrs. G. Goes to College" (1961-1962). Wickes had guest spots as well, in series such as "I Love Lucy" and "M*A*S*H." A very active person, she taught comedy acting at Washington University, The College of William and Mary, and The American Conservatory Theater. She served for many years as a nursing volunteer and held seats on the Boards of some prominent medical institutions. Mary went back to school again in the '90s, graduating from UCLA with a Master's Degree. Also in the '90s, she revived her movie career, most strongly with her role as "Sister Mary Lazarus" in **Sister Act** (1992) and

Sister Act II: Back in the Habit (1993). Then she appeared in the 1994 version of **Little Women**. Mary Wickes also did voice work for 1996 Disney animated feature **The Hunchback of Notre Dame**, which she completed just 6 weeks before her death in 1995.

WILLIAMS, ESTHER

Esther Jane Williams was born in Inglewood, California on August 8, 1923 and grew up to attend Los Angeles City College and the University of Southern California, Los Angeles. She was a member of the Los Angeles Athletic Club and became a champion swimmer, setting 1939 U.S. records. She was supposed to compete at the 1940 Olympics in Helsinki, but the war in Europe (the beginnings of World War II) caused the games to be canceled. She then began to work professionally, learning to swim in water ballet style and appearing with Johnny Weismuller and Gertrude Ederle in Billy Rose's Aquacade at the San Francisco World's Fair. Such aquatic shows were very popular at the time. Esther didn't care for her new show business life, and quit to become a model and sales clerk at the I. Magnin's department store in Los Angeles. She then married Dr. Leonard Kovner. MGM approached her a number of times to make movies, but Esther was not interested and her husband didn't like the idea either. In 1942, MGM finally convinced Williams to try film work; they trained her for a year and started her in a couple of small (non-swimming) roles. In 1944 she starred in the first movie of her own, **Bathing Beauty**, and was an overnight hit with the moviegoing public. The highlights of her films were the magnificent and colorful water ballet production numbers that came alive in Technicolor. She ranked among the Box Office Top Ten in both 1949 and 1950, and remained a major MGM star for 14 years. Her marriage to Dr. Kovner had dissolved in 1944, and she married a second time in 1945 to radio announcer Ben Gage, with whom she had three children: Benjamin, Kimball, and Susan. They divorced in 1957, and she married actor Fernando Lamas in 1967 (he died in 1982). After leaving MGM in the mid-'50s, she made a few unsuccessful dramatic films, and then retired from the movie business. In 1984, at the Olympic Games, she hosted the synchronized swimming events. That same year, she also made a video about infant water safety. Esther Williams started her own line of swim-wear, designed to flatter the figure of the average American woman. Esther has recently had knee replacement surgery, and is currently a spokeswoman for Turner Classic Movies.

WOOD, NATALIE

Natalie Wood was born Natasha Gurdin in San Francisco, California on July 20, 1938. She was the daughter of Russian immigrants; different languages and accents came easily to her as both English and Russian were spoken at home. She took dancing lessons as a young child and made her first appearance on film at the age of five. She had a natural talent and became a well-known child actress, appearing in many films, including the holiday favorite **Miracle on 34th Street** (1947). Natalie became one of the first child stars to successfully make the transition from child star to mature actress. Her trademarks were her beautiful dark hair and compelling brown eyes. She made a movie every year between 1946 and 1963, and was nominated three times for Best Actress at the Academy Awards—for **Rebel Without a Cause** (1955), **Splendor In the Grass** (1961), and **Love With a Proper Stranger** (1963). During the '60s, she tried her hand at comedy films, and in the 1970s began to work on television. After a much-publicized romance, she married actor Robert Wagner in 1957. They later divorced and she was married to British producer Richard Gregson in 1970-71 (they had a daughter, Natasha). Natalie and Robert Wagner tied the knot again in 1972 (with whom she had another daughter, Courtney). She and Wagner remained married until her untimely and tragic death in 1981 by accidental drowning. Before she died, she was planning to make her stage debut in a production of "Anastasia."

WRIGHT, TERESA
Muriel Teresa Wright was born in New York City on October 27, 1918. She graduated from Columbia High School in Maplewood, New Jersey. Teresa spent the summers of 1937 and 1938 playing in summer stock at Provincetown's Wharf Theatre. In 1938, she debuted on Broadway and went on tour in "Our Town" as understudy to Martha Scott. In 1940, she was discovered by Samuel Goldwyn while she was appearing in Broadway's "Life With Father," and he signed her to a long-term contract. In 1941, Teresa was nominated as Best Supporting Actress for her first film, "The Little Foxes." In 1942, she became the first actress to be nominated for an Academy Award in two categories simultaneously—Best Actress in **Pride of the Yankees** and Best Supporting Actress in **Mrs. Miniver** (which she won). In 1962, Teresa returned to Broadway in "Mary, Mary." She began to work in Hollywood again in 1969, where she played supporting character roles. The '70s found her working in television dramas. She also acted on Broadway in "Death of a Salesman" in 1975. Teresa married writer Niven Busch in 1942 and they had a son, Niven Terence and a daughter, Mary Kelly. Her second marriage was in 1959, to playwright Robert Anderson.

WYMAN, JANE
Jane Wyman was born Sara Jane Fulks in St. Joseph, Missouri on January 4, 1914. She attended the University of Missouri and also worked as a switchboard operator and manicurist. Using the name Jane Durrell, she became a singer on Chicago, New Orleans and Detroit radio stations. In 1932, Jane made her screen debut and from 1936-42 was under contract to Warner Brothers. In 1948, she won the Best Actress Academy Award for **Johnny Belinda**, in which she gave a performance as a deaf mute. Her movies roles ranged from comedies to melodramas. In the 1950s, she hosted and occasionally starred in her own television show, "The Jane Wyman Theater." During that decade, she was nominated twice for Best Actress at the

Academy Awards for **The Blue Veil** (1951) and **Magnificent Obsession** (1954). Over the years, she had four husbands and two children, a daughter Maureen and an adopted son Michael—both while married to Ronald Reagan. Jane enjoyed popularity in the television nighttime soap opera "Falcon Crest" during the 1980s.

WYNN, KEENAN
Keenan Wynn was born Francis Xavier Aloysius Wynn in New York City in July of 1916. His father was actor Ed Wynn, and his maternal grandfather was Frank Keenan, an actor in silent films. He studied at St. John's Military Academy. Keenan Wynn began acting in stock theater, then made his way to the Broadway stage. He also worked on radio before making his first movie in 1942. He became one of Hollywood's most solid character actors, handling a wide variety of roles, from villains to smooth-talking sidekicks. He made a long list of films for MGM, including **Without Love**, (1945), **The Hucksters** (1947), **Song of the Thin Man** (1947), **Neptune's Daughter** (1949), and **Kiss Me Kate** (1953). In the '60s and '70s, Wynn often worked in Disney feature films, such as **The Absent-Minded Professor** (1961), **Son of Flubber** (1963), and **Snowball Express** (1972). He continued to work in movies and on television well into the '80s, before passing away in 1986.

YOUNG, LORETTA
Born Gretchen Young in Salt Lake City, Utah on January 6, 1912, Loretta moved to Los Angeles with her mother and two sisters. The girls worked as movie extras to earn some income, as her father had deserted the family. In 1926, her movie career began with a small role in a silent film. She eventually landed a contract with Warner Brothers, where she was groomed for starring roles. Her excellent speaking voice made it easy for her to move into talking pictures. From 1933 to 1940, Loretta was under contract with 20th Century Fox. She worked at leading roles in the movies for 21 years before winning the Academy Award for Best Actress in **The Farmer's Daughter** (1947). She was nominated for that award again in 1949 for her performance in **Come To The Stable**. Loretta Young usually portrayed good and kind women who were full of spunk and resourcefulness. In 1953, she moved to television with the Emmy Award winning "The Loretta Young Show," which ran until 1961, and continued with "The New Loretta Young Show" from 1962 to 1963. Her autobiography, **The Things I Had to Learn**, was published in 1961. In 1986, she starred in the TV movie "Christmas Eve," which was popular and has been seen in re-runs for many years. Loretta was married very briefly to actor Grant Withers in 1932, and in 1937, became a single mother by adopting her daughter Judy. In 1940, she and television executive Thomas H.A. Lewis were married; they had two sons, Christopher and Peter and eventually divorced in 1969. Her last marriage, to designer Jean Louis, ended with his death in 1997.

YOUNG, ROBERT

Robert Young was born in Chicago on February 22, 1907, and was raised in Los Angeles, California. To support himself during his four year studies at the Pasadena Playhouse, he worked at many ordinary jobs. At the Playhouse, he appeared in more than 40 plays before getting an MGM movie contract in 1931. He starred in over 100 films, remaining an MGM star until 1944. Young started out playing romantic leads, then graduated to roles of husbands and fathers. He also worked on radio in shows such as "Good News of 1938" and in 1944, "Maxwell House Coffee Time." With Eugene Rodney, he formed Cavalier Productions in 1947. Young's popularity continued upward when he brought his radio show of four years, "Father Knows Best," to television in 1954. That show ran for six years, and later was followed with another popular series, "Marcus Welby, MD" (1969-76). Young won Emmys for his roles in both series. He married Elizabeth Louise Henderson in 1933 (she passed away in 1994), and they had four daughters: Carol, Barbara, Elizabeth, and Kathleen, and five grandchildren.

MOVIE INDEX

Title	Page

Title	Page

Title	Page

Title	Page

Title	Page

Bibliography

1. The Chronicle of the Movies, a Year-by-Year History from "The Jazz Singer" to Today, Foreword by Leonard Maltin, Reed International Books Limited, Published by Crescent Books, 1991.

2. The Film Encyclopedia, Edition, Ephraim Katz, Harper Perennial Books – a division of HarperCollins Publishers, 1994.

3. The International Dictionary of Films and Filmmakers, Second Edition, Volume III., Actors and Actresses; Nicholas Thomas, Editor; Claire Lofting, Picture Editor; St. James Press, 1992.

4. Movie Stars of the '30s, A Complete Reference Guide for the Film Historian or Trivia Buff, David Ragan, Prentice-Hall Inc., 1985.

5. Movie Stars of the '40s, A Complete Reference Guide for the Film Historian of Trivia Buff, David Ragan, Prentice-Hall Inc., 1985.